Rand McNally

PORTRAIT OF
AMERICA

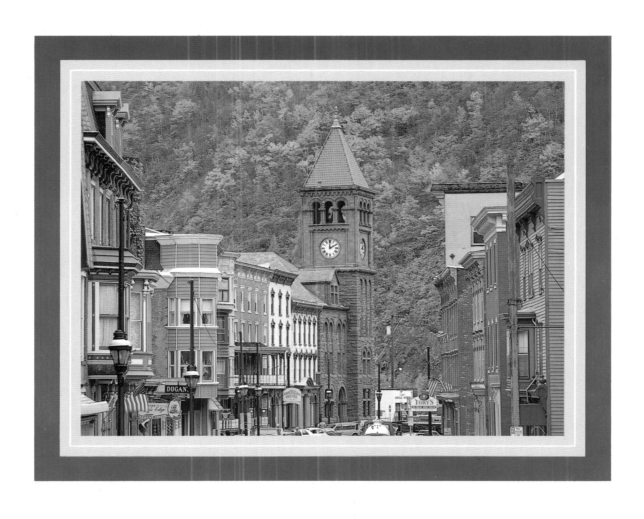

PORTRAIT OF
AMERICA

RAND McNALLY

CHICAGO · NEW YORK · SAN FRANCISCO

Contents

Rand McNally Portrait of America

General manager: Russell L. Voisin
Managing editor: Jon M. Leverenz
Editor and photo editor: Elizabeth Fagan Adelman
Writer: Jay Pridmore
Cartographic editor: V. Patrick Healy
Designer: Vito M. DePinto
Production and photo editor: Laura C. Schmidt
Manufacturing planner: Marianne Abraham

Photograph credits
10-11 Massachusetts: Josiah Davidson. 12-13 Pennsylvania: Larry Ulrich. Massachusetts: Josiah Davidson. New Hampshire: Josiah Davidson. 14-15 Baltimore: Tom Algire/Tom Stack & Associates. Connecticut: Josiah Davidson. 16-17 Pittsburgh: Steve Elmore/Tom Stack & Associates. Boston: Steve Elmore/Tom Stack & Associates. New York City: Steve Elmore/Tom Stack & Associates. Philadelphia: Tom Till. 18-19 Vermont: Jeff Gnass. 20-21 Washington, D.C.: Jeff Gnass. 22-23 New Jersey: Tom Till. Rhode Island: Jeff Gnass. Delaware: Tom Till. 28-29 Florida: Josiah Davidson. 30-31 West Virginia creek: Josiah Davidson. West Virginia mill: Larry Ulrich. 32-33 Virginia: Josiah Davidson. North Carolina: Kerry T. Givens/Tom Stack & Associates. Atlanta: Steve Elmore/Tom Stack & Associates. 34-35 Miami: Steve Elmore/Tom Stack & Associates. Orlando: Britt Runion. 36-37 North Carolina: Josiah Davidson. 38-39 South Carolina: Josiah Davidson. 42-43 Chicago: Archie Lieberman. 44-45 Illinois: Willard Clay. Minneapolis: Steve Elmore/Tom Stack & Associates. 46-47 Minnesota: Jeff Gnass. 48-49 Ohio: Tom Till. Indianapolis: Dave Willoughby. 50-51 Michigan: Willard Clay. Detroit: Detroit Convention & Visitors Bureau. 52-53 Wisconsin: Wisconsin Milk Marketing Board. Cleveland: Mort Tucker. 56-57 Louisiana: Josiah Davidson. 58-59 Alabama: Josiah Davidson. Arkansas: Tom Till. 60-61 Missouri: Jeff Gnass. Tennessee: Jeff Gnass. 62-63 Louisiana: Matt Bradley/Tom Stack & Associates. New Orleans: Port of New Orleans Photo. 64-65 Mississippi: Larry Ulrich. Kentucky: Bob Clemenz. 66-67 St. Louis: Jeff Gnass. Louisiana: Port of New Orleans Photo. 70-71 Nebraska: Willard Clay. 72-73 Nebraska: Larry Ulrich. Texas: Jeff Gnass. 74-75 Dallas: Josiah Davidson. Houston: Jim McNee/Tom Stack & Associates. 76-77 Mt. Rushmore, South Dakota: Josiah Davidson. Badlands, South Dakota: Larry Ulrich. 78-79 North Dakota: John Running. North Dakota: John Running. 80-81 Oklahoma: Fred W. Marvel. Iowa: Tom Till. Kansas: Tom Till. 86-87 Arizona: Josiah Davidson. 88-89 Arizona saguaros: Larry Ulrich. Phoenix: Brian Parker/Tom Stack & Associates. Arizona cowboy: John Running. 90-91 Utah: Josiah Davidson. New Mexico: Willard Clay. 92-93 Colorado: Josiah Davidson. 94-95 Arizona: Larry Ulrich. Colorado: Willard Clay. Utah: Jeff Gnass. 96-97 Utah: Jeff Gnass. Colorado: Nathan Bilow/Stock Imagery. 100-101 Washington: Josiah Davidson. 102-103 Wyoming: Larry Ulrich. Idaho: Larry Ulrich. Oregon: Josiah Davidson. Wyoming: Jeff Gnass. 106-107 Oregon: Josiah Davidson. Seattle: F. Stuart Westmorland/Tom Stack & Associates. 108-109 Montana: Jeff Gnass. Idaho: Jeff Gnass. Oregon: Bob Pool/Tom Stack & Associates. 110-111 Wyoming: Larry Ulrich. Oregon: Willard Clay. 114-115 San Francisco: Jeff Gnass. 116-117 Nevada: Larry Ulrich. Los Angeles: Larry Ulrich. 118-119 California redwoods: Larry Ulrich. California vineyards: Larry Ulrich. San Diego: Larry Ulrich. 120-121 California: Jeff Gnass. San Diego: Jeff Gnass. 122-123 California: Jeff Gnass. 124-125 Nevada: Larry Ulrich. 126-127 Las Vegas: Las Vegas News Bureau. Nevada: Las Vegas News Bureau. 130-131 Alaska: Jeff Gnass. 132-133 Alaska: Jeff Gnass. Hawaii: Jeff Gnass. 134-135 Alaska: Larry Ulrich. Hawaii: Larry Ulrich. 136-137 Alaska: Jeff Gnass. Hawaii: Jeff Gnass. 138-139 Hawaii: Jeff Gnass. Alaska: Larry Ulrich. 140-141 Hawaii: Larry Ulrich. Alaska: Kevin Shafer/Tom Stack & Associates.

Rand McNally Portrait of America
copyright © 1991 by Rand McNally & Company

Library of Congress Cataloging-in-Publication Data

Rand McNally and Company.
　　Portrait of America.
　　　　p.　cm.
　　Includes index.
　　ISBN 0-528-83446-0
　　1. United States—Maps.　2. United States—Description and travel.
I. Title.
G1200.R3355　1991　<G&M>
912.73—dc20
　　　　　　　　　　　　　　　91-8796
　　　　　　　　　　　　　　　　CIP
　　　　　　　　　　　　　　　　MAP

Introduction	**6**
Locator map	
Map legend	
Map of the United States	**8**
The Northeast	**10**
Connecticut	
Delaware	
Maine	
Maryland	
Massachusetts	
New Hampshire	
New Jersey	
New York	
Pennsylvania	
Rhode Island	
Vermont	
Washington, D.C.	
Maps of the Northeast	**24**
The Southeast	**28**
Florida	
Georgia	
North Carolina	
South Carolina	
Virginia	
West Virginia	
Map of the Southeast	**40**

The Great Lakes   42
    Illinois
    Indiana
    Michigan
    Minnesota
    Ohio
    Wisconsin
Map of the Great Lakes   54

The Mississippi Valley   56
    Alabama
    Arkansas
    Kentucky
    Louisiana
    Mississippi
    Missouri
    Tennessee
Map of the Mississippi Valley   68

The Great Plains   70
    Iowa
    Kansas
    Nebraska
    North Dakota
    Oklahoma
    South Dakota
    Texas
Maps of the Great Plains   82

The Southwest   86
    Arizona
    Colorado
    New Mexico
    Utah
Map of the Southwest   98

The Northwest   100
    Idaho
    Montana
    Oregon
    Washington
    Wyoming
Map of the Northwest   112

California and Nevada   114
    California
    Nevada
Map of California and Nevada   128

Alaska and Hawaii   130
    Alaska
    Hawaii
Maps of Alaska and Hawaii   142

Index to the maps   145

Introduction

America's history as a nation is relatively short, but the United States is vast in both its size and its spirit. Rand McNally's *Portrait of America* captures our nation through photographed scenes, through concise prose, and through Rand McNally's own medium—rich, detailed, full-color maps.

We see from the outset that America's landscape is ravishing. The warm colors of the South, the sculpted mountains of the West, the perpetual motion of the cities—impressions chosen for *Portrait of America* are sometimes familiar, other times surprising, always indelible.

Many details of this great land are infused with a sense of living history, such as old neighborhoods in New England or remote outposts on the West Coast. Others impart an irrepresible sense of adventure, as do the Great Lakes, once called the continent's "Sweetwater Seas." Sometimes we witness endless, faraway realms, such as Alaska's Alexander Archipelago, where conservationist John Muir made an ecstatic summertime visit more than a century ago.

Many of America's landmarks are entirely ingrained in the national consciousness. The Shenandoah Valley, the Grand Canyon, Yosemite—they amazed early Americans and even today engender swelling national pride for their size and majesty. Other landmarks are less dramatic but in some ways more sublime. The Chesapeake Bay, the lakes of northern Minnesota, the lush agricultural valleys in Oregon—these images are quieter but no less essential to the mosaic that is America.

The American character is manifest in images of physical strength and beauty, but also rises from people and the constant flow of ideals. In nine separate essays Rand McNally's *Portrait of America* penetrates the inner nature that makes each region distinct. Through images from history and literature, and an abiding sense of place, these essays point to features that define not just the landscape, but the personality that inhabits it. The Black Hills, for example, were sanctified long ago by Native Americans. Later the area figured into the picturesque career of Wild Bill Hickok and also inspired the carving of Mount Rushmore. *Portrait of America* tells the glories of California and chronicles migrations that have populated the state. Hawaii, New Mexico, Missouri, Tennessee. All the states have curious and wonderful stories to tell. For each, *Portrait of America* touches on details that make it unique, often irresistible.

An indispensable picture is revealed by the Rand McNally maps at the close of each chapter. These display spatial relationships that words and photographs can only suggest. In the Northeast, we can consider tightly packed cities and towns of the megalopolis, and then compare that region to the great distances between settled areas in the Great Plains. The broad brush of topography, we shall find, is as essential to our national character as historic buildings or inspiring landmarks.

Mountains, foothills, valleys, and other features are the canvas on which industries flourish (or fail to) and human cultures evolve. This terrain is essential to the diversity and versatility of the American character. We have lakes, rivers, prairies, and plains, and personalities drawn to such places. In so many ways our tradition is tied to our landscape, which is massive, fertile, sometimes hostile, and very often breath-taking.

Rand McNally's *Portrait of America* is about diversity, but it is about unity as well. It is about overcoming barriers and connecting one part of a vast continent to another. This portrait is about the impulse to explore rivers and build canals, and the ability to make even rugged terrain promising. It is about ideas that become inextricable from the landscape. And about an American spirit that is captured in such images as a soaring mountain, raging waterfall, or luminous urban skyline.

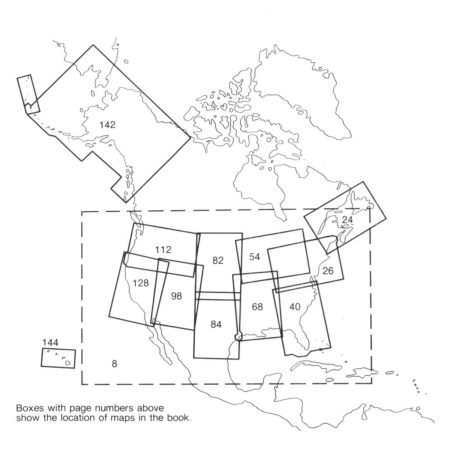

Boxes with page numbers above
show the location of maps in the book.

MAP LEGEND

Political Boundaries

— · — · —   International (first-order political unit)

————   State, Province, etc. (second-order political unit)

Capitals of Political Units

WASHINGTON   Independent Nation

Hamilton   Dependency

BERMUDA (U.K.)   Administering Country

Santa Fe   State, Province, etc.

Inhabited Localities

Map scale of 1:3,000,000, 1:6,000,000

- 0—10,000
- o 10,000—25,000
- ⊙ 25,000—100,000
- ⊡ 100,000—250,000
- ▣ 250,000—1,000,000
- ■ >1,000,000

Map scale of 1:12,000,000

- 0—50,000
- ⊙ 50,000—100,000
- ⊡ 100,000—250,000
- ▣ 250,000—1,000,000
- ■ >1,000,000

The size of type indicates the relative economic and political importance of the locality

Gatlinburg   **Flaggstaff**   **Norfolk**

Gettysburg   **Ventura**   **NEW YORK**

Miscellaneous Cultural Features

GLACIER NATIONAL PARK ▲   National or State Park or Monument

FORT CLATSOP NAT. MEM. ▲   National or State Historic(al) Site, Memorial

SEMINOLE IND. RES.   Indian Reservation

FORT DIX ▪   Military Installation

TANGLEWOOD ▲   Point of Interest (battlefield, historical site, etc.)

HOOVER DAM /   Dam

Transportation

Map scale of 1:3,000,000, 1:6,000,000 and 1:12,000,000

————   Primary Road

————   Secondary Road

————   Minor Road, Trail

—+—+—   Primary Railway

—▸—   Bridge

—◂- - -   Tunnel

- - - - -   Ferry

- - - - -   Intracoastal Waterway

DULLES INTERNATIONAL AIRPORT ✈   Airport

Hydrographic Features

Los Angeles Aqueduct   Aqueduct

SALTO ANGEL   Rapids, Falls

   Intermittent Stream

   Irrigation or Drainage Canal

The Everglades   Swamp

SEWARD GLACIER   Glacier

Lake Tahoe   Lake, Reservoir

   Salt Lake

   Dry Lake Bed

769 ▽   Depth of Water

Topographic Features

Mount McKinley ▲ 6194   Highest Elevation in Country

86 ▼   Lowest Elevation in Country

Targhee Pass 2156 ⌣   Mountain Pass

(106)   Elevation of City

   Sand Area

   Salt Flat

   Lava

Elevation and depths are given in meters

Highest Elevation and Lowest Elevation of a continent are underlined

Elevation tints shown only on 1:3,000,000 and 1:6,000,000 scale maps

Meters	Feet
3000	9843
2000	6562
1000	3281
500	1640
200	656
0	0
Land Below Sea Level 0	0
200	656
1000	3281
3000	9843
6000	19685
9000	29520

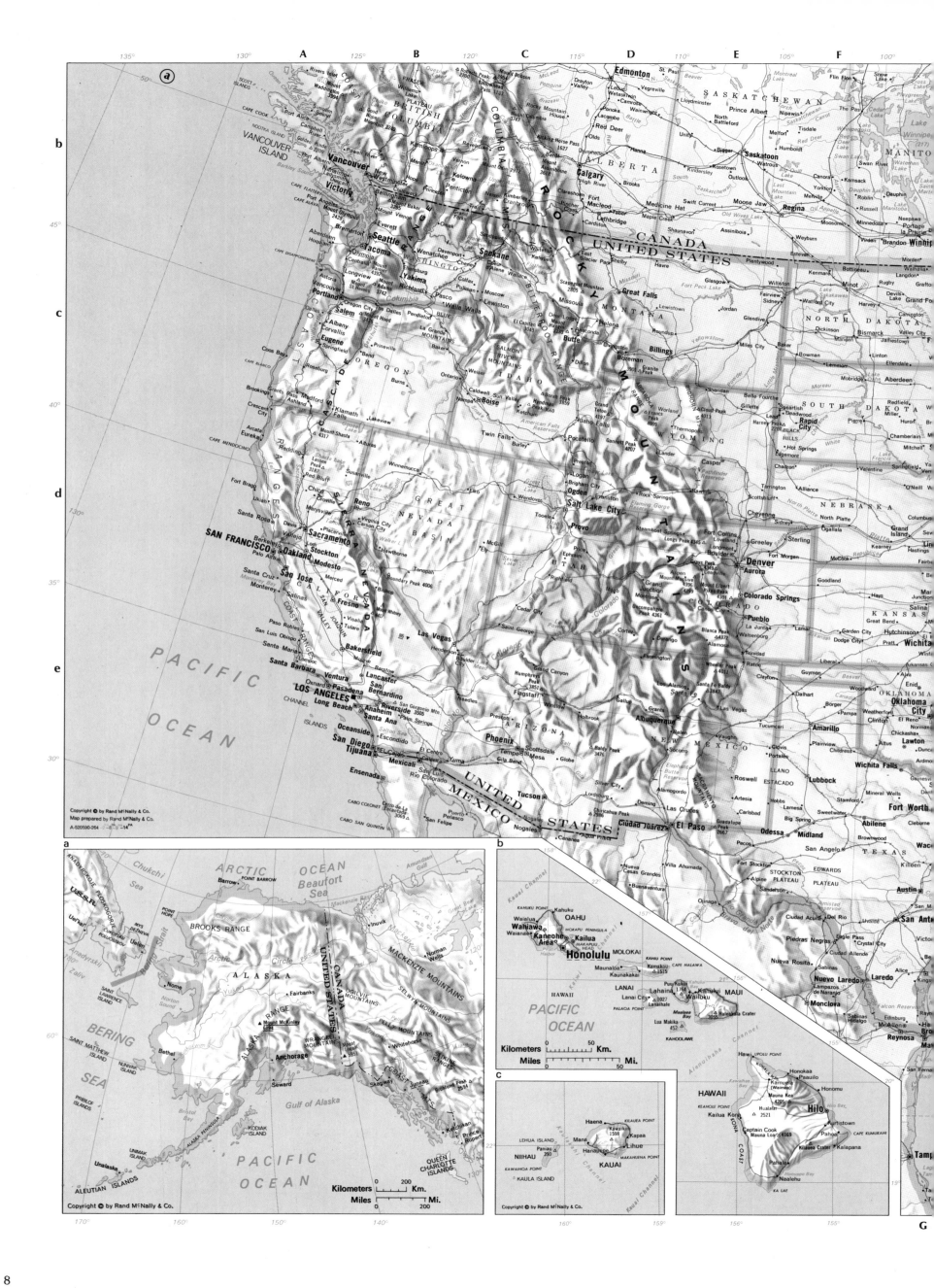

ONTARIO

QUÉBEC

MINNESOTA

Minneapolis
St. Paul

Duluth

Thunder Bay

Sault Ste. Marie

MICHIGAN

WISCONSIN

Milwaukee

Madison

CHICAGO

DETROIT

Des Moines

IOWA

MONTREAL
Ottawa
TORONTO

NEW YORK

BOSTON

Buffalo

Rochester

Syracuse

Albany

PHILADELPHIA

PITTSBURGH

Cleveland

Columbus

Cincinnati

Indianapolis

WASHINGTON

Baltimore

Kansas City

St. Louis

MISSOURI

OHIO

PENNSYLVANIA

ILLINOIS

INDIANA

KENTUCKY

Nashville

Memphis

Louisville

Knoxville

TENNESSEE

ARKANSAS

Little Rock

VIRGINIA

Richmond

Norfolk

WEST VIRGINIA

Charleston

NORTH CAROLINA

Charlotte

Raleigh

Greensboro

Columbia

SOUTH CAROLINA

Atlanta

Birmingham

GEORGIA

ALABAMA

MISSISSIPPI

LOUISIANA

Jackson

Shreveport

Baton Rouge

New Orleans

Mobile

Montgomery

Columbus

Savannah

Charleston

Jacksonville

FLORIDA

Orlando

Tampa
St. Petersburg

Miami
Miami Beach
Fort Lauderdale
West Palm Beach

Fort Myers

Key West

FLORIDA KEYS

Straits of Florida

ATLANTIC OCEAN

BERMUDA (U.K.)
Hamilton

GULF OF MEXICO

BAHAMAS

Nassau

Tropic of Cancer

WEST INDIES

CUBA

La Habana Havana

Santiago de Cuba

HAITI

DOMINICAN REPUBLIC

HISPANIOLA

Santo Domingo

Port-au-Prince

TURKS AND CAICOS ISLANDS (U.K.)
Grand Turk

CARIBBEAN SEA

CAYMAN IS. (U.K.)

Mérida

YUCATAN PENINSULA

Cancún

APPALACHIAN MOUNTAINS

NEW BRUNSWICK

NOVA SCOTIA

Halifax

NEWFOUNDLAND

CAPE BRETON ISLAND

Gulf of Saint Lawrence

PRINCE EDWARD ISLAND

Québec

Kilometers 0   200   400   600 Km.

Statute Miles 0   200   400   600 Mi.

Scale 1:12,000,000

One centimeter represents 120 kilometers.
One inch represents approximately 190 miles.

Albers Conical Equal-Area Projection

9

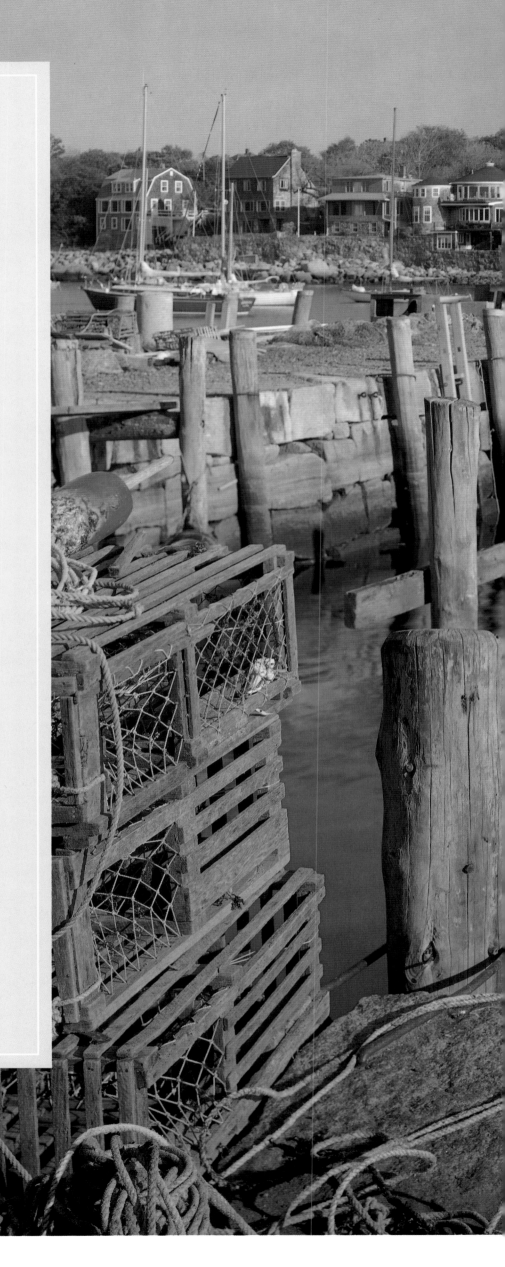

THE
Northeast

Connecticut
Delaware
Maine   New York
Maryland   Pennsylvania
Massachusetts   Rhode Island
New Hampshire   Vermont
New Jersey   Washington, D.C.

◆

"The small-paned high windows
in the peaks of their steep gables were like
knowing eyes that watched the harbor
and the far sea-line beyond, or looked
northward all along the shore and its
background of spruces and balsam firs.
When one really knows a village like this
and its surroundings, it is like becoming
acquainted with a single person."

Sandra Orne Jewett,
The Country of the Pointed Firs, 1896

◆

Rockport, Massachusetts, northeast of
Boston, was first settled in 1690. The
scenic charm of this New England
village attracts artists and makes it a
popular summer resort.

The Northeast speaks volumes about America. Its history is long and layered. Its rivers tell stories, and its families remain as tenacious as many architectural landmarks. The Northeast's countryside appears simple, and its cities are modern, yet both are swathed in vivid dramas of the past.

To make a tour of the region, one does well to start in New York City, more specifically at Grand Central Station. Grand Central, it has been suggested, serves as America's triumphal arch. Roads begin there. It is irrefutably majestic and stands as a tribute to the railroad empire of Cornelius Vanderbilt, one of America's most extravagant personalities. New York has changed all around, but Grand Central Station—modeled on the grandest of Roman baths—is still a crossroads of impressive, rushed, enormous proportions.

Other icons of America are found only blocks away. The Empire State Building, built during the Depression, became the world's tallest building for many years, and remains a monument to sheer size and mechanical power. Broadway is still rakish enough, with men and women not too different from characters inhabiting Damon Runyon stories. Central Park—Versailles-like in its way—is the most sophisticated of urban parks in a city that required relief from congestion almost from the moment it was founded.

New York was an important destination from the time Henry Hudson sailed into its harbor and north on the river named for him. Hudson was looking for China, but he shortly gave up that search. Lush terrain and plentiful beaver pelts drew early traders and colonists. Naturally, the king of England took notice and found it convenient to install a local aristocracy, then followed by a tenant class that would work the land around the river. Fine old manor houses still overlook the Hudson to memorialize that lifestyle, which declined somewhat later when the wilderness was fully opened. The limitless lands to the north and west made feudal barons relatively obsolete.

Ambition and romance drove these early Americans out from their safe hamlets, and each episode tells eloquent stories about American dreams. James Fenimore Cooper's inspiring *Leatherstocking Tales* were partly set in the wilderness frontier of central New York State, not too far from the rugged Adirondacks. The Erie Canal, completed in 1825, opened not only upstate farmland but the entire Midwest as well. By 1887, Frederick Law Olmstead, the

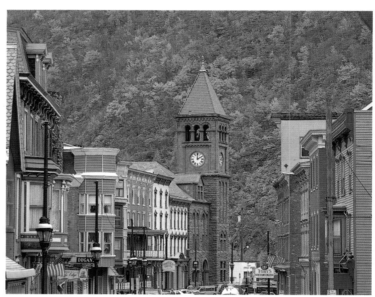

Parts of Pennsylvania are mountainous and forever remote. The modest but durable skyline of this Carbon County town suggests a moment of prosperity in an uncertain mining economy.

Near Sudbury, Massachusetts, a gristmill not unlike this one was built in 1639. Soil in New England is rarely choice, but industrious settlers were adept at building sturdy mills to grind what the fields did provide.

Woods and mountains provide frequent vistas in the White Moutains of northern New Hampshire. This gentle scene is near the village of Gorham.

Baltimore's waterfront, once dilapidated, has been revived with restaurants, an aquarium, and a spirit that values this city on one of America's most historic bays—the Chesapeake.

The old whaling port of Mystic, Connecticut, celebrates past links with the sea in this restored historic village. Coopers and sailmakers practice trades as they did when most livelihoods in Mystic concerned the old wooden vessels that plied the Eastern Seaboard.

landscape architect who built Central Park, designed the parkland around Niagara Falls so the place would reflect the majesty that many felt for America itself.

Historic dramas also lie beneath the surface of New England's calm exterior. In Massachusetts, for example, the town of Concord survives as a fine suburb of the salt-box persuasion—like so many other towns except that its very name cries out with history. It was a battlefield on the first day of fighting in the American Revolution. Memorials to that battle recall the ragtag militia that drove the Redcoats back to Boston on that occasion. Concord also was home to Henry David Thoreau. Here the writer built a small cabin on Walden Pond, convinced that he could make peace with himself in a setting close to nature. Thoreau, like those militiamen who preceded him, was the essential New Englander. He understood that life's truest objective was freedom for the human spirit.

The Yankee ideal permeates other places in New England. Old Deerfield, Massachusetts, sits agreeably in the Berkshires, with dozens of 18th-century houses restored along its main street. A quiet prep school flourishes there. It is all peaceful now, but its history includes the dreadful story of the Deerfield Massacre, an event in 1704 when Indians, bidden by the French, set out to destroy this remote outpost. They did so, but not for long. Colonists returned and built a prosperous, if remote, agricultural community.

Nantucket Island provides its own version of New England tenacity. Miles offshore from Cape Cod's low-lying dunes, Nantucket became the world's most active whaling port, so prosperous and gently governed that its residents actually resisted American independence when the rest of the colonies declared it. A mix of isolation and civilization still mingle on Nantucket as they do in many places around it.

Many other points of New England are marked by striking relationships between striking landscape and people leaving their distinct, if gentle, mark. Mount Desert Island near the furthest reaches of the Maine coast appears like a granite fortress, but it still appealed to monied Easterners who built mammoth cottages on its cliffs, and sailed schooners to get there. In northwest Connecticut, the Housatonic River Valley still serves the purpose of escape for many New Yorkers. Like much of New England, it is a place of ravishing fall foliage, stone walls, and history—in this case a portion of the old Appalachian Trail runs along its river. American history takes a different,

On Boston Common, spirits of old New England survive intact. The fifty-acre park no longer permits grazing cows, but other moments of America's past are commemorated by imposing statues. The Park Street Church carillon regularly sounds, and the gold-leaf dome of the New State House, built in 1795, crowns this historic American neighborhood.

In the 1980s, Pittsburgh overcame an industrial depression and developed one of the nation's bright new city centers. A centerpiece is the Pittsburgh Plate Glass Building, a shining postmodern tower.

Independence Hall in Philadelphia was built in 1732 as Pennsylvania's State House. The Continental Congress used it to proclaim independence from Britain, and the name was changed forever.

In 1640, Henry Hudson ventured for the first time up the river that would bear his name. Within a few years, the Hudson River attracted trappers, traders, and even aristocrats in search of their fortunes. Many found them. Now the Hudson runs past New York City, which became a world center of commerce and culture.

perhaps eccentric, turn in Newport, Rhode Island, where Gilded Age businessmen built palaces pointing out to the sea.

Boston, called the "Athens of America," also remains intimate with its past. There's Beacon Hill, reflecting the tastes of old Boston, and still inhabited by families who were founded on the social bedrock of Mayflower Pilgrims and Puritans. The personalities of North End Italians and South Boston Irish remain as vivid as they were a century ago. These people prove that Boston is no quick melting pot—even the statues of patriots on Boston Common are clustered in distinct, slightly suspicious groups.

New England is a complex weave, and no less so as one travels north. In New Hampshire, Robert Frost lived on an idyllic farm near Franconia Notch and wrote, with much self-knowledge, that "good fences make good neighbors." Vermont has its own flinty character. Shortly after American independence, it threatened to join Canada unless it were brought quickly into the Union. In 1941, a similar independent streak prompted Vermont to declare war on Germany some weeks before Congress did the same. Beneath an exterior of placid, conservative whitewashed towns (offsetting the blaze of autumn color), Vermont is a bastion of unpredictable dissent. One need only attend a town meeting in the state to witness it.

Most of the Northeast region is regarded as a single megalopolis—from Boston to Washington a single band of civilization. The population is dense, but within it are distinct pockets of history and personality. Philadelphia lives conservatively, harkening back to colonial days in the lacquered look of many buildings, and also in the Quakers who still run many of its stores and its clubs. Wilmington, Delaware, is a quiet city, and modern enough, except that it still revolves around a single family, the DuPonts, in an amicable way that brings the city's history close to the surface.

Baltimore is a city rich with memories, of American icons like Edgar Allan Poe and Babe Ruth. A recent renaissance in this city saw the redevelopment of an old harbor district, and neighborhoods of old row houses suddenly made desirable. Appropriately enough, Washington, D.C., serves as the anchor of the megalopolis; it is the most heterogeneous of cities. "Northern charm and southern efficiency" is how J.F.K. tagged it. But amidst monuments as imposing as those of Athens and Rome, Washington has the aura of being the center of the enlightened world. It attracts tourists, diplomats, and members of Con-

gress for much the same reason.

The megalopolis includes a few places of tranquility set conspicuously close to the cities. In many ways, parts of New Jersey and Pennsylvania in particular, have deliberately cut themselves off from the world. Barriers are partly geographical, but they are largely social. Some cultures are stubborn and get more so with age.

In southern New Jersey, inhabitants of the vast Pine Barrens live peacefully separate from the state's imposing industrial potential. The cultivation of cranberry bogs remains a principal occupation. The towns still do what they can to fight off development. The people of the Pine Barrens apparently know what they are missing by shunning urban ways. Nearby is Atlantic City, where not too many years ago promoters pitted men in the boxing ring against kangaroos.

In Lancaster County, Pennsylvania, simplicity also runs deep with the Amish, who call themselves the Plain People. Beyond Philadelphia's orbit, around towns named Intercourse, Paradise, and the like, Amish settled on fertile land and a set of rules that suit the people quite well. Many hold to a lifestyle of horses, buggies, and clothes made of coarse cloth. Very little distracts from the values of work, family, and devotion to God. Only one aspect of life in Lancaster County seems extravagant—cuisine drawn from the Pennsylvania Dutch. It specializes in hams, crepes, and desserts such as "shoofly" pie.

When the Spanish explorers passed through the Chesapeake Bay, they called it the "Bay of the Mother of God"—a positive response, to say the least. Even the curmudgeonly H. L. Mencken was impressed by the Chesapeake, calling it an "immense protein factory" for its shellfish and other bounty. Today it is still a lovely place where water, woods, and fields all meet. Few other bodies of water boast such a rich history.

Tucked on a perennially quiet shore, Annapolis wears its years gracefully. It's a city with more pre-Revolutionary brick structures than any other place in the country. Annapolis forms a striking historical district, but remains a youngish and active town within its ancient precincts.

History lives on Maryland's Eastern Shore as well. Separated from the cities, watermen who catch oysters and crabs still speak with an exotic accent that makes them seem like survivors of a lost tribe. How long the delicate ecology of the bay will support their livelihood, they don't know. Certainly civilization is encroaching, and if the crush of burgeoning real

The small-town charm of Vermont at twilight is enhanced by glorious fall foliage.

Thirty-six Doric columns around the
outside of the Lincoln Memorial symbolize
the 36 states of the union at the time of
the president's assassination. The memorial
was dedicated May 31, 1922, and stands
in close proximity to a number of other
Washington, D.C., memorials.

Lums Pond State Park in Delaware was assembled from former farms, old hardwood forests, and a millpond with a 200-year history.

The Kittatinny Mountains achieve their highest elevation in New Jersey. The Delaware River cuts through rugged terrain here, as does a portion of the Appalachian Trail.

The northeastern countryside still provides ample pasturage and isolation. This farm is near Kingston, Rhode Island, in a rural section of the long, populous megalopolis between Boston and Washington, D.C.

estate is not enough, some low-lying islands along the shore continue to disappear due to inscrutable natural causes. Watermen may have to find drier work. But like so many others in the Northeast, they have left their mark. This is a region where encouraging marks of humanity are frequently left and very often preserved.✩

LABRADOR SEA

ATLANTIC

OCEAN

NEWFOUNDLAND

St. John's

Corner Brook

SAINT PIERRE
AND MIQUELON
(France)

SAINT-PIERRE-
ET-MIQUELON

Sydney

Glace Bay

Scale 1:3,000,000

Kilometers
Statute Miles

One centimeter represents 30 kilometers.
One inch represents approximately 47 miles.
Lambert Conformal Conic Projection

Copyright © by Rand McNally & Co.
Map prepared by Rand McNally & Co.
A-500219-764

Kilometers
Statute Miles

Scale 1:3,000,000

One centimeter represents 30 kilometers.
One inch represents approximately 47 miles.

Copyright © by Rand McNally & Co.
Map prepared by Rand McNally & Co.
A-690596-764

Albers Conical Equal-Area Projection

THE
Southeast

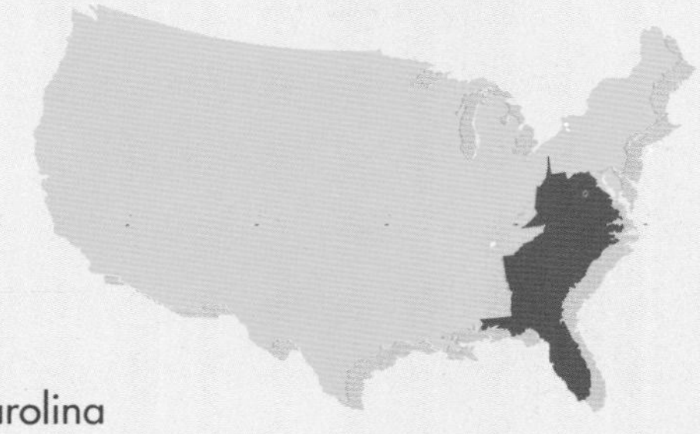

Florida
Georgia
North Carolina
South Carolina
Virginia
West Virginia

◆

"All over the land the cotton
had foamed in great white flakes
under the winter sun.
The Silver Fleece lay like a
mighty mantle across the earth...
the Fleece was goodly, gleaming
and soft, and men dreamed
of the gold it would buy."

W.E.B. Du Bois, *The Golden Fleece*, 1911

◆

Warm sunsets across calm lakes
are one reason for the growth of the
area around Winter Haven, Florida.
Pictured here is Cypress Gardens,
named for venerable old trees that
flourish throughout the South.

The notion of the New South has been evoked many times to explain change in this old and fabled part of the country. Most recently the phrase refers to the superb growth of Atlanta. It is a city of apparent harmony, substantial skyline, and the push of modern suburbs into Georgia's old plantation country. The appellation New South suits Atlantans quite well, in part because the Old South is remembered with ambivalence. Social and racial change ensued over a long, difficult period. How difficult change can be, and how eloquently it can be described, is demonstrated in the stories of Flannery O'Connor. They tell of the strength and sadness—and sometimes stubbornness—of old families and farms under the weight of modern times.

Curiously, the new Atlanta was not the first rumbling of the New South. As early as the Reconstruction the term was used to describe successive waves of change, particularly in North Carolina, where tobacco and cotton industries would grow and change the region forever. In those days, the New South was a South of larger urban centers and educational institutions, but even these harbingers of the modern met with resistance, and still do. No one argues with more conviction, even now, than a conservative Southerner.

Times continue to change, but the Old South won't be forgotten easily. Its customs and beliefs have been burned onto the consciousness of the whole nation. In some ways its culture remains as immutable as fine antiques. Secular values such as family, politics and the military take on near-religious intensity in the South even now. The closest thing to an American aristocracy lingers there, in memorable old houses with azaleas and live oaks, in such locales as Williamsburg and Charleston. Why such respect for tradition? The answer seems simple. The Old South has been forced to defend it almost from the time it was settled.

It started in the 1600s. The early planters of the Virginia Tidewater were exquisite and gentle folk, quick to replace log cabins with fine stone mansions that still dot the banks of the Chesapeake Bay. Ocean vessels came directly to their household docks, transporting cotton from the fields to ready markets in England. The same ships brought back necessities such as books, clothing, perfume, even spinets purchased in Europe. Life on the early plantations was rich but isolated, and families sought to make it more gracious by bringing portrait painters and tutors from England, and breeding horses for hunting

Cascading streams like Glade Creek cut through the mountains in Babcock State Park, West Virginia. Along the way, a gristmill recalls earlier times.

and racing.

If the Tidewater was languorous, it was often nudged by fellow Virginians not far away in the Piedmont and the Shenendoah Valley. This was harder country, and perhaps more emotional. Patrick Henry, a Piedmont native, cried "Give me liberty or give me death" while Virginia delegates met in Richmond. Cyrus McCormick later invented his reaper on the family farm in the valley. Aptly, the area drew some of the Civil War's most intense activity. John Brown chose Harper's Ferry as a place to attempt an uprising of slaves. Numerous battles were fought in this area, and Appomattox was the setting for the war's last act.

Still farther west, the gentle South was altered more radically. Mountain people are often known for rough and colorful lives, and those of Appalachia are no exception. West Virginians, for their part, had long promised to secede from Virginia proper, and did so when the Civil War began. Even today they are stoic people who face the difficulties of a mining economy with folkways—music and other arts—that are among the most durable in the nation. They say West Virginia speech patterns go back to Scotch-Irish roots deeper in the English language than Shakespeare. This is remote country with traditions all its own.

Other battles peculiar to the South were played out in the mind of Virginia's most famous writer, Edgar Allan Poe. Poe was born in Richmond in 1809. He was a restless youth who often traveled north, but he was forever drawn back to his home. He even attempted to follow the footsteps of many Southern families by attending West Point, but he was a failure there and dropped out. On the surface, Poe sought the qualities of a Southern gentleman, but something dark, even medieval, ruminated in his literary mind. Poe's gothic tales may not have been set in the South, but they sprang from this society.

Recent chapters of history show how the two Souths can and do live harmoniously together. In North Carolina, for example, education is revered and strong, by virtue of the nation's oldest state university and numerous other institutions. Today its result is the "research triangle" of Chapel Hill, Durham and Raleigh, with universities and a fast-expanding high-tech industry.

At the same time the state is large enough, and its history long enough, to support a bucolic rural life outside the modern world. The state is still dependent on tobacco and sweet potatoes in large

Thomas Jefferson found peace at Monticello, his "little mountain." Panoramas, gardens, a house of classical perfection—these features made the Virginia estate a perfect retreat.

In such places as Apex, North Carolina, industry and agriculture have coexisted since the days of the earliest textile mills. Here is evidence that cotton still thrives in the Southeast.

Atlanta's gleaming glass towers have the look of unmistakable prosperity. This city is the center of the New South, and its suburbs spread out over eighteen Georgia counties.

It may be our most polyglot city. Latin Americans flock to Miami for vacations. Europeans come for its climate and invest lavishly in its real estate. The skyline is reminiscent of Manhattan, as if to welcome its many retirees from northern cities.

Orlando is a place for the imagination. In the 1960s, it boomed because of its proximity to Cape Canaveral. Now it is home to Disney World. Visitors can witness twilight in a Chinese pagoda while a colored fountain shines in the calm waters of Lake Eola.

Wilmington, North Carolina, was a substantial cotton port in colonial times. Fine homes were built on hills overlooking the Cape Fear River, and Orton Plantation, shown here, was known for great hospitality. The house survived Spanish, British, and Union invasions of Wilmington.

measure. It also draws outsiders to the solitude of the Blue Ridge Mountains, where stately resorts were built by Eastern moguls, and where Carl Sandburg made a more modest home near Asheville. The Outer Banks of North Carolina include Cape Hatteras National Seashore and provide enough space for a herd of wild ponies to run amidst windy surf and flats with wildflowers, pines, and even lusty live oaks.

On the southern edge of this region, Florida continues to witness changes that are both gradual and jarring. This warm land has mystified people from the time Spanish explorers first set foot here in the 1500s. They wondered if its rivers would lead them to China. In colonial times it continued to ignite the imagination and was a destination for travelers and naturalists. One of the earliest visitors to the area, William Bartram, wandered the savanna and river basins of North Florida around what is now the Ocala National Forest. He wrote of "crystal waters, half-encircled by swelling hills, clad with Orange and odoriferous Illisium [sic] groves," along with other descriptions. Bartram published his journal in Philadelphia in 1791. George Washington, John Adams, and Thomas Jefferson all owned copies of his *Travels*. Later J.J. Audubon accused the book, quite wrongly, of causing a land boom in Florida in the mid-1800s.

The land boom actually began later and not because of naturalists. The grandest speculator-developer of all was a man named Henry Morrison Flagler, who built hotels (the first Breakers in Palm Beach in 1901), railroads, and a citrus industry. There followed retirees and tourists. Development continued variously and with few restraints right up to the opening of Disney World in 1971.

Serious environmental concerns came late to Florida, perhaps because the ecology of the wetland of the interior is truly mysterious. Efforts have been made of late toward the preservation of the Everglades, the wildest of Florida's swamplands at the southern end of the state. This area represents a succession of ecologies, from hardwood hammocks to mangrove and estuary. Its waters flow south from Lake Okeechobee, spreading out in a wide, slow-moving sheet. In the past, canals and dikes have converted Everglades wetlands to farmlands. Unfortunately, this has proved devastating to areas that were once home to fauna as diverse as turkey buzzards and panthers. Only recently have efforts begun to restore swamps from former farms.

Cypress Gardens, near Charleston, lies in marshland once laced with rice fields. Today, plantation life is mostly erased, but the beauty of South Carolina low country and the antique elegance of Charleston itself make this coastal area a popular tourist destination.

Amidst images of change, the Old South retains some of the country's finest old cities. Charleston, South Carolina, is one, a city whose constitution was drafted in colonial times by philosopher John Locke to encourage religious and economic freedom. Charleston enjoyed a period of great wealth, beginning around 1760 when the slave trade flourished and its streets were lined with private mansions. As time went on, Charleston survived earthquakes and hurricanes, and protected images of its splendid past. With the modern impulse to restore historic landmarks, Charleston is one place where the high polish of preservation appears appropriate and authentic.

Savannah, Georgia, seen from a distance, looks similar to Charleston; it is antique and prosperous now, as it was when "acres of bales" of cotton sat on its wharves and railway stations. But Savannah, one finds, is different. It is less lavish with images of private wealth. It has more public squares, open gardens and places for small crowds to gather. This detail, it comes as no surprise, shows up in the personality of Savannahans. It is the kind of thing that one sees in the South time and again—life is reflected, however subtly, in a feature of topography. It leads to the most reasonable kind of conservatism. It makes change a matter to undertake only slowly and with grace.☆

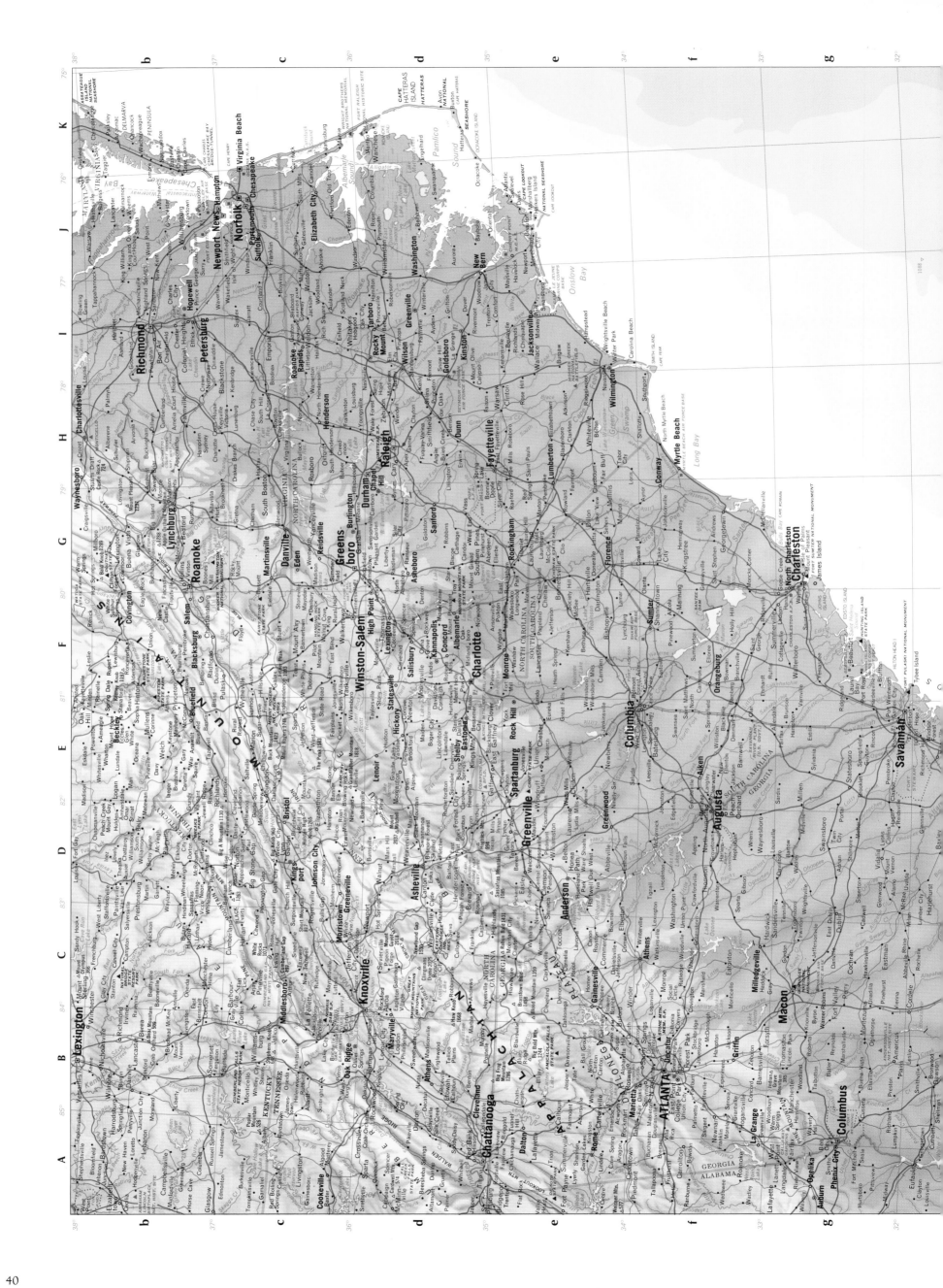

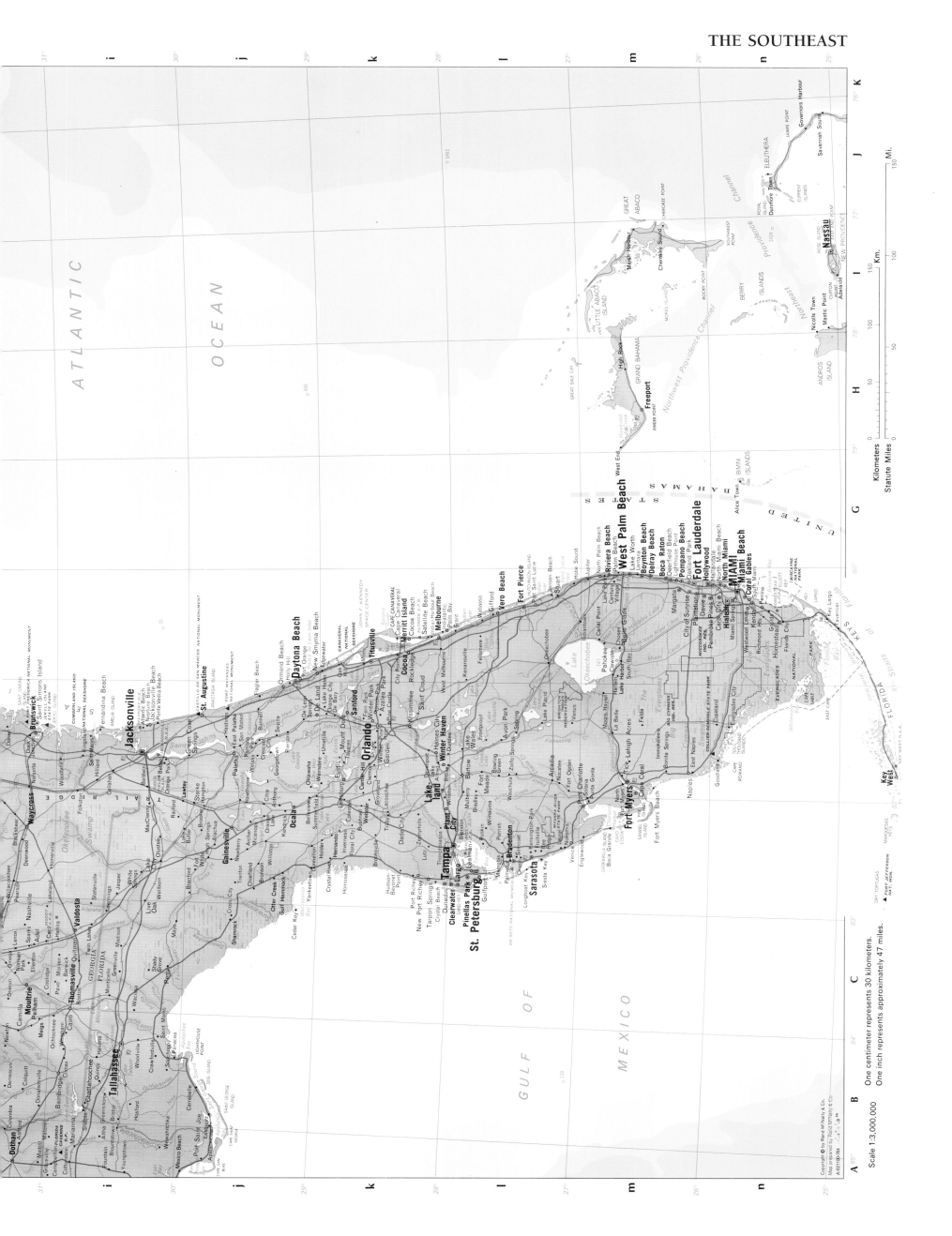

THE
Great Lakes

Illinois
Indiana
Michigan
Minnesota
Ohio
Wisconsin

"...Those grand fresh-water seas of ours –
Erie, and Ontario, and Huron,
and Superior, and Michigan – possess
an ocean-like expansiveness, with
many of the ocean's noblest traits....
They contain round archipelagoes
of romantic isles, even as Polynesian
waters do; in large part are shared by
contrasting nations as the Atlantic is;
they furnish long maritime approaches
to our numerous territorial colonies,
dotted all round their banks..."

Herman Melville, *Moby Dick*, 1851

Even from above—in this case from atop the Sears Tower—the Chicago skyline is impressive. In the 1880s, this great city on Lake Michigan took the lead in building skyscrapers rising ten stories above the street. It never looked back.

Of all the regions in the country, the Great Lakes states could by themselves form the most perfect nation. They have ample resources—minerals in the north, fertile soil in the heartland. They have industrial centers and giant waterways to connect them. Perhaps most important, the region shares a set of values borne by its rich history.

The unity of the Midwestern states is real, yet so is the diversity that has woven it. The southernmost reaches of Indiana and Illinois remain as Southern in their way as Minnesota remains Scandinavian. Staunch conservatism in parts of the region is offset by unabashed progressivism elsewhere. Conflict has tempered this society. Mild discomfort—with neighbors as well as climate—has built character. In this way history has been good to the Midwest.

The region's true strength shows up in its villages and towns that still hold their own against the push of aggressive cities. In central Illinois, for example, Petersburg may seem like a remote Victorian outpost, but its history is far from quiet. By the early 1900s it had seen business tycoons, dirty politics, and a chronicler in Edgar Lee Masters who wrote about it in *Spoon River Anthology*. The book was a national success when it came out in 1915 and bared the soul of small-town America. In it, verse-epitaphs of not-so-fictional citizens reveal their lives beneath the surface. A prohibitionist really died of cirrhosis of the liver. Ann Rutledge, Abraham Lincoln's first sweetheart, implies that their romantic flame burned long after he left this part of Illinois. *Spoon River Anthology* caused a local scandal for a hundred reasons when it came out. But in Petersburg, that's relatively forgotten. What's remembered of Petersburg is a certain worldliness in a place that remains pleasant for its farms and flower-strewn prairies.

Small cities in this region are far from flat, tedious towns. Galesburg, Illinois, had its history written by the poet Carl Sandburg, who spent his youth pondering the differences between the English–, German–, Swedish–, and African–Americans living in this old railroad town. Later he asked, "Did I know America because I knew Galesburg?" Also in the Great Lakes states is New Glarus, Wisconsin. It was settled in 1845 by Swiss immigrants with the intention to raise a town much like the one they left in Europe. Years and interstates have passed, but they still celebrate the local Swiss cheese, retain vestiges of the old language, and stage the legend of William Tell each summer. There's also

The farms of Illinois sometimes seem inexhaustible. Soybeans (growing here in LaSalle County) actually assist fertility, as this relatively new import from the Orient returns nitrogen to soil that might otherwise be depleted.

*Minneapolis is a city of commerce—witness the
IDS Tower. Across the river is St. Paul, where the
domes of the state capitol and St. Paul's Cathedral
compose a more antique, but no less impressive, skyline.*

Glaciers moved the earth and carved this lovely landscape in Minnesota's Voyageurs National Park. French fur traders were the first Europeans to venture this deep into the wilderness.

Rochester, Minnesota, a farm town that saw beyond the vagaries of weather that made farmers rich one year and poor the next. It grew a great medical center, the Mayo Clinic, and a surprising cultural environment of symphony and art.

Curiously, the earliest settlement of the Great Lakes states concentrated not on the lakes at all, but on those parts close to the Ohio River. The Ohio is the region's undergirding and was at one time the nation's most convenient avenue to the West. Cincinnati grew up early on its banks with an economy that owed both to ambitious farmers who settled the fertile land, and sophisticated traders from the not-too-distant East. Cincinnati today is a gently antique city with innate conservatism that harkens back to its vigilance against abundant temptations that floated down the river.

Contrasts between Cincinnati and the parts of Indiana just beyond it are striking. Southern Hoosiers turn out to be independent sorts whose forebears didn't come on boats—they walked and rode through the Cumberland Gap. Their terrain is lovely but stingy, made of stony ridges and wooded hollows. Some people in this area still subsist on farming and rabbits when they can shoot them. Many still enjoy the old and rich folk culture of music and crafts that have been passed down. The isolation of the place also attracted, and still attracts, its share of utopians. New Harmony was established in 1814 with scientists and philosophers, and the town retains an otherworldly feel even if the apostles are long gone. Recent communes have set up in this area, and live happily by cutting their own wood and steering clear of too-modern ways.

Mastering the Great Lakes themselves was difficult, but its hardships have embroidered the "sweetwater seas" (as 17th-century Jesuits called them) with a long, imaginative history. French voyageurs were the first to record explorations, and they canoed well into the frozen north. Jean Nicolet passed into Lake Michigan for the first time in 1634, and when he arrived at Wisconsin's Door Peninsula, he was convinced he had found China. Door County, of course, lacked spices. But it was rich with fish, and was hospitable to cherry orchards—all of which made Icelandic and Scandinavian immigrants more than comfortable 200 years later. Door County remains cold but lovely, a place for peaceful retreat from modern life. The eminent landscape architect Jens Jensen built a home here on limestone bluffs amid cedar and pines—it's now an arts and edu-

Duesenbergs, Marmons, and Stutzes were
manufactured in Indianapolis in the days
before Detroit rose to become America's
Motor City. Indianapolis Motor Speedway
was built in 1909 as a proving ground for
new cars.

Ohio's oldest lighthouse, on
Marblehead Peninsula on Lake
Erie, was built in 1821. This
area near Sandusky has witnessed
much American history.

cation center. A preserve near the shore called the Ridges is known for primeval terrain and dozens of kinds of wild orchids.

Not finding China, the French were still enchanted with the wilderness, particularly the area around the Straits of Mackinac, separating Lake Huron from Lake Michigan. In ancient times, the area was a rendezvous for Indian tribes, and then became a center for voyageurs and fur trading. During the French and Indian Wars, English soldiers took over the stronghold, and after a succession of costly scrapes with Indians, built an imposing fort amidst limestone bluffs on Mackinac Island. This later became a strategic point for Americans, who needed to pass through this point to extend their influence westward. It was secured only with the Treaty of Ghent in 1814, and then a Congressional act forbidding foreigners from trading furs with Indians. Fur trading proved transient, but Mackinac's most dependable commerce owed to its persistent remoteness. Tourists discovered it, and one of the nation's largest wooden structures, the Grand Hotel, was built there in 1887. It has weathered several economic depressions. Today it remains remote and grand.

The maritime history of the lakes is too often neglected, but it includes vivid stories and even a few feats of American heroism. In the War of 1812, for example, Commodore Oliver Perry built a fleet of war vessels from timbers cut near Erie, Pennsylvania. These he launched near Put-in-Bay, Ohio, and went on to defeat the British in the Battle of Lake Erie. Other milestones were of a commercial nature. Iron ore was discovered far north, in Michigan's Upper Peninsula and Minnesota's Mesabi Range, and transporting it initially required putting lake boats on rollers to cross from Lake Superior to Lake Huron at Sault Sainte Marie. A canal was needed, and locks were finally cut through granite bedrock. When the mines were connected to the steel mills at the southern edge of the lakes, production increased, and railroads were built. These and other events mingled to make Chicago one of the world's truly great centers of commerce.

The story of Chicago is one of the fastest growth imaginable. Of all its products—from steel, to corn, to farm implements—its most important one was people. Immigrants arrived here by boat and by train, and settled in a city that was sometimes bleak but always bustling. In 1893, city fathers built a stupendous World's Fair—a ''White City'' bedazzled by electric lights—with European architecture, extrav-

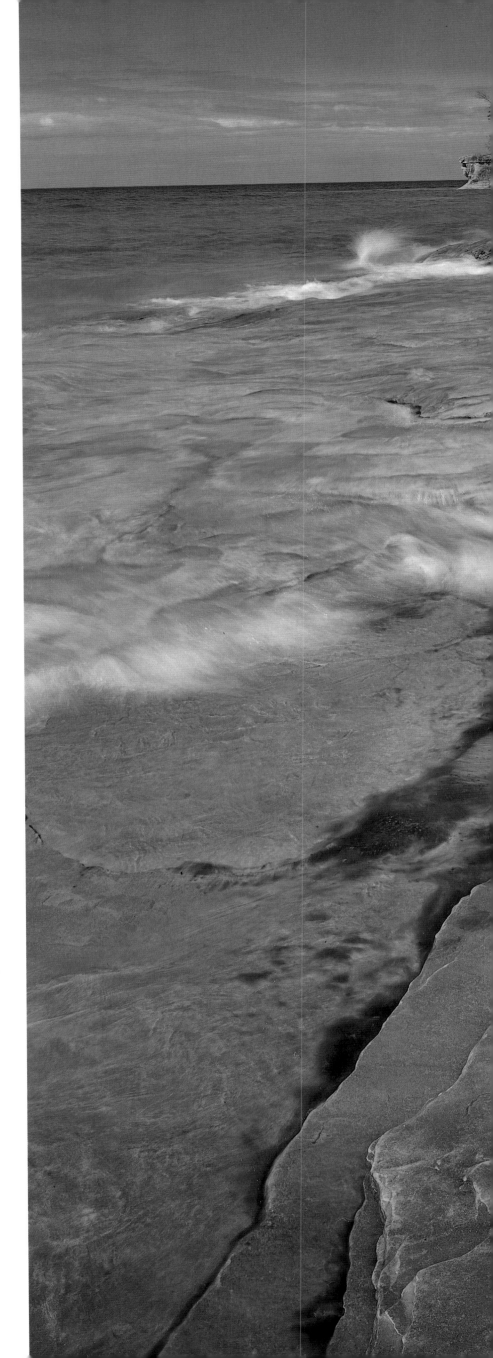

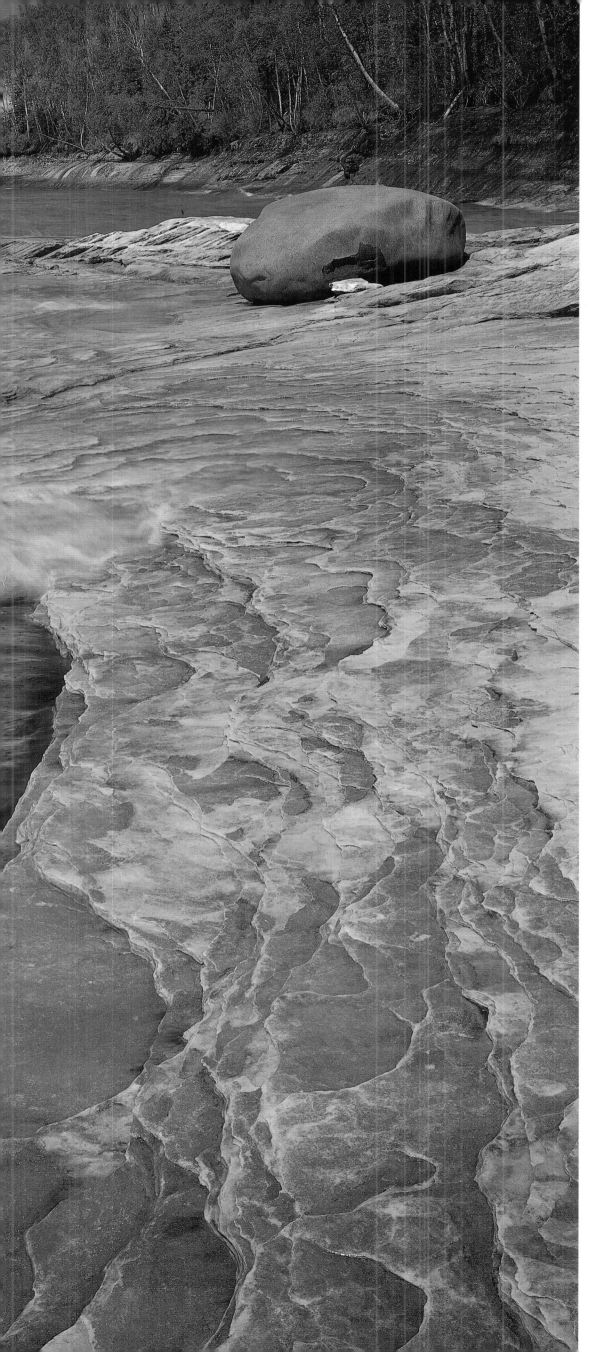

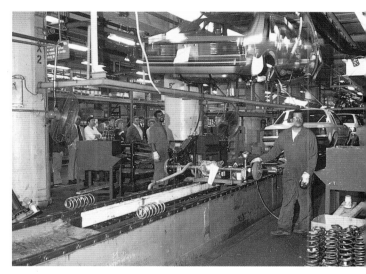

America's romance with the automobile begins right here in Detroit.

Pictured Rocks National Lakeshore, on Lake Superior in Michigan's Upper Peninsula, features cliffs and palisades of Cambrian limestone. The topography of the area is so evocative in some places that American Indians believed that gods lived here.

"A good dairy cow should have large nostrils, because milk is evolved from the blood, and the blood is vitalized by the air the cow breathes." So said William D. Hoard about dairy farming. He was made governor of Wisconsin between 1889 and 1891.

Cleveland, like many neighboring Great Lakes metropolises, boasts perennially exciting professional-sports seasons. The Indians and Browns play ball in its stadium.

agant landscapes, and pavilions of industry from around the world. Jackson Park in Chicago retains vestiges of this glamorous event, which took place in the midst of a serious economic depression.

Culturally, a powerful ambivalence often beset Chicago—it was seen as a harsh city with a brilliant future. Novelist Nelson Algren wrote about Polish slums and said that living in Chicago was like loving a woman with a broken nose. Other literature was more rambunctious, such as the plays of Hecht and MacArthur who wrote *The Front Page*. Appropriately, Chicago also spawned the settlement house movement, and the University of Chicago quickly evolved into one of the nation's leading schools of social investigation. By design, Chicago was an intellectual center as well as an industrial one. Its leaders wanted the city's destiny clearly in its own hands.

Milwaukee has watched some of its beer industry sift away. This is normal enough—brewing derived originally from heavy German immigration and ice that could be cut from the lake. Industries shift, but people remain, and Milwaukee's people lately have built one of the most active arts communities of any city its size in the country. The Milwaukee Ballet and Milwaukee Art Museum draw admirers from much larger cities. Old beer money still funds lakefront festivals, and the Milwaukee Symphony Orchestra thrives in Uihlein Hall, a fine old auditorium named for the family that once owned Schlitz.

Cleveland was called the "come back city" of the 1980s. Previous to that it was saddled with industries almost uniformly vulnerable to foreign competition—steel, auto parts, machine tools. After some initial convulsions, it made a swift transition into a service-based economy, with financial, legal, transportation, and other industries based there. Cleveland is once again a success, though bearing the brunt of dislocations caused by the change.

Detroit, for its part, still faces the challenges brought on by 20th century industry. History was both kind and cruel to the Motor City. It brought great fortunes and powerful waves of migration. It also compressed union battles and ethnic tensions into a period of only a few decades. Modern Detroit is calling for entirely new solutions—and crossing old political boundaries that have separated rich and poor, city and suburb. The objective is to make the burdens of a city's diversity a positive strength. It is a typically Midwestern story. ☆

Kilometers

Statute Miles

Scale 1:3,000,000

One centimeter represents 30 kilometers.
One inch represents approximately 47 miles.

Albers Conical Equal Area Projection

THE
Mississippi Valley

Alabama
Arkansas
Kentucky
Louisiana
Mississippi
Missouri
Tennessee

◆

"[The Mississippi River]
had a new story to tell every day.
Throughout the long twelve hundred
miles there never was a page
that was void of interest,
never one that you leave unread
without some loss."

Mark Twain, *Life on the Mississippi*, 1863

◆

The sugar planters who built this house in the 1830s preferred its French name, Bon Séjours, meaning "good rest." But river-boat passengers who gazed through its corridor of live oaks gave it the name that stuck: Oak Alley. It is still resplendent, on the banks of the Mississippi, in Vacherie, Louisiana, between New Orleans and Baton Rouge.

Traveling downstream on the Mississippi River, somewhere near St. Louis, the North ends and the South begins. The change can be seen in the river itself. The Upper Mississippi is tucked safely between bluffs and limestone cliffs. The Lower Mississippi becomes Old Man River, rolling over low-lying farmland, sometimes even washing towns entirely away. It's laid-back but powerful, romantic but sometimes tragic. These words could also describe the South itself.

Missouri begins the South, but the state is not entirely of it. St. Louis is indeed an old river town, and the St. Louis Art Museum is known for genre scenes such as George Caleb Bingham's "Jolly Boatmen in Port." Yet St. Louis also looks west; as one does by gazing through the Gateway Arch, part of the Jefferson National Expansion Memorial. The fact is that St. Louis has a split personality, and so does Missouri. The north half of the state is Yankee, with "bottomless" glacial soil and settlement by purposeful European immigrants. The southern half, where the Ozark Mountains begin, is more rugged. It drew Virginians and Tennesseeans who were looking for solitude, not comfort. Missouri was divided during the Civil War; residents have been a mite suspicious of outsiders and of each other ever since.

Ozark reticence has abated in recent years, in part because quiet lakes and the hot springs have brought pockets of wealth to this broadly mountainous area. Life is more modern especially in parts of Arkansas, where large industries in manufacturing, forest products, and agriculture punctuate the woods and lowland plains. Little Rock has adopted the look and customs of a true financial center. But throughout Arkansas, there also remains a closeness to the land, an old, indigenous folk culture that seems as authentic as anyplace in the country.

There are cultural estuaries in the region, but most of all there's still the Mississippi. Mark Twain understood it properly as one of the most powerful, not to mention fascinating, forces in American history. Some pages were more interesting than others, of course, and one stop not to be missed was Memphis. From its earliest days, this city was a depot for lumber and cotton, and as the only good port between the Ohio River and Vicksburg, it was something more. When lavish gambling boats plied the river at the turn of the century, black musicians got off in Memphis for rest and relaxation. They met in their particular bars, played their own mu-

Bellingrath Gardens, a major stop on Alabama's Mobile Azalea Trail, features many different species and profuse color year-round.

The Ozark Plateau was formed a million years ago when the earth thrust a former ocean bed skyward. Rivers and streams have since sculpted the limestone, dolomite, sandstone, and shale into picturesque forms. Here the Buffalo River in Arkansas flows beneath ancient cliffs.

sic in their distinctive way. So it was that Beale Street in Memphis became the cradle of down-home rhythm and blues. The neighborhood is still a fine piece of Americana. It is remembered for free black families who lived there before the Civil War, for '30s-style diners serving ham hocks and collard greens, and for a style of blues that employed not one lead guitar, but two. The sound was unique, and even influenced the big bands that made Memphis a regular stop, and always took a little of the city away with them when they left.

Farther on down the Mississippi, images of the Old South grow more eloquent, and its history more complex. A major town along the way was Natchez, Mississippi, where lumbermen and grain dealers often unloaded their goods after floating hundreds of miles downriver. Natchez's lower city was famous for gambling and other unsavory delights—just as well that the river finally ripped it from the banks. The upper city remains, with antebellum mansions of the most ornate Greek Revival style. Many such homes have been maintained and still open their doors to the public. They reflect the splendor and hospitality of former times, despite the fact that the town is now laced with the more utilitarian trappings of a gas and oil industry.

In old Natchez, boatmen would sell their barges, then set off to walk or ride north on the Natchez Trace—one of the earliest important trails of America. The Natchez Trace went to Nashville and completed the triangle (or nearly so) with the Lower Mississippi and Ohio rivers. The history of the Trace suggests, for one thing, why so many strains of homespun country music settled in Nashville, which became a major music center as soon as radio began broadcasting performances of the Grand Ole Opry. The Trace also explains why a pair of Kentucky icons—bourbon and thoroughbreds—are intimately related as part of the same Southern pedigree.

The reason for whiskey in Kentucky goes back to Thomas Jefferson, who as president offered 60 acres in Kentucky to anyone who would use it to grow America's native grain, corn. The land was fertile but remote. Grain often spoiled in transport, but whiskey endured. Legend has it that distillers floated their bourbon (named for Bourbon County, Kentucky, now dry) down the river, and took partial payment in Arabian horses to ride back up the Natchez Trace. Back home, Kentucky's phosphorus-rich soil did as much for the horses as it did for the hootch—from these roots sprang the ritual of mint juleps at the

Grand Glaize Arm, in Lake of the Ozarks, Missouri, typifies the landscape throughout the Ozark Plateau. Quiet waters like these are punctuated by hotels and resort towns.

Tennessee autumn in Great Smoky Mountains National Park produces a ravishing display in America's largest hardwood forest. Beech, birch, ash, black oak, and elm are among species that cover the steep foothills through which passes the Appalachian Trail.

Where southern Louisiana melts gradually into the Gulf of Mexico, Cajuns once plied swamps and bayous in dugout boats called pirogues. Today, oil rigs dot the marshland, which otherwise resists most human penetration.

New Orleans is a city of skyscrapers and the
Louisiana Superdome (the world's largest indoor
sports arena) but also of history, folk culture,
and genuine mystery.

Kentucky Derby.

In New Orleans the past is never so orderly. Laden with sediments of Spanish, French, Yankees, Africans, Cajuns, and others, it is America's most exotic city largely because of the Mississippi River. Geography made New Orleans a destination where abundant trailings of culture could accumulate. The river also created a marshland that encircled the city, making it insular and cocoonlike. Music, cuisine, architecture, and other arts developed distinctive New Orleans character as a result.

Different strains in the local personality have made New Orleanians secretive and demonstrative in relatively equal measure. This fine paradox ascends to a crescendo at the city's Mardi Gras, when societies called "krewes" assemble for a period of intense revelry. If Mardi Gras looks like a pagan ritual, so be it. A modicum of voodoo also reigns in this city. Certain New Orleans houses are reputed to be haunted. And the notes of jazz funerals still resonate in the French Quarter.

Beyond New Orleans, Cajuns live in and amongst the swamps and bayous toward the Gulf. Descended from bands of French who were chased from Canada 300 years ago, Cajuns chose this territory essentially because it was coveted by no one else. These are people who adapted to their environment in unique ways. Not so long ago many lived in houses on stilts, and got around in dugout boats called pirogues. Today a system of levies makes a clearer distinction between land and water, but most people realize that the big river seems unwilling to cooperate in this respect. Nature's clear intention is to turn the Mississippi away from New Orleans and toward the calm Cajun swamplands near Lafayette. Frankly this issue is more remarkable to New Orleanians than it is to Cajuns, who, if the Mississippi ever did change course, would cope quite well, thank you. Bayou waters are always shifting, and Cajuns have negotiated them with what amounts to a sixth sense.

You can't help but remember the Mississippi River's impact when you talk about a new public project that the government has built along the Mississippi–Alabama state line. The Tennessee–Tombigbee Waterway is designed to bring prosperity to a country that hasn't seen much wealth in a century. The Tenn–Tom connects the Tennessee and Tombigbee rivers, creating a wide, commercial water route from Eastern states to Mobile. It was a long-controversial project that turned out to be one of the most ambitious engineering projects ever—more earth was moved for the

This peaceful glade in Mississippi includes a portion of Lake Lee, one of the oxbow lakes created by erosion and floods along the Mississippi River.

In Kentucky bluegrass country, thoroughbreds benefit from lush meadows, mineral-rich water, and the attentions of people who take these magnificent beasts very seriously indeed.

Tenn–Tom than ever before in a single project, even the Panama Canal.

The question is, will this waterway change those parts of Mississippi and Alabama that remain as remote in many ways as William Faulkner's fictional Yoknapatawpha County? Before the Civil War, Upper Tombigbee country was rich with cotton, and steamboats carried the crop from towns with names like Corinth, Aberdeen, and Demopolis to the seaport at Mobile. With greater prosperity in the antebellum period, the railroad came through, and then with the war, Union armies arrived, bent in part on destroying the railroad. After Shiloh and a succession of other battles, the area never recovered. Like Faulkner's world of shabby gentry and odd intellectuals, its connections to the rest of the world were largely broken.

Since the Tenn–Tom was completed several years ago, some industry has improved. There's a more prosperous wood-chip industry, and more soybeans from the area's farms are sold. But truth be told, progress in this part of the South won't come quickly down a river. Change is arriving from other directions. It came to Alabama by blows in the 1960s when a number of its cities were flashpoints in the civil rights movement. Other images of backwardness have been overturned: there's an advanced medical center at the state university, and a fair-sized music recording industry at Muscle Shoals.

The Delta Queen was built in Glasgow, Scotland, in 1924, and then shipped to California to work the Sacramento River. Only in 1947 was it hauled to New Orleans, via the Panama Canal. Now restored to a state of authentic old elegance, it carries time-travelers up the Mississippi River, usually as far north as Vicksburg.

Gateway Arch is the centerpiece of the Jefferson National Expansion Memorial in St. Louis. The arch commemorates America's westward thrust, and also adorns the banks of the Mississippi River, the nation's link to the South.

Rivers, for their part, change places only gradually, and usually not in ways that can be predicted. The Upper Tombigbee is less isolated today because of the waterway, but still poor. Mobile's industry has been enhanced, but it still treats azaleas with as much reverence as commerce, and still celebrates Mardi Gras with as much abandon as New Orleans (where the Mobile-born celebration was imported). Miles of soggy marshland still separate the old farms upriver from the city and the open gulf. In the bayous, life's greatest luxury is a fresh duck and sack of oysters. Old ways endure in the Deep South. These delta swamplands, and its old pleasures, provide a substantial buffer against progress moving too quickly up or down this or any other river. ☆

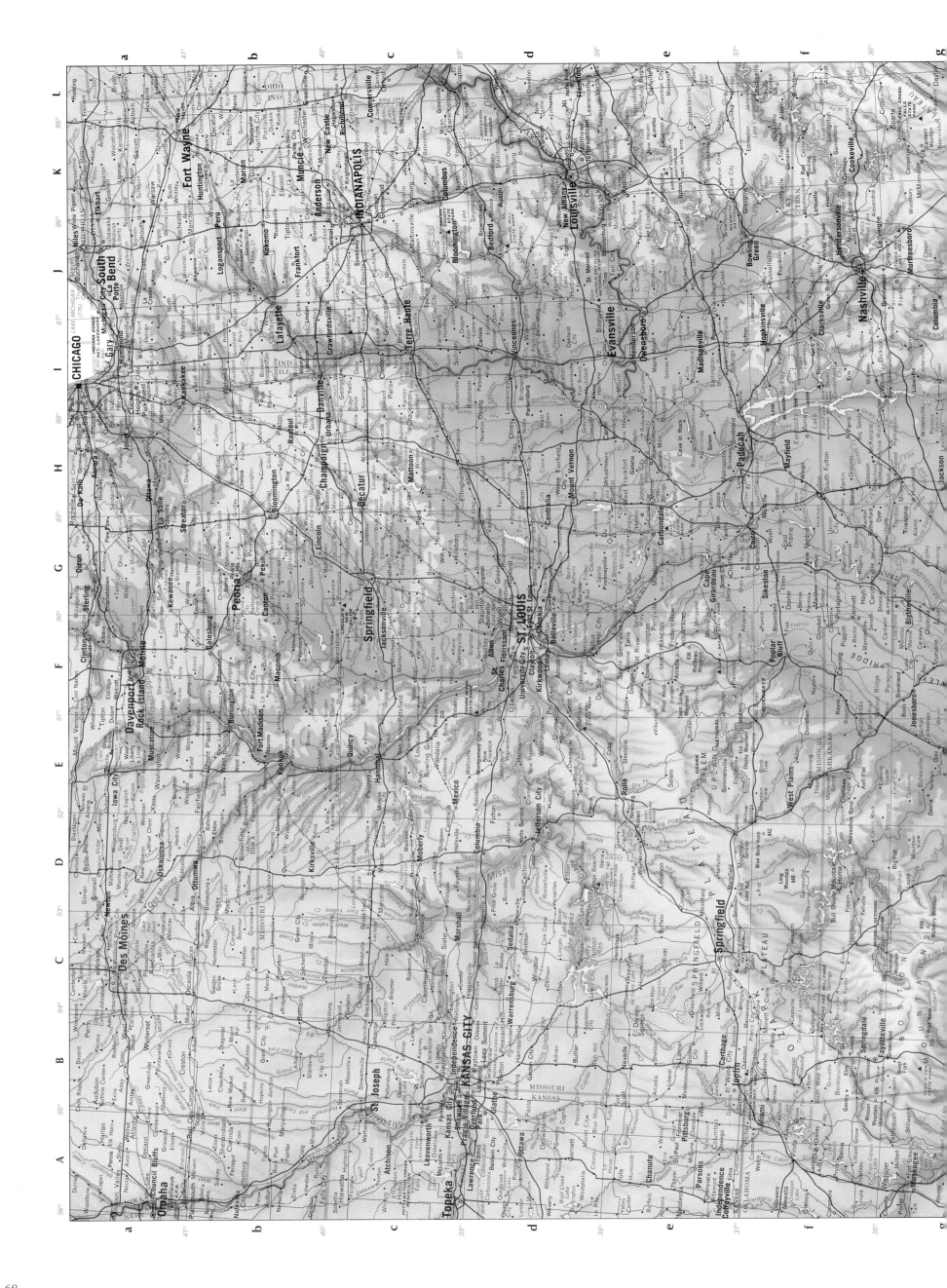

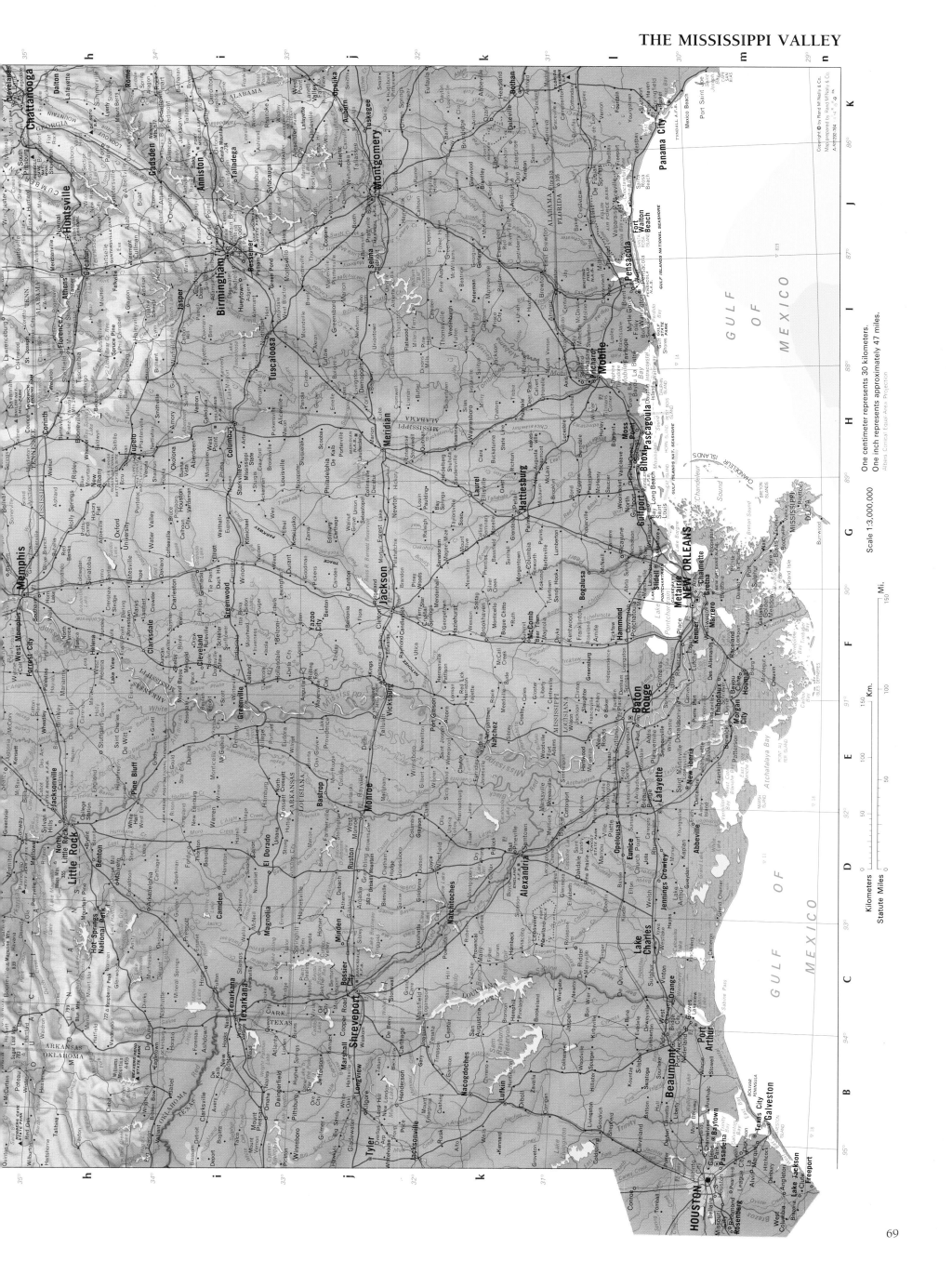

Scale 1:3,000,000

One centimeter represents 30 kilometers.
One inch represents approximately 47 miles.

Albers Conical Equal Area Projection

Kilometers
Statute Miles

Km.
Mi.

THE
Great Plains

Iowa
Kansas
Nebraska
North Dakota
Oklahoma
South Dakota
Texas

◆

*"...More than anything else
I felt motion in the landscape;
in the fresh, easy-blowing
morning wind, and in the earth
itself, as if the shaggy grass were a
sort of loose hide, and underneath
it herds of wild buffalo were
galloping, galloping..."*

Willa Cather, My Antonia, 1918

◆

In the high plains of western Nebraska, the land's gentle roll gradually rises to become mesas and rocky cliffs. Scotts Bluff National Monument is one of the most prominent of such landmarks and was a milepost for passersby on the Oregon Trail.

Explorers called it the Great American Desert because of its endless, arid tablelands of grass. Later, author Frank L. Baum found a new way of viewing the Great Plains when he wrote *The Wizard of Oz*. Baum lived for a time on South Dakota farmland and doubtlessly witnessed its tornadoes and floods. He also learned that this widest and most open of country could caress the imagination like ocean waves.

The Wizard of Oz, which penetrates the soul of Kansas, also captures the essential contradiction of the plains. They appear monotonous, bereft of diversity, even harsh. Yet they are also beautiful and historic. Their expansiveness engenders a sort of independence. A special character has always shown up in its plants and animals, and does today in its people.

The ancient prairies of this region are among the most remarkable creations of the American landscape. In modern times, they have been mostly plowed under by farmers, but their rare, iridescent flora still flourishes in specks of land throughout these states. Prairies created some of the world's most fertile soil, built up year after year by organic decay. Where they remain, prairies are often protected in state and federal preserves, such as Ft. Niobrara National Wildlife Refuge in Nebraska. These areas evoke a time when buffalo, elk, and even cougars ran these ranges, and when grass fires nourished the deep-rooted plants like big bluestem, wild orchids, and prairie gentian.

Human culture has taken hold on the prairie with surprising diversity in places that are still distinctly Dutch, Czech, Swedish, Amish, or otherwise. Such people are known for making a pact with their land and maintaining it through good times and bad. The Amana Colonies in Iowa, for example, are still run by a closed joint-stock corporation. It is owned mostly by descendants of the German religious sect that first settled seven communal villages in 1855. These farm settlements thrive today because they are industrious and have enough work not only for colony members, but to attract outsiders as well. Amanaites have always been comfortable in the real world, enough so that members founded Amana Refrigeration Company in 1934. (It since has been sold to a larger corporation.) Life is good in these "colonies" without being too ascetic or too modern. "Amana martinis" are consumed using strong rhubarb wine as the main ingredient, and local bread is still baked in wood-burning ovens.

Prairie and plains have always brought

The site of an ancient coral reef, Guadalupe Mountains National Park contains Texas's El Capitan, shown here. The park contains one of the most extensive reef systems held in the fossil record.

The Platte River, shown here near Kearney, Nebraska, is wide and shallow. Its generous valley showed settlers the way west as many Americans made that often difficult trek across the country.

out the resourcefulness of the people who live there. Indians who roamed the area built their lives around migrating herds of bison. The first European settlers were also hardy souls. They lived in earth lodges and collected buffalo chips for fuel because wood was so scarce. They often lived near rivers that trickled in summer, but could rush and sweep their earthly possessions away come spring. They survived on dairy farms, and grew grains that flourished nicely even west of the 100th meridian— the line between the lush east and the much drier plains.

In the western parts of the region, small farmers eventually turned to ranching. The story goes that their herds broke away and were left for lost—only to survive the winter like bison on wild grass. So it was that durable ranchers in Texas, Kansas, Nebraska and farther west grazed their cattle across areas as large as some New England states. At the turn of the century, cowboys from throughout the Great Plains drove herds as far as needed to reach old Elgin, Kansas, gone today but once "The Greatest Cattle Shipping Point in the World."

Despite shifting economies and customs, the grassland empire continued to evolve. As ranchers needed a big city, power passed to Dallas, on the edge of the range but also close enough to farm country to be a large cotton exchange as well. Some cities would fade, but others change with the times. Just how much is shown by the fact that Dallas grew not just with cattle and cotton, but lately as a center of high fashion. It became a marvelously diverse city. Cowpunching receded into memory, but a part of its spirit lives on.

Away from population centers, the range remains much as it was in former times. Far north in North Dakota, wheat farming dominates the land as it did 100 years ago when railroads sold off right-of-way to some of the biggest farming outfits America had ever seen. Plains cattle ranchers can be polite and prosperous folk these days, but their world has changed only in the details. On the Sand Hills of Nebraska, fifty thousand acres is a good size for a spread on endless, rolling grasslands. Ranchers say that the land is too rough even for pickup trucks, so their preferred mode of transportation is single-engine airplane, or, naturally, the horse.

This region supports its people, but life on the plains could still be transient. Oklahoma typifies this aspect of its history very well. It was relatively empty territory until the Five Civilized Tribes from east of the Mississippi River moved to lands set aside for them in what was called Indian

Inside its starry globe, Reunion Tower in Dallas revolves and looks out over the edge of the Great Plains. Dallas has vestiges of the Old West, but the modern city is also known for fashion and a legendary love of opulence.

Around the turn of the century, the east Texas skyline was made up of oil derricks and small towns. Then oil corporations entered Texas, and Houston mushroomed.

Begun in 1927, Mount Rushmore in South Dakota is the work of sculptor Gutzon Borglum, instructed by President Coolidge to execute "a distinctively national monument...decidedly American in its conception, in its magnitude, in its meaning and altogether worthy of our country."

For thousands of years, soft rock and clay in the Badlands of South Dakota have been chiseled by erosion. Spires, turrets, and other imaginative forms are the result of unique conditions.

Territory in the 1830s. Later, Oklahoma was known for the mad dashes of settlers racing into newly opened homesteading lands, and for "Sooners" who actually sneaked in before the appointed time. Then in the 1930s, a combination of depleted soil and Depression led to the Dust Bowl days. "Okies" were displaced persons who left Oklahoma and neighboring states for the promise of California. It was oil that finally gave Oklahoma a more settled life. As if grateful for something that anchored people to their land, the state even placed derricks on the grounds of its Capitol in Oklahoma City.

On the margins of this region is the Big Thicket of East Texas. This area was settled early, in the 1820s, by people from Georgia and Tennessee. They were first attracted by the hardwoods, a resource that was scarce as people moved farther west. This land, streaked with bayous, is actually blessed by the most amazing diversity of flora anywhere—orchids, ferns, and even a large selection of carnivorous plants. Bootlegging and hunting for razorback pigs was traditional in this area—still is in some parts. But they also found oil underneath, and that led to settlers of a different sort. After the first big strike, at Spindletop in 1901, tall derricks were clustered in towns filled with wildcatters. Later, the oil companies staked their claims, and by 1930 they had established an authentic skyscraper town, Houston.

South and west, between the Pecos River and the Rio Grande, Texas was home to other cultures, some ancient, others relatively raw. The country was once was filled with bison, and home to some of the earliest Indian communities in North America, going back ten thousand years. Later it appealed to settlers in times when its grasslands were lush and attractive for cattle. Quickly overgrazed, it became dry, rugged territory. It now evokes characters like Judge Roy Bean, a tavern owner and self-styled justice of the peace in Langtry, Texas. Roy Bean's brand of law was legendary if not always just. He knew courtroom procedure from his own frequent brushes with the law. His most famous escapade was staging a championship bout between Peter Maher and Bob Fitzsimmons on an island in the Rio Grande, so as to avoid laws in Texas and Mexico against prizefighting.

The Great Plains are not known for distinctive topography, yet they are punctuated by some of America's most striking features. As the high plains of South Dakota rise from east to west, they break into one of the most striking landscapes in the en-

North Dakota is the most intensively farmed state in the nation. Wheat, as harvested here, leads the way, followed by barley, rye, and flax.

In the late 1800s, North Dakota "bonanza farming" was the name for huge agricultural enterprises that grew wheat on land purchased from the railroads. Some farms were spectacularly profitable. Their stories drew thousands of homesteaders who wanted just a small piece of what North Dakota allegedly held.

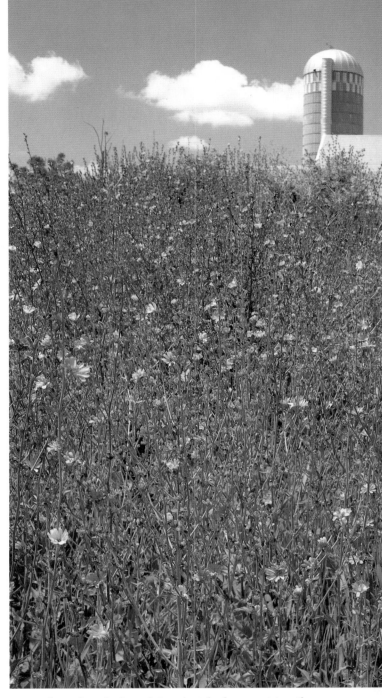

Despite being heavily farmed, Iowa's rich, deep, prairie soil still harbors patches of wildflowers, which provide marvelous signals of the changing seasons, especially spring.

Oklahoma was the grassy highway connecting Texas ranches with stock-shipping yards in Kansas. Today, cattle drives are largely over, but rodeos and colorful costumes recall days when the range was governed by cattle barons, and cowboys were their skillful knights.

The Flint Hills of Kansas, shown here a few moments after sunrise, were once a place of long cattle drives. Today the area still features wide open spaces, with sections of tall grass prairie, and distant views of large limestone mesas.

tire country: the Badlands. *Les mauvaises terres*, so named by French explorers, are a sudden valley of jagged, blade-like peaks, sculpted of eroding clay. Farther west are the Black Hills, which were pushed up by underground volcanic exertions millions of years ago. The Black Hills are considered sacred Indian grounds—so impressive are its dimensions. Americans memorialized a similar emotion when the federal government created Mt. Rushmore. The idea of colossal heads carved from a granite mountain might seem like a glib feat of engineering. But in person they produce a kind of majesty akin, if not equal, to nature itself.

Many epic American stories were set in this spacious high country. Plains Indians—Sioux and Pawnees—practiced the Sun Dance, where braves would hang by skewers until their flesh ripped away from the chest. This ceremony was meant to produce inspired visions of powerful spirits. Later, visions of a different kind—wealth wrought from gold—prompted whites to violate treaties protecting the Black Hills as Indian lands. The nation's bloodiest Indian war ensued, during which General George Custer set out on a strange personal crusade, ending at Little Big Horn. Wounded Knee, South Dakota, was the site of the Indians' final sad encounter with the U.S. Army.

As time went on, additional heroes emerged from this country. Wild Bill Hickok was an Indian fighter and U.S. Marshal in Kansas. He was drawn to the Black Hills by the prospect of gold. He might have mined some, but he spent much time in Deadwood City, South Dakota, playing cards. A more savory character, Theodore Roosevelt, prefaced his political career with attempts to raise cattle on the North Dakota frontier by the Badlands. He failed at cattle, but his manifest pioneering spirit won the hearts of the voters. Roosevelt's time in the state is memorialized by Theodore Roosevelt National Park, part river valley, part badlands.

If we are drawn to the plains and prairie today, it is for a sense of freedom that still thrives in this region. It appears to be something that the people who live here will fight for. The spirit is demonstrated these days by ardent battles of farm families to keep their farms and work the land where their forebears lived. Preserving a relationship with the land remains as important now as it was when America was still an endless and optimistic frontier. ☆

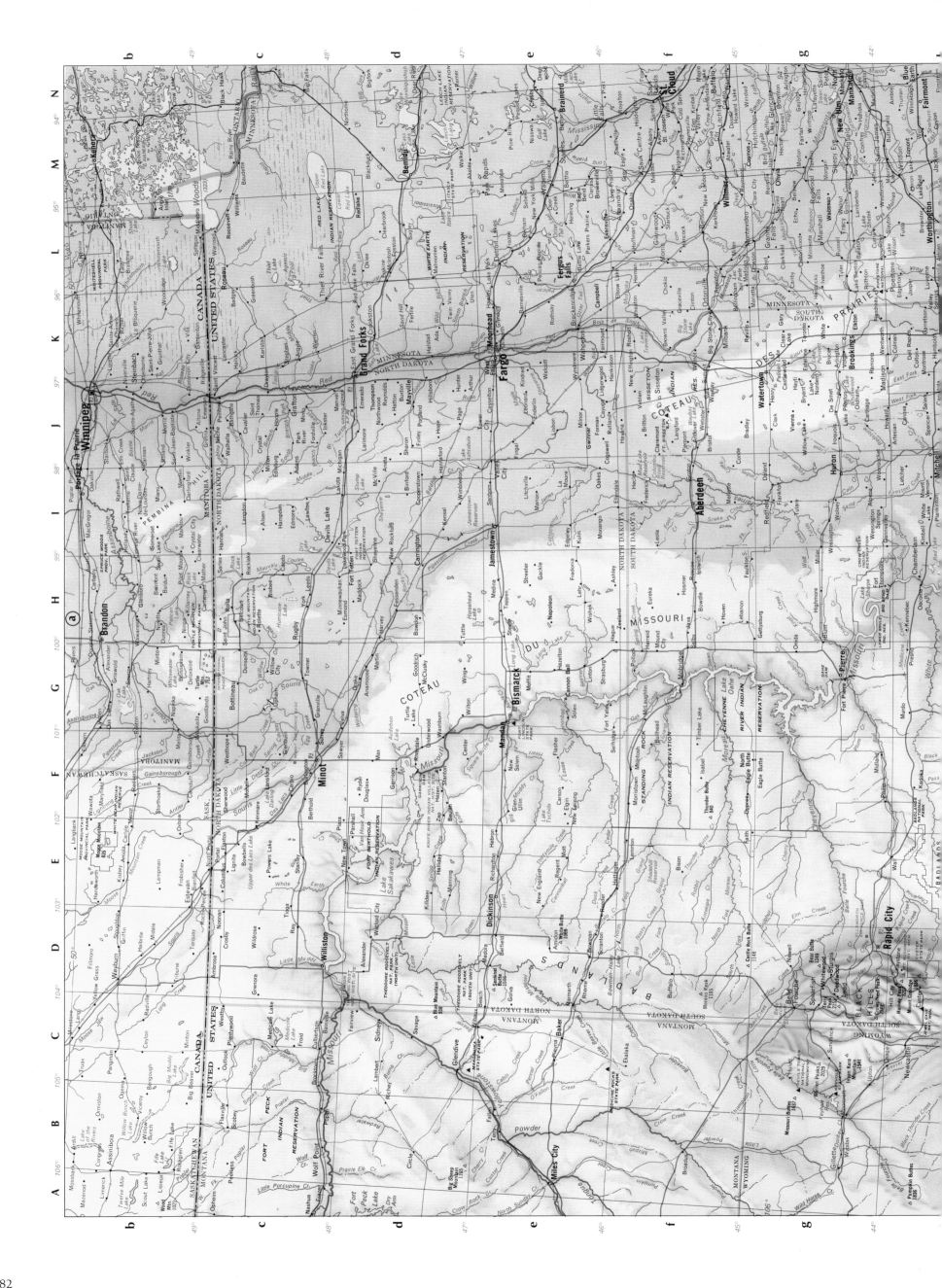

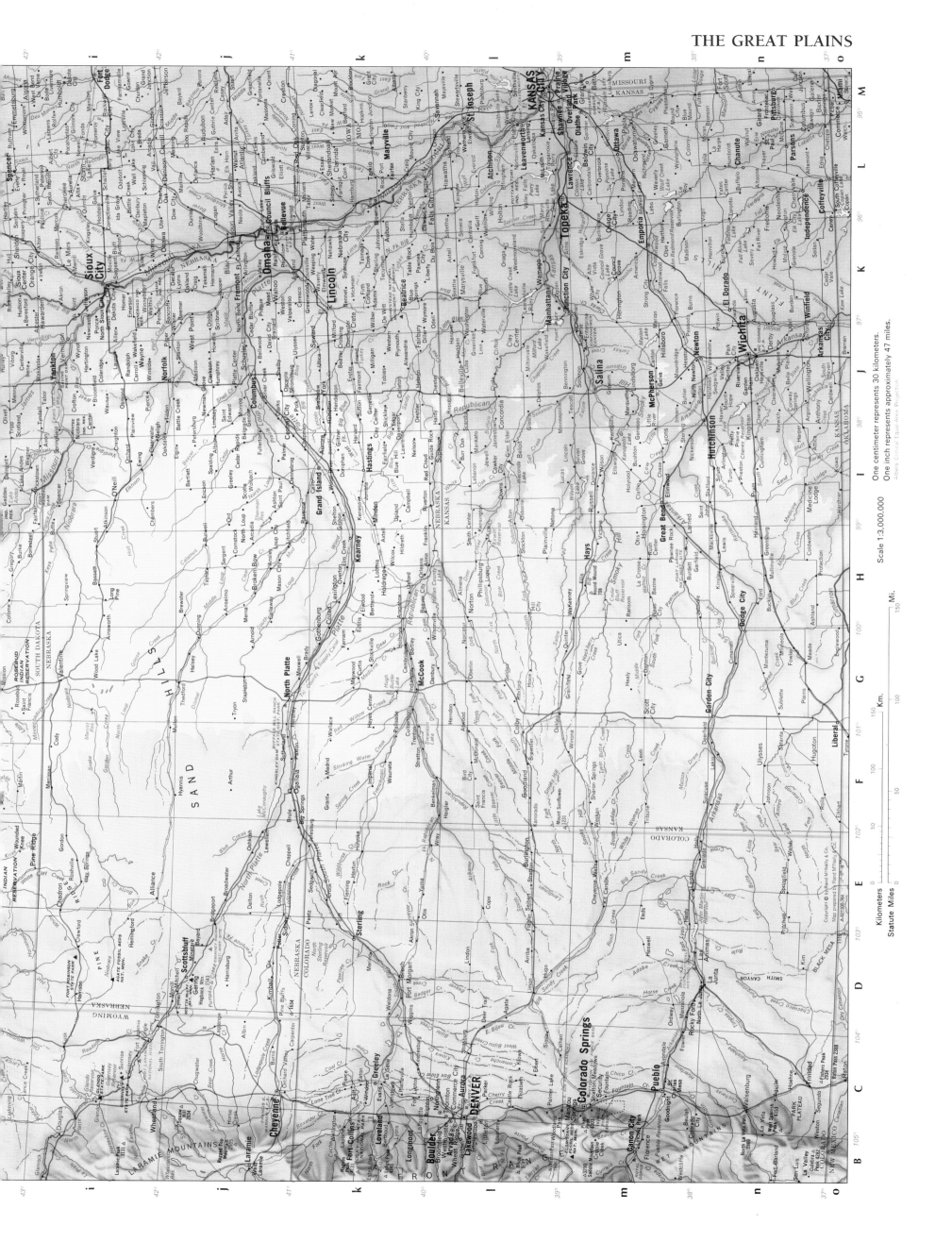

Scale 1:3,000,000

One centimeter represents 30 kilometers.
One inch represents approximately 47 miles.

Albers Conical Equal-Area Projection

Copyright © by Rand McNally & Co.
Made in U.S.A. A-821300-784

Kilometers

Statute Miles

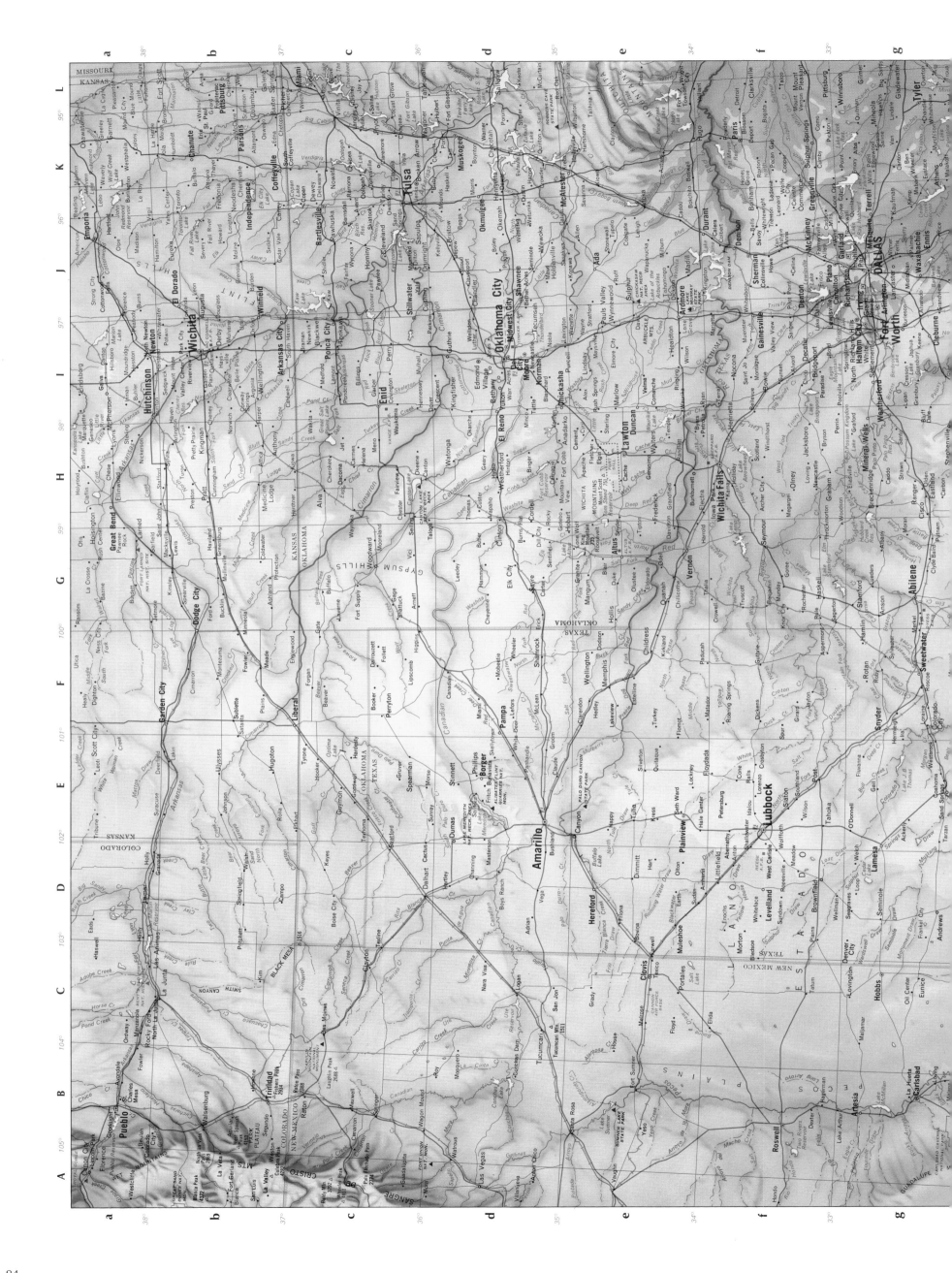

84

One centimeter represents 30 kilometers.
One inch represents approximately 47 miles.

Albers Conical Equal-Area Projection

Scale 1:3,000,000

Copyright by Rand McNally & Co.

GULF OF MEXICO

T H E
Southwest

Arizona
Colorado
New Mexico
Utah

◆

"*Everywhere the aerial gradations*
and sky-effects inimitable;
nowhere else such perspectives,
such transparent lilacs and greys.
I can conceive of some superior
landscape painter, some fine colorist,
after sketching a while out here,
discarding all his previous work...
as muddy, raw and artificial."

Walt Whitman, *Aerial Effects*, 1879

◆

Towers at Red Rock Crossing,
Arizona, rise above a shallow
crossing point in Oak Creek,
a few miles from the old
crossroads town of Sedona.

In modern Aspen, Colorado, the Old West survives mainly in old photos of a distant and far different past. Aspenites of the late 1800s were miners who lived amid mud and manure. There were booms and there were busts, but rarely much in the way of luxury or even romance. It might well be a ghost town today except for a quirk of topography that made it one of the world's most lavish resorts.

Aspen is a special case, but making the Southwest safe and sound for polite society was a long and curious journey. Civilization here began centuries ago with ancient pueblos, continued in exotic Spanish towns, and survived lawless mining outposts in Arizona. Cities sprang up, but until recent times, they were too isolated to flourish.

Colorado eventually grew, and the way it did was typical. For most of its life the state capital at Denver was an agricultural market and little more—people called it "the town that time forgot." Then after World War II, Easterners began noticing the mountains' charms. Air travel made the city accessible. A more mobile, increasingly restless society found it attractive, and business followed. "I'd rather make one dollar in Denver than three dollars in New York," said one businessman.

The beauty of Colorado seemed transcendent, but there was also, finally, wealth. Real estate boomed in Denver. Oil was discovered. Then an army veteran found that a narrow cut in the mountains where his unit once trained reminded him of the Austrian Tyrol. This was Aspen itself, where investors were brought in, ski slopes cut, and development took on a charmed life of its own. In 1949 a festival to commemorate the bicentennial of Goethe, of all things, was held there. It attracted Artur Rubinstein, Albert Schweitzer, and other luminaries. Aspen was being called the American Salzburg. So it goes in the American West.

This was not the first time that Americans rushed in this direction. Back in the 1820s, Americans who cared little for comfortable travel went west on a trail named for the old settlement of Santa Fe, even then a worthwhile destination. Santa Fe was set on a wide plain with a full, open view of the Sangre de Cristo Mountains, the southern tail of the Rockies. Long settled by the Spanish, Santa Fe's markets were filled with food and other merchandise. Travelers described plazas lined with strings of red peppers and fresh wild turkeys. Churches glimmered with gold and silver. Festivals were characterized by wild

A pair of saguaro cacti frame the Superstition Mountains in Arizona. The reason for this name is not certain—it might be that Pima Indians lived in constant fear of Apaches who would pour without warning from these rocky heights.

Gila Bend, Arizona, is known for ancient societies and the mystery of a 900-year old pyramid. In more recent times, cattle production has led some settlers to choose a life on the range.

Downtown Phoenix is relatively compact compared with the rest of this sprawling city. It began as a small western settlement with a hopeful name from antiquity. Today Phoenix is a sophisticated urban center in a region that was once considered too harsh for polite society.

Geologists debate the origin of these strange and spectacular formations in Canyonlands National Park, Utah. What is known is that Indians once lived here and outlaw Butch Cassidy once hid out here.

These finely sculpted peaks, known as Maroon Bells, near Aspen, Colorado, are only a few miles from the world-famous resort.
But the narrow valley remains a relative wilderness, inaccessible by road in winter and swathed in endless wildflowers in spring.

Gila Cliff Dwellings National Monument, New Mexico, is one of many vivid archaeological sites in the Southwest.

fandangos and alleged licentiousness. Today a kind of otherworldliness still prevails in this town. Artists migrate to Santa Fe, inspired by the dramatic dappled landscape and living history of the place. Around the restored Palace of Governors, Indian crafts are sold in a market as timeless as the old pueblos that are still inhabited nearby in Taos.

In the late 1800s, further reports of the American Southwest told of exotic cultures and amazing terrain. Among those bringing this message was a Harvard dropout and journalist by the name of Charles Fletcher Lummins, who took his first walking trip through Arizona in 1884. "We read a vast amount about the wonders of foreign lands; but very few writers—and still fewer reliable ones—tell us of the marvelous secrets of our own," Lummins wrote. He was bewitched by Hopi rituals, and particularly a snake dance that he compared to feats he knew of in India. He described mesas with rough walls of worn sandstone capped with cornices of hard lava. One hundred years ago, Lummins exhorted his readers to see America first, and held up the Southwest as testimony.

Civilization had existed there for a long time. The pueblos of Oraibi, Arizona, America's oldest continuously inhabited place, have hung on to sharp cliffs for over 800 years. But real understanding of the territory came slowly to most Americans. Early images of the region were drawn by the artist Frederic Remington, who began his career by illustrating magazine stories of battles between the cavalry and Apache war bands. Remington got reports secondhand, which led to elaborate, oft-fictitious narratives. Soldiers were gallant heroes. Indians were picturesque savages. An imaginative chap, the young New Yorker adopted the rough dialect of a frontiersman, and declared that Europe was a "10-cent sideshow" compared to a visit to the American Southwest. Later, as Remington's affection for the West deepened he portrayed it more realistically. He painted the harsh realities of cowboy life and even chronicled massacres of Indians by whites.

Various other views of the region were transmitted by journalists, sensational and otherwise. Gold and silver mining possessed a fascination for turn-of-the-century Americans, even those who never left their safe Eastern cities. Mining towns in Arizona, for example, were populated by indisputably tough characters. The gunfight at the O.K. Corral became legend even though it was always unclear which side the villains were on. In another episode, legislators from Tucson were pelted with

dead cats after winning the state university for their city. That mining town's good citizens really wanted the prison, a more lucrative project, instead.

Gentler forms of civilization came to the region with dams and irrigation. Projects of the U.S. Water Reclamation Act turned dry desert into citrus orchards and other kinds of farms. Importantly, they also made cities desirable places to live. Little by little, Phoenix became a place attractive not because of its reputation as a frontier town, but for the comforts of a warm, arid climate. Like other Sun Belt cities, growth came after World War II (accelerated by the development of air conditioning). Intellectual institutions migrated there; it became a place for pure research in sciences, particularly astronomy, and new technological industries. For its part, Tucson also grew comfortable with itself as a college town, and the University of Arizona (especially its Museum of Anthropology) now has substantial impact on the life of the city.

Various forms of culture flourished in the desert, perhaps because of its history, certainly because of its stirring panoramas and color. Frank Lloyd Wright moved there and refined Prairie School architecture in a place where the land had haunting architectural shapes of its own. Georgia O'Keeffe was attracted by the sensuality of form and color. Contemporary artists such as R.C. Gorman have brought Indian motifs to international markets. Even the Cowboy Artists of America boast a large following and astonishing prices for their wistful works of a romantic West.

The romance of the Southwest persists in its dramatic and sometimes impenetrable landscape. Among the great landmarks, the Grand Canyon exerts the most majestic, even frightening profile, yet until very recently it sheltered an Indian village deep inside. Canyon de Chelly National Monument is smaller in scale, but it has been sculpted by nature with such apparent purpose that the Navajos regard it as sacred. In the Painted Desert, broad layers of shale, sandstones, and mineral oxides create bands of color resembling the fluid lines of Indian blankets, jewelry, and other art.

Utah is nearby, in some ways a place apart. For one thing it was separated from Arizona by the formidable canyons of the Colorado River—bridges to make an easy drive across it are relatively new. More to the point, the state was settled by Mormons who migrated to this hard territory because they craved isolation. That they had in Utah—along with equal mea-

"I have seen people rave over it; better people struck dumb with it; but, have never yet seen the man or woman who expected it," wrote Charles F. Lummins, one of the first journalists to describe the Grand Canyon, Arizona.

One of the first explorers of Colorado's western slope was Captain John W. Gunnison, for whom Gunnison National Forest is named. His concern was to find a likely route for the railroad. Minerals were later discovered, with the predictable rush of prospectors.

In Bryce Canyon National Park, Utah, exotic sandstone towers have been sculpted by centuries of erosion. Here, Thor's Hammer is seen from the Navajo Loop Trail, an undulating path weaving amongst this and other formations.

Morning pastels on the Great Salt Lake belie the bleak desert that Mormons found when they arrived to create their own society in Utah.

sures of beauty and desolation. The intriguing formations of Bryce Canyon and the colors of Zion National Park testified vividly enough that the state was touched by extraordinary forces. Still, the land the Mormons found was dry and hard to till, and the lake around which they settled is one of the world's saltiest bodies of water.

From this landscape, Mormon leader Brigham Young endeavored to build a prosperous society, and one with the most limited contact with the outside world. By the turn of the century he had done so, with banking, agriculture, manufacturing, and transportation all well established. As prosperity grew, larger portions of the desert were irrigated and made into productive farmland. Much of the state had the qualities of an oasis, built around the gray granite spires of the Mormon Temple.

Utah's development reflected an idea that evolved as a matter of faith to Mormons. It was also something Native Americans understood, and even rough-hewn miners could not help but realize. This was that the lands of the Southwest possessed a responsive spirit. A certain amount of reverence toward it was helpful. Persistence and steady labor seemed more important still.☆

Acrobatics and skiboarding have become fashionable, but nothing in Colorado is quite like a long, smooth run through fresh powder.

One centimeter represents 30 kilometers.
One inch represents approximately 47 miles.

Albers Conical Equal Area Projection

Scale 1:3,000,000

THE
Northwest

Idaho
Montana
Oregon
Washington
Wyoming

◆

"While this equable and bland temperature

prevails through the lower country,

the peaks and ridges of the vast mountains

by which it is dominated,

are covered with perpetual snow.

This renders them discernible at a great

distance, shining at times like bright

summer clouds, at other times assuming

the most aerial tints, and always forming

brilliant and striking features

in the vast landscape."

Washington Irving, *Astoria*, 1836

◆

Mount Shuksan, in Washington's
Mount Baker National Forest, is
one of the peaks of the Northwest
that attracts fishermen, hikers,
and cross-country skiers.

The American frontier was built through a chorus of myths, and those revolving around the Northwest attracted particular attention. Legends of explorers, and later of cowboys, cast the nation's attention to these promising, but remote and dangerous, territories. Many stories were true, some extravagant, but all of them pointed out that the land was open, rough, and romantic as the American spirit itself.

Buffalo Bill was one such man whose image, like the high Wyoming country he finally called home, became bigger than mere life. Born in Iowa, William F. Cody's tale began when he rode for the Pony Express at the age of 14. He probably did, though it's clear that Cody later had a press agent par excellence to embellish such details. Will's next jobs were as an Indian scout for generals such as Sheridan and Custer, then a guide for buffalo hunters from more civilized climes. After leading a massively successful hunt with a party that included Russian royalty, Buffalo Bill was rewarded with a huge overcoat made of Russian fur from Grand Duke Alexis. Cody became one of the most baroque characters the West ever produced. He wore extravagant buckskin suits on the streets of New York. When his Wild West Show became world famous, he trundled Indians in full regalia off to Europe, and had their photographs made sitting in gondolas in Venice.

If Buffalo Bill was a caricature, he said he wanted to be remembered as a "pioneer and developer of civilization." He founded Cody, Wyoming, reputed to be rich with gold. It was also close to Yellowstone Park, with geysers and hot springs that were awesome even to him. Cody poured money into the town. He himself came up relatively empty, but today Cody is the home of the Buffalo Bill Historical Center, a true shrine of Western history and art.

Perhaps more than any other part of the country, the Northwest has stirred the most far-flung ambitions of Americans. Thomas Jefferson regarded it as a mission of his presidency to establish a route to the Pacific Coast, where trappers and traders had settlements that could be reached only after a long sea voyage. For an overland passage Jefferson appropriated $2,500, a sum that went to a pair of army officers, Lewis and Clark. They believed, like geographers of the day, that they needed only to cross the summit of the Rockies, then glide down gentle rivers to the coast.

The fact that over 1,000 miles separated the Continental Divide from the ocean might have discouraged lesser souls. But

Clepsydra Geyser in Yellowstone National Park in Wyoming often hisses and bubbles. Beneath the surface of geysers, water is heated by volcanic gases. In complicated underground chambers, pressure builds until it explodes into steam and blasts violently through cooler waters at the surface.

"The soil improves somewhat," wrote Meriwether Lewis after crossing the Continental Divide and into Idaho, Oregon, and Washington. The fertility attracted a stream of later settlers. Today, potatoes, wheat, barley (being harvested here in Idaho), and other crops make agriculture the most important industry by far in parts of the Northwest.

after paddling the Missouri River to the high country of Montana, they found their way to Idaho's Snake River, cutting between steep slopes of Ponderosa pine, and giant gorges lined by red cliffs. As they approached the Columbia River, the land opened. The explorers noted in their diaries that the soil, like their spirits, improved. Indeed they saw places of remarkable fertility, and in later years they would draw pioneers by the thousands, attracted by grazing land and conditions to make Idaho potatoes and Washington apples famous.

The writings of Lewis and Clark must have provided curious reading to Easterners. Theirs was a perilous journey. They often were bewildered by multiple forks in the river. At times they faced starvation, and members of the party even shot and wounded each other while hunting. Ultimately they reached the ocean, and Lewis was so elated by their success that he promised, "in the course of 10 or 12 years a tour across the Continent by this route will be undertaken with as little concern as a voyage across the Atlantic is at present."

An easy trek was wishful thinking, but difficulties did not stop others from making it. A succession of men and women braved the wilderness and increasingly suspicious Indians. Some of their exploits were recorded by Washington Irving in his narrative of the West, *Astoria*, written in 1836. Irving was the first serious writer to chronicle the region. His narrative was drawn from stories told by people such as John Jacob Astor, a fur merchant who founded the settlement of Astoria at the mouth of the Columbia. Overland explorers were included in Irving's book, and their adventures provided marvelously vivid pictures for readers. One reviewer wrote that Irving's accounts were as striking and sometimes appalling as "the adventures of explorers of the Middle Ages."

The uplands of Montana and Idaho—opened by the Oregon Trail—became ripe for legends of their own. This was hard country, made even more so by the discovery of minerals and arrival of miners. Previously furs and agriculture brought quiet, tenacious souls, but gold brought a rush of impatient and often unscrupulous sorts, and greed grew far faster than anything like law and order. Thus it was that bands of outlaws roamed freely and eventually evolved into de facto crime syndicates. Bandits were elected sheriff in frontier towns, as, for example, one Henry Plummer in a place called Bannack, Montana. Plummer was a handsome, winning fellow,

On the Cascades' western slope, Sweet Home, Oregon, was settled by loggers in the 1800s. The surrounding streams are filled with chinook salmon and steelhead trout.

Wyoming's portion of the Black Hills includes Devil's Tower National Monument, a 600-foot stump of volcanic rock.

The Oregon coast, shown here at Cannon Beach, is enchanting when at rest but ferocious when frequent storms kick up.

The city on Puget Sound, Seattle here hosts a sailboat race while it sits silently glowing in the sun.

which allowed townspeople initially to overlook his conviction record. Before long rumor had it that he was in cahoots with a band that rustled cattle, murdered prospectors, and cheated at cards. The only way to deal with such a situation was to do what eventually was done. Vigilante squads were recruited from Montana all the way to Oregon. They were relentless in tracking down offenders. Plummer himself was detained the Avengers, as the vigilantes were called, hastily tried, and then made to do a "rope dance," all of which was lavishly covered in newspapers around the country. The Avengers were known as one of the first and most effective "detective agencies" in the West. Their brand of rough justice is remembered rather fondly by many even now.

Describing Washington and Oregon, geographers talk constantly about contrasts in history, in terrain, and in personality. The eastern portions of these two states are indeed different from common conceptions of the Pacific Northwest. They have wide, open, arid panoramas. Their ranges have known wheat farming, sheep ranching, and a history, not of cowboys, but of imported Mexican vaqueros. Wildlife teems in lakes that fill with spring runoff. Antelope are plentiful in some places, and stir ancient memories of this austere country that is so different from the pine forests west of the Cascade Mountains.

Oregon and Washington also represent separate worlds. Oregon was settled by New Englanders, frugal, conservative, and civilized. Early Oregonians named Portland after the city in Maine. Even today Portland remains villagelike in some ways. It is well loved for shaded streets and famous for its roses. Washington's history harkens back to "Mercer girls"— wagonloads of eligible females brought out to marry lumberjacks and others who "turned out looking like grizzlies in store clothes with their hair slicked down like sea otters."

Differences abound in these two states, but in many ways their coasts are of a single spirit. Rich resources and gentle climate imply that they are largely at peace with nature. They share the Columbia River gorge, which cuts through the Cascade Mountains beneath long falls of water and massive limestone cliffs. Within view of Seattle, Mount Rainier makes hearty outdoorsmen of city dwellers. Long trails skirt high glaciers and penetrate miles of virgin forest. In southwest Oregon, Crater Lake lies marvelously azure, high in an old volcano, attracting large numbers of people to

Just west of the high plains in northern Montana is Glacier National Park. The region was created by the uplift of the earth's limestone crust and subsequent erosion by glaciers and streams. The result is valleys, lakes, and a fine spring palette of wildflowers.

*The forests of Washington and Oregon have long
served the nation as a source for lumber and wood products.
Today, there are protected forest lands in both states.*

*Another strange and wonderful corner of the Rocky Mountains is
Idaho's City of Rocks, near the border with Utah.*

Hood River County in northern Oregon is peaceful country. It is favored by climate and volcanic soil as a place for fruit orchards and other kinds of agriculture.

Not far from the Continental Divide, the earliest explorers passed panoramas such as this on the Snake River in Wyoming. Beneath the Grand Tetons' jagged peaks, the land is embroidered with pines and autumn-tinged aspens.

otherwise remote country.

The region's compact with nature includes the wealth of hydroelectric energy. At one time the resource was considered a munificent gift from heaven, providing ample electricity, which led to the manufacture of aluminum and thus Seattle's aircraft industry. Utilities even built stepped "ladders" so salmon could pass over artificial barriers like the Bonneville Dam and complete their annual migrations up the Columbia. The region's relationship with the environment is far more complex today. Salmon have been the subject of sometimes bitter politics. Another compelling issue has involved the spotted owl, whose numbers have been diminishing for some time. Saving owls is important to many people because the species is considered an indicator species—as it goes so go an abundance of other less visible flora and fauna. The outcome of this battle has been laws for the preservation of Washington's old growth forests; logging continues only in areas that have been replanted in modern times.

Nature in this region moves other people in other ways. Oregon is known increasingly as an epicurean paradise. In the subtly colored richness of the Willamette Valley, viticulture of certain grapes, principally Pinot noir, ranks with the most successful in the world. Moreover, white truffles and chanterelles grow in nearby woods. Local sturgeon caviar and Dungeness crab compete for the palate's attention. Oregon lamb, much appreciated by connoisseurs, is raised on plains just east of the Cascades.

Puget Sound is still one of those wonderful bodies of water with endless inlets and wooded harbors. But despite the success of environmentalists, the untouched coast is being pushed farther and farther from Seattle. So for many Washingtonians the westering urge continues. Some have found their way well beyond the city and to the San Juan Islands, some points of which are still best reached by plane. It is a place where vast stands of Douglas firs stand cathedral-like, and in summer snorkelers cavort with harbor seals. It recalls a time when few Europeans ventured here, when survival itself demonstrated a remarkable relationship with nature. It remains one of America's romantic hideaways.☆

Kilometers 0   50   100   150   Km.

Statute Miles 0   50   100   150   Mi.

Scale 1:3,000,000   One centimeter represents 30 kilometers.
                     One inch represents approximately 47 miles.
                     Albers Conical Equal-Area Projection

California
AND
Nevada

California
Nevada

◆

"We carried life out here
and set it down the way those
ants carry eggs. And I was the leader.
The westering was as big as God,
and the slow steps that made
the movement piled up and piled up
until the continent was crossed."

John Steinbeck, *The Grapes of Wrath*, 1939

◆

*San Francisco's Golden Gate Bridge
was built in 1937, helping transform
Marin County from a remote web of
cowpaths into one of the most thickly
settled places in the United States.*

California. The word alone evokes an abundance of images—rocky coasts, lush vineyards, sprawling cities. But the place, most of all, calls up a personality. California, a virtual paradise of nature, would be much diminished without its people. Californians are seekers, they are ambitious, and all panoramas of this state are touched by their enthusiasm for life.

Prevailing opinion marks Californians as eccentrics, as perpetual strangers in a strange land. But in reality they are the quintessential Americans, living the quintessential American dream, heightened only slightly by something in the warm air or their richly woven history.

The attractions to California have never been particularly subtle—and perhaps its critics would prefer the more sublime blandishments of other states. The first European settlers were missionaries, drawn there to save souls in a place that already seemed close to paradise. Later it was gold, a fever that began in 1848 when a workman found nuggets while building a millrace in the foothills of the Sierra Nevada. Within ten years, gold changed San Francisco from a rickety outpost into a city of some splendor and even ostentation. The alleged Dauphin of France, a shipwrecked English baronet, and all manner of Easterners arrived and contributed heartily to its growth.

The agriculture of the San Joaquin Valley provided additional fortunes after settlers discovered the fertility of its soil and perfection of its climate for grain, cotton, orchards, grapes, and endless other crops. Petroleum was later discovered in the valley, bringing more wealth and another wave of migration to the far end of the unfinished nation.

Not all of California's early migrants came for economic reasons. Many were attracted simply by the landscape, by beauty that seemed sacred in its intensity. As writers descended on Yosemite, they compared its rock formations to cathedrals, and straight pines to towering columns. Horace Greeley, publisher of the New York *Tribune* and no particular romantic, brought back extravagant reports. "The modicum of moonlight that fell into this awful gorge," he wrote, "gave to that precipice a vagueness of outline, an indefinite vastness, a ghostly and weird spirituality."

Other unique splendors of California included its giant redwoods, the world's tallest trees, and sequoias, the world's largest. Conservationist John Muir said that the sequoia "seems the very god of the woods." Lumbermen would harvest them with

Los Angeles was once a "sprawl of suburbs in search of a city." Then a network of highways gradually wove the area together, with its hub near the old downtown district. By 1959, a law prohibiting buildings of more than 13 stories was changed, as skyscrapers could be made earthquake-proof.

Scenes like this at Red Rock Canyon, Nevada, were witnessed by travelers en route to California. Their appreciation of this desert's stark beauty increased when gold, silver, and copper were discovered amidst the yucca and rocky peaks.

blasting powder. Today redwoods grow protected in dozens of parks from Big Sur on the central coast all the way north to Jedediah Smith State Park near Crescent City. Sequoias are concentrated inland in the Sierra Nevada, notably in Kings Canyon National Park, where the trees embroider some of California's most massive granite forms.

Californians have nurtured their relationship to the land in other ways. North of San Francisco, small farmers work the soil using organic techniques that yield finely wrought, expensive crops. A wine industry has evolved particularly in Napa and Sonoma counties and competes in quality with the much older vineyards of Europe. Sonoma also grows apples with such care that some growers blend their ciders to achieve perfect balance. An industry of exotic vegetables caters to gourmets and the restaurant trade, which has taken hold in this area with much enthusiasm. Some say that the culture of this area resembles Provence in France. Others point out that this is rural America at its most romantic.

Unique landmarks in California provide something for every state of mind. Mount Shasta, best seen from a distance, is a snowy volcanic cone of near-perfect form. It stands on the remote northern extremity of the Sierra range, which then extends south 600 miles. The Mojave Desert and Death Valley attract visitors for the variety of textures, colors, and silence found there. Jet-black volcanic mass, red granite, and bluish minerals in sandstone paint extraordinary pictures of natural history. Mosaic Canyon and Dante's View are descriptive names of two famous features in Death Valley National Monument.

Quite naturally Californians have concluded that their lives should be as dramatic and seamless as the landscape. Thus the state is fertile ground for groups seeking spiritual solace—including those seeking experiences of Eastern mysticism and cults devoted to rock and roll bands. Nevertheless, those who seek unity in this life have their work cut out for them in California, for it remains almost maddeningly diverse.

Consider its two major cities. Los Angeles is a world of splendid self-consciousness—a result, perhaps, of wealth based largely on images of itself. In the earliest days the city's major industry was real estate. Then it was entertainment. Both pursuits are dedicated to creating hard reality from mere perception. A curious sidelight on L.A. is that it was chosen as a setting for the most hard-boiled characters imagi-

The damp and foggy area around Del Norte Coast Redwoods State Park, in northern California, is home to giant redwoods, western rhododendrons, and much other plant life.

Napa Valley, California, features microclimates that make it one of the world's greatest grape-growing areas. Length of season, temperature, humidity, and other factors mark certain points in the valley as optimal for many varieties.

The history of San Diego is represented here at Mission San Diego de Alcala. In 1769, Father Junipero Serra (whose statue appears here) founded the original mission on this site.

Mono Lake, east of Yosemite National Park, is a volcanic creation. This comparative wasteland is punctuated by wooded clusters and wildlife.

nable: the private eyes of Raymond Chandler and Dashiell Hammett. In California the highs were higher, and the serpents more deadly, than anyplace else on earth. Many came only to witness, but so many ended up staying and finding a home.

Then there is San Francisco, with a question of its own. How can a city so relatively young conjure such feelings of Old World charm? Is it real or is this, too, an illusion? In some ways San Francisco resembles Hong Kong, a vast trading center, or old Vienna, civilized despite chaos. San Francisco is unlike any other American city, perhaps because of its enchanting natural beauty, or perhaps because, as writer Brett Harte said, it is "serene and indifferent to fate." Indeed, the nervousness of other American cities has been expiated somehow from San Francisco.

Other conceptions of the culture prevail in California. San Diego has Balboa Park, built for the 1915 World's Fair and still a centerpiece of the city's ornate Spanish architecture. There's San Simeon, the work of one man, William Randolph Hearst, whose power to assemble eclectic antiquities equaled even that of the popes and Medici princes. There's also the Monterey Peninsula where vestiges of Steinbeck's Cannery Row have been restored and are joined with one of the world's most fascinating aquariums.

The glitter of San Diego at sunset is here viewed across its vast harbor.

California's El Capitan, a 3,000-foot granite face in Yosemite National Park, is affected by the play of shadows, mists, and other variables that have long enchanted artists.

On the border of California and Nevada lies magnificent Lake Tahoe. It is encircled with national forests, resorts, and stunning views.

Astride the Colorado River, Nevada's Hoover Dam still ranks among the world's largest dams. Its creation, Lake Mead, provides water to regions as far away as southern California.

*Some of the nation's
most famous neon glows here
in Las Vegas.
Perhaps only fireworks
could be more dazzling.*

Next door to California is Nevada, long considered a geographic companion of California, but with a fascinating history of its own. The first visitors to Nevada's Great Basin came in the 1850s when the dry, ancient, rugged range was regarded mostly as an obstacle between gold-crazed California and the rest of the world. Nevada's Comstock Lode, with its wealth of unmined silver, later attracted a rough and ready kind of prospector—settling in places that are now monochromatic ghost towns.

The dryness and unpromising landscape of Nevada has been expressed in many ways. Writers used to claim that God had left it unfinished, given it up as a bad job. Some people even suggested that Nevada was actually un-American in its unproductiveness. Yet others saw something lovely in the desert. "This strange, weird land never looked so attractive to our eyes," said one amazed visitor about dry and ancient formations of the earth. Mark Twain, too, found something exhilarating here. On his way to Carson City, where he went when his Mississippi River days were interrupted by the Civil War, one could see "buffaloes and Indians, and prairie dogs and antelopes, and have all kinds of adventures, and maybe get hanged or scalped, and have ever such a fine time, and write home and tell us all about it, and be a hero..."

That was Twain. As time wore on, and the ups and downs of mining adventures failed to produce a stable economy, it was clear that prosperity would require still more extraordinary efforts. In Utah, also in the Great Basin, Mormons created a kind of garden in the desert, driven as one by a spiritual mission. Nevada chose not to follow down this path, so it took another: divorce and gambling. The result was propitious. Since 1940, Nevada's population has increased tenfold, to well over one million. It changed from an invisible netherworld to a place where, among other traits, a whole genre of popular culture evolved.

Physically, little binds Nevada and the many parts of California together, except lines drawn on a map. It's the broad brush of human nature that distinguishes this region as something that coheres. The people are outspoken, ambitious, sometimes askew, and absolutely determined to find their own corner of paradise. The land provides, after all, so many titillating glimpses. ☆

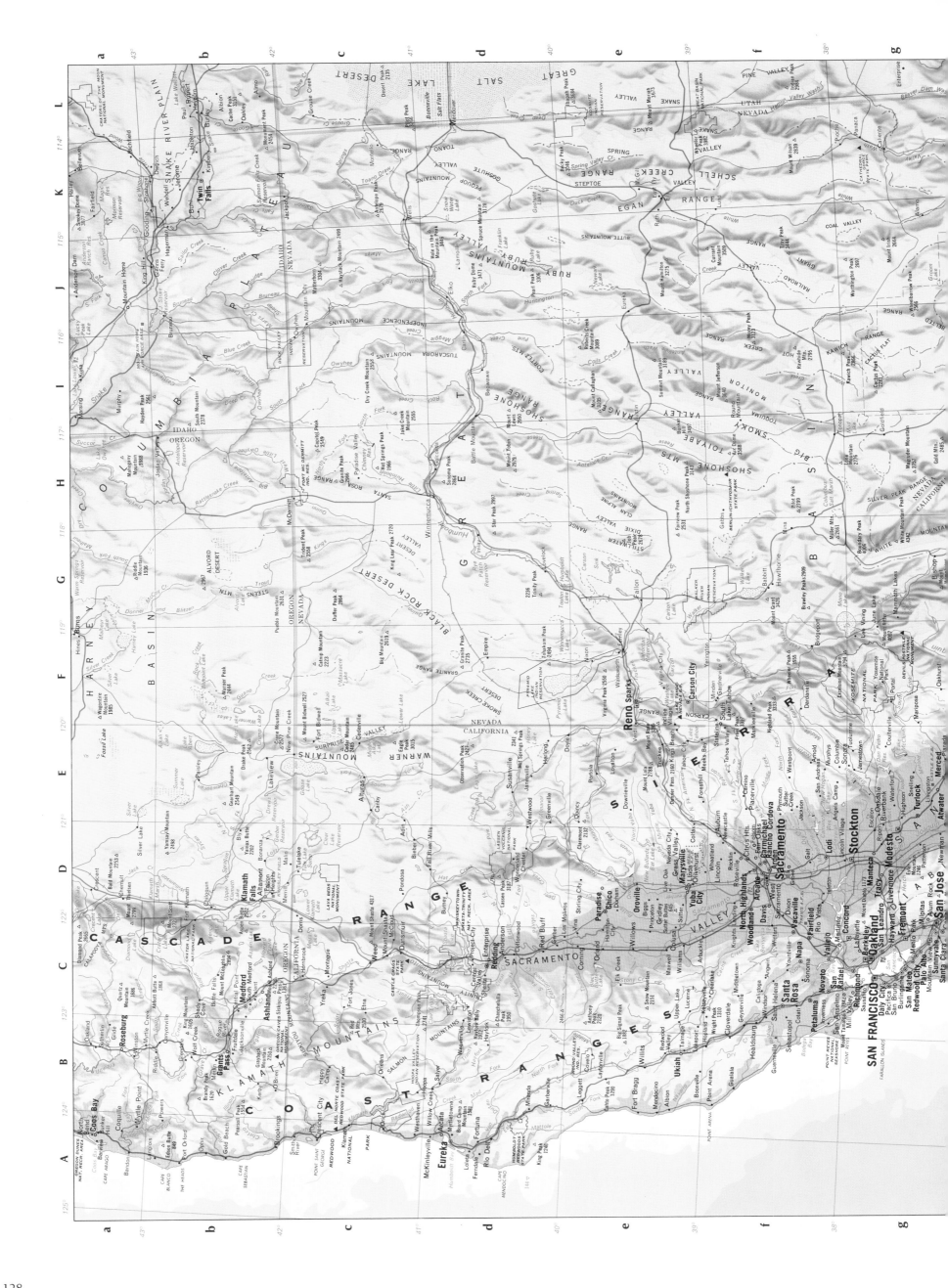

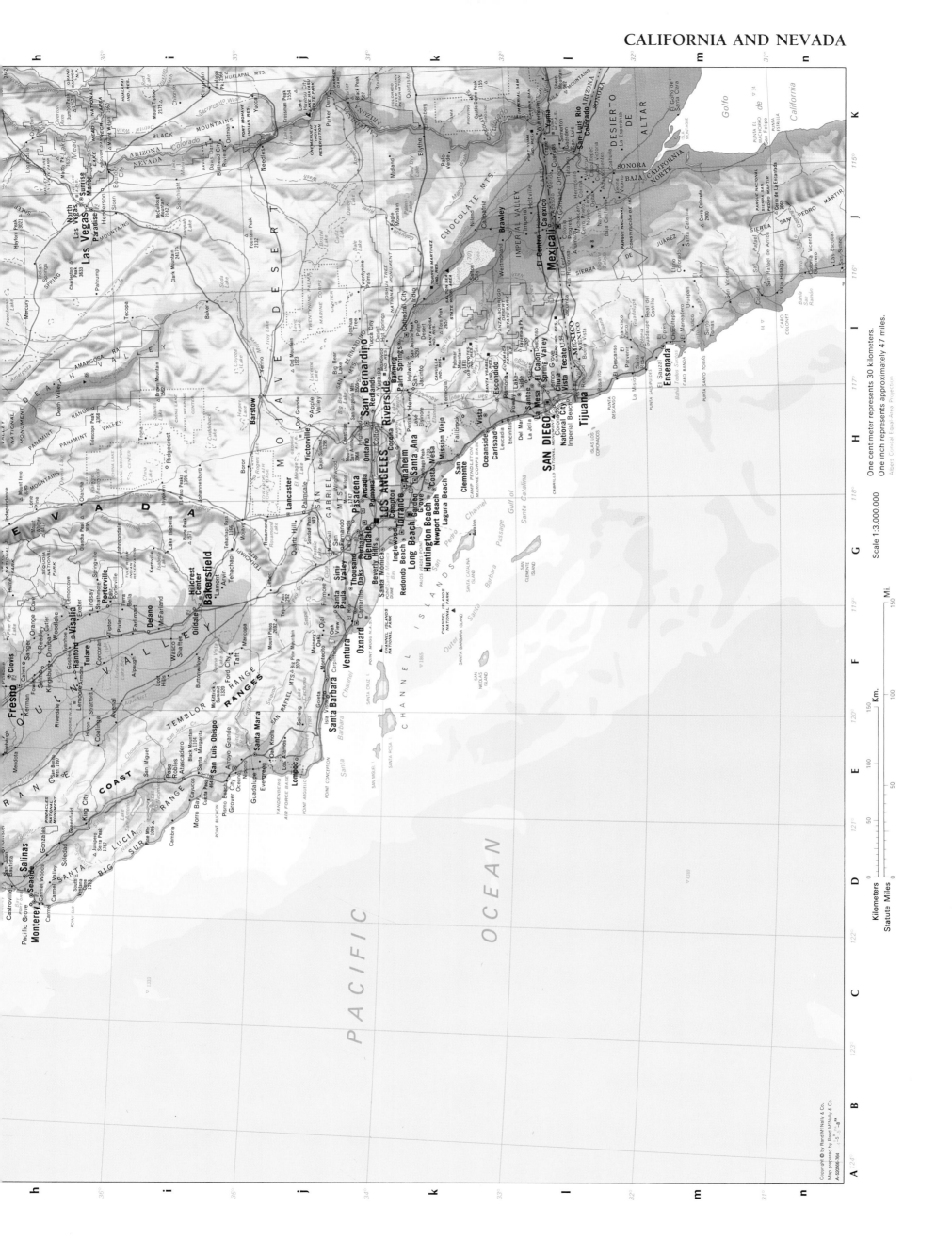

Scale 1:3,000,000

One centimeter represents 30 kilometers.
One inch represents approximately 47 miles.

Albers Conical Equal-Area Projection

Kilometers
Statute Miles

Km.
Mi.

Alaska
AND
Hawaii

Alaska
Hawaii

"North and South, as far as the eye could see, it was unbroken white, save for a dark hairline that curved and twisted from around the spruce-covered island to the south, and that curved and twisted away into the north, where it disappeared behind another spruce-covered island. This dark hairline was the trail..."

Jack London, *To Build a Fire*, 1910

Alaska's Denali National Park is named after the Athabaskan Indian word for "the high one." It refers to Mount McKinley, North America's highest peak, which displays nearly all of its 20,000-foot altitude from a relatively low base.

On the surface, so little ties Alaska to Hawaii that only the contrasts call for attention. Alaska is vast, forbidding, and sparsely settled. Hawaii is warm and swathed in color. Its habitat is so gentle that untold species of birds and flowers, along with a harmonious hybrid society, flourish there.

Yet, despite differences, Alaska and Hawaii constitute America's last frontiers. When they became states in 1959, they were exotic as the most farflung lands, and they remain physically and spiritually distinct. Both states are insulated from the rest of the world. They are special environments that make special demands on their people, and there's little evidence that this will soon change.

Most frontiers are gradually, naturally, converted into civilized pastures by the ruggedness and inventiveness of the people who go there. Yet something in the terrain of Alaska, or in its history, has arrested this development. Alaska can be as dangerous as the surface of the moon, ethereal as Mt. McKinley, or even irascible as a town of brawling miners.

Only a few settlements qualify as cities in this huge state. Anchorage is by far the most populous, and its rowdy past is not far behind it. (A trucking firm once advertised itself with the words: "Displays of violence are merely manifestations of frustrations due to lack of vigorous activity and we are here to provide that activity.") As Anchorage grew it was highly distrusted by the rest of Alaska, perhaps with reason. Over the years, it wrested the District Court from Valdez, displaced Seward as Alaska's principal seaport, and drew a large portion of the state's college students from Fairbanks. An initiative to move the state capital from Juneau to a neutral site closer to Anchorage proved too divisive and ornery to continue. It has been suggested that the cities of Alaska constitute a confederation not unlike Greek city-states.

There's a brilliance to life in Alaska, and no one captured it better than conservationist John Muir who traveled here three times in the late 1800s. In the Coast Mountains near Juneau, Muir found abundant dwarfed conifers. He described "flat, fan-shaped plumes thickly foliaged and imbricated by snow pressure, forming a smooth handsome thatch which bears cones and thrives as if this repressed condition were its very best." He found mountain wildflowers, bright as if each plant were making up for its distressingly short season. All of which made him wildly enthusiastic for this wilderness. "When night was drawing

Many parts of Gates of the Arctic National Park are accessible only by air or by foot. Its eight million acres consist of vertical granite cliffs and valleys that in summer are filled with grassy, flowered meadows.

Many visitors regard the island of Kauai as the most striking of the Hawaiian Islands. It has lush, green valleys, majestic peaks, and the sea cliffs of Na Pali Coast State Park.

near," Muir writes in *Travels in Alaska*, "I ran down the flowery slopes exhilarated, thanking God for the gift of this great day. The setting sun fired the clouds. All the world seemed new-born."

Much of Alaska is too hostile and mountainous to be graded for roads or even mapped. This circumstance has given rise to a peculiar kind of pioneer on the range: the bush pilot. Some fly full-time for enterprises like the Alaska Pipeline. Others use their airplanes much as earthbound cowboys use pickup trucks. Alaska depends upon this sort of transportation to close the great distances. Bush pilots are curious souls, combining basic common sense with monstrous pride, even hubris. Legends are made of foolhardy types who escape death by acts of heroism.

People rise to the challenges of Alaska. On the very edge of North America, for example, Eskimos on Little Diomede Island still hunt seal and walrus running through the Bering Straits, and even net birds on high, rocky outcroppings. On the Interior Plateau, north of the southerly Alaska Range (and Mount McKinley), migrants from the lower 48 endure long winters miles from the closest town. Stark isolation is rewarded by short summers in areas filled with water and soil as fertile as a river delta.

Another constant in Alaska is gold, the pursuit of which persists long after the first strikes in 1899. Even long-time Alaskans catch gold fever, and the phenomenon requires a particular understanding of Alaskans, or of gold, or of the livid mix of the two. In *Coming Into the Country*, author John McPhee introduces an outdoorsman otherwise known as "a man of maximum practical application" coaxing equipment over treacherous frozen ridges to mine a claim of only moderate promise. For hardened Alaskans, the fever is explainable only as a way of getting a little hard cash to sustain their needs in a land where money is relatively rare.

The Hawaiian frontier is less treacherous by outward appearances, but that is deceptive. Volcanoes on the islands remain active and can still alter the terrain decisively. Hawaii's charms and its powers were obvious to the first settlers who arrived there—it is said around A.D. 750 from the western edge of Polynesia. To them, land of good soil and sufficient rain seemed like a paradise, albeit a volatile one. To appease the gods who governed such a place, the first Hawaiians created a system of *kapu*, or taboo, a society ordered according to divine rights and strict rules of behavior. Deities were soothed, apparently,

Taro farms like this one on the island of Maui are diminishing, partly because they must compete with urban developers for water. Taro, a tuber vegetable, is used to make traditional poi, a pasty staple that earns mixed reviews from haoles.

Sitka, Alaska, lies in the Alexander Archipelago. These islands, "with the straits, channels, canals, sounds, passages, and fiords, form an intricate web of land and water embroidery," wrote the great conservationist John Muir after his first visit to Alaska in 1879.

and a royal dynasty that was noted for its intelligence was established on the islands.

Later, the first Caucasian visitors, *haoles*, treated Hawaii carelessly. They came as missionaries, contemptuous of kapu, and intent on spreading their own religious message. Missionaries amended ancient concepts of private land ownership for their own benefit; their sons and daughters became the islands' first landed aristocracy. Since then traditional Hawaiian life has been fairly well lost. A limited number of owners even now control most of the land. Original Hawaiians are now almost entirely absorbed by haoles and orientals who were brought there to work sugar and pineapple fields.

Still, the old gods are in evidence. On the Big Island of Hawaii, the Waipaio Valley was once the natural enclosure for the homes of Hawaiian kings. It remains powerfully beautiful, with steep green hillsides, laced with long ribbons of falling water. Some volcanoes provide silent backdrops to gentle climes, as old Diamondhead near the populous beaches of Oahu. Others are more frightening. On Maui, Haleakala, "House of the Sun," is a huge volcanic basin so desolate that astronauts tested their moon-landing gear there.

The wrath of Hawaiian spirits is not unknown. Pele, the Fire Goddess, occasionally lets loose with new eruptions. The famous volcano Kilauea is powerful and capricious, rolling over towns but at least once in memory diverting its massive flow to spare an orchid garden in seemingly deliberate fashion. Pele's sister Namakaokahai, the Sea Goddess, also acts up occasionally with *tsunamis*, tidal waves, sent from thousands of miles away to destroy coastal towns. Events such as these are remembered today more distinctly than the ancient deities are understood.

In some ways, the gods have been kind, as they have in Honolulu, the one place where true urban life has stuck on these exotic islands. So many ethnic groups have coalesced harmoniously in this city, and today it represents a model of equality for older cities on the U.S. mainland. But Honolulu also is a crowded city that demonstrates the difficulties of civilization superimposed on paradise.

Indeed, Hawaii's charmed environment appears ever more fragile with the passing of time. As if Hawaiian gods hold its fate in the balance, ancient customs once again command the respect they deserve, even from those without a drop of Hawaiian blood. New resorts are being laid out according to *mauka-makai*, an ancient principle of holding land in narrow strips from

Kenai Fjords National Park shows signs of life on an afternoon in July as clusters of plants break through the edges of a glacier. Scenes such as this one are so fragile that 100 million acres of Alaska have been set aside as federal parks, monuments, forests, and refuges.

*Honolulu's high-rise buildings are well suited to tourists and
others who prefer dramatic views of Diamond Head and Waikiki Beach,
plus efficient air conditioning, to Hawaii's other charms.*

The Trans-Alaskan Pipeline delivers 25 percent of U.S. oil production from Prudhoe Bay in the north to Valdez in the south. It crosses some of the most remote wilderness on earth, including a range that is home to Alaska's largest caribou herds.

Bougainvillea thrives a few feet from a secluded beach on the Big Island. Tourism contributes more to the Hawaiian economy than any other sector, and visitors can still find their own personal paradise if they look for it.

shore to mountain. Thus the occupant can enjoy all the land has to offer—from the ocean to coastal fields, to cool wooded mountains. On the Big Island the mysterious landscapes and forests of Hawaii Volcanoes National Park have been set aside for many decades. Nearby, the coastal village of Honaunau more recently was added as part of the parks system. Honaunau, "City of Refuge" to ancient Hawaiians, was a sanctuary on a quiet wooded bay for sinners and defeated soldiers.

Whether or not America has come to grips with its paradise is still an open question. The military still bombs remote islands in the chain for target practice. The pineapple and sugarcane industries are thoroughly industrialized, and gigantic irrigation schemes now score the volcanic ground for maximum productivity. Tourism is the main industry of the islands, and this seems appropriate. Tourism provides millions of people with a glimpse of this spiritual frontier, and then whisks them quickly away before its splendors become too familiar. The islands are too delicate and the gods too powerful to risk offending them. ☆

Petersberg, in the Wrangell Narrows of the Alexander Archipelago, is considered the shrimp capital of Alaska. Logging and trapping are other traditional occupations for hardy Norwegians who were the majority of the town's early settlers.

Pu'uhonua o Honaunau National Historic Park, on Hawaii, was sacred to ancient Hawaiians, and the park features temples, tikis, and other restored landmarks peculiar to the old kapu system.

Scale 1:6,000,000

One centimeter represents 60 kilometers.
One inch represents approximately 95 miles.
Lambert Conformal Conic Projection

ALASKA AND HAWAII

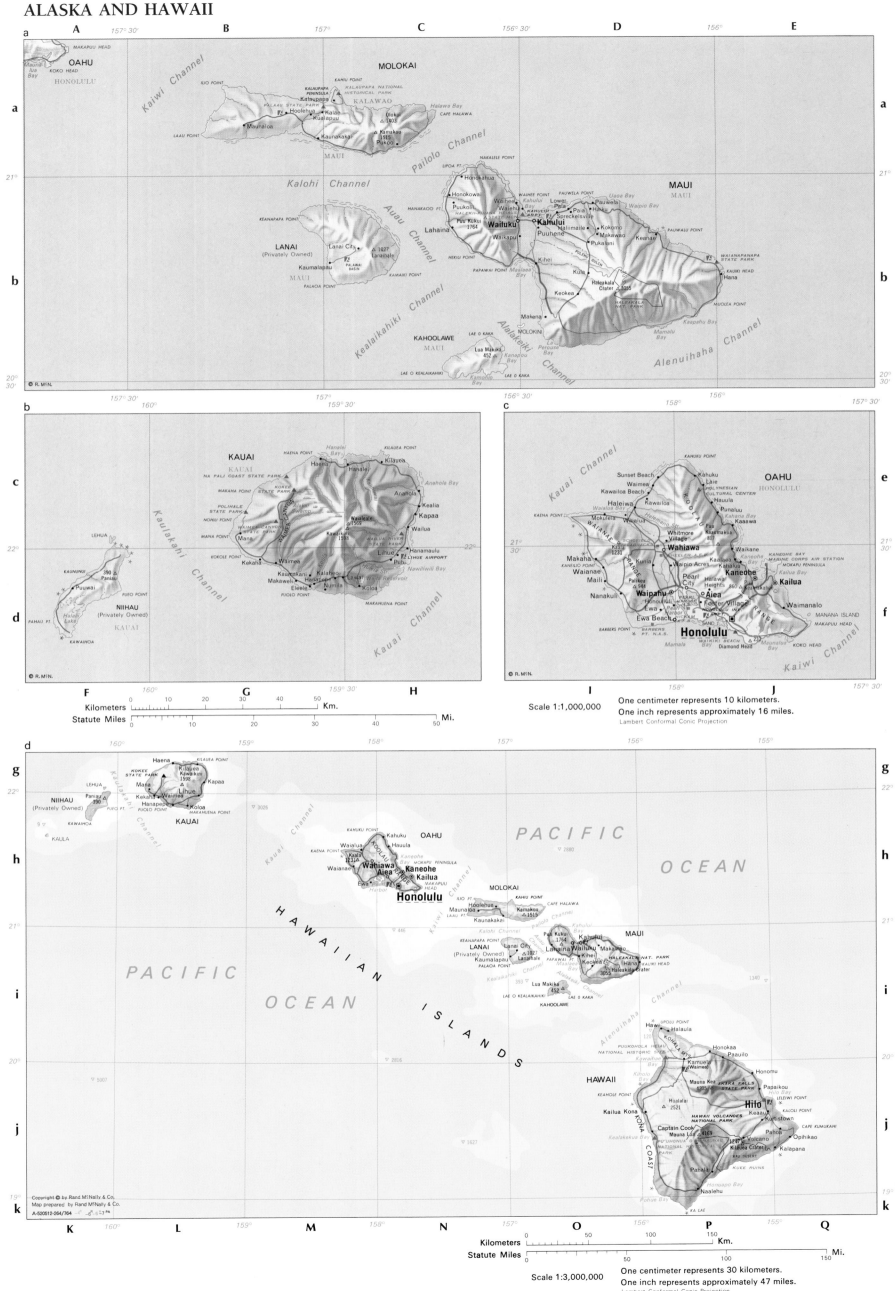

Scale 1:1,000,000
One centimeter represents 10 kilometers.
One inch represents approximately 16 miles.
Lambert Conformal Conic Projection

Kilometers
Statute Miles

Scale 1:3,000,000
One centimeter represents 30 kilometers.
One inch represents approximately 47 miles.
Lambert Conformal Conic Projection

Introduction to the Index

In a single alphabetical list, this index includes names of more than 15,000 features that appear on the reference maps. These features include populated places and physical features—such as lakes, rivers, and mountain ranges. Each name is followed by a map-reference key and a page reference.

Alphabetization and Abbreviation

The names of cities and towns appear in regular type. The names of all other features appear in *italics*. The names of physical features may be inverted, since they are always alphabetized under the proper, not the generic, part of the name. For example, Lake Erie is listed as *Erie, Lake*. Otherwise every entry, whether consisting of one word or more, is alphabetized as a single continuous entity. "Lake City", for example, appears after "Lafayette" and before "Lakehurst."

In the case of identical names, towns are listed first, followed by states, then physical features. Entries that are completely identical are sequenced alphabetically by state name. Each name is followed by a state abbreviation. Exceptions are features that cross state or interational boundaries, which are, therefore, not wholly contained within one state. The state abbreviations are those used by the United States Postal Service (see list below). Other abbreviations have been adopted by Rand McNally.

On the map, abbreviations may be used in a name, but the full name will appear in the index: for example *Mt. St. Helens* on the map is *Saint Helens, Mount,* in the index.

Map-Reference Keys and Page References

The map-reference keys and page references are found in the last two columns of each entry.

Each map-reference key consists of a lowercase letter followed by one or two uppercase letters. The lowercase letters appear along the side of each map and the uppercase letters appear across the top and bottom. Inset maps are keyed separately.

Map-reference keys for point features, such as towns, cities and mountain peaks, indicate the positions of the symbols. For extensive features, such as countries or mountain ranges, positions are given for the approximate center of the feature. Those for linear features, such as canals and rivers, are given for the position of the name.

The page number generally refers to the map that shows the feature at the best scale. Countries, mountain ranges and other extensive features are usually indexed to maps that both show the features completely and also show them in their relationship to broad areas. Page references to two-page maps always refer to the left-hand page. If a page contains several maps or insets, a small letter after the page number identifies the specific map or inset.

List of Abbreviations

AK	Alaska	DE	Delaware	KS	Kansas	MO	Missouri	NJ	New Jersey	*r.*	*river*	UT	Utah		
AL	Alabama	FL	Florida	KY	Kentucky	MS	Mississippi	NM	New Mexico	RI	Rhode Island	VA	Virginia		
AR	Arkansas	GA	Georgia	LA	Louisiana	MT	Montana	NV	Nevada	SC	South Carolina	VT	Vermont		
AZ	Arizona	HI	Hawaii	MA	Massachusetts	NA	North America	NY	New York	SD	South Dakota	WA	Washington		
CA	California	IA	Iowa	MD	Maryland	NC	North Carolina	OH	Ohio	TN	Tennessee	WI	Wisconsin		
CO	Colorado	ID	Idaho	ME	Maine	ND	North Dakota	OK	Oklahoma	TX	Texas	WV	West Virginia		
CT	Connecticut	IL	Illinois	MI	Michigan	NE	Nebraska	OR	Oregon	US	United States	WY	Wyoming		
DC	District of Columbia	IN	Indiana	MN	Minnesota	NH	New Hampshire	PA	Pennsylvania						

Index

Name — Map Ref. — Page

A

Abajo Peak, UT g G 98
Abbeville, GA h C 40
Abbeville, LA m D 68
Abbeville, MS h G 68
Abbeville, SC e D 40
Abbotsford, WI f E 54
Aberdeen, ID h M 112
Aberdeen, MD h J 26
Aberdeen, MS i H 68
Aberdeen, NC d G 40
Aberdeen, SD f I 82
Aberdeen, WA d B 112
Abernathy, TX f E 84
Abilene, KS m J 82
Abilene, TX g G 84
Abingdon, IL j E 54
Abingdon, VA c E 40
Abiquiu, NM h J 98
Abita Springs, LA I F 68
Absaroka Range, US f O 112
Absarokee, MT e P 112
Absecon, NJ h L 26
Acadia National Park, ME c R 26
Accomac, VA b K 40
Accoville, WV b E 40
Ackerly, TX g E 84
Ackerman, MS i G 68
Ackley, IA h B 54
Acworth, GA e B 40
Ada, MN d K 82
Ada, OH g C 26
Ada, OK e J 84
Adair, IA j M 82
Adair, OK f A 68
Adairsville, GA e B 40
Adairville, KY f J 68
Adak, AK k F 142
Adak Island, AK k F 142
Adams, MA e M 26
Adams, MN g C 54
Adams, NE k K 82
Adams, NY d J 26
Adams, ND c I 82
Adams, TN f I 68
Adams, WI g F 54
Adams, Mount, WA d D 112
Adamsville, TN g H 68
Addis, LA I E 68
Addison, MI i K 54
Adel, GA h C 40
Adel, IA i A 54
Adin, CA c E 128
Adirondack Mountains, NY d L 26
Admiralty Island, AK h AA 142
Adrian, GA g D 40
Adrian, MI i K 54
Adrian, MN h L 82
Adrian, MO d B 68
Adrian, OR g H 112
Adrian, TX d D 84
Adrian, WV i F 26
Advance, MO e G 68
Affton, MO d F 68
Afognak Island, AK g R 142
Afton, IA a B 68
Afton, NY e K 26
Afton, OK f B 68
Afton, WY b F 98
Agate, CO I D 82
Agate Beach, OR f A 112
Agency, IA j C 54
Agua Dulce, TX I I 84
Agua Fria, r., AZ k D 98
Aguila, AZ k C 98
Aguilar, CO n C 82
Ahklun Mountains, AK g N 142
Ahoskie, NC c J 40
Aiea, HI f J 144c
Aiken, SC f E 40
Ainsworth, NE i H 82
Aitkin, MN d B 54
Ajo, AZ I D 98
Akaka Falls State Park, HI j P 144d
Akeley, MN c A 54
Akiachak, AK f N 142
Akron, CO k D 82
Akron, IN a J 68
Akron, IA i K 82
Akron, NY d H 26
Akron, OH f E 26
Akron, PA g J 26
Alabama, state, US e I 8
Alabama, r., AL k I 68
Alabaster, AL i J 68
Alachua, FL j D 40
Alakai Swamp, HI c G 144b
Alalakeiki Channel, HI b C 144a
Alameda, CA g C 128
Alameda, NM i J 98
Alamo, GA g D 40
Alamo, NV g J 128
Alamo, TN g G 68
Alamo, r., CA k J 128
Alamogordo, NM I K 98
Alamo Heights, TX j H 84
Alamo Lake, AZ j C 98
Alamosa, CO g K 98
Alamosa, r., CO g J 98
Alamosa East, CO g K 98
Alanson, MI e K 54
Alapaha, GA h C 40
Alapaha, r., US i C 40
Alaska, state, US d R 142
Alaska, Gulf of, AK g V 142
Alaska Peninsula, AK h O 142
Alaska Range, AK e S 142
Alava, Cape, WA b A 112
Alba, MI f K 54
Alba, TX g K 84
Albany, GA h B 40
Albany, IL i E 54
Albany, IN b K 68
Albany, KY f K 68
Albany, MN e A 54
Albany, MO b B 68
Albany, NY e M 26
Albany, OH h D 26
Albany, OR f B 112
Albany, TX g G 84
Albany, WI h F 54
Albemarle, NC d F 40
Albemarle Sound, NC c J 40
Alberene, VA b H 40
Alberta, AL j I 68
Albert City, IA i M 82
Albert Lea, MN g B 54
Alberton, MT c K 112
Albertville, AL h J 68
Albia, IA i C 54
Albin, WY j C 82
Albion, CA e B 128
Albion, ID h L 112
Albion, IL d H 68
Albion, IN a K 68
Albion, IA h C 54
Albion, MI h K 54
Albion, NE j I 82
Albion, NY d H 26
Albion, PA f F 26
Albion, WA d H 112
Albuquerque, NM i J 98
Alburg, VT c M 26
Alcalde, NM h J 98
Alcester, SD h K 82
Alcoa, TN d C 40
Alcolu, SC f F 40
Alcorn, MS k E 68
Alcovy, r., GA f C 40
Alden, IA h B 54
Alden, MN g B 54
Alderson, WV b F 40
Aledo, IL i E 54
Alegres Mountain, NM j H 98
Aleknagik, AK g O 142
Alenuihaha Channel, HI i O 144d
Aleutian Islands, AK j F 142
Aleutian Range, AK g Q 142
Alex, OK e I 84
Alexander, ND d D 82
Alexander Archipelago, AK h AA 142
Alexander City, AL j K 68
Alexandria, IN b K 68
Alexandria, KY i B 26
Alexandria, LA k D 68
Alexandria, MN f L 82
Alexandria, MO b E 68
Alexandria, NE k J 82
Alexandria, SD h J 82
Alexandria, TN f J 68
Alexandria, VA i I 26
Alexandria Bay, NY c K 26
Alexis, IL i E 54
Alfred, ME d P 26
Alfred, NY e I 26
Alger, OH g C 26
Algodones, NM i J 98
Algoma, WI f H 54
Algona, IA g A 54
Algona, WA c C 112
Algonac, MI h M 54
Algonquin, IL h G 54
Algood, TN f K 68
Alice, TX I H 84
Aliceville, AL i H 68
Aliquippa, PA g F 26
Allardt, TN f L 68
Allegan, MI h J 54
Allegany, NY e H 26
Allegheny, r., US g G 26
Allegheny Mountains, US i F 26
Allegheny Plateau, US g H 26
Allegheny Reservoir, US f H 26
Allemands, Lac Des, LA m F 68
Allen, NE i K 82
Allen, OK e J 84
Allen, SD h F 82
Allen, TX f J 84
Allen, Mount, AK e W 142
Allendale, IL d I 68
Allendale, SC f E 40
Allentown, PA g K 26
Allerton, IA j B 54
Alliance, NE i E 82
Alliance, OH g E 26
Alligator, r., NC d J 40
Allison, IA h C 54
Allouez, WI f G 54
Allyn, WA c C 112
Alma, AR g B 68
Alma, GA h D 40
Alma, KS I K 82
Alma, MI g K 54
Alma, NE k H 82
Alma, WI f D 54
Alma Center, WI f E 54
Almena, KS I H 82
Almira, WA c G 112
Almo, ID h L 112
Almond, WI f F 54
Almont, MI h L 54
Alpaugh, CA i F 128
Alpena, AR f C 68
Alpena, MI e L 54
Alpena, SD g I 82
Alpha, IL i E 54
Alpha, MI d G 54
Alpharetta, GA e B 40
Alpine, AZ k G 98
Alpine, CA I I 128
Alpine, TX i C 84
Alsea, OR f B 112
Alsea, r., OR f B 112
Alsen, ND c I 82
Alta, IA i L 82
Altamaha, r., GA h E 40
Altamont, IL c H 68
Altamont, KS n L 82
Altamont, OR h D 112
Altamont, TN g K 68
Alta Vista, KS m K 82
Altavista, VA b G 40
Altha, FL i A 40
Altheimer, AR h E 68
Alto, TX h K 84
Alton, IL d F 68
Alton, IA i K 82
Alton, KS I I 82
Alton, MO f E 68
Alton, NH d O 26
Altoona, AL h J 68
Altoona, IA i B 54
Altoona, KS n L 82
Altoona, PA g H 26
Altoona, WI f D 54
Alturas, CA c E 128
Altus, AR g C 68
Altus, OK e G 84
Alum Rock, CA g D 128
Alva, OK c H 84
Alvarado, TX g I 84
Alvin, TX j K 84
Alvord, TX f I 84
Amagansett, NY g N 26
Amana, IA i D 54
Amanda, OH h D 26
Amargosa, r., US h I 128
Amargosa Range, CA h I 128
Amarillo, TX d E 84
Amasa, MI d G 54
Amberg, WI e H 54
Amboy, IL i F 54
Amboy, MN g A 54
Ambridge, PA g F 26
Ambrose, ND c D 82
Ambrosia Lake, NM i I 98
Amchitka Island, AK k D 143a
Ameagle, WV b E 40
Amelia Court House, VA b I 40
Amelia Island, FL i E 40
American Falls, ID h M 112
American Falls Reservoir, ID h M 112
American Fork, UT d E 98
Americus, GA g B 40
Americus, KS m K 82
Amery, WI e C 54
Ames, IA h B 54
Amesbury, MA e P 26
Amherst, MA e N 26
Amherst, NY e H 26
Amherst, OH f D 26
Amherst, TX e D 84
Amherst, VA b G 40
Amherst, WI f F 54
Amherstdale, WV j E 26
Amidon, ND e D 82
Amistad Reservoir (Presa de la Amistad), NA j E 84
Amite, LA I F 68
Amite, r., LA I F 68
Amity, AR h C 68
Amity, OR e B 112
Ammon, ID g N 112
Ammonoosuc, r., NH c O 26
Amnicon, r., WI d D 54
Amory, MS i H 68
Amsterdam, NY e L 26
Anacoco, LA k C 68
Anaconda, MT d M 112
Anacortes, WA b C 112
Anadarko, OK d H 84
Anaheim, CA k H 128
Anahola, HI c H 144b
Anahola Bay, HI c H 144b
Anahuac, TX j L 84
Anamoose, ND d G 82
Anamosa, IA h D 54
Anastasia Island, FL j E 40
Anawalt, WV b E 40
Anchorage, AK f T 142
Anchor Point, AK g S 142
Andalusia, AL k J 68
Anderson, AL h I 68
Anderson, CA d C 128
Anderson, IN b K 68
Anderson, MO f B 68
Anderson, SC e D 40
Anderson, TX i K 84
Anderson Dam, ID g J 112
Andover, ME c P 26
Andover, MA e O 26
Andover, NY e I 26
Andover, OH f F 26
Andover, SD f J 82
Andreanof Islands, AK j F 142
Andrews, IN b K 68
Andrews, NC d C 40
Andrews, SC f G 40
Andrews, TX g D 84
Androscoggin, r., ME c P 26
Anegam, AZ I D 98
Aneta, ND d J 82
Angelina, r., TX k B 68
Angels Camp, CA f E 128
Angier, NC d H 40
Angle Inlet, MN b L 82
Angleton, TX j K 84
Angola, IN a L 68
Angola, NY e G 26
Angoon, AK h AA 142
Anguilla, MS j F 68
Angwin, CA f C 128
Aniak, AK f O 142
Animas, NM m H 98
Animas, r., US h I 98
Animas Peak, NM m H 98
Anita, IA j M 82
Ankeny, IA i B 54
Anna, IL e G 68
Anna, TX f J 84
Anna, Lake, VA a I 40
Annandale, MN e A 54
Annapolis, MD i J 26
Ann Arbor, MI h L 54
Annette, AK i CC 142
Anniston, AL i K 68
Annville, KY b C 40
Annville, PA g J 26
Anoka, MN e B 54
Anselmo, NE j H 82
Ansley, NE j H 82
Anson, TX g G 84
Ansonville, NC d F 40
Ansted, WV i E 26
Antelope Island, UT d D 98
Antelope Peak, NV c K 128
Anthon, IA i L 82
Anthony, FL j D 40
Anthony, KS n I 82
Anthony, NM I J 98
Anthony, TX m J 98
Antigo, WI e F 54
Antimony, UT f E 98
Antioch, IL h G 54
Antlers, OK e K 84
Anton, TX f D 84
Anton Chico, NM i K 98
Antonito, CO g J 98
Antwerp, OH f B 26
Anvik, AK e N 142
Apache, OK e H 84
Apache Junction, AZ k E 98
Apache Peak, AZ m F 98
Apalachicola, FL j B 40
Apalachicola, r., FL i A 40
Apalachicola Bay, FL j A 40
Apex, NC d H 40
Apollo, PA g G 26
Apostle Islands, WI d E 54
Appalachia, VA c D 40
Appalachian Mountains, NA c K 8
Apple, r., US h E 54
Apple, r., WI e C 54
Applegate, r., OR b B 128
Appleton, MN f K 82
Appleton, WI f G 54
Appleton City, MO d B 68
Apple Valley, CA j H 128
Appling, GA f D 40
Appomattox, VA b H 40

Name	Map Ref.	Page
Appomattox, r., VA	b H	40
Aquilla, TX	h I	84
Arab, AL	h J	68
Arabi, LA	m F	68
Aragon, GA	e A	40
Aransas, r., TX	k l	84
Aransas Pass, TX	l l	84
Arapaho, OK	d H	84
Arapahoe, NE	k H	82
Arbuckle, CA	e C	128
Arc, Bayou des, r., AR	g E	68
Arcade, CA	j G	128
Arcade, NY	e H	26
Arcadia, CA	j G	128
Arcadia, FL	l E	40
Arcadia, IN	b J	68
Arcadia, LA	i L	82
Arcadia, KS	n M	82
Arcadia, LA	j D	68
Arcadia, MO	e F	68
Arcadia, NE	j H	82
Arcadia, PA	g H	26
Arcadia, SC	e E	40
Arcadia, WI	f D	54
Arcanum, OH	h B	26
Arcata, CA	d A	128
Arc Dome, NV	f H	128
Archbold, OH	f B	26
Archdale, NC	d G	40
Archer, FL	j D	40
Archer City, TX	f H	84
Arco, ID	g L	112
Arcola, IL	c H	68
Arcola, MS	i F	68
Arctic Village, AK	b V	142
Arden, CA	f D	128
Ardmore, AL	h J	68
Ardmore, OK	e l	84
Ardmore, PA	g K	26
Argenta, IL	n J	82
Argonia, WI	e G	54
Argos, IN	a J	68
Argyle, MN	c K	82
Arikaree, r., US	l E	82
Ariton, AL	k K	68
Arizona, state, US	e D	8
Arjay, KY	c C	40
Arkadelphia, AR	h C	68
Arkansas, state, US	d H	8
Arkansas, r., US	d H	8
Arkansas City, AR	i E	68
Arkansas City, KS	n J	82
Arkoma, OK	g B	68
Arkport, NY	e l	26
Arlee, MT	c K	112
Arlington, GA	h B	40
Arlington, IA	h D	54
Arlington, KS	l J	82
Arlington, KY	f G	68
Arlington, MN	f A	54
Arlington, NE	j K	82
Arlington, OH	g C	26
Arlington, OR	e E	112
Arlington, SD	g J	82
Arlington, TN	g G	68
Arlington, TX	g l	84
Arlington, VT	d M	26
Arlington, VA	i l	26
Arlington, WA	b C	112
Arlington Heights, IL	h H	54
Arma, KS	n M	82
Armada, MI	h M	54
Armijo, NM	i J	98
Armona, CA	h F	128
Armour, SD	h l	82
Armstrong, IA	h M	82
Armstrong, MO	c D	68
Arnaudville, LA	l E	68
Arnett, OK	c G	84
Arnold, CA	f E	128
Arnold, MN	d C	54
Arnold, MO	d F	68
Arnold, NE	j G	82
Arnolds Park, IA	h L	82
Arp, TX	g K	84
Arrey, NM	l l	98
Arriba, CO	l D	82
Arrowrock Reservoir, ID	g J	112
Arroyo Grande, CA	i E	128
Arroyo Hondo, NM	h K	98
Artesia, MS	i H	68
Artesia, NM	g B	84
Artesian, SD	c H	68
Arthur, IL	c H	68
Arthur, NE	j F	82
Arthur, ND	d J	82
Arthur, TN	c C	40
Arvada, CO	e K	98
Arvin, CA	i G	128
Arvon, Mount, MI	d G	54
Arvonia, VA	b H	40
Asbury Park, NJ	g L	26
Ashburn, GA	h C	40
Ashdown, AR	i B	68
Asheboro, NC	d G	40
Asherton, TX	k G	84
Asheville, NC	d D	40
Ash Flat, AR	f E	68
Ashford, AL	k K	68
Ash Fork, AZ	i D	98
Ash Grove, MO	e C	68
Ashland, AL	i J	68
Ashland, KS	n H	82
Ashland, KY	i D	26
Ashland, MS	h G	68
Ashland, MO	d D	68
Ashland, MT	e S	112
Ashland, NE	j K	82
Ashland, NH	d O	26
Ashland, OH	g D	26
Ashland, OR	h C	112
Ashland, PA	g J	26
Ashland, WI	d E	54
Ashland, Mount, OR	h C	112
Ashland City, TN	f l	68
Ashley, IL	d G	68
Ashley, MI	g K	54
Ashley, ND	e H	82
Ashley, OH	g D	26
Ashmore, IL	c H	68
Ashtabula, OH	f F	26
Ashtabula, Lake, ND	f N	112
Ashton, ID	f N	112
Ashton, IA	h L	82
Ashton, NE	j l	82
Ashuelot, r., NH	e N	26
Ashville, AL	i J	68
Ashville, OH	h D	26
Ashwaubenon, WI	f G	54
Asotin, WA	d H	112
Aspen, CO	e J	98
Aspen Butte, OR	h C	112
Aspermont, TX	f F	84
Assateague Island, US	i K	26
Assumption, IL	c G	68
Astoria, IL	b F	68
Astoria, OR	d B	112
Atascadero, CA	i E	128
Atascosa, r., TX	k H	84
Atchafalaya, r., LA	l E	68
Atchafalaya Bay, LA	m E	68
Atchison, KS	i L	82
Athena, OR	e G	112
Athens, AL	h J	68
Athens, GA	f C	40
Athens, IL	c G	68
Athens, LA	j C	68
Athens, MI	h J	54
Athens, NY	e K	26
Athens, OH	h C	26
Athens, PA	f J	26
Athens, TN	d B	40
Athens, TX	g K	84
Athens, WV	b E	40
Athens, WI	e E	54
Athol, MA	e N	26
Atigun Pass, AK	b T	142
Atka, AK	j G	142
Atkins, AR	g D	68
Atkinson, IL	i E	54
Atkinson, NE	i H	82
Atkinson, NC	e H	40
Atlanta, GA	f B	40
Atlanta, IL	b G	68
Atlanta, MO	c D	68
Atlanta, TX	i B	68
Atlantic, IA	j L	82
Atlantic, NC	g E	40
Atlantic Beach, FL	i E	40
Atlantic City, NJ	h L	26
Atlantic Ocean	e L	8
Atlantic Peak, WY	h P	112
Atmore, AL	k l	68
Atoka, OK	e J	84
Atrisco, NM	j J	98
Attalla, AL	h J	68
Attica, IN	b l	68
Attica, KS	n l	82
Attica, NY	f D	26
Attica, OH	g D	26
Attleboro, MA	f O	26
Attoyac, r., TX	k B	68
Attu Island, AK	j A	143a
Atwater, CA	g E	128
Atwater, MN	f M	82
Atwood, IL	c H	68
Atwood, KS	i F	82
Atwood, TN	g H	68
Auau Channel, HI	b C	144a
Aubrey Cliffs, AZ	i C	98
Auburn, AL	j K	68
Auburn, CA	f D	128
Auburn, IL	c G	68
Auburn, IN	a K	68
Auburn, KY	e J	68
Auburn, ME	c P	26
Auburn, MA	e O	26
Auburn, MI	g K	54
Auburn, NE	k L	82
Auburn, NY	e J	26
Auburn, WA	c C	112
Aucilla, r., US	i C	40
Audubon, IA	j M	82
Auglaize, r., OH	f B	26
Au Gres, MI	f L	54
Au Gres, r., MI	f L	54
Augusta, AR	g E	68
Augusta, GA	f D	40
Augusta, IL	b F	68
Augusta, KS	n J	82
Augusta, KY	i B	26
Augusta, ME	c Q	26
Augusta, MT	c M	112
Augusta, WI	f D	54
Aulander, NC	c l	40
Ault, CO	d L	98
Aurelia, IA	i L	82
Aurora, CO	e L	98
Aurora, IL	i G	54
Aurora, IN	c L	68
Aurora, MN	c C	54
Aurora, MO	f C	68
Aurora, NE	k l	82
Aurora, NC	d J	40
Aurora, OH	f E	26
Aurora, UT	f E	98
Aurora, WV	h G	26
Au Sable, r., MI	f L	54
Au Sable Forks, NY	c M	26
Austin, IN	d K	68
Austin, MN	g C	54
Austin, NV	e H	128
Austin, PA	f H	26
Austin, TX	i l	84
Austinville, VA	c F	40
Auxier, KY	b D	40
Auxvasse, MO	c E	68
Ava, IL	d H	68
Ava, MO	e E	68
Avalon, CA	k G	128
Avant, OK	c J	84
Avenal, CA	h E	128
Avery, ID	d J	112
Avery, TX	i B	68
Avery Island, LA	m E	68
Avis, PA	f l	26
Avoca, IA	j L	82
Avoca, NY	e l	26
Avon, IL	j E	54
Avon, MN	e A	54
Avon, MT	d M	112
Avon, NC	d K	40
Avon, SD	h l	82
Avondale, AZ	k D	98
Avondale, CO	m C	82
Avonmore, PA	g G	26
Avon Park, FL	l E	40
Axis, AL	l H	68
Axtell, KS	i K	82
Axtell, NE	k H	82
Ayden, NC	d l	40
Ayer, MA	e O	26
Aynor, SC	f G	40
Azalea Park, FL	k E	40
Aztec, NM	h l	98
Aztec Peak, AZ	k l	98

B.

Babbitt, MN	c D	54
Babbitt, NV	f G	128
Baboquivari Peak, AZ	m E	98
Baconton, GA	h B	40

Bad, r., MI	g K	54
Bad, r., SD	g F	82
Bad, r., WI	d E	54
Bad Axe, MI	g L	54
Badger, MN	c K	82
Badlands, US	e D	82
Badlands, SD	h E	82
Badlands National Park, SD	h E	82
Baffin Bay, TX	l l	84
Bagdad, AZ	j C	98
Bagdad, FL	i l	68
Baggs, WY	i R	112
Bagley, MN	d L	82
Bailey, NC	d H	40
Bainbridge, GA	i B	40
Bainbridge, NY	e K	26
Bainbridge, OH	h C	26
Bainville, MT	c C	82
Baird, TX	g G	84
Baird, Mount, ID	g N	112
Bairoil, WY	b l	98
Baker, CA	i l	128
Baker, FL	i J	68
Baker, LA	l E	68
Baker, MT	c l	82
Baker, OR	f H	112
Baker, Mount, WA	b D	112
Bakersfield, CA	i F	128
Bakersville, NC	c D	40
Balaton, MN	g L	82
Balcones Escarpment, TX	i F	84
Bald Knob, AR	g E	68
Bald Mountain, OR	g D	112
Baldwin, FL	i E	40
Baldwin, LA	m E	68
Baldwin, MI	g J	54
Baldwin, WI	f C	54
Baldwin City, KS	c M	82
Baldwin Peninsula, AK	c M	142
Baldwinsville, NY	d J	26
Baldwinville, MA	e N	26
Baldwyn, MS	h J	68
Baldy Mountain, MT	b P	112
Baldy Mountain, NM	h K	98
Baldy Peak, AZ	k G	98
Balfour, ND	d D	82
Ball, LA	k D	68
Ballantine, MT	e Q	112
Ball Ground, GA	e B	40
Ballinger, TX	h G	84
Ballston Spa, NY	d M	26
Ballville, OH	f C	26
Balmorhea, TX	i C	84
Balsam Lake, WI	e C	54
Baltimore, MD	h J	26
Baltimore, OH	h D	26
Bamberg, SC	f E	40
Banana River, FL	k F	40
Bancroft, ID	h N	112
Bancroft, IA	h M	82
Bancroft, NE	a K	68
Banded Peak, CO	g J	98
Bandera, TX	j G	84
Bandon, OR	g A	112
Bangor, ME	c R	26
Bangor, MI	h l	54
Bangor, PA	g K	26
Bangs, TX	h G	84
Banks, AL	k K	68
Banks Lake, WA	c F	112
Banner Elk, NC	e J	40
Bannertown, NC	c F	40
Banning, CA	k l	128
Bannock Peak, ID	h M	112
Bapchule, AZ	k E	98
Baraboo, WI	g F	54
Baraboo, r., WI	g F	54
Baraga, MI	d G	54
Baranof Island, AK	h AA	142
Barataria, LA	m F	68
Barataria Bay, LA	m G	68
Barbers Point, HI	f l	144c
Barbers Point Naval Air Station, HI	f l	144c
Barberton, OH	f E	26
Barboursville, WV	i G	26
Barbourville, KY	c C	40
Bardstown, KY	e K	68
Bardwell, KY	f G	68
Bar Harbor, ME	c R	26
Bark, r., WI	h G	54
Barkley, Lake, US	f l	68
Barksdale, TX	j F	84
Barling, AR	g B	68
Barlow, KY	f G	68
Barnegat, NJ	h L	26
Barnegat Bay, NJ	h L	26
Barnesboro, PA	g G	26
Barnesville, GA	f B	40
Barnesville, MN	e K	82
Barnesville, OH	h F	26
Barnhart, TX	h E	84
Barnsdall, OK	c J	84
Barnstable, MA	f P	26
Barnwell, SC	f E	40
Barques, Pointe aux, MI	f M	54
Barracksville, WV	h F	26
Barre, VT	c N	26
Barren, r., KY	e J	68
Barren Islands, AK	i N	142
Barren River Lake, KY	f J	68
Barron, WI	e D	54
Barrow, AK	a P	142
Barrow, Point, AK	a P	142
Barry, IL	c E	68
Barryton, MI	g J	54
Barstow, CA	j H	128
Barstow, TX	h C	84
Bartholomew, Bayou, r., US	i E	68
Bartlesville, OK	c K	84
Bartlett, NE	j l	82
Bartlett, NH	c O	26
Bartlett, TN	g G	68
Bartlett, TX	i l	84
Bartley, NE	k G	82
Barton, VT	c N	26
Bartonville, IL	j F	54
Bartow, FL	l E	40
Bartow, GA	g D	40
Barview, OR	e A	112
Barwick, GA	i C	40
Basile, LA	l D	68
Basin, WY	d M	112
Bassett, NE	i G	82
Bassett, VA	c F	40
Bassett Peak, AZ	l G	98
Bassfield, MS	k G	68
Bass Harbor, ME	c R	26
Bastian, VA	b E	40
Bastrop, LA	j E	68
Bastrop, TX	i l	84

Batavia, IL	i G	54
Batavia, IA	j C	54
Batavia, NY	e H	26
Batavia, OH	h B	26
Batesburg, SC	f E	40
Batesville, AR	g E	68
Batesville, IN	c K	68
Batesville, MS	h G	68
Batesville, TX	k G	84
Bath, ME	d Q	26
Bath, NY	e l	26
Bathgate, ND	c J	82
Baton Rouge, LA	l E	68
Batson, TX	i L	84
Battle Creek, IA	i L	82
Battle Creek, MI	h J	54
Battle Ground, IN	b J	68
Battle Ground, WA	e C	112
Battle Lake, MN	e L	82
Battlement Mesa, CO	e H	98
Battle Mountain, NV	d l	128
Baudette, MN	b A	54
Bauxite, AR	h D	68
Baxley, GA	h D	40
Baxter, IA	i B	54
Baxter, MN	d A	54
Baxter, TN	f K	68
Baxter Springs, KS	n M	82
Baxterville, MS	k G	68
Bay, AR	g F	68
Bayard, IA	j M	82
Bayard, NE	j D	82
Bayard, NM	l H	98
Bayard, WV	h G	26
Bayboro, NC	d J	40
Bay City, MI	g L	54
Bay City, OR	e B	112
Bay City, TX	k K	84
Bayfield, CO	g l	98
Bayfield, WI	d E	54
Bay Minette, AL	l l	68
Bayonne, NJ	h l	26
Bayou Bodcau Reservoir, LA	j C	68
Bayou Cane, LA	m F	68
Bayou D'Arbonne Lake, LA	j D	68
Bayou La Batre, AL	l H	68
Bay Port, MI	g L	54
Bayport, MN	e C	54
Bay Saint Louis, MS	l G	68
Bay Shore, NY	g M	26
Bay Springs, MS	k G	68
Baytown, TX	j L	84
Bazine, KS	m H	82
Beach, ND	e C	82
Beach Haven, NJ	i L	26
Beacon, NY	f M	26
Beacon Hill, WA	d C	112
Beal City, MI	g K	54
Bear, r., US	b E	98
Bear, r., CA	e D	128
Bearden, AR	i D	68
Beardstown, IL	b F	68
Bear Lake, US	c E	98
Bear Mountain, OR	g C	112
Bear River Range, US	j G	84
Beartooth Pass, WY	f P	112
Bear Town, MS	k F	68
Beatrice, AL	k l	68
Beatrice, NE	k K	82
Beattie, KS	i K	82
Beatty, NV	h l	128
Beattyville, KY	b C	40
Beaufort, NC	e J	40
Beaufort, SC	g F	40
Beaumont, CA	k l	128
Beaumont, MS	k H	68
Beaumont, TX	i B	68
Beaver, AK	c U	142
Beaver, OK	c F	84
Beaver, PA	g E	26
Beaver, UT	f D	98
Beaver, WV	b E	40
Beaver, r., NY	d K	26
Beaver, r., PA	g F	26
Beaver, r., UT	f D	98
Beaver City, NE	k H	82
Beaver Crossing, NE	k J	82
Beaver Dam, KY	e J	68
Beaver Dam, WI	g G	54
Beaver Falls, PA	g F	26
Beaverhead, r., MT	e M	112
Beaverhead Mountains, US	e L	112
Beaver Island, AK	e L	112
Beaver Lake, AR	f B	68
Beaver Mountains, AK	e P	142
Beaverton, MI	g K	54
Beaverton, OR	e C	112
Beckley, WV	j E	26
Beckville, TX	j B	68
Becky Peak, NV	e K	128
Bedford, IN	d J	68
Bedford, IA	k M	82
Bedford, KY	d K	68
Bedford, PA	g H	26
Bedford, VA	b G	40
Bedias, TX	i K	84
Beebe, AR	g E	68
Beech, r., TN	g H	68
Beech Creek, KY	e l	68
Beecher, IL	i H	54
Beech Fork, r., KY	e K	68
Beech Grove, IN	c J	68
Beemer, NE	j K	82
Bee Ridge, FL	l D	40
Beersheba Springs, TN	g K	68
Beeville, TX	k l	84
Beggs, OK	d J	84
Bel Air, MD	h J	26
Belcher, LA	j C	68
Belcourt, ND	c H	82
Belding, MI	g J	54
Belen, NM	j J	98
Belfast, ME	c Q	26
Belfield, ND	e D	82
Belfry, KY	b D	40
Belfry, MT	f P	112
Belgrade, ME	c P	26
Belgrade, MT	e N	112
Belgrade, NE	j l	82
Belhaven, NC	d J	40
Belington, WV	h G	26
Belknap Crater, OR	f C	112
Belkofski, AK	i E	142
Bellair, FL	f J	54
Bellaire, MI	f J	54
Bellaire, OH	g F	26
Bellaire, TX	j K	84
Bellamy, AL	j H	68
Belle, MO	d E	68
Belle, WV	i E	26
Belle, r., LA	m E	68
Bellefontaine, OH	g C	26
Bellefonte, PA	g l	26
Belle Fourche, SD	g D	82

Belle Fourche, r., US	g E	82
Belle Glade, FL	m F	40
Belle Plaine, IA	i C	54
Belle Plaine, KS	n J	82
Belle Plaine, MN	f B	54
Belleview, FL	j D	40
Belleville, IL	d G	68
Belleville, KS	i J	82
Belleville, PA	g l	26
Belleville, WI	h F	54
Bellevue, ID	g K	112
Bellevue, IA	h E	54
Bellevue, MI	h J	54
Bellevue, NE	j L	82
Bellevue, OH	f D	26
Bellevue, TX	f H	84
Bellevue, WA	c C	112
Bellingham, MN	f K	82
Bellingham, WA	b C	112
Bell Island Hot Springs, AK	b C	24
Bellmead, TX	h l	84
Bellows Falls, VT	d N	26
Bells, TN	g G	68
Bells, TX	f J	84
Bellville, OH	g D	26
Bellville, TX	j J	84
Bellwood, NE	j J	82
Bellwood, PA	g H	26
Belmond, IA	h B	54
Belmont, MS	h H	68
Belmont, NH	d O	26
Belmont, NY	e H	26
Belmont, SC	e E	40
Belmont, WI	h E	54
Beloit, KS	i J	82
Beloit, WI	h F	54
Belpre, OH	h E	26
Belspring, VA	b F	40
Belt, MT	c O	112
Belton, MO	d B	68
Belton, SC	e D	40
Belton, TX	h l	84
Belvidere, IL	h G	54
Belvidere, NJ	g K	26
Belview, MN	f L	82
Belzoni, MS	i F	68
Bement, IL	c H	68
Bemidji, MN	c A	54
Bemis, TN	g H	68
Benavides, TX	l H	84
Ben Bolt, TX	l H	84
Bend, OR	f D	112
Benham, KY	c D	40
Benjamin, TX	f G	84
Benkelman, NE	k F	82
Ben Lomond, CA	g C	128
Benndale, MS	l H	68
Bennet, NE	k K	82
Bennettsville, SC	e G	40
Bennington, KS	i J	82
Bennington, VT	e M	26
Benoit, MS	i E	68
Benson, AZ	m F	98
Benson, MN	f L	82
Benson, NC	d H	40
Benton, AR	h D	68
Benton, IL	d H	68
Benton, KY	f H	68
Benton, LA	j C	68
Benton, MS	j F	68
Benton, MO	e G	68
Benton, PA	f J	26
Benton, TN	d B	40
Benton City, WA	d F	112
Benton Harbor, MI	h l	54
Bentonia, MS	j F	68
Bentonville, AR	f B	68
Ben Wheeler, TX	g K	84
Beowawe, NV	d l	128
Berclair, TX	k l	84
Berea, KY	b B	40
Berea, OH	f E	26
Berea, SC	e D	40
Beresford, SD	h K	82
Bergen, NY	d l	26
Bergland, MI	d F	54
Bergoo, WV	i F	26
Bering Glacier, AK	f W	142
Bering Sea	g G	142
Bering Strait	e D	142
Berkeley, CA	g C	128
Berkeley Springs, WV	h H	26
Berkshire Hills, MA	e M	26
Berlin, MD	i K	26
Berlin, NH	c O	26
Berlin, NJ	h L	26
Berlin, PA	h H	26
Berlin, WI	g G	54
Berlin Lake, OH	f E	26
Bernalillo, NM	i J	98
Berne, IN	b L	68
Bernice, LA	j D	68
Bernie, MO	f G	68
Berry, AL	i l	68
Berryessa, Lake, CA	f C	128
Berryville, AR	f C	68
Bertha, MN	e L	82
Berthold, ND	c F	82
Berthoud, CO	d K	98
Berthoud Pass, CO	e K	98
Bertram, TX	i H	84
Bertrand, MO	f G	68
Bertrand, NE	k H	82
Berwick, LA	m E	68
Berwick, ME	d P	26
Berwick, PA	f J	26
Berwyn, IL	i H	54
Bessemer, AL	i J	68
Bessemer, MI	d E	54
Bessemer City, NC	d E	40
Bethalto, IL	d F	68
Bethany, IL	c H	68
Bethany, MO	b B	68
Bethany, OK	d l	84
Bethel, AK	f M	142
Bethel, CT	f M	26
Bethel, MN	e B	54
Bethel, NC	d l	40
Bethel, OH	h B	26
Bethel Acres, OK	d l	84
Bethel Springs, TN	h H	68
Bethesda, MD	b J	26
Bethlehem, PA	g K	26
Bethlehem, WV	g F	26
Bethune, SC	e F	40
Betsy Layne, KY	b D	40
Bettendorf, IA	i E	54
Bettles Field, AK	c S	142
Beulah, CO	l B	82
Beulah, MI	f l	54
Beulah, MS	i E	68
Beulah, ND	d F	82
Beulaville, NC	e l	40

B. Everett Jordan Lake, NC	d G	40
Beverly, MA	e P	26
Beverly Hills, CA	j G	128
Bevier, MO	c D	68
Bexley, OH	h D	26
Bibb City, GA	g B	40
Bicknell, IN	d l	68
Bicknell, UT	f E	98
Biddeford, ME	d P	26
Bieber, CA	c D	128
Big, r., MO	d F	68
Big Bay, MI	d H	54
Big Bay De Noc, MI	e l	54
Big Bear Lake, CA	j l	128
Big Bear Lake, CA	j l	128
Big Belt Mountains, MT	d N	112
Big Bend National Park, TX	j C	84
Big Black, r., MS	j F	68
Big Blue, r., US	i K	82
Big Canyon, TX	i D	84
Big Clifty, KY	e J	68
Big Creek, CA	g F	128
Big Creek Peak, ID	f L	112
Big Cypress Swamp, FL	m E	40
Big Delta, AK	d V	142
Big Eau Pleine, r., WI	f E	54
Bigelow Bight, US	d P	26
Big Falls, MN	b B	54
Big Flat, AR	f D	68
Bigfork, MN	c B	54
Bigfork, MT	b K	112
Big Fork, r., MN	b B	54
Big Frog Mountain, TN	d B	40
Biggers, AR	f F	68
Biggs, CA	e D	128
Big Hole, r., MT	e L	112
Bighorn, r., US	e R	112
Bighorn Basin, US	f Q	112
Big Horn Lake, US	e Q	112
Bighorn Mountains, US	e R	112
Big Island, VA	b G	40
Big Lake, MN	e B	54
Big Lake, TX	h E	84
Big Lookout Mountain, OR	f H	112
Big Lost, r., ID	g L	112
Big Mountain, NV	c F	128
Big Muddy, r., IL	e G	68
Big Otter, r., VA	b G	40
Big Pine, CA	g G	128
Big Pine Mountain, CA	i F	128
Big Piney, WY	h O	112
Big Piney, r., MO	e D	68
Bigpoint, MS	l H	68
Big Rapids, MI	g J	54
Big Rib, r., WI	e F	54
Big Sable, r., MI	f l	54
Big Sable Point, MI	f l	54
Big Sandy, MT	b O	112
Big Sandy, TN	f H	68
Big Sandy, TX	g K	84
Big Sandy, r., US	j D	26
Big Sandy, r., AZ	j C	98
Big Sandy, r., TN	f H	68
Big Sandy, r., WY	i P	112
Big Sioux, r., US	i B	54
Big Sky, MT	e N	112
Big Smoky Valley, NV	f H	128
Big Spring, TX	g E	84
Big Springs, NE	j E	82
Big Spruce Knob, WV	i F	26
Big Stone City, SD	f K	82
Big Stone Gap, VA	c D	40
Big Stone Lake, US	f K	82
Big Sunflower, r., MS	j E	68
Big Sur, CA	i D	128
Big Thompson, r., CO	d K	98
Big Timber, MT	e P	112
Big Water, UT	g E	98
Big Wells, TX	k G	84
Big Wood, r., ID	g L	112
Billings, MO	e C	68
Billings, MT	e Q	112
Billings, OK	c l	84
Billings Heights, MT	e Q	112
Bill Williams, r., AZ	j C	98
Bill Williams Mountain, AZ	i D	98
Billy Chinook, Lake, OR	f D	112
Biloxi, MS	l H	68
Biloxi, r., MS	l G	68
Biltmore Forest, NC	d D	40
Binford, ND	d l	82
Bingham, ME	b Q	26
Binghamton, NY	e K	26
Binger, OK	d H	84
Birch, r., WV	i F	26
Birch Run, MI	g L	54
Birch Tree, MO	e E	68
Birchwood, WI	e D	54
Bird City, KS	i F	82
Bird Island, MN	g M	82
Birmingham, AL	i J	68
Birmingham, IA	j D	54
Birmingham, MI	h L	54
Birnamwood, WI	f F	54
Bisbee, AZ	m G	98
Bisbee, ND	c H	82
Biscayne Bay, FL	n F	40
Biscoe, NC	d G	40
Bishop, CA	g G	128
Bishop, TX	l l	84
Bishopville, SC	e F	40
Bismarck, MO	e F	68
Bismarck, ND	e G	82
Bison, SD	f E	82
Bison Peak, CO	e K	98
Bistineau, Lake, LA	j C	68
Bitterroot Range, US	d K	112
Bivins, TX	i B	68
Biwabik, MN	c C	54
Bixby, OK	d J	84
Black, r., US	g E	68
Black, r., AK	c V	142
Black, r., AZ	k F	98
Black, r., LA	k D	68
Black, r., MI	g M	54
Black, r., NY	d K	26
Black, r., SC	f G	40
Black, r., VT	c N	26
Black, r., WI	g D	54
Black Butte, MT	f N	112
Black Diamond, WA	c D	112
Blackduck, MN	c A	54
Black Eagle, MT	c N	112
Blackfoot, ID	g M	112

Blackfoot, r., ID	g N	112
Blackfoot, r., MT	d L	112
Blackfoot Reservoir, ID	h N	112
Black Hawk Creek, r., IA	h C	54
Black Hills, US	g D	82
Black Lake, NY	c K	26
Black Lake Bayou, r., LA	j C	68
Black Mesa, US	h B	84
Black Mesa, AZ	h C	98
Blackmore, Mount, MT	e N	112
Black Mountain, NC	d D	40
Black Mountain, US	c D	40
Black Mountain, WY	f R	112
Black Mountains, AZ	i B	98
Black Range, NM	k l	98
Black River, NY	c K	26
Black River Falls, WI	f E	54
Black Rock, AR	f E	68
Black Rock Desert, NV	c G	128
Blacksburg, SC	d E	40
Blacksburg, VA	b F	40
Blackshear, GA	h D	40
Blackstone, VA	b l	40
Blackville, SC	f E	40
Black Warrior, r., AL	i l	68
Blackwater, r., MO	d C	68
Blackwell, OK	c l	84
Blackwell, TX	g F	84
Bladenboro, NC	e H	40
Blaine, ME	b C	112
Blaine, WA	b C	112
Blair, NE	i K	82
Blair, OK	e G	84
Blair, WI	f D	54
Blairstown, IA	i C	54
Blairsville, GA	e C	40
Blairsville, PA	g G	26
Blakely, GA	h B	40
Blakesburg, IA	j C	54
Blanca, CO	g K	98
Blanca Peak, CO	g K	98
Blanchard, r., OH	f C	26
Blanchard, LA	j C	68
Blanchardville, WI	h F	54
Blanchester, OH	h C	26
Blanco, TX	i H	84
Blanco, r., TX	i H	84
Blanco, Cañon, NM	i K	98
Blanco, Cape, OR	h A	112
Blanco, Rio, r., CO	g J	98
Bland, MO	d E	68
Bland, VA	b E	40
Blanding, UT	g G	98
Blandinsville, IL	a E	68
Blanket, TX	h H	84
Blasdell, NY	f F	26
Bledsoe, TX	f C	84
Blessing, TX	k J	84
Blissfield, MI	i L	54
Block Island, RI	f O	26
Block Island, RI	f O	26
Blockton, IA	k M	82
Bloomer, WI	e D	54
Bloomfield, IN	c J	68
Bloomfield, IA	j C	54
Bloomfield, KY	e K	68
Bloomfield, MO	f G	68
Bloomfield, NM	h l	98
Blooming Grove, TX	g l	84
Blooming Prairie, MN	g B	54
Bloomington, IL	b G	68
Bloomington, IN	c J	68
Bloomington, MN	f B	54
Bloomington, TX	k J	84
Bloomington, WI	h E	54
Bloomsburg, PA	f J	26
Bloomville, OH	f C	26
Blossburg, PA	f l	26
Blossom, TX	f K	84
Blountstown, FL	i A	40
Blountsville, AL	h J	68
Blountville, TN	c D	40
Blowing Rock, NC	c E	40
Blue, r., CO	e J	98
Blue, r., KS	k G	98
Blue, r., IN	d J	68
Blue, r., OK	e J	84
Blue Creek, WA	b H	112
Blue Earth, MN	g A	54
Blue Earth, r., MN	g A	54
Bluefield, VA	b E	40
Bluefield, WV	b E	40
Blue Hill, ME	c R	26
Blue Hill, NE	k l	82
Blue Hill Bay, ME	c R	26
Blue Island, IL	i H	54
Blue Mound, IL	c G	68
Blue Mound, KS	m L	82
Blue Mountain, MS	h H	68
Blue Mountain, PA	g l	26
Blue Mountains, US	f G	112
Blue Rapids, KS	i K	82
Blue Ridge, GA	e B	40
Blue Ridge, US	d J	8
Blue Springs, NE	k K	82
Bluestone, r., US	b E	40
Bluestone Lake, US	b E	40
Bluewater, NM	i l	98
Bluff, UT	g G	98
Bluff City, TN	c D	40
Bluff Dale, TX	g H	84
Bluff Park, AL	i J	68
Bluffs, IL	c F	68
Bluffton, IN	b K	68
Bluffton, OH	g C	26
Blunt, SD	g H	82
Bly, OR	h D	112
Blythe, CA	k K	128
Blytheville, AR	g G	68
Boardman, r., MI	f F	26
Boardman, r., MI	f J	54
Boaz, AL	h J	68
Bobtown, PA	h F	26
Boca de Quadra, AK	b D	24
Boca Grande, FL	m D	40
Boca Raton, FL	m F	40
Bode, IA	i M	82
Boerne, TX	j H	84
Bogachiel, r., WA	c A	112
Bogalusa, LA	l G	68
Bogata, TX	f K	84
Boger City, NC	d E	40
Bogue Chitto, MS	k F	68
Bogue Chitto, r., US	k F	68
Bogue Phalia, r., MS	i F	68
Boiling Springs, NC	d E	40
Bois Blanc Island, MI	e K	54
Bois Brule, r., WI	d D	54
Bois de Sioux, r., US	e K	82
Boise, ID	g l	112

Name	Map Ref.	Page
Boise, r., ID	g I	112
Boise City, OK	c D	84
Bokchito, OK	e J	84
Boles, AR	h B	68
Boley, OK	d J	84
Boligee, AL	j H	68
Boling, TX	j K	84
Bolingbrook, IL	i G	54
Bolivar, MO	e C	68
Bolivar, NY	e H	26
Bolivar, TN	g H	68
Bolivar Peninsula, TX	j L	84
Bolton, MS	j F	68
Bolton, NC	e H	40
Bon Air, VA	b I	40
Bonanza, OR	h D	112
Bonanza, UT	d G	98
Bonaparte, IA	j D	54
Bond, MS	I G	68
Bonduel, WI	f G	54
Bonesteel, SD	h I	82
Bonham, TX	f J	84
Bonifay, FL	I K	68
Bonita, LA	j E	68
Bonita Springs, FL	m E	40
Bonito, Rio, r., NM	k K	98
Bonner, MT	d L	112
Bonners Ferry, ID	b I	112
Bonne Terre, MO	e F	68
Bonneville Peak, ID	h M	112
Bonneville Salt Flats, UT	d C	98
Bonnie Doone, NC	d H	40
Bono, AR	g F	68
Bon Secour, AL	I I	68
Bon Wier, TX	I C	68
Book Cliffs, US	e G	98
Booker, TX	c F	84
Boomer, WV	i E	26
Boone, IA	h B	54
Boone, NC	c E	40
Boone, r., IA	h B	54
Boones Mill, VA	b G	40
Booneville, AR	g C	68
Booneville, KY	b C	40
Booneville, MS	h H	68
Boonsboro, MD	h I	26
Boonville, CA	e B	128
Boonville, IN	d I	68
Boonville, MO	d D	68
Boonville, NY	d K	26
Booth, AL	j J	68
Boothbay Harbor, ME	d Q	26
Boothville, LA	m G	68
Borah Peak, ID	f L	112
Borger, TX	d E	84
Borgne, Lake, LA	I G	68
Boron, CA	j H	128
Boscobel, WI	g E	54
Bosque Farms, NM	j J	98
Bossier City, LA	j C	68
Boston, GA	i C	40
Boston, MA	e O	26
Boston Mountains, AR	g C	68
Boswell, IN	b I	68
Boswell, OK	e K	84
Boswell, PA	g G	26
Bosworth, MO	c C	68
Botkins, OH	g B	26
Bottineau, ND	c G	82
Boulder, CO	d K	98
Boulder, MT	d M	112
Boulder, r., MT	d M	112
Boulder City, NV	i K	128
Boundary, AK	d X	142
Boundary Peak, NV	g G	128
Bountiful, UT	d E	98
Bourbeuse, r., MO	d E	68
Bourbon, IN	a J	68
Bourbon, MO	d E	68
Bourg, LA	m F	68
Bouse, AZ	k B	98
Bovey, MN	c B	54
Bovill, ID	d I	112
Bovina, TX	e D	84
Bowbells, ND	c E	82
Bowdle, SD	f H	82
Bowdon, GA	f A	40
Bowdon, ND	d H	82
Bowen, IL	b E	68
Bowie, AZ	I G	98
Bowie, MD	h J	26
Bowie, TX	f I	84
Bowling Green, FL	I E	40
Bowling Green, KY	f J	68
Bowling Green, MO	c E	68
Bowling Green, OH	f C	26
Bowling Green, VA	a I	40
Bowman, GA	e C	40
Bowman, ND	e D	82
Bowman, SC	f F	40
Box Elder, MT	b O	112
Boyce, LA	k D	68
Boyceville, WI	e C	54
Boyd, MN	g L	82
Boyd, TX	f I	84
Boydton, VA	c H	40
Boyer, r., IA	j L	82
Boyertown, PA	g K	26
Boykins, VA	d I	40
Boyle, MS	i F	68
Boylston, AL	j J	68
Boyne City, MI	e J	54
Boynton, OK	d K	84
Boynton Beach, FL	m F	40
Boysen Reservoir, WY	g Q	112
Boys Ranch, TX	d D	84
Bozeman, MT	e N	112
Brackettville, TX	j F	84
Bradenton, FL	I D	40
Bradford, AR	g E	68
Bradford, IL	i F	54
Bradford, OH	g B	26
Bradford, PA	f H	26
Bradford, TN	f H	68
Bradford, VT	d N	26
Bradley, AR	i C	68
Bradley, FL	I E	40
Bradley, IL	i H	54
Bradley, SD	f J	82
Bradshaw, NE	k J	82
Bradshaw, WV	b E	40
Brady, MT	b N	112
Brady, NE	j G	82
Brady, TX	h G	84
Braham, MN	e B	54
Braidwood, IL	i G	54
Brainard, NE	j J	82
Brainerd, MN	d A	54
Braman, OK	c I	84
Branchville, SC	f F	40
Brandenburg, KY	d J	68
Brandon, FL	I D	40
Brandon, MS	j G	68
Brandon, SD	h K	82
Brandon, VT	d M	26
Brandon, WI	g G	54
Branford, FL	j D	40
Branson, MO	f C	68
Brant Lake, NY	d M	26
Brantley, AL	k J	68
Brasstown Bald, GA	e C	40
Brattleboro, VT	e N	26
Brave, PA	h F	26
Bravo del Norte (Rio Grande), r., NA	f F	8
Brawley, CA	I J	128
Brawley Peaks, NV	f G	128
Braymer, MO	c C	68
Brazil, IN	c I	68
Brazoria, TX	j K	84
Brazos, r., TX	j K	84
Brea, CA	k H	128
Breaux Bridge, LA	I E	68
Breckenridge, CO	e J	98
Breckenridge, MI	g K	54
Breckenridge, MN	e K	82
Breckenridge, MO	c C	68
Breckenridge, TX	g H	84
Breda, IA	i M	82
Breese, IL	d G	68
Bremen, GA	f A	40
Bremen, IN	a J	68
Bremen, OH	h D	26
Bremerton, WA	c C	112
Bremond, TX	h J	84
Brenham, TX	i J	84
Brent, AL	j I	68
Brent, FL	I I	68
Brentwood, NY	g M	26
Brentwood, TN	f J	68
Breton Islands, LA	m G	68
Breton Sound, LA	m G	68
Brevard, NC	d D	40
Brewer, ME	c R	26
Brewster, KS	I F	82
Brewster, MN	h L	82
Brewster, NE	j H	82
Brewster, OH	g E	26
Brewster, WA	b F	112
Brewton, AL	k I	68
Brian Head, UT	g D	98
Bricelyn, MN	g B	54
Briceville, TN	c B	40
Bridge City, TX	I C	68
Bridgeport, AL	h K	68
Bridgeport, CA	f F	128
Bridgeport, CT	f M	26
Bridgeport, IL	d I	68
Bridgeport, MI	g L	54
Bridgeport, NE	j D	82
Bridgeport, TX	f I	84
Bridgeport, WA	b F	112
Bridgeport, WV	h F	26
Bridgeport, Lake, TX	f I	84
Bridger, MT	e Q	112
Bridgeton, NJ	h K	26
Bridgeville, DE	i K	26
Bridgewater, MA	f P	26
Bridgewater, SD	h J	82
Bridgewater, VA	i H	26
Bridgman, MI	i I	54
Bridgton, ME	c P	26
Briggs, TX	i I	84
Brigham City, UT	c D	98
Brighton, CO	e L	98
Brighton, IL	c F	68
Brighton, IA	i D	54
Brighton, MI	h L	54
Brighton, NY	d I	26
Brilliant, AL	h I	68
Brillion, WI	f H	54
Brinkley, AR	h E	68
Bristol, CT	f N	26
Bristol, FL	i B	40
Bristol, NH	d O	26
Bristol, PA	g L	26
Bristol, RI	f O	26
Bristol, SD	f J	82
Bristol, TN	c D	40
Bristol, VT	c M	26
Bristol, VA	c D	40
Bristol Bay, AK	g O	142
Bristol Lake, CA	j J	128
Bristow, OK	d J	84
Britt, IA	g B	54
Britton, SD	f J	82
Broad, r., US	e E	40
Broadalbin, NY	d L	26
Broadus, MT	f B	82
Broadwater, NE	j E	82
Broadway, VA	i H	26
Brockport, NY	d I	26
Brockton, MA	e O	26
Brockton, MT	c C	82
Brockway, PA	f H	26
Brocton, NY	e G	26
Brodhead, KY	b B	40
Brodhead, WI	h F	54
Brodnax, VA	c H	40
Brogan, OR	f H	112
Broken Arrow, OK	c K	84
Broken Bow, NE	j H	82
Broken Bow, OK	h B	68
Broken Bow Lake, OK	h B	68
Bronson, FL	j D	40
Bronson, KS	n L	82
Bronson, MI	i J	54
Bronson, TX	k B	68
Bronte, TX	h F	84
Bronwood, GA	h B	40
Brook, IN	b I	68
Brookeland, TX	k B	68
Brooker, FL	j D	40
Brookfield, MO	c C	68
Brookfield, WI	g G	54
Brookford, NC	d E	40
Brookhaven, MS	k F	68
Brookings, OR	h A	112
Brookings, SD	g K	82
Brookland, AR	g F	68
Brooklet, GA	g E	40
Brooklyn, IA	i C	54
Brooklyn, MI	h K	54
Brooklyn, MS	k G	68
Brooklyn Center, MN	e B	54
Brookneal, VA	b H	40
Brookport, IL	e H	68
Brooks, ME	c Q	26
Brooks, Mount, AK	e S	142
Brookshire, TX	j K	84
Brooks Range, AK	c P	142
Brooksville, FL	k D	40
Brooksville, KY	i B	26
Brooksville, MS	i H	68
Brookville, IN	c K	68
Brookville, PA	f G	26
Brookville Lake, IN	c K	68
Broomfield, CO	e K	98
Brooten, MN	f L	82
Browerville, MN	e M	82
Brown City, MI	g M	54
Brown Deer, WI	g H	54
Brownfield, TX	f D	84
Browning, MO	b C	68
Browning, MT	b L	112
Brownlee Reservoir, US	f H	112
Brownsburg, IN	c J	68
Brownsdale, MN	g C	54
Brownstown, IL	d H	68
Brownstown, IN	d J	68
Browns Valley, MN	f K	82
Brownsville, KY	e J	68
Brownsville, LA	j D	68
Brownsville, OR	f C	112
Brownsville, PA	g G	26
Brownsville, TN	g G	68
Brownsville, TX	n I	84
Brownton, MN	f A	54
Brownville, AL	i I	68
Brownville, ME	b Q	26
Brownville, NE	k L	82
Brownville Junction, ME	b Q	26
Brownwood, TX	h H	84
Broxton, GA	h D	40
Bruce, MS	i G	68
Bruce, SD	g K	82
Bruce, WI	e D	54
Bruin Point, UT	e F	98
Brule, NE	j F	82
Brule, r., US	e G	54
Brundidge, AL	k K	68
Bruneau, ID	h J	112
Bruneau, r., US	h J	112
Brunson, SC	g E	40
Brunswick, GA	h E	40
Brunswick, ME	d Q	26
Brunswick, MD	h I	26
Brunswick, MO	c C	68
Brunswick, OH	f E	26
Brush, CO	k D	82
Bryan, OH	f B	26
Bryan, TX	i J	84
Bryant, AR	h D	68
Bryant, SD	g J	82
Bryce Canyon National Park, UT	g D	98
Bryson, TX	f H	84
Bryson City, NC	d C	40
Buchanan, GA	f A	40
Buchanan, MI	i I	54
Buchanan, VA	b G	40
Buchanan, Lake, TX	i H	84
Buckatunna, MS	k H	68
Buckeye, AZ	k D	98
Buckeye Lake, OH	h D	26
Buckhannon, WV	i F	26
Buckholts, TX	i I	84
Buckingham, VA	b H	40
Buckland, AK	d N	142
Buckley, IL	j G	54
Buckley, WA	c C	112
Bucklin, KS	n H	82
Bucklin, MO	c D	68
Bucksport, ME	c R	26
Bucyrus, OH	g D	26
Buda, IL	i F	54
Buda, TX	i I	84
Bude, MS	k F	68
Buena Vista, CO	f J	98
Buena Vista, GA	g B	40
Buena Vista, MS	i H	68
Buena Vista, VA	b G	40
Buffalo, KS	n L	82
Buffalo, MN	e B	54
Buffalo, MO	e C	68
Buffalo, NY	e H	26
Buffalo, OH	h E	26
Buffalo, OK	c G	84
Buffalo, SC	e E	40
Buffalo, SD	f D	82
Buffalo, TX	h J	84
Buffalo, WY	f S	112
Buffalo, r., AR	f D	68
Buffalo, r., MN	d K	82
Buffalo, r., MS	k E	68
Buffalo, r., TN	g I	68
Buffalo, r., WI	f D	54
Buffalo Center, IA	g B	54
Buffalo Lake, MN	g M	82
Buford, GA	e B	40
Buhl, ID	h K	112
Buhl, MN	c C	54
Buhler, KS	m J	82
Bulan, KY	b C	40
Bullard, TX	g K	84
Bullhead, SD	f F	82
Bullhead City, AZ	i B	98
Bull Mountain, MT	d M	112
Bullock, NC	c H	40
Bulls Gap, TN	c C	40
Bull Shoals, AR	f D	68
Bull Shoals Lake, US	f D	68
Buna, TX	I C	68
Bunavista, TX	d E	84
Bunceton, MO	d D	68
Bunker, MO	e E	68
Bunker Hill, IL	c G	68
Bunker Hill, IN	b J	68
Bunker Hill, OR	g A	112
Bunker Hill, NV	e H	128
Bunkie, LA	I D	68
Bunnell, FL	j E	40
Buras, LA	m G	68
Burbank, CA	j G	128
Burbank, WA	d F	112
Burden, KS	n K	82
Burdett, KS	m H	82
Burgaw, NC	e I	40
Burgess, VA	b J	40
Burgettstown, PA	g F	26
Burgin, KY	e L	68
Burien, WA	c C	112
Burkburnett, TX	e H	84
Burke, SD	h H	82
Burkesville, KY	f K	68
Burleson, TX	g I	84
Burley, ID	h L	112
Burlingame, CA	g C	128
Burlingame, KS	m L	82
Burlington, CO	I E	82
Burlington, IA	j D	54
Burlington, KS	m L	82
Burlington, NJ	g L	26
Burlington, NC	c G	40
Burlington, ND	c F	82
Burlington, VT	c M	26
Burlington, WA	b C	112
Burlington, WI	h G	54
Burlington, WY	f Q	112
Burlington Junction, MO	b A	68
Burnet, TX	i H	84
Burney, CA	d D	128
Burnham, PA	g I	26
Burns, KS	m K	82
Burns, OR	g F	112
Burns, TN	f I	68
Burns, WY	j C	82
Burns Flat, OK	d G	84
Burnside, KY	c B	40
Burnsville, AL	j J	68
Burnsville, MS	h H	68
Burnsville, NC	d D	40
Burnsville, WV	i F	26
Burnt, r., OR	f H	112
Burr Oak, KS	I I	82
Burro Peak, NM	I H	98
Burrton, KS	m J	82
Burrwood, LA	n G	68
Burt, IA	h M	82
Burt Lake, MI	e K	54
Burton, MI	g L	54
Burton, TX	i J	84
Burwell, NE	j H	82
Busby, MT	e S	112
Bush, r., SC	e E	40
Bushland, TX	d D	84
Bushnell, FL	k D	40
Bushnell, IL	j E	54
Bushton, KS	m I	82
Bussey, IA	i C	54
Butler, AL	j H	68
Butler, GA	g B	40
Butler, IN	a L	68
Butler, MO	d B	68
Butler, OH	g D	26
Butler, OK	d G	84
Butler, PA	g G	26
Butner, NC	c H	40
Butte, MT	d M	112
Butte, NE	i I	82
Butte Creek, r., CA	e D	128
Butte Falls, OR	h C	112
Butterfield, MN	h M	82
Butternut, WI	d E	54
Buttonwillow, CA	i F	128
Buxton, NC	d K	40
Buxton, ND	d J	82
Byers, TX	e H	84
Byesville, OH	h E	26
Byhalia, MS	h G	68
Bylas, AZ	k F	98
Bynum, NC	d G	40
Byrdstown, TN	f K	68
Byron, GA	g C	40
Byron, IL	h F	54
Byron, WY	f Q	112
C		
Caballo Reservoir, NM	I I	98
Cable, WI	d D	54
Cabool, MO	e D	68
Cabot, AR	h D	68
Cacapon, r., WV	h H	26
Cache, OK	e H	84
Cache, r., IL	e G	68
Cache la Poudre, r., CO	d K	98
Cache Peak, ID	h L	112
Cactus, TX	c D	84
Cactus Peak, NV	g I	128
Caddo, OK	e J	84
Caddo, TX	g H	84
Caddo, r., AR	h C	68
Caddo Lake, US	j B	68
Caddo Mills, TX	f J	84
Cadillac, MI	f J	54
Cadiz, KY	f I	68
Cadiz, OH	g F	26
Cadott, WI	f D	54
Cadwell, GA	g C	40
Cahaba, r., AL	j I	68
Cahokia, IL	d F	68
Cainsville, MO	b C	68
Cairo, GA	i B	40
Cairo, IL	e G	68
Cairo, NE	j I	82
Cairo, WV	h E	26
Cajon Summit, CA	j H	128
Calais, ME	b S	26
Calamus, r., NE	j H	82
Calaveras, r., CA	f D	128
Calcasieu, r., LA	I D	68
Calcasieu Lake, LA	m C	68
Caldwell, ID	g I	112
Caldwell, KS	n J	82
Caldwell, OH	h E	26
Caldwell, TX	i J	84
Caledonia, MN	g D	54
Caledonia, MS	i H	68
Caledonia, NY	e I	26
Caledonia, OH	g D	26
Calera, AL	i J	68
Calera, OK	f J	84
Calexico, CA	I J	128
Calfkiller, r., TN	f K	68
Calfpasture, r., VA	i G	26
Calhan, CO	I C	82
Calhoun, AL	j J	68
Calhoun, GA	e B	40
Calhoun, KY	e I	68
Calhoun, MO	d C	68
Calhoun, TN	d B	40
Calhoun City, MS	i G	68
Calhoun Falls, SC	e D	40
Calico Rock, AR	f D	68
Caliente, NV	g K	128
California, MO	d D	68
California, PA	g G	26
California, state, US	d B	8
California Aqueduct, CA	h E	128
Calion, AR	i D	68
Calipatria, CA	k J	128
Calispell Peak, WA	b H	112
Calistoga, CA	f C	128
Callaghan, Mount, NV	e I	128
Callahan, FL	i E	40
Callaway, NE	j H	82
Calliham, TX	k H	84
Calmar, IA	g D	54
Caloosahatchee, r., FL	m E	40
Calumet, MI	c G	54
Calumet, MN	c B	54
Calumet City, IL	a I	68
Calvert, AL	k H	68
Calvert, TX	i J	84
Calvin, OK	e J	84
Calwa, CA	h F	128
Calypso, NC	d H	40
Camanche, IA	i E	54
Camarillo, CA	j F	128
Cambria, CA	i D	128
Cambria, WI	g F	54
Cambridge, ID	f I	112
Cambridge, IL	i E	54
Cambridge, IA	i B	54
Cambridge, MD	i J	26
Cambridge, MA	e O	26
Cambridge, MN	e B	54
Cambridge, NE	k G	82
Cambridge, NY	d M	26
Cambridge, OH	g E	26
Cambridge City, IN	c K	68
Cambridge Springs, PA	f F	26
Camden, AL	k I	68
Camden, AR	i D	68
Camden, DE	h K	26
Camden, ME	c Q	26
Camden, MS	j G	68
Camden, NJ	h K	26
Camden, NY	d K	26
Camden, NC	c J	40
Camden, OH	h B	26
Camden, SC	e F	40
Camden, TN	f H	68
Camdenton, MO	d D	68
Cameron, LA	m C	68
Cameron, MO	c B	68
Cameron, SC	f F	40
Cameron, TX	i J	84
Cameron, WV	h F	26
Cameron, WI	e D	54
Camilla, GA	h B	40
Camino, CA	f E	128
Campaign, TN	g K	68
Campbell, CA	g D	128
Campbell, MN	e K	82
Campbell, MO	f F	68
Campbell, NE	k I	82
Campbell Hill, OH	g C	26
Campbellsport, WI	g G	54
Campbellsville, KY	e K	68
Campbellton, FL	i A	40
Camp Douglas, WI	g E	54
Camp Hill, AL	j K	68
Camp Hill, PA	g J	26
Campo, CO	n E	82
Camp Point, IL	b E	68
Campti, LA	k C	68
Campton, KY	b C	40
Camp Verde, AZ	j E	98
Camp Wood, TX	j F	84
Canaan, CT	e M	26
Canaan, VT	c O	26
Canadian, TX	d F	84
Canadian, r., US	d J	84
Canadian, r., CO	d J	98
Canajoharie, NY	e L	26
Canal Fulton, OH	g E	26
Canal Point, FL	m F	40
Canal Winchester, OH	h D	26
Canandaigua, NY	e I	26
Canaseraga, NY	e I	26
Canastota, NY	d K	26
Canaveral, Cape, FL	k F	40
Canby, CA	c E	128
Canby, MN	g K	82
Canby, OR	e C	112
Candle, AK	d N	142
Candlestick, MS	j F	68
Candlewood, Lake, CT	f M	26
Cando, ND	c H	82
Candor, NY	e J	26
Candor, NC	d G	40
Cane, r., LA	k D	68
Caney, KS	n L	82
Caney, r., US	c K	84
Canisteo, NY	e I	26
Canisteo, r., NY	e I	26
Canistota, SD	h J	82
Cannel City, KY	b C	40
Cannelton, IN	e J	68
Cannon, r., MN	f B	54
Cannon Ball, r., ND	e G	82
Cannonball, r., ND	e G	82
Cannon Beach, OR	e B	112
Cannon Falls, MN	f C	54
Canon, GA	e C	40
Canon City, CO	f K	98
Canonsburg, PA	g F	26
Canoochee, r., GA	g E	40
Canova, SD	h J	82
Canova Beach, FL	k F	40
Canton, GA	e B	40
Canton, IL	j E	54
Canton, KS	m J	82
Canton, MN	g D	54
Canton, MS	j F	68
Canton, MO	b E	68
Canton, NY	c K	26
Canton, NC	d D	40
Canton, OH	g E	26
Canton, OK	c H	84
Canton, PA	f J	26
Canton, SD	h K	82
Canton, TX	g K	84
Canton Lake, OK	c H	84
Cantonment, FL	I I	68
Cantwell, AK	e T	142
Canutillo, TX	m J	98
Canyon, TX	e E	84
Canyon City, OR	f G	112
Canyon Ferry Lake, MT	d N	112
Canyonlands National Park, UT	f G	98
Canyonville, OR	h B	112
Capac, MI	g M	54
Cape Canaveral, FL	k F	40
Cape Charles, VA	b J	40
Cape Cod Bay, MA	f P	26
Cape Coral, FL	m E	40
Cape Elizabeth, ME	d P	26
Cape Fear, r., NC	e H	40
Cape Girardeau, MO	e G	68
Cape Lisburne, AK	b K	142
Cape May, NJ	i L	26
Cape May Court House, NJ	h L	26
Cape Pole, AK	i BB	142
Cape Porpoise, ME	d P	26
Cape Romanzof, AK	f L	142
Cape Vincent, NY	c J	26
Cape Yakataga, AK	f W	142
Capitan, NM	k K	98
Capitan Peak, NM	k K	98
Capitola, CA	h D	128
Capitol Peak, NV	c H	128
Capitol Reef National Park, UT	f E	98
Capitol View, SC	f F	40
Capron, IL	h G	54
Captain Cook, HI	j P	144d
Caraway, AR	g F	68
Carbon, TX	g H	84
Carbon, r., WA	c D	112
Carbondale, CO	e I	98
Carbondale, IL	e G	68
Carbondale, KS	m L	82
Carbondale, PA	f K	26
Carbon Hill, AL	i I	68
Cardington, OH	g D	26
Cardwell, MO	f F	68
Carencro, LA	I D	68
Caretta, WV	b E	40
Carey, OH	g C	26
Caribou Mountain, ID	g N	112
Carleton, MI	h L	54
Carleton, NE	k J	82
Carlin, NV	d I	128
Carlinville, IL	c G	68
Carlisle, AR	h E	68
Carlisle, IN	d I	68
Carlisle, IA	i B	54
Carlisle, KY	i B	26
Carlisle, PA	g I	26
Carl Junction, MO	e B	68
Carlsbad, CA	k H	128
Carlsbad, NM	g B	84
Carlsbad, TX	h F	84
Carlsbad Caverns National Park, NM	g B	84
Carlton, MN	d C	54
Carlton, OR	e B	112
Carlton, TX	h H	84
Carlyle, IL	d G	68
Carlyle Lake, IL	d G	68
Carmel, CA	h D	128
Carmel, IN	c J	68
Carmel, NY	f M	26
Carmel Valley, CA	h D	128
Carmel Woods, CA	h D	128
Carmen, OK	c H	84
Carmi, IL	d H	68
Carmichael, CA	f D	128
Carmine, TX	i J	84
Carnegie, OK	d H	84
Caro, MI	g L	54
Carol City, FL	n F	40
Caroleen, NC	d E	40
Carolina Beach, NC	e I	40
Carp, r., MI	d K	54
Carpenter, WY	j C	82
Carpentersville, IL	h G	54
Carpinteria, CA	j F	128
Carpio, ND	c F	82
Carrabelle, FL	j B	40
Carrboro, NC	d G	40
Carriere, MS	I G	68
Carriers Mills, IL	e H	68
Carrington, ND	d H	82
Carrizo Mountain, NM	k K	98
Carrizo Springs, TX	k G	84
Carrizozo, NM	k K	98
Carroll, IA	i M	82
Carroll, NE	i J	82
Carrollton, AL	i H	68
Carrollton, GA	f A	40
Carrollton, IL	c F	68
Carrollton, KY	d K	68
Carrollton, MI	g L	54
Carrollton, MS	i G	68
Carrollton, MO	c C	68
Carrollton, OH	g E	26
Carrollton, TX	g J	84
Carrolltown, PA	g H	26
Carrville, AL	j K	68
Carson, ND	e F	82
Carson, WA	e D	112
Carson, r., NV	e F	128
Carson City, MI	g K	54
Carson City, NV	e F	128
Carson Range, US	e F	128
Carson Sink, NV	e G	128
Carter, OK	d G	84
Carter Lake, IA	j L	82
Carter Mountain, WY	f P	112
Cartersville, GA	e B	40
Carterville, IL	e G	68
Carthage, AR	h D	68
Carthage, IL	j D	54
Carthage, IN	c K	68
Carthage, MS	j G	68
Carthage, MO	e B	68
Carthage, NY	d K	26
Carthage, NC	d G	40
Carthage, SD	g J	82
Carthage, TN	f K	68
Carthage, TX	j B	68
Caruthersville, MO	f G	68
Cary, MS	j F	68
Cary, NC	d H	40
Caryville, FL	I K	68
Caryville, TN	c B	40
Casa Grande, AZ	I E	98
Casas Adobes, AZ	I F	98
Cascade, ID	f I	112
Cascade, IA	h D	54
Cascade, MT	c N	112
Cascade, WI	g G	54
Cascade Locks, OR	e D	112
Cascade Range, NA	c B	8
Cascade Reservoir, ID	f I	112
Casco Bay, ME	d P	26
Caseville, MI	g L	54
Casey, IL	c I	68
Casey, IA	j M	82
Cashiers, NC	d C	40
Cashmere, WA	c E	112
Cashton, WI	g E	54
Casper, WY	b J	98
Caspian, MI	d G	54
Cass, r., MI	g L	54
Cass City, MI	g L	54
Casselton, ND	e J	82
Cass Lake, MN	c A	54
Cassopolis, MI	i I	54
Cassville, MO	f C	68
Cassville, WI	h E	54
Castalia, OH	f D	26
Castile, NY	e H	26
Castine, ME	c R	26
Castleberry, AL	k I	68
Castle Dale, UT	e F	98
Castle Hills, TX	j H	84
Castle Peak, CO	e J	98
Castle Peak, ID	f K	112
Castle Rock, CO	e L	98
Castle Rock, WA	d C	112
Castle Rock, OR	f G	112
Castle Rock Lake, WI	g F	54
Castleton, VT	d M	26
Castlewood, SD	g J	82
Castlewood, VA	c D	40
Castor, r., MO	e F	68
Castroville, CA	h D	128
Castroville, TX	j H	84
Catahoula Lake, LA	k D	68
Catawba, r., US	e F	40
Catawissa, PA	g J	26
Cathedral City, CA	k I	128
Cathlamet, WA	d B	112
Cat Island, MS	I G	68
Catlettsburg, KY	i D	26
Catlin, IL	b I	68
Catnip Mountain, NV	c F	128
Catonsville, MD	h J	26
Catoosa, OK	c K	84
Catskill, NY	e M	26
Catskill Mountains, NY	e L	26
Cattaraugus, NY	e H	26
Cavalier, ND	c J	82
Cave City, AR	g E	68
Cave City, KY	e K	68
Cave In Rock, IL	e H	68
Cave Run Lake, KY	i C	26
Cave Spring, GA	e A	40
Cawker City, KS	I I	82
Cawood, KY	c C	40
Cayce, SC	f E	40
Cayucos, CA	i E	128
Cayuga, IN	c I	68
Cayuga, ND	e J	82
Cayuga, TX	h K	84
Cayuga Heights, NY	e J	26
Cayuga Lake, NY	e J	26
Cazenovia, NY	e K	26
Cebollita Peak, NM	j I	98
Cecil, GA	h C	40
Cecilia, KY	e K	68
Cedar, r., US	i D	54
Cedar, r., MI	f K	54
Cedar, r., NE	j I	82
Cedar, r., NY	d L	26
Cedar Bluff Reservoir, KS	m H	82
Cedar Bluffs, NE	j K	82
Cedarburg, WI	g H	54
Cedar City, MO	d D	68
Cedar City, UT	g C	98
Cedar Creek Reservoir, TX	g J	84
Cedaredge, CO	f I	98
Cedar Falls, IA	h C	54
Cedar Grove, WV	i E	26
Cedar Grove, WI	g H	54
Cedar Hill, TN	f J	68
Cedar Key, FL	j C	40
Cedar Lake, IN	a I	68
Cedar Mountain, CA	c E	128
Cedar Rapids, IA	i D	54
Cedar Rapids, NE	j I	82
Cedar Springs, MI	g J	54
Cedartown, GA	e A	40
Cedar Vale, KS	n K	82
Cedarville, CA	c E	128
Cedarville, MI	d K	54
Cedarville, NJ	h K	26
Celeste, TX	f J	84
Celina, OH	g B	26
Celina, TN	f K	68
Celina, TX	f J	84
Cement, OK	e H	84
Centennial Mountains, US	f N	112
Center, CO	g J	98
Center, MO	c E	68
Center, NE	j I	82
Center, ND	d F	82
Center, TX	k B	68
Centerburg, OH	g D	26
Center City, MN	e C	54
Center Hill, FL	k E	40
Center Hill Lake, TN	f K	68
Center Moriches, NY	g N	26
Center Mountain, ID	e J	112
Center Point, AL	i J	68
Center Point, IA	h D	54
Center Point, TX	j G	84
Centerville, IN	c L	68
Centerville, IA	j C	54
Centerville, MO	e F	68
Centerville, PA	g G	26
Centerville, SD	h K	82
Centerville, TN	g I	68
Centerville, TX	h K	84
Centerville, UT	d E	98
Central, AZ	I G	98
Central, NM	I H	98
Central, SC	e D	40
Central City, IL	d G	68
Central City, IA	h D	54
Central City, KY	e I	68
Central City, NE	j I	82
Central City, PA	g H	26
Central Heights, AZ	k F	98
Centralia, IL	d G	68
Centralia, KS	I K	82
Centralia, MO	c D	68
Centralia, WA	d C	112
Central Lake, MI	e J	54
Central Point, OR	h C	112
Central Square, NY	d J	26
Central Valley, CA	d C	128
Centre, AL	h K	68
Centreville, AL	j I	68
Centreville, MD	h J	26
Centreville, MI	i J	54
Centreville, MS	k E	68
Century, FL	I I	68
Century, WV	h F	26
Century Village, FL	m F	40
Ceresco, NE	j K	82
Cerrillos, NM	i J	98
Cerro Gordo, IL	c H	68
Ceylon, MN	h M	82
Chaco, r., NM	h H	98
Chacon, Cape, AK	c B	24
Chadbourn, NC	e H	40
Chadron, NE	i D	82
Chadwick, IL	h F	54
Chaffee, MO	e G	68
Chalkyitsik, AK	c W	142
Challis, ID	f K	112
Chalmette, LA	m G	68
Chama, NM	h J	98
Chama, Rio, r., US	h J	98
Chamberlain, SD	h H	82
Chambers, AZ	i G	98
Chambers, NE	i I	82
Chambersburg, PA	h I	26
Chamblee, GA	f B	40
Chamois, MO	d E	68
Champaign, IL	b H	68
Champion, MI	d H	54
Champion, OH	f F	26
Champlain, NY	c M	26
Champlain, Lake, NA	c M	26
Chandalar, r., AK	c U	142
Chandeleur Islands, LA	m H	68
Chandeleur Sound, LA	m G	68
Chandler, AZ	k E	98
Chandler, IN	d I	68
Chandler, OK	d J	84
Chandler, TX	g K	84
Chandler Lake, AK	b R	142
Chandlerville, IL	c F	68
Channel Islands, CA	k F	128
Channelview, TX	j K	84
Channing, MI	d G	54
Channing, TX	d D	84
Chanute, KS	n L	82
Chapel Hill, NC	d G	40
Chapel Hill, TN	g J	68
Chapin, IL	c F	68
Chaplin, r., KY	e K	68
Chapman, KS	m J	82
Chapman, NE	j I	82
Chapmanville, WV	j D	26
Chappell, NE	j E	82

Map
Name · Ref. · Page

Chappell Hill, TX i J 84
Chardon, OH f E 26
Chariton, IA i B 54
Chariton, r., US c D 82
Charles, Cape, VA b K 40
Charles City, IA g C 54
Charles City, VA b I 40
Charles Mound, IL h E 54
Charleston, AR g B 68
Charleston, IL c H 68
Charleston, MS h F 68
Charleston, MO f G 68
Charleston, SC g G 40
Charleston, WV i E 26
Charleston Peak, NV h J 128
Charlestown, IN d K 68
Charlestown, NH d N 26
Charlevoix, MI e J 54
Charlevoix, Lake, MI e J 54
Charlotte, MI h K 54
Charlotte, NC d F 40
Charlotte, TN f I 68
Charlotte, TX k H 84
Charlotte Court House, VA b H 40
Charlotte Harbor, FL m D 40
Charlottesville, VA a H 40
Charter Oak, IA i L 82
Chase, KS m I 82
Chase City, VA c H 40
Chaska, MN f B 54
Chatanika, r., AK d T 142
Chateaugay, NY c L 26
Chatfield, MN g C 54
Chatham, IL c G 68
Chatham, LA j D 68
Chatham, MA j D 26
Chatham, NY e M 26
Chatham, VA c G 40
Chatham Strait, AK h AA 142
Chatom, AL k H 68
Chatsworth, GA e B 40
Chatsworth, IL j G 54
Chattahoochee, FL i B 40
Chattahoochee, r., US h B 40
Chattanooga, TN g K 68
Chattaroy, WV b D 40
Chauncey, OH h D 26
Chautauqua Lake, NY e G 26
Chauvin, LA m F 68
Chazy, NY c M 26
Cheaha Mountain, AL i K 68
Cheat, r., US h G 26
Cheat, Shavers Fork, r., WV i G 26
Chebanse, IL i H 54
Cheboygan, MI e K 54
Checotah, OK d K 84
Cheektowaga, NY e H 26
Chefornak, AK f L 142
Chehalis, WA c E 112
Chehalis, r., WA d B 112
Chelan, WA c E 112
Chelan, Lake, WA c E 112
Chelsea, IA i C 54
Chelsea, MI h K 54
Chelsea, OK c K 84
Chelsea, VT d N 26
Chelyan, WV i E 26
Chemult, OR g D 112
Chenango, r., NY e K 26
Chenango Bridge, NY e K 26
Cheney, KS n J 82
Cheney, WA c H 112
Cheney Reservoir, KS n J 82
Cheneyville, LA k D 68
Chenoa, IL i H 54
Cheraw, SC e G 40
Cheriton, VA b K 40
Cherokee, AL h I 68
Cherokee, IA i L 82
Cherokee, KS n M 82
Cherokee, OK c H 84
Cherokee, TX i H 84
Cherokee Lake, TN c C 40
Cherokees, Lake O' The, OK c L 84
Cherokee Village, AR f E 68
Cherry Hill, NJ h K 26
Cherryvale, KS n L 82
Cherry Valley, AR g F 68
Cherryville, NC d F 40
Chesaning, MI g K 54
Chesapeake, VA c J 40
Chesapeake Bay, US c J 8
Chesapeake Beach, MD i J 26
Cheshire, MA e M 26
Chesnee, SC d E 40
Chester, CA d D 128
Chester, IL e G 68
Chester, MT b O 112
Chester, NE k J 82
Chester, OK c H 84
Chester, PA h K 26
Chester, SC e E 40
Chester, VT d N 26
Chester, WV b I 26
Chesterfield, SC e F 40
Chesterfield, VA b I 40
Chesterhill, OH h E 26
Chesterton, IN a I 68
Chestertown, MD h J 26
Chesuncook Lake, ME a D 26
Chetco, r., OR b A 128
Chetek, WI e D 54
Chetopa, KS n M 82
Chevak, AK f L 142
Cheviot, OH h G 26
Chewaucan, r., OR h E 112
Chewelah, WA b H 112
Cheyenne, OK d G 84
Cheyenne, WY c L 98
Cheyenne, r., US g F 82
Cheyenne Wells, CO m E 82
Chicago, IL i H 54
Chicago Heights, IL i H 54
Chichagof Island, AK h AA 142
Chickahominy, r., VA b I 40
Chickaloon, AK f T 142
Chickamauga, GA e A 40
Chickamauga Lake, TN d A 40
Chickasaw, AL i H 68
Chickasaw Bogue, r., AL j I 68
Chickasawhay, r., MS k H 68
Chickasha, OK d H 84
Chico, CA e D 128
Chico, TX i I 84
Chicopee, GA e C 40
Chicopee, MA e M 26
Chiefland, FL j D 40
Chignik, AK h O 142
Chignik Lake, AK h O 142
Chikaskia, r., US b I 84
Childersburg, AL i J 68

Childress, TX e F 84
Chilhowie, VA c E 40
Chillicothe, IL j F 54
Chillicothe, MO c C 68
Chillicothe, OH h D 26
Chillicothe, TX e G 84
Chiloquin, OR h D 112
Chilton, WI f G 54
Chimayo, NM h K 98
China Grove, NC d F 40
Chinati Peak, TX j B 84
Chincoteague, VA b K 40
Chinle, AZ h G 98
Chino, CA j H 128
Chinook, MT b P 112
Chino Valley, AZ e I 98
Chinquapin, NC e I 40
Chipley, FL i K 68
Chippewa, r., MI g K 54
Chippewa, r., MN f L 82
Chippewa, r., WI f D 54
Chippewa, Lake, WI e C 54
Chippewa Falls, WI f D 54
Chireno, TX k B 68
Chiricahua Mountains, AZ m G 98
Chiricahua Peak, AZ m G 98
Chirikof Island, AK i Q 142
Chisago City, MN e C 54
Chisholm, AL j J 68
Chisholm, ME c P 26
Chisholm, MN d C 54
Chisos Mountains, TX j C 84
Chistochina, AK e V 142
Chitina, AK f W 142
Chitina, r., AK f W 142
Chloride, AZ i B 98
Chocolate Mountains, US k J 128
Choctawhatchee Bay, FL i J 68
Chokio, MN f K 82
Chosen, FL m F 40
Choteau, MT c M 112
Chouteau, OK c K 84
Chowchilla, CA g E 128
Chowan, r., NC c J 40
Chrisman, IL c I 68
Christiansburg, VA b F 40
Christopher, IL e G 68
Christoval, TX h F 84
Chubbuck, ID h M 112
Chugach Islands, AK g S 142
Chugach Mountains, AK f U 142
Chugwater, WY c L 98
Chugwater Creek, r., WY c K 98
Chula Vista, CA l H 128
Chunchula, AL l H 68
Church Hill, TN c D 40
Church Point, LA l D 68
Church Rock, NM i H 98
Churdan, IA i M 82
Churubusco, IN a K 68
Chuska Mountains, NM i H 98
Cibecue, AZ j F 98
Cicero, IL a I 68
Cicero, IN b J 68
Cimarron, KS n G 82
Cimarron, NM h L 98
Cimarron, r., US d I 84
Cimarron, r., NM h K 98
Cincinnati, IA j C 54
Cincinnati, OH h B 26
Circle, AK d V 142
Circle, MT c T 112
Circleville, OH h D 26
Circleville Mountain, UT f D 98
Cisco, TX g H 84
Cisne, IL d H 68
Cissna Park, IL j H 54
Citra, FL j D 40
Citronelle, AL k H 68
Citrus Heights, CA f D 128
City of Refuge, see Pu'uhonua o Honaunau National Historic Site, HI j P 144d
City Point, FL k F 40
Clackamas, r., OR e C 112
Claflin, KS m I 82
Claiborne, AL k I 68
Clair Engle Lake, CA b C 128
Clairton, PA g G 26
Clam, r., MI f J 54
Clam, r., WI e C 54
Clanton, AL j J 68
Clara, MS k H 68
Clara City, MN g L 82
Clare, MI g K 54
Claremont, CA j H 128
Claremont, NH d N 26
Claremont, SD f I 82
Claremont, CA e E 128
Claremore, OK c K 84
Clarence, IA i D 54
Clarence, MO c D 68
Clarendon, AR h E 68
Clarendon, PA f G 26
Clarendon, TX e F 84
Clarinda, IA k L 82
Clarion, IA h B 54
Clarion, PA f G 26
Clarion, r., PA f G 26
Clarissa, MN e M 82
Clark, SD g J 82
Clark, Lake, AK f Q 142
Clark Fork, ID b I 112
Clark Fork, r., US c J 112
Clarkdale, AZ j D 98
Clarkesville, GA e C 40
Clarkfield, MN g L 82
Clarks, LA j D 68
Clarks, NE j J 82
Clarks, r., KY f H 68
Clarksburg, WV h F 26
Clarksdale, MS h F 68
Clarks Hill, IN b I 68
Clarks Hill Lake, US f D 40
Clarkson, KY c B 40
Clarkson, NE k I 82
Clarks Point, AK g O 142
Clarks Summit, PA f K 26
Clarkston, WA d H 112
Clarksville, AR g B 68
Clarksville, IN d K 68
Clarksville, IA h C 54
Clarksville, TN f I 68
Clarksville, TX f K 84
Clarkton, MO f G 68
Clarkton, NC e H 40
Clatskanie, OR d B 112
Claude, TX d E 84

Claxton, GA g E 40
Clay, KY e I 68
Clay, TX i J 84
Clay, WV i E 26
Clay Center, KS i J 82
Clay Center, NE k I 82
Clay City, IL d H 68
Clay City, IN c I 68
Clay City, KY b C 40
Claymont, DE h K 26
Claypool, AZ k F 98
Claysburg, PA g H 26
Clay Springs, AZ j F 98
Clayton, AL k K 68
Clayton, DE h K 26
Clayton, GA e C 40
Clayton, IL b F 68
Clayton, LA k E 68
Clayton, MO d F 68
Clayton, NM c C 84
Clayton, NY c J 26
Clayton, NC d H 40
Clayton, OK e K 84
Clearbrook, MN d L 82
Clearfield, IA k M 82
Clearfield, PA f H 26
Clearfield, UT c D 98
Clearlake, CA f C 128
Clear Lake, IA g B 54
Clear Lake, SD g K 82
Clear Lake, WI e C 54
Clear Lake, CA e C 128
Clear Lake Reservoir, CA c D 128
Clermont, WY f S 112
Clearwater, FL l D 40
Clearwater, KS n J 82
Clearwater, NE i l 82
Clearwater, SC f E 40
Clearwater, r., ID d l 112
Clearwater, r., MN d L 82
Clearwater, r., MT c L 112
Clearwater Mountains, ID d J 112
Clebit, OK e L 84
Cleburne, TX g l 84
Cle Elum, WA c E 112
Cle Elum, r., WA c D 112
Clemson, SC e D 40
Clendenin, WV i E 26
Clermont, FL k E 40
Cleveland, AL i J 68
Cleveland, GA e C 40
Cleveland, MS i F 68
Cleveland, NC d F 40
Cleveland, OH f E 26
Cleveland, OK c J 84
Cleveland, TN g L 68
Cleveland, TX i K 84
Cleveland, Mount, MT b L 112
Clewiston, FL m F 40
Clifton, AZ k G 98
Clifton, IL j H 54
Clifton, KS i J 82
Clifton, TN g l 68
Clifton, TX h l 84
Clifton Forge, VA b G 40
Climax, CO e J 98
Climax, GA i B 40
Climax, MI h J 54
Clinch, r., US c C 40
Clinchco, VA b D 40
Clingmans Dome, US d C 40
Clinton, AL j H 68
Clinton, AR g B 68
Clinton, CT f N 26
Clinton, IL b H 68
Clinton, IA i E 54
Clinton, KY f H 68
Clinton, LA l E 68
Clinton, ME c O 26
Clinton, MA e O 26
Clinton, MI h L 54
Clinton, MN f K 82
Clinton, MS j F 68
Clinton, MO d C 68
Clinton, NC e H 40
Clinton, OK d H 84
Clinton, SC e E 40
Clinton, TN c B 40
Clinton, WI h G 54
Clinton Lake, KS m L 82
Clintonville, WI f G 54
Clintwood, VA b D 40
Clio, AL k K 68
Clio, MI g L 54
Clio, SC e G 40
Cloquet, MN c C 54
Cloquet, r., MN c C 54
Cloudcroft, NM l K 98
Cloud Peak, WY f R 112
Clover, SC d E 40
Cloverdale, AL h l 68
Cloverdale, CA f B 128
Cloverdale, IN c J 68
Clover Pass, AK i CC 142
Cloverport, KY e J 68
Clovis, CA g F 128
Clovis, NM e C 84
Clute, TX j K 84
Clyde, KS i J 82
Clyde, NY d J 26
Clyde, NC d D 40
Clyde, OH f D 26
Clyde, TX g G 84
Clyde, r., VT c N 26
Clyde Park, MT e O 112
Clymer, PA g H 26
Coachella, CA k l 128
Coahoma, TX g E 84
Coal City, IL i G 54
Coal Fork, WV i E 26
Coalgate, OK e J 84
Coal Grove, OH i D 26
Coal Hill, AR g B 68
Coalinga, CA h E 128
Coalport, PA g H 26
Coalville, UT d E 98
Coast Ranges, US c B 8
Coatesville, PA h K 26
Cobden, IL e G 68
Cobleskill, NY e L 26
Cochise Head, AZ l G 98
Cochran, GA g C 40
Cochrane, WI f D 54
Cochranton, PA f F 26
Cocoa, FL k F 40
Cocoa Beach, FL k F 40
Coconino Plateau, AZ i D 98
Cod, Cape, MA f P 26
Cody, NE i F 82
Cody, WY f P 112
Coeburn, VA c D 40
Coeur d'Alene, ID c l 112
Coeur d'Alene, r., ID c l 112

Coeur d'Alene Lake, ID c l 112
Coffeen, IL c G 68
Coffeeville, MS i G 68
Coffeyville, KS n L 82
Coggon, IA h D 54
Cogswell, ND e J 82
Cohocton, r., NY e l 26
Cohoe, AK f S 142
Cohoes, NY e M 26
Coin, IA k L 82
Cokato, MN e A 54
Cokeville, WY h O 112
Colbert, OK f J 84
Colby, KS l F 82
Colby, WI f E 54
Colchester, CT f N 26
Colchester, IL j E 54
Cold Bay, AK i M 142
Cold Spring, MN e A 54
Coldspring, TX i K 84
Coldwater, KS n H 82
Coldwater, MI i J 54
Coldwater, MS h G 68
Coldwater, OH g B 26
Coldwater, r., MS h F 68
Colebrook, NH c O 26
Cole Camp, MO d C 68
Coleman, FL k D 40
Coleman, MI g K 54
Coleman, TX h G 84
Coleman, WI e G 54
Coleman, Lake, TX g G 84
Coleraine, MN c B 54
Coleridge, NE i l 82
Coles, MS k E 68
Colfax, CA f E 128
Colfax, IL j G 54
Colfax, IN b J 68
Colfax, IA i B 54
Colfax, LA k D 68
Colfax, WA d H 112
Colfax, WI f D 54
Collbran, CO e l 98
College, AK d U 142
Collegedale, TN g K 68
College Park, GA g B 40
College Place, WA d G 112
College Station, AR h D 68
College Station, TX i l 84
Collegeville, IN b l 68
Colleyville, TX g l 84
Collierville, TN g G 68
Collins, GA g D 40
Collins, IA i B 54
Collins, MS k G 68
Collins, r., TN g K 68
Collinston, LA j E 68
Collinsville, AL h K 68
Collinsville, MS j H 68
Collinsville, OK c K 84
Collinsville, TX f J 84
Collinwood, TN g l 68
Collister, ID g l 112
Colman, SD h K 82
Colmesneil, TX l B 68
Colo, IA h B 54
Cologne, MN f B 54
Coloma, MI h l 54
Coloma, WI f F 54
Colome, SD h H 82
Colon, MI i J 54
Colonial Heights, VA b l 40
Colony, KS m l 82
Colorado, state, US d E 8
Colorado, r., NA m A 98
Colorado, r., TX j J 84
Colorado City, AZ h D 98
Colorado City, CO g L 98
Colorado City, TX g F 84
Colorado River Aqueduct, CA k J 128
Colorado Springs, CO f L 98
Colquitt, GA i B 40
Colstrip, MT e S 112
Colt, AR g F 68
Colton, CA j H 128
Colton, SD h K 82
Columbia, AL j J 68
Columbia, CA f E 128
Columbia, IL d F 68
Columbia, KY e K 68
Columbia, LA j D 68
Columbia, MD h J 26
Columbia, MS k G 68
Columbia, MO d D 68
Columbia, NC d J 40
Columbia, PA g J 26
Columbia, SC e E 40
Columbia, TN g J 68
Columbia, r., NA b B 8
Columbia City, IN a K 68
Columbia Falls, ME c S 26
Columbia Falls, MT b K 112
Columbia Mountains, NA d N 24
Columbiana, AL i J 68
Columbiana, OH g F 26
Columbiaville, MI g L 54
Columbus, GA h A 40
Columbus, IN c K 68
Columbus, KS n M 82
Columbus, MS i H 68
Columbus, MT e P 112
Columbus, NE j l 82
Columbus, NM m l 98
Columbus, ND c E 82
Columbus, OH h C 26
Columbus, TX j J 84
Columbus, WI g F 54
Columbus Grove, OH g B 26
Columbus Junction, IA j D 54
Colusa, CA e C 128
Colville, WA b H 112
Colville, r., AK b S 142
Colville, r., WA b H 112
Comanche, OK e l 84
Comanche, TX h H 84
Combahee, r., SC g F 40
Comer, GA e C 40
Comfort, NC e l 40
Comfort, TX i H 84
Comfrey, MN g M 82
Commerce, GA e C 40
Commerce, OK c L 84
Commerce, TX f K 84
Commerce City, CO f L 98
Como, MS h G 68
Como, TX f K 84
Compton, CA k G 128
Comstock, MI h J 54
Comstock, TX i E 84
Comstock Park, MI g J 54
Conasauga, r., US e B 40
Concho, AZ j G 98

Concho, r., TX h G 84
Concord, CA g C 128
Concord, IL c G 68
Concord, MI h K 54
Concord, NH d O 26
Concord, NC d F 40
Concordia, KS i J 82
Concordia, MO d C 68
Concrete, WA b D 112
Conde, SD f l 82
Condon, OR e F 112
Conecuh, r., US k J 68
Conejos, CO g J 98
Conejos, r., CO g J 98
Confluence, PA h G 26
Congaree, r., SC f F 40
Conneaut, OH f F 26
Conneautville, PA f F 26
Connell, WA d G 112
Connellsville, PA g G 26
Connersville, IN c K 68
Conover, NC d E 40
Conrad, IA h C 54
Conrad, MT b N 112
Conroe, TX i K 84
Conroe, Lake, TX i K 84
Constantine, MI i J 54
Continental, OH f B 26
Convent, LA l F 68
Converse, IN b K 68
Convoy, OH g B 26
Conway, AR g D 68
Conway, NH c O 26
Conway, NC c l 40
Conway, SC f G 40
Conway Springs, KS n J 82
Conyers, GA g B 40
Cook, MN c C 54
Cook, NE k K 82
Cookes Peak, NM l l 98
Cookeville, TN f K 68
Cook Inlet, AK f R 142
Cooleemee, NC d F 40
Coolidge, AZ l E 98
Coolidge, GA h C 40
Coolidge, TX h J 84
Coolin, ID b l 112
Coon Rapids, IA j M 82
Coon Rapids, MN e B 54
Coon Valley, WI g D 54
Cooper, TX f K 84
Cooper Landing, AK f T 142
Cooper Mountain, AK f T 142
Cooper Road, LA j C 68
Coopers, AL j J 68
Cooperstown, NY e L 26
Cooperstown, ND d l 82
Coopersville, MI g J 54
Coosa, r., US h K 68
Coosawhatchie, r., SC g E 40
Coos Bay, OR g A 112
Coos Bay, OR g A 112
Copan, OK c K 84
Cope, CO l E 82
Copeland, FL n E 40
Copenhagen, NY d l 26
Copper, r., AK f V 142
Copperas Cove, TX h l 84
Copper Butte, WA b G 112
Copper Harbor, MI c H 54
Coquille, OR g A 112
Coquille, r., OR g A 112
Coral Gables, FL n F 40
Coral City, CO g L 98
Coralville, IA i D 54
Coralville Lake, IA i D 54
Coram, MT b K 112
Corbin, KY c B 40
Corcoran, CA h F 128
Cordele, GA h C 40
Cordell, OK d H 84
Cordell Hull Reservoir, TN f K 68
Corder, MO c C 68
Cordova, AL i l 68
Cordova, AK f V 142
Corinne, UT c D 98
Corinne, WV b E 40
Corinth, MS h H 68
Corinth, NY d M 26
Cornelia, GA e C 40
Cornelius, NC d F 40
Cornell, WI e D 54
Cornersville, TN g J 68
Corning, AR f F 68
Corning, CA e C 128
Corning, IA k M 82
Corning, KS l K 82
Corning, NY e l 26
Corning, OH h D 26
Cornish, ME d P 26
Corona, CA j H 128
Corona, NM j K 98
Coronado, CA l H 128
Corpus Christi, TX l l 84
Corpus Christi, Lake, TX k l 84
Corpus Christi Bay, TX l l 84
Correctionville, IA i L 82
Corrigan, TX i B 68
Corry, PA f G 26
Corsica, SD h l 82
Corsicana, TX g J 84
Cortez, CO g H 98
Cortland, NE k K 82
Cortland, NY e J 26
Cortland, OH f F 26
Corunna, MI h K 54
Corvallis, MT d K 112
Corvallis, OR f B 112
Corwith, IA h B 54
Corydon, IA j B 54
Corydon, IN d K 68
Corydon, KY e l 68
Coshocton, OH g E 26
Cosmos, MN f M 82
Cossatot, r., AR h B 68
Costa Mesa, CA k H 128
Costilla, NM h K 98
Cosumnes, r., CA f D 128
Cotati, CA g B 128
Cottage Grove, OR g B 112
Cottageville, SC f F 40
Cotter, AR f D 68
Cotton Plant, AR g E 68
Cottonport, LA l D 68
Cotton Valley, LA j C 68
Cottonwood, AZ j D 98
Cottonwood, CA d C 128
Cottonwood, ID d l 112

Cottonwood, MN g L 82
Cottonwood, r., KS m K 82
Cottonwood, r., MN g M 82
Cottonwood Falls, KS m K 82
Cotulla, TX k G 84
Coudersport, PA f H 26
Coulee City, WA c F 112
Coulee Dam, WA c G 112
Coulterville, CA f E 128
Coulterville, IL d G 68
Council, ID f l 112
Council Bluffs, IA j L 82
Council Grove, KS m K 82
Country Homes, WA c H 112
Coupeville, WA b C 112
Courtland, AL h l 68
Courtland, CA c l 68
Coushatta, LA j C 68
Cove, OR e H 112
Covelo, CA e B 128
Covert, MI h l 54
Covington, GA f C 40
Covington, IN b l 68
Covington, KY h B 26
Covington, LA l F 68
Covington, OH g B 26
Covington, TN g G 68
Covington, VA b G 40
Cowan, TN g J 68
Coward, SC f G 40
Cowden, IL c H 68
Cowen, WV i F 26
Cowen, Mount, MT e O 112
Coweta, OK d K 84
Cowley, WY f Q 112
Cowlitz, r., WA c C 112
Cowpasture, r., VA i G 26
Cowpens, SC d E 40
Coxsackie, NY e M 26
Cozad, NE k H 82
Crab Orchard, KY b B 40
Crab Orchard, TN d B 40
Craig, AK b A 24
Craig, CO d l 98
Craig, MO b A 68
Craig, MT d M 112
Craigmont, ID d l 112
Craigsville, VA a G 40
Craigsville, WV i F 26
Crandon, WI d E 54
Crane, AZ l B 98
Crane, IN d J 68
Crane, MO e B 68
Crane, TX h D 84
Crane Mountain, OR h E 112
Cranston, RI f O 26
Crater Lake, OR h C 112
Crater Lake National Park, OR h C 112
Crawford, CO f l 98
Crawford, MS i H 68
Crawford, NE i D 82
Crawford, TX h l 84
Crawfordsville, AR g F 68
Crawfordsville, IN b J 68
Crawfordville, FL i B 40
Crawfordville, GA f D 40
Crazy Woman Creek, r., WY f S 112
Creal Springs, IL e H 68
Creede, CO g J 98
Creedmoor, NC c H 40
Creighton, NE i J 82
Crenshaw, MS h F 68
Cresapton, MD h H 26
Cresco, IA g C 54
Cresson, PA g H 26
Cresson, TX g l 84
Crested Butte, CO f J 98
Crestline, CA j H 128
Crestline, OH f D 26
Creston, IA j M 82
Crestview, FL i l 68
Crestwood Hills, TN d B 40
Creswell, OR g B 112
Crete, IL i H 54
Crete, NE k K 82
Creve Coeur, IL j F 54
Crewe, VA b H 40
Cricket, NC c E 40
Cridersville, OH g B 26
Cripple Creek, CO f K 98
Crisfield, MD i K 26
Crivitz, WI e G 54
Crocker, MO e D 68
Crockett, TX h K 84
Crofton, KY e l 68
Crofton, NE i J 82
Croghan, NY d l 26
Croix, Lac la, NA b C 54
Cromwell, IN a J 68
Crook, CO k E 82
Crooked, r., OR e C 112
Crooked Creek, AK f O 142
Crookston, MN d K 82
Crooksville, OH h D 26
Crosby, MN d B 54
Crosby, MS k E 68
Crosby, ND c D 82
Crosby, Mount, WY g P 112
Crosbyton, TX f E 84
Cross City, FL j C 40
Crossett, AR i E 68
Cross Plains, TX g G 84
Cross Plains, WI g E 54
Cross Sound, AK g Z 142
Crossville, IL d H 68
Crossville, TN d A 40
Croswell, MI g M 54
Crothersville, IN c K 68
Crow, r., MN e M 82
Crow Agency, MT e R 112
Crowder, OK d K 84
Crowder, MS h F 68
Crowell, TX f G 84
Crowley, LA l D 68
Crowleys Ridge, US g F 68
Crown Point, IN a l 68
Crown Point, NM i H 98
Crown Point, NY d M 26
Crow Wing, r., MN d M 82
Crozet, VA a H 40
Cruger, MS i F 68
Crystal, ND c J 82
Crystal, r., CO e J 98
Crystal Beach, FL l D 40
Crystal City, MO d F 68
Crystal City, TX k G 84
Crystal Falls, MI d G 54

Crystal Lake, IL h G 54
Crystal River, FL k D 40
Crystal Springs, MS k F 68
Cuba, AL j H 68
Cuba, IL j E 54
Cuba, KS i J 82
Cuba, MO d E 68
Cuba, NM h J 98
Cuba, NY e l 26
Cudahy, WI h H 54
Cuero, TX j l 84
Cuesta Pass, CA i E 128
Culbertson, MT c C 82
Culbertson, NE k G 82
Culebra Peak, CO g K 98
Cullen, LA j C 68
Culleoka, TN g J 68
Cullman, AL h J 68
Cullom, IL j G 54
Cullowhee, NC d C 40
Culpeper, VA i l 26
Culver, IN a J 68
Culver, OR f D 112
Cumberland, IA j M 82
Cumberland, KY c D 40
Cumberland, MD h H 26
Cumberland, WI d D 54
Cumberland, r., US d l 8
Cumberland, Lake, KY f L 68
Cumberland City, TN f l 68
Cumberland Gap, US c C 40
Cumby, TX f K 84
Cumming, GA e B 40
Cunningham, KS n I 82
Currant Mountain, NV f J 128
Current, r., US f F 68
Currie, MN g L 82
Currituck, NC c K 40
Currituck Sound, NC c K 40
Curtis, AR i C 68
Curtis, NE k G 82
Curwensville, PA f H 26
Cushing, OK d J 84
Cushing, TX k B 68
Cushman, AR g E 68
Cusseta, GA h B 40
Custer, MI g l 54
Custer, MT e R 112
Custer, OK d H 84
Custer, SD h D 82
Cut Bank, MT b M 112
Cuthbert, GA h B 40
Cutler, CA h F 128
Cutler, ME c S 26
Cutlerville, MI g J 54
Cuyahoga Falls, OH f E 26
Cynthiana, KY i B 26
Cypress, LA k C 68
Cyril, OK e H 84

D

Dacoma, OK c H 84
Dade City, FL k D 40
Dadeville, AL j K 68
Dahlgren, IL d H 68
Dahlonega, GA e B 40
Daingerfield, TX f B 84
Daisetta, TX i L 84
Dakota City, IA i M 82
Dakota City, NE i K 82
Dale, IN d J 68
Dale Hollow Lake, US c A 40
Daleville, AL k K 68
Daleville, IN b K 68
Dalhart, TX c D 84
Dallas, AL i l 68
Dallas, GA f A 40
Dallas, NC d E 40
Dallas, OR f B 112
Dallas, PA f K 26
Dallas, TX g J 84
Dallas, WI e D 54
Dallas Center, IA i M 82
Dallas City, IL j D 54
Dall Island, AK c B 24
Dalton, GA e A 40
Dalton, MA e M 26
Dalton, NE j E 82
Dalton, PA f K 26
Dalton Gardens, ID c I 112
Daly City, CA g C 128
Damascus, AR g D 68
Damascus, GA h B 40
Damascus, MD h I 26
Damascus, VA c E 40
Dan, r., US c G 40
Dana, IN c I 68
Danbury, CT f M 26
Danbury, IA i L 82
Danbury, NE k G 82
Danbury, NC c F 40
Danbury, TX j K 84
Danby Lake, CA j I 128
Dandridge, TN c C 40
Danforth, ME b S 26
Danforth Hills, CO d H 98
Daniel, WY g P 112
Danielson, CT f O 26
Daniels Pass, UT d E 98
Danielsville, GA e C 40
Dannebrog, NE j I 82
Dannemora, NY c M 26
Dansville, NY e I 26
Dante, VA c D 40
Danvers, IL j F 54
Danville, AR g C 68
Danville, GA g C 40
Danville, IL b I 68
Danville, IN c J 68
Danville, KY e L 68
Danville, OH g D 26
Danville, PA g J 26
Danville, VA c G 40
Danville, VT c N 26
Daphne, AL l I 68
Darby, MT d K 112
Dardanelle, AR g C 68
Dardanelle, CA f E 128
Dardanelle Lake, AR g C 68
Darien, GA h E 40
Darling, MS h F 68
Darlington, SC e F 40
Darlington, WI h E 54
Darrington, WA b D 112
Darrouzett, TX c F 84
Dassel, MN e A 54
Dauphin Island, AL l H 68
Dauphin Island, AL l H 68
Davant, LA m G 68
Davenport, FL k E 40
Davenport, IA i E 54
Davenport, NE k J 82
Davenport, WA c G 112

Name Map Ref. Page

David City, NE j J 82
Davidson, NC d F 40
Davidson, OK e G 84
Davie, FL m F 40
Davis, CA f D 128
Davis, NC e J 40
Davis, OK e I 84
Davis, WV h G 26
Davis, Mount, PA h G 26
Davisboro, GA g D 40
Davis City, IA j B 54
Davis Dam, AZ i B 98
Davy, WV b E 40
Dawson, GA h B 40
Dawson, MN g K 82
Dawson, NE k L 82
Dawson, TX h J 84
Dawson Springs, KY e I 68
Dawsonville, GA e B 40
Dayton, IA h A 54
Dayton, OH h B 26
Dayton, OR e B 112
Dayton, PA g G 26
Dayton, TN g K 68
Dayton, TX i L 84
Dayton, VA i H 26
Dayton, WA d H 112
Dayton, WY f R 112
Daytona Beach, FL j E 40
Dayville, OR f F 112
Dead, r., MI d H 54
Deadwood, SD g D 82
Deadwood, r., ID f J 112
Deale, MD i J 26
Deal Island, MD i K 26
Dearborn, MI h L 54
Dearborn, r., MT c M 112
Death Valley, CA h I 128
Death Valley, CA h I 128
Deatsville, AL j J 68
De Bary, FL k E 40
De Beque, CO e H 98
De Berry, TX j B 68
Decatur, AL h J 68
Decatur, GA f B 40
Decatur, IL c H 68
Decatur, IN b L 68
Decatur, MI h J 54
Decatur, MS j G 68
Decatur, NE i K 82
Decatur, TN d B 40
Decatur, TX f I 84
Decaturville, TN g H 68
Decherd, TN g J 68
Deckerville, MI g M 54
Decorah, IA g D 54
Deenwood, GA h D 40
Deep River, CT f N 26
Deep River, IA i C 54
Deepwater, MO d C 68
Deer Creek, MN e L 82
Deerfield, IL h H 54
Deerfield, KS n F 82
Deerfield Beach, FL m F 40
Deer Isle, ME c R 26
Deer Lodge, MT d M 112
Deer Park, AL k H 68
Deer Park, WA c H 112
Deer River, MN c B 54
Deer Trail, CO l C 82
Deerwood, MN d B 54
Defiance, IA j L 82
Defiance, OH f B 26
De Forest, WI g F 54
De Funiak Springs, FL l J 68
De Graff, OH g C 26
De Gray Lake, AR h C 68
De Kalb, IL i G 54
De Kalb, MS j H 68
De Kalb, TX i B 68
De Land, FL j E 40
Delano, CA i F 128
Delano, MN e B 54
Delano Peak, UT f D 98
Delavan, IL b G 68
Delaware, OH g C 26
Delaware, OK c K 84
Delaware, state, US d K 8
Delaware, r., US f L 26
Delaware, r., KS l L 82
Delaware Bay, US h K 26
Delaware City, DE h K 26
Delcambre, LA m E 68
Del City, OK d I 84
De Leon, TX g H 84
De Leon Springs, FL j E 40
Delhi, IA h D 54
Delhi, LA j E 68
Delhi, NY e L 26
Delight, AR h C 68
Dell City, TX m K 98
Dell Rapids, SD h K 82
Del Mar, CA l H 128
Delmar, DE i K 26
Delmar, IA h E 54
Delmar, MD i K 26
Del Mar Hills, TX l G 84
Delmarva Peninsula, US i K 26
Delmont, SD h I 82
Del Norte, CO g J 98
Delphi, IN j I 54
Delphos, KS l J 82
Delphos, OH g B 26
Delray Beach, FL m F 40
Del Rio, TX j F 84
Delta, CO f H 98
Delta, MO e G 68
Delta, OH f B 26
Delta, UT e D 98
Delta City, MS i F 68
Delta Junction, AK d V 142
Del Valle, TX i I 84
Demarcation Point, AK b X 142
Deming, NM l I 98
Demopolis, AL j I 68
Demorest, GA e C 40
Demotte, IN a I 68
Denali National Park, AK e T 142
Denali National Park, AK e S 142
Denham Springs, LA l F 68
Denison, IA i L 82
Denison, TX f J 84
Denmark, SC f E 40
Denmark, WI f H 54
Dennison, OH g E 26
Dennis Port, MA f P 26
Denton, MD i K 26
Denton, MT c P 112
Denton, NC d F 40
Denton, TX f I 84
Denver, CO e L 98
Denver, IA h C 54
Denver, PA g J 26
Denver City, TX g D 84
De Pere, WI f G 54
Depew, NY e H 26
Depew, OK d J 84
Depoe Bay, OR f A 112
Deport, TX f K 84
Deposit, NY e K 26
Depue, IL i F 54
De Queen, AR h B 68
De Quincy, LA l C 68
Derby, KS n J 82
Derby, ME b R 26
Derby, NY e H 26
Derby Line, VT b N 26
De Ridder, LA l C 68
Dermott, AR i E 68
Dernieres, Isles, LA m F 68
Derry, NH e O 26
Des Allemands, LA m F 68
Des Arc, AR h E 68
Descanso, CA l I 128
Deschutes, r., OR e E 112
Deschutes, r., WA d C 112
Deseret Peak, UT d D 98
Desert Hot Springs, CA k I 128
Desert Peak, UT c C 98
Desha, AR g E 68
Deshler, NE k J 82
Deshler, OH f C 26
Desloge, MO e F 68
De Smet, SD g J 82
Des Moines, IA i B 54
Des Moines, NM c C 84
Des Moines, r., US j C 54
De Soto, IL e G 68
De Soto, MO d F 68
Des Plaines, IL h H 54
Destin, FL l J 68
Detour, Point, MI e I 54
De Tour Village, MI d L 54
Detroit, MI h L 54
Detroit, OR f C 112
Detroit, TX i A 68
Detroit Beach, MI i L 54
Detroit Lakes, MN e L 82
De Valls Bluff, AR h E 68
De View, Bayou, r., AR g E 68
Devils, r., TX j E 84
Devils Lake, ND c I 82
Devils Lake, ND c H 82
Devils Tower, WY g C 82
Devine, TX j H 84
Dewar, OK d K 84
Dewey, OK c K 84
Deweyville, TX l C 68
De Witt, AR h E 68
De Witt, IA i E 54
De Witt, MI h K 54
De Witt, NE k K 82
De Witt, NY d J 26
Dexter, ME b Q 26
Dexter, MI e C 26
Dexter, MO f G 68
Dexter, NM f B 84
Dexter, NY c J 26
D'Hanis, TX j G 84
Diablo Range, CA g D 128
Diagonal, IA k M 82
Diamond, MO e B 68
Diamond Head, HI f J 144c
Diamond Peak, ID f L 112
Diamond Peak, OR g C 112
Diamondville, WY c F 98
Diaz, AR g E 68
D'Iberville, MS l H 68
Diboll, TX k B 68
Dickens, TX f F 84
Dickinson, ND e E 82
Dickinson, TX j K 84
Dickson, OK e J 84
Dickson, TN f I 68
Dierks, AR h B 68
Dietrich, ID h K 112
Dighton, KS m G 82
Dike, IA h C 54
Dill City, OK d G 84
Diller, NE k K 82
Dilley, TX k G 84
Dillingham, AK g O 142
Dillon, CO e J 98
Dillon, MT e M 112
Dillon, SC e G 40
Dillon Lake, OH g D 26
Dillon Mountain, NM k H 98
Dillwyn, VA b H 40
Dilworth, MN e K 82
Dime Box, TX i J 84
Dimmitt, TX e D 84
Dinosaur, CO d G 98
Dinuba, CA h F 128
Dinwiddie, VA b I 40
Diomede, AK d J 142
Dirty Devil, r., UT f F 98
Disappointment, Cape, WA d A 112
Dishman, WA c H 112
Dismal, r., NE j G 82
Disney, OK c K 84
District of Columbia, district, US i I 26
Divernon, IL c G 68
Dix, NE j D 82
Dix, r., KY b B 40
Dixfield, ME c P 26
Dixie Valley, NV d G 128
Dixon, CA f D 128
Dixon, IL i F 54
Dixon, KY e I 68
Dixon, MO e D 68
Dixon, NM h K 98
Dixon Entrance, NA c B 24
Dixons Mills, AL j I 68
Dobson, NC c F 40
Dock Junction, GA h E 40
Doddridge, AR i C 68
Doddsville, MS i F 68
Dodge, NE j K 82
Dodge Center, MN f C 54
Dodge City, KS n G 82
Dodgeville, WI i F 54
Dodson, LA j D 68
Dodson, MT b Q 112
Dodson, TX e F 84
Doerun, GA h C 40
Doland, SD g I 82
Dolgeville, NY d L 26
Dolores, CO g H 98
Dolores, r., US f H 98
Dona Ana, NM l J 98
Donaldson, AR h D 68
Donaldsonville, LA l F 68
Donalsonville, GA h B 40
Doneraile, SC e G 40
Donie, TX h J 84
Doniphan, MO f F 68
Doniphan, NE k I 82
Donna, TX m H 84
Donnelly, ID f I 112
Donner, LA m F 68
Donner Pass, CA e E 128
Donner und Blitzen, r., OR g G 112
Donora, PA g G 26
Doon, IA h K 82
Door Peninsula, WI f H 54
Dora, AL i I 68
Doraville, GA f B 40
Dorcheat, Bayou, r., US i C 68
Dorchester, NE k J 82
Dorchester, WI e E 54
Dorena, OR g C 112
Dorrance, KS m I 82
Dorris, CA c D 128
Dorton, KY b D 40
Dos Palos, CA h E 128
Dothan, AL k K 68
Double Springs, AL h I 68
Doubletop Peak, WY g O 112
Douglas, AK g AA 142
Douglas, AZ m G 98
Douglas, GA h D 40
Douglas, ND d F 82
Douglas, WY d K 98
Douglas, Cape, AK g R 142
Douglas, Mount, AK g R 142
Douglas Lake, TN c C 40
Douglass, KS n J 82
Douglasville, GA f B 40
Dove Creek, CO g H 98
Dover, AR g C 68
Dover, DE h K 26
Dover, ID b I 112
Dover, NH d P 26
Dover, NJ g L 26
Dover, NC d I 40
Dover, OH g E 26
Dover, OK d I 84
Dover, TN f I 68
Dover-Foxcroft, ME b Q 26
Dowagiac, MI i I 54
Dowagiac, r., MI h I 54
Dow City, IA j L 82
Downey, ID h M 112
Downieville, CA e E 128
Downing, MO b D 68
Downingtown, PA g K 26
Downs, KS l I 82
Downs Mountain, WY e P 112
Downsville, NY e L 26
Dows, IA h B 54
Doyle, CA d E 128
Doylestown, OH g E 26
Doylestown, PA g K 26
Doyline, LA j C 68
Dozier, AL k J 68
Dracut, MA e O 26
Dragoon, AZ l F 98
Drain, OR g B 112
Drake, ND d G 82
Drake Peak, OR h E 112
Drakesboro, KY e I 68
Drakes Branch, VA c H 40
Draper, NC c G 40
Draper, UT d E 98
Drayton, ND c J 82
Drayton, SC e E 40
Dresden, OH g D 26
Dresden, TN f H 68
Drew, MS i F 68
Driftwood, r., IN c J 68
Driggs, ID g N 112
Driscoll, TX l I 84
Driskill Mountain, LA j D 68
Drummond, MT d L 112
Drummond, WI d D 54
Drummond Island, MI d L 54
Drumright, OK d J 84
Dry Bay, AK g Y 142
Dry Cimarron, r., US c C 84
Dry Creek Mountain, NV c I 128
Dry Devils, r., TX j F 84
Dry Fork, r., MO e E 68
Dry Prong, LA k D 68
Dry Ridge, KY i B 26
Dry Tortugas, FL o D 40
Dubach, LA j D 68
Dublin, GA g D 40
Dublin, TX g H 84
Dublin, VA b F 40
Dubois, ID f M 112
Dubois, IN d J 68
Du Bois, NE k K 82
Du Bois, PA f H 26
Dubois, WY a G 98
Dubuque, IA h E 54
Duchesne, UT d F 98
Duchesne, r., UT d F 98
Duck, r., TN g I 68
Duck Hill, MS i G 68
Dudleyville, AZ l F 98
Due West, SC e D 40
Duffer Peak, NV c G 128
Dufur, OR e D 112
Dugdemona, r., LA j D 68
Dugger, IN c I 68
Duke, OK e G 84
Dulce, NM h J 98
Duluth, GA e B 40
Duluth, MN d C 54
Dumas, AR i E 68
Dumas, TX d E 84
Dumont, IA h C 54
Dunbar, WV i E 26
Duncan, AZ l G 98
Duncan, MS h F 68
Duncan, OK e I 84
Duncannon, PA g I 26
Dundalk, MD h J 26
Dundas, MN f B 54
Dundee, FL k E 40
Dundee, MI i L 54
Dundee, MS h F 68
Dundee, NY e J 26
Dunedin, FL k D 40
Dungannon, VA c D 40
Dunkirk, IN b K 68
Dunkirk, NY e G 26
Dunkirk, OH g C 26
Dunlap, IA j L 82
Dunlap, TN g K 68
Dunmore, PA f K 26
Dunn, NC d H 40
Dunnellon, FL j D 40
Dunning, NE j G 82
Dunseith, ND c G 82
Dunsmuir, CA c C 128
Du Page, r., IL i G 54
Dupree, SD f F 82
DuQuoin, IL e G 68
Duran, NM j K 98
Durand, IL h F 54
Durand, MI h L 54
Durand, WI f D 54
Durango, CO g I 98
Durant, IA i E 54
Durant, MS i G 68
Durant, OK f J 84
Durbin, WV i G 26
Durham, CA e D 128
Durham, NH d P 26
Durham, NC d H 40
Dushore, PA f J 26
Duson, LA l D 68
Dustin, OK d J 84
Dutch Harbor, AK j K 142
Dutch John, UT d G 98
Dutton, MT c N 112
Dutton, Mount, UT f D 98
Dwight, IL i G 54
Dworshak Reservoir, ID d J 112
Dyer, TN f H 68
Dyersburg, TN f G 68
Dyersville, IA h D 54
Dysart, IA h C 54

E

Eads, CO m E 82
Eagar, AZ j G 98
Eagle, AK d X 142
Eagle, CO e J 98
Eagle, r., CO e J 98
Eagle Bend, MN e L 82
Eagle Butte, SD f F 82
Eagle Grove, IA h B 54
Eagle Lake, TX j J 84
Eagle Lake, CA d E 128
Eagle Mountain, CA k J 128
Eagle Mountain, ID d J 112
Eagle Mountain, MN c E 54
Eagle Pass, TX k F 84
Eagle Peak, CA c E 128
Eagle River, MI c G 54
Eagle River, WI e F 54
Eagle Rock, VA b G 40
Eagleton Village, TN d C 40
Eagletown, OK h B 68
Eagle Village, AK d X 142
Earle, AR g F 68
Earlham, IA a B 68
Earlimart, CA f I 128
Earlington, KY e I 68
Earl Park, IN b I 68
Earlville, IL i G 54
Earlville, NY e K 26
Early, IA i L 82
Early, TX h H 84
Earth, TX e D 84
Easley, SC e D 40
East Alton, IL d F 68
East Aurora, NY e H 26
East Bay, TX j L 84
East Bend, NC c F 40
East Berlin, PA h J 26
East Bernard, TX j J 84
East Bernstadt, KY b B 40
East Brady, PA g G 26
East Brewton, AL k I 68
East Carbon, UT e F 98
East Chicago, IN a I 68
East Dublin, GA g D 40
East Dubuque, IL h E 54
East Ely, NV e K 128
East Fayetteville, NC d H 40
East Flat Rock, NC d D 40
East Gaffney, SC d E 40
East Gallatin, r., MT e N 112
East Glacier Park, MT b L 112
East Grand Forks, MN d J 82
East Grand Rapids, MI h J 54
East Greenwich, RI f O 26
Easthampton, MA e N 26
East Helena, MT d N 112
East Jordan, MI e J 54
Eastlake, MI f I 54
Eastlake, OH f E 26
Eastland, TX g H 84
East Lansing, MI h K 54
East Laurinburg, NC e G 40
East Liverpool, OH g F 26
East Lynn Lake, WV i D 26
Eastman, GA g C 40
East Millinocket, ME b R 26
East Missoula, MT d L 112
East Moline, IL i E 54
East Naples, FL m E 40
East Nishnabotna, r., IA k L 82
East Olympia, WA d C 112
Easton, MD i J 26
Easton, PA g K 26
Eastover, SC f F 40
East Palatka, FL j E 40
East Palestine, OH g F 26
East Pecos, NM i K 98
East Peoria, IL f J 54
Eastpoint, FL j B 40
East Point, GA f B 40
Eastport, ID a I 112
Eastport, ME c T 26
East Porterville, CA h G 128
East Prairie, MO f G 68
East Rockingham, NC e G 40
East Saint Louis, IL d F 68
East Spencer, NC d F 40
East Stroudsburg, PA g K 26
East Tawas, MI f L 54
East Troy, WI h G 54
Eastville, VA b K 40
East Wenatchee, WA c E 112
East Wilmington, NC e I 40
Eaton, CO d L 98
Eaton, IN b K 68
Eaton, OH h B 26
Eaton Rapids, MI h K 54
Eatonton, GA f C 40
Eatonville, WA d C 112
Eau Claire, WI f D 54
Eau Claire, r., WI f D 54
Eau Galle, r., WI f C 54
Eben Junction, MI d I 54
Ebensburg, PA g H 26
Eccles, WV b E 40
Echo, MN g L 82
Eclectic, AL j J 68
Ecru, MS h G 68
Eddyville, IA i C 54
Eddyville, KY e H 68
Eden, MS j F 68
Eden, TX h G 84
Eden, WY b G 98
Edenton, NC c J 40
Eden Valley, MN e A 54
Edgar, NE k J 82
Edgar, WI f F 54
Edgard, LA l F 68
Edgartown, MA f P 26
Edgefield, SC f E 40
Edgeley, ND e I 82
Edgemont, SD h D 82
Edgerton, MN h K 82
Edgerton, OH f B 26
Edgerton, WI h F 54
Edgerton, WY a J 98
Edgewater, AL i J 68
Edgewater, FL k F 40
Edgewood, IL d H 68
Edgewood, IA h D 54
Edgewood, MD h J 26
Edgewood, TX g K 84
Edina, MN f B 54
Edina, MO b D 68
Edinboro, PA f F 26
Edinburg, IL c G 68
Edinburg, IN c K 68
Edinburg, MS j G 68
Edinburg, ND c J 82
Edinburg, TX m H 84
Edinburg, VA i H 26
Edison, GA h B 40
Edisto, r., SC g F 40
Edisto Island, SC g F 40
Edmond, OK d I 84
Edmonds, WA c C 112
Edmonton, KY f K 68
Edmore, MI g J 54
Edmore, ND c I 82
Edna, KS n L 82
Edna, TX k J 84
Edna Bay, AK i BB 142
Edwards, MS j F 68
Edwards, NY c K 26
Edwards, r., IL i E 54
Edwards Plateau, TX i F 84
Edwardsville, IL d G 68
Eek, AK f M 142
Eel, r., CA d A 128
Eel, r., IN c I 68
Eel, r., IN b J 68
Effingham, IL c H 68
Effingham, KS l L 82
Egan Range, NV e K 128
Egegik, AK g P 142
Egg Harbor City, NJ h L 26
Ehrenberg, AZ k B 98
Ehrhardt, SC f E 40
Ekalaka, MT f C 82
Ekwok, AK g P 142
Elaine, AR h F 68
Elba, AL k J 68
Elbert, CO l C 82
Elbert, Mount, CO e J 98
Elberta, MI f I 54
Elberton, GA e D 40
Elbow Lake, MN f L 82
El Cajon, CA l I 128
El Campo, TX j J 84
El Capitan, MT d K 112
El Centro, CA l J 128
Elcho, WI e F 54
Eldon, IA j C 54
Eldon, MO d D 68
Eldora, IA h B 54
El Dorado, AR i D 68
Eldorado, IL e H 68
El Dorado, KS n K 82
Eldorado, OK e G 84
Eldorado, TX i F 84
El Dorado Springs, MO e B 68
Eldred, PA f H 26
Eldridge, IA i E 54
Eleanor, WV i E 26
Electra, TX e H 84
Electric City, WA c F 112
Eleele, HI d G 144b
Elephant Butte Reservoir, NM k I 98
Eleva, WI f D 54
Eleven Point, r., US f E 68
Elfrida, AZ m G 98
Elgin, IL h G 54
Elgin, IA h D 54
Elgin, MN f C 54
Elgin, NE j I 82
Elgin, ND e F 82
Elgin, OK e H 84
Elgin, OR e H 112
Elgin, TX i I 84
Eliasville, TX g H 84
Elida, NM f C 84
Elim, AK d M 142
Eliot, ME d P 26
Elizabeth, CO e L 98
Elizabeth, IL h E 54
Elizabeth, LA l D 68
Elizabeth, NJ g L 26
Elizabeth, WV h E 26
Elizabeth City, NC c J 40
Elizabethton, TN c D 40
Elizabethtown, IL e H 68
Elizabethtown, KY e K 68
Elizabethtown, NY c M 26
Elizabethtown, NC e H 40
Elizabethtown, PA g J 26
El Jebel, CO e I 98
Elk, r., US g J 68
Elk, r., CO d J 98
Elk, r., KS n K 82
Elk, r., MN e B 54
Elk, r., MO f B 68
Elk, r., WV i E 26
Elk, r., WI e E 54
Elkader, IA h D 54
Elk City, OK d G 84
Elk Creek, CA e C 128
Elk Grove, CA f D 128
Elkhart, IN a K 68
Elkhart, KS n F 82
Elkhart, TX h K 84
Elkhart Lake, WI g G 54
Elkhead Mountains, CO d I 98
Elk Horn, IA j L 82
Elkhorn, WI h G 54
Elkhorn, r., NE j J 82
Elkhorn City, KY b D 40
Elkin, NC c F 40
Elkins, WV i G 26
Elkland, PA f I 26
Elk Mountain, WY c J 98
Elk Mountain, WY c J 98
Elko, NV d J 128
Elk Point, SD i K 82
Elk Rapids, MI f J 54
Elk River, ID d I 112
Elk River, MN e B 54
Elkton, KY f I 68
Elkton, MD h K 26
Elkton, MI g L 54
Elkton, SD g K 82
Elkton, VA i H 26
Elkville, IL e G 68
Ellaville, GA g B 40
Ellen, Mount, UT f F 98
Ellendale, MN g B 54
Ellendale, ND e I 82
Ellensburg, WA d E 112
Ellenton, GA h C 40
Ellenville, NY f L 26
Ellerbe, NC d G 40
Ellettsville, IN c J 68
Ellicott City, MD h J 26
Ellicottville, NY e H 26
Ellijay, GA e B 40
Ellington, MO e F 68
Ellinwood, KS m I 82
Elliott, IA j L 82
Elliott, MS i G 68
Elliott Key, FL n F 40
Ellis, KS m H 82
Elliston, MT d M 112
Ellisville, MS k G 68
Elloree, SC f F 40
Ellsworth, KS m I 82
Ellsworth, ME c R 26
Ellsworth, MI e J 54
Ellsworth, MN h K 82
Ellsworth, WI f C 54
Ellwood City, PA g F 26
Elm, r., US f I 82
Elm, r., ND d J 82
Elma, IA g C 54
Elma, WA c B 112
Elm City, NC d I 40
Elm Creek, NE k H 82
Elmer, NJ h K 26
Elmhurst, IL i H 54
Elmira, NY e J 26
El Mirage, AZ k D 98
Elmira Heights, NY e J 26
Elmore, MN g A 54
Elmore, OH f C 26
Elmore City, OK e I 84
Elm Springs, AR f B 68
Elmwood, IL j F 54
Elmwood, NE k K 82
Elmwood, WI f C 54
Elnora, IN d I 68
Eloise, FL l E 40
Elora, TN g J 68
Eloy, AZ l E 98
El Paso, IL j F 54
El Paso, TX m J 98
El Portal, CA g F 128
El Reno, OK d I 84
El Rio, CA j F 128
El Rito, NM h J 98
El Rito, r., NM h J 98
Elroy, WI g E 54
Elsa, TX m I 84
Elsberry, MO c F 68
Elsie, MI g K 54
Elsinore, UT f D 98
Elsmere, DE h K 26
Elton, LA l D 68
Elvins, MO e F 68
Elwell, Lake, MT b N 112
Elwood, IN b K 68
Elwood, KS l M 82
Elwood, NE k H 82
Ely, MN c D 54
Ely, NV e K 128
Elyria, OH f D 26
Embarras, r., IL d I 68
Embarrass, WI f G 54
Embarrass, r., MN c C 54
Embarrass, r., WI f G 54
Embreeville, TN c D 40
Emden, IL b G 68
Emelle, AL j H 68
Emerado, ND d J 82
Emerson, AR i C 68
Emerson, GA e B 40
Emerson, IA j L 82
Emerson, NE i K 82
Emery, SD h J 82
Emery, UT e E 98
Eminence, KY d K 68
Eminence, MO e E 68
Emlenton, PA f G 26
Emmaus, PA g K 26
Emmet, AR i C 68
Emmetsburg, IA h M 82
Emmett, ID g I 112
Emmitsburg, MD h I 26
Emmonak, AK e L 142
Emory, TX g K 84
Emory, r., TN c B 40
Emory Peak, TX j C 84
Empire, LA m G 68
Empire, NV d F 128
Emporia, KS m K 82
Emporia, VA c I 40
Emporium, PA f H 26
Encampment, WY c J 98
Encampment, r., US c J 98
Encinal, TX k G 84
Encinitas, CA k H 128
Encino, NM j K 98
Encino, TX m H 84
Endeavor, WI g F 54
Enderlin, ND e J 82
Endicott, NY e J 26
Endicott, WA d H 112
Enfield, NH d N 26
Enfield, NC c I 40
Engelhard, NC d K 40
England, AR h E 68
Englewood, CO e L 98
Englewood, FL m D 40
Englewood, KS n H 82
Englewood, TN d B 40
English, IN d J 68
English, r., IA i D 54
English Bay, AK g S 142
Enid, OK c I 84
Enka, NC d D 40
Ennis, MT e N 112
Ennis, TX g J 84
Enochs, TX f D 84
Enon, OH h C 26
Enosburg Falls, VT c N 26
Enterprise, AL k K 68
Enterprise, CA e D 128
Enterprise, KS m J 82
Enterprise, MS j H 68
Enterprise, OR e H 112
Enterprise, UT g C 98
Entiat, r., WA c E 112
Enumclaw, WA c D 112
Eolia, MO c E 68
Epes, AL j H 68
Ephraim, UT e E 98
Ephrata, PA g J 26
Ephrata, WA c F 112
Epping, NH d O 26
Equality, IL e H 68
Erath, LA m D 68
Erick, OK d G 84
Ericson, NE j I 82
Erie, CO d K 98
Erie, IL i E 54
Erie, KS n L 82
Erie, PA e F 26
Erie, Lake, NA h O 54
Erie Canal, see New York State Barge Canal, NY d H 26
Erin, TN f I 68
Errol Heights, OR e C 112
Erskine, MN d K 82
Erwin, NC d H 40
Erwin, TN c D 40
Escalante, UT g E 98
Escalante, r., UT g E 98
Escalante Desert, UT g C 98
Escalon, CA g E 128
Escambia, r., FL l I 68
Escanaba, MI e H 54
Escanaba, r., MI d H 54
Escatawpa, r., US l H 68
Escondido, CA k H 128
Eskdale, WV i E 26
Eskridge, KS m K 82
Esmond, ND c H 82
Espanola, NM i J 98
Essex, IA k L 82
Essex, MD h J 26
Essex, MO f G 68
Essex Junction, VT c M 26
Essexville, MI g L 54
Estacada, OR e C 112
Estacado, Llano, US f D 84
Estancia, NM j J 98
Estelline, SD g K 82
Estelline, TX e F 84
Estes Park, CO d K 98
Estherville, IA h M 82
Estill, SC g E 40
Ethan, SD h J 82
Ethel, MS i G 68
Ethel, Mount, CO d J 98
Ethridge, MT b M 112
Ethridge, TN g I 68
Etna, CA c C 128
Etna, WY a E 98
Etowah, TN d B 40
Etowah, r., GA e A 40
Ettrick, VA b I 40
Euclid, OH f E 26
Eudora, AR i E 68
Eudora, KS m L 82
Eufaula, AL k K 68
Eufaula, OK d K 84
Eufaula Lake, OK d K 84
Eugene, OR f B 112
Eunice, LA l D 68
Eunice, NM g C 84
Eupora, MS i G 68
Eureka, CA d A 128
Eureka, IL j F 54
Eureka, KS n K 82
Eureka, MT b J 112
Eureka, NV e J 128
Eureka, SC e E 40
Eureka, SD f H 82
Eureka, UT e D 98
Eureka Springs, AR f C 68
Eustace, TX g J 84
Eustis, FL k E 40
Eustis, NE k G 82
Eutaw, AL j I 68
Eva, AL h J 68
Evadale, TX l B 68
Evans, CO d L 98
Evans, Mount, CO e K 98
Evans City, PA g F 26
Evansdale, IA h C 54
Evanston, IL h H 54
Evanston, WY c F 98
Evansville, IL d G 68
Evansville, IN e I 68
Evansville, MN e L 82
Evansville, WI h F 54
Evansville, WY b J 98
Evant, TX h H 84
Evart, MI g J 54
Evarts, KY c C 40
Eveleth, MN c C 54
Evening Shade, AR f E 68
Everest, KS l L 82
Everett, PA g H 26
Everett, WA c C 112
Everglades City, FL n E 40
Everglades National Park, FL n F 40
Evergreen, AL k J 68
Evergreen, CA i E 128
Evergreen, MT b K 112
Everly, IA h L 82
Ewa, HI f I 144c
Ewa Beach, HI f I 144c
Ewen, MI d F 54
Ewing, NE i I 82
Ewing, VA c C 40
Excelsior Mountain, CA f F 128
Excelsior Springs, MO c B 68
Exeter, CA h F 128
Exeter, NE k J 82
Exeter, NH e P 26
Exeter, r., NH d O 26
Exira, IA j M 82
Exmore, VA b K 40
Experiment, GA f B 40
Eyota, MN g C 54

F

Fabens, TX m J 98
Factoryville, PA f K 26
Fairbank, IA h C 54
Fairbanks, AK d U 142
Fairbanks, LA l D 68
Fair Bluff, NC e G 40
Fairborn, OH h B 26
Fairburn, GA f B 40
Fairbury, IL j G 54
Fairbury, NE k J 82
Fairchance, PA h G 26
Fairchild, WI f E 54
Fairfax, AL j K 68
Fairfax, MN g M 82
Fairfax, MO b A 68
Fairfax, OK c J 84
Fairfax, SC g E 40
Fairfax, SD h I 82
Fairfax, VT c M 26
Fairfax, VA i I 26
Fairfield, AL i J 68
Fairfield, CA f C 128
Fairfield, ID g K 112
Fairfield, IL d H 68
Fairfield, IA i D 54

Name	Map Ref.	Page
Fairfield, ME	c Q	26
Fairfield, MT	c N	112
Fairfield, NE	k l	82
Fairfield, OH	h B	26
Fairfield, TX	h J	84
Fairgrove, MI	g L	54
Fairhaven, MA	f P	26
Fair Haven, NY	d J	26
Fair Haven, VT	d M	26
Fairhope, AL	l l	68
Fairland, IN	c K	68
Fairland, OK	c L	84
Fairmont, MN	h M	82
Fairmont, NE	k J	82
Fairmont, NC	e G	40
Fairmont, WV	h F	26
Fairmount, GA	e B	40
Fairmount, IL	b l	68
Fairmount, IN	b K	68
Fairmount, ND	e K	82
Fair Oaks, CA	f D	128
Fair Oaks, CA	f B	40
Fair Plain, MI	h I	54
Fairplains, NC	c E	40
Fairplay, CO	e J	98
Fairview, GA	e A	40
Fairview, IL	j E	54
Fairview, KS	l L	82
Fairview, MI	f K	54
Fairview, MT	d C	82
Fairview, OK	c H	84
Fairview, TN	g l	68
Fairview, UT	f E	98
Fairview, WV	h F	26
Fairview Park, IN	c l	68
Fairview Peak, NV	e G	128
Fairweather Mountain, NA	g Z	142
Faison, NC	d H	40
Faith, SD	f E	82
Falcon Heights, OR	h D	112
Falcon Reservoir (Presa Falcón), NA	m G	84
Falfurrias, TX	l H	84
Falkville, AL	h J	68
Fall, r., KS	n L	82
Fallbrook, CA	k H	128
Fall Creek, WI	b H	40
Falling, r., MT	e B	40
Fallon, MT	e B	82
Fallon, NV	e G	128
Fall River, KS	n K	82
Fall River, MA	f O	26
Fall River, WI	g F	54
Fall River Mills, CA	c D	128
Falls City, NE	k L	82
Falls City, OR	f B	112
Falls Creek, PA	i H	26
Falmouth, KY	i B	26
Falmouth, ME	d P	26
Falmouth, MA	f P	26
Falmouth, VA	i l	26
Fanny, Mount, OR	e H	112
Farallon Islands, CA	g B	128
Fargo, ND	e K	82
Faribault, MN	f B	54
Farina, IL	d H	68
Farley, IA	b H	54
Farmer City, IL	b H	68
Farmersburg, IN	c l	68
Farmersville, CA	c G	68
Farmersville, TX	f J	84
Farmerville, LA	j D	68
Farmington, IL	j D	54
Farmington, IA	j D	54
Farmington, ME	c P	26
Farmington, MN	f B	54
Farmington, MO	e F	68
Farmington, NH	d O	26
Farmington, NM	h H	98
Farmington, UT	d E	98
Farmville, NC	d l	40
Farmville, VA	b H	40
Farnam, NE	k G	82
Farnhamville, IA	i M	82
Farragut, IA	k L	82
Farrell, PA	h F	26
Farwell, MI	g K	54
Farwell, TX	l C	84
Faulkton, SD	f H	82
Fayette, AL	i l	68
Fayette, IA	h D	54
Fayette, MS	k E	68
Fayette, MO	c D	68
Fayette, OH	f B	26
Fayetteville, AR	f B	68
Fayetteville, GA	f B	40
Fayetteville, NC	d E	40
Fayetteville, TN	g J	68
Fayetteville, WV	i E	26
Fear, Cape, NC	f l	40
Feather, r., CA	d E	128
Federalsburg, MD	i K	26
Felda, FL	m E	40
Felix, Rio, r., NM	k K	98
Fellsmere, FL	l F	40
Fennimore, WI	h E	54
Fennville, MI	h l	54
Fenton, MI	h L	54
Fenton, MO	e F	68
Fentress, TX	j l	84
Fenwick, WV	i F	26
Ferdinand, IN	d J	68
Fergus Falls, MN	g l	54
Ferguson, KY	b B	40
Ferguson, MO	d F	68
Fernandina Beach, FL	i E	40
Ferndale, CA	a D	128
Ferndale, WA	b C	112
Fernley, NV	e F	128
Fern Park, FL	k E	40
Fernwood, ID	c l	112
Ferriday, LA	k E	68
Ferris, TX	g J	84
Ferron, UT	e E	98
Ferrysburg, MI	g l	54
Fertile, MN	d K	82
Fessenden, ND	d H	82
Festus, MO	d F	68
Fife Lake, MI	f J	54
Fifield, WI	e E	54
Fillmore, CA	j G	128
Fillmore, UT	f D	98
Fincastle, VA	c H	40
Findlay, IL	c H	68
Findlay, OH	f B	26
Fingal, ND	e J	82
Finley, ND	d J	82
Finley, NE	k K	82
Firebaugh, CA	h E	128
Firth, NE	k K	82
Fish, r., AL	l l	68
Fisher, AR	g F	68
Fisher, IL	b H	68
Fisher, LA	j C	68
Fisher, r., MT	b J	112
Fishers Island, NY	f O	26
Fishing Creek, MD	i J	26
Fisk, MO	f F	68
Fitchburg, MA	e O	26
Fitzgerald, GA	h C	40
Five Points, NM	i J	98
Flagler, CO	l D	82
Flagler Beach, FL	i E	40
Flagstaff, AZ	d F	98
Flagstaff Lake, ME	b P	26
Flambeau, r., WI	e D	54
Flaming Gorge Reservoir, US	c G	98
Flanagan, IL	j G	54
Flandreau, SD	g K	82
Flasher, ND	e F	82
Flat, TX	h l	84
Flat, r., MI	g J	54
Flat Lick, KY	c C	40
Flatonia, TX	j l	84
Flat River, MO	e F	68
Flat Rock, IL	h K	68
Flat Rock, IL	d l	68
Flattery, Cape, WA	b A	112
Flatwood, AL	j J	68
Flatwoods, KY	i D	26
Flaxton, ND	c E	82
Flaxville, MT	c B	82
Fleetwood, PA	g K	26
Fleming, CO	k E	82
Fleming-Neon, KY	b D	40
Flemingsburg, KY	i C	26
Fletcher, NC	d D	40
Fletcher, OK	e H	84
Fletcher Pond, MI	f L	54
Flint, MI	g L	54
Flint, r., US	h J	68
Flint, r., GA	i B	40
Flint, r., MI	g L	54
Flintville, TN	g J	68
Flippin, AR	f D	68
Flomaton, AL	k l	68
Flomot, TX	e F	84
Floodwood, MN	d C	54
Flora, IL	d H	68
Flora, IN	b J	68
Flora, MS	j F	68
Florala, AL	k J	68
Floral City, FL	k D	40
Floral Park, MT	e M	112
Flora Vista, NM	h H	98
Florence, AL	h l	68
Florence, AZ	k E	98
Florence, CO	f K	98
Florence, KS	m K	82
Florence, OR	g A	112
Florence, SC	e G	40
Florence, WI	e G	54
Floresville, TX	j H	84
Florida, state, US	f J	8
Florida, r., CO	g l	98
Florida Bay, FL	n F	40
Florida City, FL	n F	40
Florida Keys, FL	o E	40
Florida, Straits of, NA	k C	60
Florien, LA	j C	68
Florissant, MO	d F	68
Flowery Branch, GA	e C	40
Floyd, NM	h C	84
Floyd, VA	c F	40
Floyd, r., IA	i K	82
Floydada, TX	f E	84
Floyds Fork, r., KY	d K	68
Flushing, MI	g L	54
Fluvanna, TX	g E	84
Foley, AL	l l	68
Foley, MN	e B	54
Folkston, GA	i D	40
Follett, TX	c F	84
Folsom, CA	f D	128
Folsom Lake, CA	f D	128
Fonda, IA	i M	82
Fonda, NY	e L	26
Fond du Lac, WI	g G	54
Fontana, CA	j H	128
Fontana Lake, NC	d C	40
Fontanelle, IA	j M	82
Footville, WI	h F	54
Foraker, Mount, AK	e S	142
Ford, KS	n H	82
Ford, r., MI	d H	54
Ford City, CA	i F	128
Ford City, PA	g G	26
Fordsville, KY	e J	68
Fordville, ND	c J	82
Fordyce, AR	i D	68
Foreman, AR	i B	68
Forest, MS	j G	68
Forest, OH	f B	26
Forest Acres, SC	e F	40
Forest City, IA	g B	54
Forest City, NC	d E	40
Forest City, PA	f K	26
Forest Home, AL	k J	68
Forest Lake, MN	e C	54
Forest Park, GA	f B	40
Forestville, WI	f H	54
Forgan, OK	c F	84
Forked Deer, r., TN	f E	68
Forks, WA	c A	112
Forman, ND	e J	82
Forney, TX	g J	84
Forrest, IL	j G	54
Forrest City, AR	g F	68
Forreston, IL	h F	54
Forsan, TX	g E	84
Forsyth, GA	f C	40
Forsyth, MO	f C	68
Forsyth, MT	d S	112
Fort Adams, MS	k E	68
Fort Atkinson, WI	h G	54
Fort Benton, MT	c O	112
Fort Bidwell, CA	c E	128
Fort Bragg, CA	e B	128
Fort Branch, IN	d l	68
Fort Bridger, WY	c F	98
Fort Calhoun, NE	j K	82
Fort Cobb, OK	d K	84
Fort Collins, CO	k D	98
Fort Covington, NY	c L	26
Fort Davis, AL	j K	68
Fort Davis, TX	h C	84
Fort Defiance, AZ	i G	98
Fort Deposit, AL	k l	68
Fort Dodge, IA	h A	54
Fort Duchesne, UT	d F	98
Fort Edward, NY	d M	26
Fort Gaines, GA	i d	68
Fort Garland, CO	g K	98
Fort Gay, WV	h D	26
Fort Gibson, OK	d K	84
Fort Gibson Lake, OK	d K	84
Fort Hall, ID	g M	112
Fort Jones, CA	c C	128
Fort Klamath, OR	h B	112
Fort Laramie, WY	b L	98
Fort Lauderdale, FL	m F	40
Fort Loramie, OH	g B	26
Fort Loudoun Lake, TN	d B	40
Fort Lupton, CO	d L	98
Fort Madison, IA	j E	54
Fort Meade, FL	l E	40
Fort Mill, SC	d F	40
Fort Mitchell, AL	g A	40
Fort Morgan, CO	k D	82
Fort Myers, FL	m E	40
Fort Myers Beach, FL	m E	40
Fort Ogden, FL	l E	40
Fort Payne, AL	h K	68
Fort Peck, MT	b S	112
Fort Peck Lake, MT	c S	112
Fort Pierce, FL	l F	40
Fort Pierre, SD	g G	82
Fort Plain, NY	e L	26
Fort Recovery, OH	g B	26
Fort Scott, KS	n M	82
Fort Smith, AR	g B	68
Fort Stockton, TX	i D	84
Fort Sumner, NM	h F	98
Fort Supply, OK	c G	84
Fort Thomas, AZ	l E	98
Fort Thompson, SD	g H	82
Fort Totten, ND	d l	82
Fort Towson, OK	e K	84
Fortuna, CA	d A	128
Fortuna Ledge (Marshall), AK	f M	142
Fort Valley, GA	g C	40
Fortville, IN	c K	68
Fort Walton Beach, FL	l J	68
Fort Washakie, WY	a H	98
Fort Wayne, IN	a K	68
Fort White, FL	j D	40
Fort Worth, TX	g l	84
Fort Yates, ND	f G	82
Fort Yukon, AK	c V	142
Fossil, OR	f E	112
Fosston, MN	d L	82
Fosters, AL	i l	68
Foster Village, HI	f A	144c
Fostoria, OH	f C	26
Fouke, AR	i C	68
Fountain, CO	m C	82
Fountain, FL	i A	40
Fountain City, WI	f D	54
Fountain Green, UT	e E	98
Fountain Inn, SC	e D	40
Fountain Peak, CA	j J	128
Fountain Place, LA	l E	68
Fourche LaFave, r., AR	h D	68
Fourche Maline, r., OK	e L	84
Four Corners, OR	f C	112
Four Mountains, Islands of, AK	j l	142
Four Oaks, NC	d H	40
Fowler, CA	h F	128
Fowler, CO	m C	82
Fowler, IN	b l	68
Fowler, MI	g K	54
Fowlerton, TX	k H	84
Fowlerville, MI	h K	54
Fox, r., US	b E	68
Fox, r., IL	d H	68
Fox, r., WI	f G	54
Fox Islands, AK	j J	142
Fox Lake, IL	h G	54
Fox Lake, WI	g G	54
Foxpark, WY	c J	98
Foxworth, MS	k G	68
Framingham, MA	e O	26
Francesville, IN	b J	68
Francis Case, Lake, SD	h H	82
Francs Peak, WY	g P	112
Frankel City, TX	g D	84
Frankenmuth, MI	g L	54
Frankford, MO	c E	68
Frankfort, IN	b J	68
Frankfort, KS	k B	82
Frankfort, KY	d L	68
Frankfort, MI	f l	54
Frankfort, NY	d K	26
Frankfort, OH	h C	26
Frankfort, SD	g l	82
Franklin, AZ	l G	98
Franklin, GA	f A	40
Franklin, ID	h N	112
Franklin, IL	c F	68
Franklin, IN	c J	68
Franklin, KY	f J	68
Franklin, LA	m E	68
Franklin, MA	e O	26
Franklin, MN	g M	82
Franklin, NE	k l	82
Franklin, NH	d O	26
Franklin, NJ	f L	26
Franklin, NC	c H	40
Franklin, PA	f G	26
Franklin, TN	f J	68
Franklin, TX	h J	84
Franklin, VA	c J	40
Franklin, WV	i G	26
Franklin, WI	h G	54
Franklin D. Roosevelt Lake, WA	b G	112
Franklin Grove, IL	i F	54
Franklinton, LA	l F	68
Franklinton, NC	c H	40
Franklinville, NY	e H	26
Frankston, TX	g K	84
Frankton, IN	b K	68
Frankville, AL	k H	68
Fraser, CO	e K	98
Fraser, r., CO	d K	98
Frazee, MN	d K	82
Frazer, MT	b S	112
Frederic, WI	d C	54
Frederica, DE	h K	26
Frederick, MD	h l	26
Frederick, OK	e H	84
Frederick, SD	f l	82
Fredericksburg, IA	h C	54
Fredericksburg, TX	i H	84
Fredericksburg, VA	i l	26
Fredericktown, MO	e F	68
Fredericktown, OH	g D	26
Fredonia, AZ	h D	98
Fredonia, KS	n L	82
Fredonia, NY	e G	26
Fredonia, ND	d F	82
Freeburg, IL	d G	68
Freeburg, MO	d E	68
Freehold, NJ	g L	26
Freeland, MI	g K	54
Freeland, PA	f K	26
Freeman, SD	h J	82
Freeport, FL	l J	68
Freeport, IL	h F	54
Freeport, ME	d P	26
Freeport, NY	g M	26
Freeport, PA	g G	26
Freeport, TX	k K	84
Freer, TX	l H	84
Fremont, CA	g D	128
Fremont, IN	a L	68
Fremont, IA	i C	54
Fremont, MI	g J	54
Fremont, NE	j K	82
Fremont, NC	d l	40
Fremont, OH	f C	26
Fremont, WI	f F	54
Fremont, r., UT	f F	98
French Broad, r., US	d D	40
Frenchburg, KY	b C	40
French Lick, IN	d J	68
Frenchman Bay, ME	c R	26
Frenchman, r., US	d D	82
Fresno, CA	h F	128
Fresno, r., CA	h E	128
Fresno Reservoir, MT	b P	112
Frewsburg, NY	e G	26
Friant, CA	h F	128
Friars Point, MS	h F	68
Friday Harbor, WA	b B	112
Fridley, MN	e B	54
Friend, NE	k J	82
Friendship, NY	e H	26
Friendship, TN	g G	68
Friendship, WI	g F	54
Fries, VA	c F	40
Frio, r., TX	k H	84
Friona, TX	e D	84
Frisco, TX	g J	84
Frisco City, AL	k l	68
Fritch, TX	d E	84
Froid, MT	c C	82
Fromberg, MT	e Q	112
Frontenac, KS	n M	82
Frontier, WY	c F	98
Front Range, CO	d K	98
Front Royal, VA	i H	26
Frost, TX	g J	84
Frostburg, MD	h H	26
Frostproof, FL	l E	40
Fruita, CO	e H	98
Fruitdale, AL	k H	68
Fruitdale, OR	h B	112
Fruithurst, AL	i K	68
Fruitland, ID	f l	112
Fruitland, MD	i K	26
Fruitport, MI	g l	54
Fruitvale, WA	d E	112
Fruitville, FL	l D	40
Fryeburg, ME	c P	26
Fryingpan, r., CO	e J	98
Fulda, MN	h M	82
Fullerton, CA	k H	128
Fullerton, NE	j J	82
Fulton, AL	k l	68
Fulton, AR	i C	68
Fulton, IL	i E	54
Fulton, KS	m M	82
Fulton, MS	h H	68
Fulton, MO	d E	68
Fulton, NY	d J	26
Fulton, TX	k l	84
Fultondale, AL	i J	68
Fuquay-Varina, NC	d H	40

G

Name	Map Ref.	Page
Gabbs, NV	f l	128
Gackle, ND	e H	82
Gadsden, AL	h J	68
Gadsden, AZ	l B	98
Gaffney, SC	d E	40
Gage, OK	c G	84
Gail, TX	g E	84
Gainesboro, TN	f K	68
Gainesville, FL	j D	40
Gainesville, GA	e C	40
Gainesville, MO	f D	68
Gainesville, TX	f l	84
Gaithersburg, MD	h l	26
Galatia, IL	e H	68
Galax, VA	c F	40
Galena, AK	d P	142
Galena, IL	h E	54
Galena, KS	n M	82
Galena, MO	f C	68
Galena Park, TX	j K	84
Galesburg, IL	j E	54
Galesburg, IL	h J	54
Galesville, WI	f D	54
Galeton, PA	f l	26
Galion, OH	g D	26
Galiuro Mountains, AZ	l F	98
Gallatin, MO	c C	68
Gallatin, TN	f J	68
Gallatin, r., US	e N	112
Gallinas, r., NM	d B	84
Gallinas Peak, NM	j K	98
Gallipolis, OH	i D	26
Gallup, NM	i H	98
Galt, CA	f D	128
Galva, IL	i E	54
Galva, IA	i L	82
Galva, KS	m J	82
Galveston, TX	j L	84
Galveston Bay, TX	j L	84
Galveston Island, TX	j L	84
Gamaliel, TX	g J	68
Gambell, AK	e l	142
Gambier, OH	g D	26
Ganado, AZ	i G	98
Ganado, TX	j K	84
Gannett Peak, WY	g P	112
Gannvalley, SD	g l	82
Gantt, AL	k J	68
Garber, OK	d H	84
Garberville, CA	d B	128
Garden City, GA	g E	40
Garden City, KS	n G	82
Garden City, KS	m J	82
Garden City, TX	h E	84
Gardendale, AL	i J	68
Garden Grove, CA	k B	128
Garden Grove, IA	j B	54
Garden Peninsula, MI	e H	54
Garden Plain, KS	m K	82
Gardiner, ME	c Q	26
Gardiner, MT	e O	112
Gardiner, OR	g A	112
Gardiners Bay, NY	f N	26
Gardner, KS	m M	82
Gardner, MA	e N	26
Gardnerville, NV	f F	128
Garfield, KS	m H	82
Garfield, NM	i l	98
Garfield, WA	c H	112
Garfield Mountain, MT	f M	112
Garibaldi, OR	e B	112
Garland, AL	k J	68
Garland, TX	g J	84
Garland, UT	c D	98
Garnavillo, IA	h D	54
Garner, IA	g B	54
Garner, NC	d H	40
Garnett, KS	m K	82
Garretson, SD	h K	82
Garrett, IN	a K	68
Garrett, KY	b D	40
Garrison, MT	d M	112
Garrison, ND	d F	82
Garrison, TX	k B	68
Garwin, IA	h C	54
Garwood, TX	j J	84
Gary, IN	a l	68
Gary, SD	g K	82
Gary, TX	j B	68
Gary, WV	b E	40
Gas City, IN	b K	68
Gasconade, r., MO	d E	68
Gassaway, WV	i F	26
Gaston, NC	c l	40
Gaston, Lake, US	c H	40
Gastonia, NC	d E	40
Gate, OK	c F	84
Gate City, VA	c D	40
Gatesville, NC	c J	40
Gatesville, TX	h l	84
Gateway, CO	f H	98
Gatlinburg, TN	d C	40
Gauley, r., WV	i E	26
Gauley Bridge, WV	i E	26
Gause, TX	i J	84
Gaylord, MI	e K	54
Gaylord, MN	f A	54
Gays Mills, WI	g E	54
Gearhart Mountain, OR	h E	112
Geary, OK	d H	84
Geddes, SD	h l	82
Geiger, AL	j H	68
Geistown, PA	h H	26
Geneseo, ID	d l	112
Geneseo, r., US	h R	54
Geneseo, IL	i E	54
Geneseo, KS	m K	82
Geneseo, NY	e l	26
Geneva, AL	k K	68
Geneva, IL	i G	54
Geneva, IN	b L	68
Geneva, NE	k J	82
Geneva, NY	e l	26
Geneva, OH	f F	26
Genoa, IL	h G	54
Genoa, NE	j J	82
Genoa, OH	f C	26
Genoa, WI	g D	54
Gentry, AR	f B	68
George, IA	h K	82
George, Lake, FL	j E	40
George, Lake, NY	d M	26
Georgetown, CO	e K	98
Georgetown, DE	h K	26
Georgetown, FL	j E	40
Georgetown, GA	h A	40
Georgetown, ID	h N	112
Georgetown, IL	c l	68
Georgetown, KY	i B	26
Georgetown, MS	k F	68
Georgetown, OH	i C	26
Georgetown, SC	f G	40
Georgetown, TX	i l	84
George West, TX	k H	84
Georgia, state, US	e J	8
Georgia, Strait of, NA	h	24
Georgiana, AL	k J	68
Geraldine, MT	c O	112
Gerber, CA	d E	128
Gerdine, Mount, AK	f R	142
Gering, NE	j D	82
Germantown, IL	d G	68
Germantown, TN	h G	68
Germantown, WI	g G	54
Germfask, MI	d J	54
Geronimo, OK	e H	84
Gettysburg, PA	h l	26
Gettysburg, SD	f H	82
Geyser, MT	c O	112
Geyserville, CA	f C	128
Gibbon, MN	f A	54
Gibbon, NE	k l	82
Gibbonsville, ID	e L	112
Gibson, GA	f D	40
Gibson City, IL	j G	54
Gideon, MO	f G	68
Gifford, FL	l F	40
Gila, r., US	b B	98
Gila Bend, AZ	l D	98
Gila Bend Mountains, AZ	k C	98
Gila Mountains, AZ	l G	98
Gilbert, AZ	k D	98
Gilbert, LA	k H	68
Gilbert, MN	c C	54
Gildford, MT	b O	112
Gillespie, IL	c G	68
Gillett, AR	h E	68
Gillett, WI	f G	54
Gillette, WY	g B	82
Gills Rock, WI	e H	54
Gilman, IA	i C	54
Gilman, IL	j H	54
Gilman, WI	e E	54
Gilmer, TX	f K	84
Gilmore City, IA	i M	82
Gilroy, CA	g D	128
Giltner, NE	k l	82
Girard, IL	c G	68
Girard, KS	n M	82
Girard, OH	f F	26
Girard, PA	e F	26
Girard, TX	f F	84
Glacier, WA	b D	112
Glacier National Park, MT	b L	112
Glacier Peak, WA	b D	112
Gladbrook, IA	h C	54
Glade Spring, VA	c E	40
Gladewater, TX	f L	68
Gladstone, MI	e H	54
Gladstone, MO	c D	68
Gladwin, MI	g K	54
Glasco, KS	l J	82
Glasgow, KY	f K	68
Glasgow, MO	c D	68
Glasgow, MT	b S	112
Glasgow, VA	b G	40
Glassboro, NJ	h K	26
Gleason, TN	g H	68
Glen Alpine, NC	d E	40
Glenburn, ND	c F	82
Glen Burnie, MD	h J	26
Glencoe, AL	h J	68
Glencoe, MN	f A	54
Glen Cove, NY	g M	26
Glendale, AZ	k D	98
Glendale, CA	j G	128
Glendale, MS	k G	68
Glendale, OR	h B	112
Glendale, UT	g D	98
Glendale, WI	g H	54
Glendive, MT	d C	82
Glendo, WY	b K	98
Gleneden Beach, OR	f A	112
Glen Elder, KS	l l	82
Glen Flora, TX	j J	84
Glenmora, LA	l D	68
Glennallen, AK	e V	142
Glenns Ferry, ID	h J	112
Glennville, GA	h E	40
Glenoma, WA	d C	112
Glenrock, WY	b K	98
Glen Rose, TX	g l	84
Glens Falls, NY	d M	26
Glen Ullin, ND	e F	82
Glenville, MN	g B	54
Glenville, WV	i F	26
Glen White, WV	b E	40
Glenwood, AL	k J	68
Glenwood, GA	g D	40
Glenwood, IA	j L	82
Glenwood, MN	f L	82
Glenwood, NM	k H	98
Glenwood, UT	f E	98
Glenwood City, WI	c C	54
Glenwood Springs, CO	e l	98
Glidden, IA	i M	82
Glidden, WI	d E	54
Glide, OR	g B	112
Globe, AZ	k E	98
Glorieta, NM	j K	98
Gloster, MS	k E	68
Gloucester, MA	e P	26
Gloucester, VA	b J	40
Glouster, OH	h D	26
Glover, r., OK	e L	84
Gloversville, NY	d L	26
Glyndon, MN	e K	82
Goat Mountain, MT	c L	112
Gobles, MI	h J	54
Godfrey, IL	d F	68
Goffstown, NH	d O	26
Gogebic, Lake, MI	d F	54
Golconda, IL	e H	68
Golconda, NV	d H	128
Gold Beach, OR	h A	112
Golden, CO	e K	98
Golden, IL	c E	68
Golden City, MO	e E	68
Goldendale, WA	e E	112
Golden Meadow, LA	m F	68
Goldfield, IA	h B	54
Goldfield, NV	g H	128
Goldonna, LA	j D	68
Goldsboro, NC	d l	40
Goldsmith, TX	h D	84
Goldston, NC	d G	40
Goldthwaite, TX	h H	84
Goleta, CA	j F	128
Goliad, TX	k l	84
Golovin, AK	d M	142
Golva, ND	e D	82
Gonzales, CA	h D	128
Gonzales, LA	l F	68
Gonzales, TX	j l	84
Goochland, VA	b l	40
Goodhue, MN	f C	54
Gooding, ID	h K	112
Goodland, IN	b l	68
Goodland, KS	l F	82
Goodman, MS	j G	68
Goodman, WI	e G	54
Goodnews Bay, AK	g N	142
Goodnight, CO	f L	98
Goodrich, ND	d G	82
Goodrich, TX	i L	84
Good Thunder, MN	f A	54
Goodview, MN	f D	54
Goodwater, AL	i J	68
Goodwell, OK	c E	84
Goodyear, AZ	k D	98
Goose, r., ND	d J	82
Goose Creek, SC	g F	40
Goose Lake, US	c E	128
Gordo, AL	i l	68
Gordon, GA	g C	40
Gordon, NE	g D	82
Gordon, WI	d D	54
Gordonsville, VA	i H	26
Goree, TX	f G	84
Goreville, IL	e H	68
Gorham, ME	d P	26
Gorham, NH	c O	26
Gorman, TX	g H	84
Goshen, IN	a K	68
Goshen, NY	f L	26
Gosport, IN	c J	68
Gotebo, OK	d G	84
Gothenburg, NE	k G	82
Gould, AR	i E	68
Gould City, MI	d J	54
Goulds, FL	n F	40
Gouverneur, NY	c K	26
Gove, KS	m G	82
Gowanda, NY	e H	26
Gower, MO	c C	68
Gowrie, IA	i M	82
Grace, ID	h N	112
Graceville, FL	i A	40
Graceville, MN	f K	82
Grady, AR	h E	68
Grady, NM	e C	84
Graettinger, IA	h M	82
Graford, TX	f H	84
Grafton, IL	d F	68
Grafton, ND	c J	82
Grafton, OH	f E	26
Grafton, WV	h F	26
Grafton, WI	f H	54
Graham, TX	f H	84
Graham, Mount, AZ	l G	98
Grainfield, KS	l G	82
Grambling, LA	j D	68
Granada, CO	m E	82
Granby, CO	d K	98
Granby, MO	f B	68
Granby, Lake, CO	d K	98
Grand, r., US	c C	68
Grand, r., MI	g l	54
Grand, r., OH	f E	26
Grand, r., SD	f G	82
Grand, r., WI	g G	54
Grand Bay, AL	l H	68
Grand Blanc, MI	h L	54
Grand Cane, LA	i C	68
Grand Canyon, AZ	h C	98
Grand Canyon, AZ	h D	98
Grand Canyon National Park, AZ	h D	98
Grand Coulee, WA	c F	112
Grand Coulee Dam, WA	c G	112
Grande, Rio (Bravo del Norte), r., NA	f G	8
Grande Ronde, r., US	e H	112
Grandfalls, TX	h D	84
Grandfield, OK	e H	84
Grand Forks, ND	d J	82
Grand Haven, MI	g l	54
Grand Island, NE	k l	54
Grand Isle, LA	m G	68
Grand Junction, CO	e H	98
Grand Junction, IA	i M	82
Grand Junction, TN	g G	68
Grand Lake, CO	d K	98
Grand Lake, LA	m E	68
Grand Lake, LA	m D	68
Grand Lake, OH	g B	26
Grand Ledge, MI	h K	54
Grand Marais, MI	d J	54
Grand Marais, MN	c E	54
Grand Meadow, MN	g C	54
Grand Mesa, CO	e H	98
Grand Portage, MN	c F	54
Grand Prairie, TX	g J	84
Grand Rapids, MI	h J	54
Grand Rapids, MN	c B	54
Grand Saline, TX	g K	84
Grand Teton, WY	a F	98
Grand Teton National Park, WY	g O	112
Grand Tower, IL	e G	68
Grand Traverse Bay, MI	e J	54
Grandview, MO	d B	68
Grandview, TX	g J	84
Grand View, WI	d D	54
Granger, TX	i l	84
Granger, WA	d E	112
Granger, WY	c G	98
Grangeville, ID	e l	112
Granite, OK	e G	84
Granite City, IL	d F	68
Granite Falls, MN	g L	82
Granite Falls, NC	d E	40
Granite Peak, MT	e Q	112
Graniteville, SC	n D	40
Graniteville, VT	c N	26
Grant, FL	l F	40
Grant, MI	g J	54
Grant, NE	k F	82
Grant, r., WI	g D	54
Grant, Mount, NV	f G	128
Grant City, MO	b B	68
Grant Park, IL	i H	54
Grants, NM	i l	98
Grantsburg, WI	c C	54
Grants Pass, OR	h B	112
Grantsville, UT	d D	98
Grantsville, WV	i E	26
Grantville, GA	f B	40
Granville, IL	i F	54
Granville, NY	d M	26
Granville, ND	c G	82
Granville, OH	g D	26
Granville, WV	h F	26
Grapeland, TX	h K	84
Grapevine Lake, TX	g l	84
Grasonville, MD	i J	26
Grass, r., NY	c K	26
Grass Creek, WY	g Q	112
Grassflat, PA	g H	26
Grass Lake, MI	h K	54
Grass Range, MT	c Q	112
Grass Valley, CA	c D	128
Grave Peak, ID	d K	112
Gravette, AR	f B	68
Gray, GA	f C	40
Gray, KY	c B	40
Grayback Mountain, OR	h B	112
Grayling, AK	e N	142
Grayling, MI	f K	54
Grays Harbor, WA	c A	112
Grayson, AL	h l	68
Grayson, KY	i D	26
Grayson, LA	j D	68
Grays Peak, CO	e K	98
Graysville, AL	i J	68
Grayville, IL	e H	68
Great Barrington, MA	e M	26
Great Basin, US	c C	8
Great Bend, KS	m l	84
Great Dismal Swamp, US	c J	40
Great Divide Basin, WY	h Q	112
Great Falls, MT	c N	112
Great Falls, SC	e F	40
Great Miami, r., US	h B	26
Great Pee Dee, r., SC	f G	40
Great Sacandaga Lake, NY	d L	26
Great Salt Lake, UT	c D	98
Great Salt Lake Desert, UT	d C	98
Great Smoky Mountains, US	d C	40
Great Smoky Mountains National Park, US	d C	40
Greece, NY	d l	26
Greeley, CO	d L	98
Greeley, KS	m L	82
Greeley, NE	j l	82
Greeleyville, SC	f G	40
Green, r., IL	i F	54
Green, r., KY	e J	68
Green, r., ND	d D	82
Green, r., WA	c C	112
Greenacres, WA	c H	112
Green Bay, WI	f H	54
Green Bay, US	f H	54
Greenbrier, AR	g D	68
Green Brier, TN	f J	68
Greenbrier, r., WV	b F	40
Greenburg, LA	l F	68

Name	Map Ref.	Page
Greenbush, MN	c K	82
Greencastle, IN	c J	68
Greencastle, PA	h I	26
Green City, MO	b D	68
Green Cove Springs, FL	j E	40
Greendale, IN	c L	68
Greene, IA	h C	54
Greene, NY	e K	26
Greeneville, TN	c D	40
Greenfield, CA	h D	128
Greenfield, IL	c F	68
Greenfield, IA	j M	82
Greenfield, MA	e N	26
Greenfield, MO	e C	68
Greenfield, OH	h C	26
Greenfield, TN	f H	68
Green Forest, AR	f C	68
Green Lake, WI	g G	54
Greenland, AR	g B	68
Greenland, MI	d F	54
Greenleaf, KS	i K	82
Green Mountains, VT	d N	26
Green Peter Lake, OR	f C	112
Green Pond, AL	i I	68
Greenport, NY	f N	26
Green River, UT	f F	98
Green River, WY	c G	98
Green River Lake, KY	e K	68
Greensboro, AL	j I	68
Greensboro, FL	i B	40
Greensboro, GA	f C	40
Greensboro, MD	i K	26
Greensboro, NC	c G	40
Greensburg, IN	c K	68
Greensburg, KS	h J	82
Greensburg, KY	e K	68
Greensburg, PA	g G	26
Greens Peak, AZ	j G	98
Green Springs, OH	f C	26
Green Swamp, NC	e H	40
Greentown, IN	b K	68
Greenup, IL	c H	68
Greenup, KY	i D	26
Green Valley, AZ	m F	98
Green Valley, IL	j F	54
Greenview, IL	b G	68
Greenville, AL	k J	68
Greenville, CA	d E	128
Greenville, FL	i C	40
Greenville, GA	f B	40
Greenville, IL	d G	68
Greenville, KY	e I	68
Greenville, ME	b Q	26
Greenville, MI	i E	54
Greenville, MS	i E	68
Greenville, MO	e F	68
Greenville, NH	e O	26
Greenville, NC	d I	40
Greenville, OH	g B	26
Greenville, PA	f F	26
Greenville, SC	e D	40
Greenville, TX	f J	84
Greenwich, CT	f M	26
Greenwich, NY	d M	26
Greenwich, OH	f D	26
Greenwood, AR	g B	68
Greenwood, IN	c J	68
Greenwood, MS	i F	68
Greenwood, NE	k K	82
Greenwood, SC	e D	40
Greenwood, WI	f E	54
Greenwood, Lake, SC	e D	40
Greer, SC	e D	40
Greers Ferry Lake, AR	g D	68
Gregory, MI	h F	54
Gregory, SD	h H	82
Gregory, TX	i I	84
Grenada, MS	i G	68
Grenola, KS	n K	82
Grenora, ND	c D	82
Gresham, OR	c E	112
Gresham Park, GA	f B	40
Gretna, LA	m F	68
Gretna, VA	c G	40
Greybull, WY	f Q	112
Greybull, r., WY	f Q	112
Grey Eagle, MN	e M	82
Greylock, Mount, MA	e M	26
Greys, r., WY	g O	112
Gridley, CA	d E	128
Gridley, IL	j G	54
Griffin, GA	d I	40
Grifton, NC	d I	40
Griggsville, IL	c F	68
Grinnell, IA	i C	54
Griswold, IA	j L	82
Groesbeck, TX	h J	84
Groom, TX	e I	84
Grosse Pointe, MI	h M	54
Gros Ventre, r., WY	g O	112
Groton, CT	f N	26
Groton, NY	e J	26
Groton, SD	f I	82
Grottoes, VA	i H	26
Grove, OK	c L	84
Grove City, MN	f M	82
Grove City, OH	h C	26
Grove City, PA	f F	26
Grove Hill, AL	k I	68
Groveland, FL	k E	40
Grover City, CA	i E	128
Groves, TX	m C	68
Groveton, NH	c O	26
Groveton, TX	h K	84
Grovetown, GA	f D	40
Gruetli-Laager, TN	g K	68
Grulla, TX	m H	84
Grundy, VA	b D	40
Grundy Center, IA	h C	54
Gruver, TX	c E	84
Gu Achi, AZ	l D	98
Guadalupe, CA	j E	128
Guadalupe, r., TX	k I	84
Guadalupe Mountains National Park, TX	h B	84
Guadalupe Peak, TX	h B	84
Guadalupita, NM	h K	98
Gualala, CA	f B	128
Guerneville, CA	f B	128
Guernsey, WY	b L	98
Gueydan, LA	l D	68
Guide Rock, NE	k I	82
Guildhall, VT	c O	26
Guilford, ME	b Q	26
Guin, AL	h I	68
Gulf Hammock, FL	j D	40
Gulfport, FL	l G	40
Gulfport, MS	l G	68
Gulf Shores, AL	l I	68
Gunnison, CO	f J	98
Gunnison, UT	e E	98
Gunnison, r., CO	f H	98
Guntersville, AL	h J	68
Guntersville Lake, AL	h J	68
Gurdon, AR	i C	68
Gustavus, AK	g AA	142
Gustine, CA	g E	128
Gustine, TX	h H	84
Guthrie, KY	f I	68
Guthrie, OK	c J	84
Guthrie, TX	f F	84
Guthrie Center, IA	j M	82
Guttenberg, IA	h D	54
Guyandotte, r., WV	b I	40
Guymon, OK	c E	84
Guyot, Mount, US	d C	40
Guyton, GA	g E	40
Gwinn, MI	d H	54
Gwinner, ND	i I	98
Gym Peak, NM	e J	98
Gypsum, CO	e J	98
Gypsum, KS	m J	82

H

Name	Map Ref.	Page
Hackberry, AZ	i C	98
Hackberry, LA	m C	68
Hackensack, NJ	g L	26
Hackett, AR	g B	68
Hackettstown, NJ	g L	26
Hackleburg, AL	h I	68
Haddam, KS	i J	82
Haddock, GA	f C	40
Hadlock, WA	b C	112
Haena Point, HI	c G	144b
Hagan, GA	g E	40
Hagerman, ID	h K	112
Hagerman, NM	f B	84
Hagerstown, IN	b L	68
Hagerstown, MD	h I	26
Haggin, Mount, MT	d L	112
Hague, ND	e H	82
Hagues Peak, CO	d K	98
Hahira, GA	i C	40
Haiku, HI	b D	144a
Hailey, ID	g K	112
Haileyville, OK	e K	84
Haines, AK	g AA	142
Haines, OR	f H	112
Haines City, FL	k E	40
Halalii Lake, HI	d F	144b
Halaula, HI	i P	144d
Halawa, Cape, HI	a C	144a
Halawa Heights, HI	f J	144c
Hale, MO	c C	68
Haleakala Crater, HI	b D	144a
Haleakala National Park, HI	b D	144a
Haleiwa, HI	e I	144c
Halekii-Pihana Heiaus State Monument, HI	b D	144a
Haleyville, AL	h I	68
Halfway, MD	h I	26
Halfway, OR	f H	112
Halifax, NC	c I	40
Halifax, VA	c H	40
Haliimaile, HI	b D	144a
Hallandale, FL	n F	40
Hallettsville, TX	j J	84
Halliday, ND	d E	82
Hallock, MN	c K	82
Hallowell, ME	c Q	26
Halls, TN	g G	68
Hallstead, PA	f K	26
Hallsville, MO	c B	68
Hallsville, TX	j B	68
Halsey, NE	j G	82
Halsey, OR	f B	112
Halstad, MN	d K	82
Halstead, KS	m J	82
Haltom City, TX	g I	84
Hamburg, AR	i E	68
Hamburg, IA	k L	82
Hamburg, NJ	f L	26
Hamburg, NY	e H	26
Hamburg, PA	g K	26
Hamden, CT	f N	26
Hamden, OH	h D	26
Hamilton, AL	h I	68
Hamilton, GA	g B	40
Hamilton, IL	j D	54
Hamilton, KS	n K	82
Hamilton, MI	h I	54
Hamilton, MO	c C	68
Hamilton, MT	d K	112
Hamilton, NY	e K	26
Hamilton, NC	d I	40
Hamilton, OH	h B	26
Hamilton, TX	h H	84
Hamilton, Mount, NV	e J	128
Hamilton City, CA	e C	128
Hamilton Dome, WY	a H	98
Hamlet, NC	e G	40
Hamlin, TX	g F	84
Hamlin, WV	i D	26
Hammon, OK	d G	84
Hammond, IN	a I	68
Hammond, LA	l F	68
Hammond, WI	f C	54
Hammondsport, NY	e I	26
Hammonton, NJ	h L	26
Hampden, ME	c R	26
Hampden, ND	c I	82
Hampden Sydney, VA	b H	40
Hampshire, IL	h G	54
Hampstead, NC	e I	40
Hampton, AR	i D	68
Hampton, FL	j D	40
Hampton, GA	f B	40
Hampton, IA	h B	54
Hampton, NE	k J	82
Hampton, NH	e P	26
Hampton, SC	g D	40
Hampton, TN	c D	40
Hampton, VA	b J	40
Hampton Bays, NY	g N	26
Hampton Butte, OR	e F	112
Hams Fork, r., WY	c F	98
Hana, HI	b E	144a
Hanahan, SC	g F	40
Hanakaoo Point, HI	b C	144a
Hanalei, HI	c G	144b
Hanamaulu, HI	d H	144b
Hanapepe, HI	d G	144b
Hanceville, AL	h H	68
Hancock, MD	h H	26
Hancock, MI	c G	54
Hancock, MN	f L	82
Hancock, NY	f K	26
Hancock, WI	f F	54
Hanford, CA	h F	128
Hankinson, ND	e K	82
Hanna, WY	c J	98
Hanna City, IL	j F	54
Hannaford, ND	d I	82
Hannah, ND	c I	82
Hannibal, MO	c E	68
Hanover, IL	h E	54
Hanover, IN	d K	68
Hanover, KS	i K	82
Hanover, NH	d N	26
Hanover, NM	i H	98
Hanover, PA	h J	26
Hanska, MN	g M	82
Hapeville, GA	f B	40
Happy, TX	e E	84
Happy Camp, CA	c B	128
Happy Jack, AZ	j E	98
Harbor, OR	h A	112
Harbor Beach, MI	g M	54
Harbor Springs, MI	e K	54
Harcuvar Mountains, AZ	k C	98
Hardeeville, SC	g E	40
Hardesty, OK	c E	84
Hardin, IL	c F	68
Hardin, MT	e R	112
Hardinsburg, KY	e J	68
Hardtner, KS	n I	82
Hardwick, GA	f C	40
Hardwick, VT	c N	26
Hardwood, LA	l E	68
Hardy, AR	f E	68
Hardy, NE	k J	82
Harkers Island, NC	e J	40
Harlan, IA	j L	82
Harlan, KY	c C	40
Harlan County Lake, NE	k H	82
Harlem, FL	m F	40
Harlem, GA	f D	40
Harlem, MT	b Q	112
Harlingen, TX	m I	84
Harlowton, MT	d P	112
Harman, WV	i G	26
Harmony, IN	c I	68
Harmony, MN	g C	54
Harney Peak, SD	h D	82
Harper, KS	n I	82
Harper, TX	i G	84
Harrell, AR	i D	68
Harriman, TN	d B	40
Harrington, DE	i K	26
Harrington, ME	c S	26
Harrington, WA	c G	112
Harris, MN	e C	54
Harrisburg, AR	g F	68
Harrisburg, IL	e H	68
Harrisburg, NE	j D	82
Harrisburg, OR	f B	112
Harrisburg, PA	g J	26
Harrison, AR	f C	68
Harrison, ID	c I	112
Harrison, MI	f K	54
Harrison, NE	i D	82
Harrisonburg, LA	k E	68
Harrisonburg, VA	i H	26
Harrisonville, MO	d B	68
Harriston, MS	k E	68
Harrisville, MI	f L	54
Harrisville, NY	c K	26
Harrisville, WV	h E	26
Harrodsburg, KY	e L	68
Harrold, TX	e G	84
Harry S. Truman Reservoir, MO	d C	68
Hart, TX	e D	84
Hart, MI	g I	54
Hartford, AL	k K	68
Hartford, AR	g B	68
Hartford, CT	f N	26
Hartford, KS	m L	82
Hartford, KY	e J	68
Hartford, MI	h I	54
Hartford, SD	h K	82
Hartford, WI	g G	54
Hartford City, IN	b K	68
Hartington, NE	i J	82
Hartland, ME	c Q	26
Hartley, IA	h L	82
Hartley, TX	d D	84
Hartselle, AL	h J	68
Hartshorne, OK	e K	84
Hartsville, SC	e F	40
Hartville, MO	e D	68
Hartwell, GA	e D	40
Hartwell Lake, US	e D	40
Harvard, IL	h G	54
Harvard, NE	k I	82
Harvey, IL	i H	54
Harvey, ND	d H	82
Haskell, OK	d K	84
Haskell, TX	f G	84
Hasperos Canyon, NM	k K	98
Hastings, FL	j E	40
Hastings, MI	h J	54
Hastings, MN	f C	54
Hastings, NE	k I	82
Hasty, CO	m E	82
Haswell, CO	m D	82
Hatch, NM	l I	98
Hatch, UT	g D	98
Hatchie, r., US	g G	68
Hatfield, AR	h B	68
Hatfield, MA	e N	26
Hatteras, NC	d K	40
Hatteras, Cape, NC	d K	40
Hatteras Island, NC	d K	40
Hattiesburg, MS	k G	68
Hatton, AL	h I	68
Hatton, ND	d J	82
Hauala, HI	e J	144c
Havana, AR	g C	68
Havana, FL	i B	40
Havana, IL	b F	68
Havana, ND	f J	82
Havasu Lake, US	j B	98
Havelock, NC	e J	40
Haven, NJ	n J	82
Haverhill, MA	e O	26
Haverhill, NH	d N	26
Havre, MT	b P	112
Havre de Grace, MD	h J	26
Havre North, MT	b P	112
Haw, r., NC	e G	40
Hawaii, HI	j P	144d
Hawaiian Islands, HI	h N	144d
Hawaii Volcanoes National Park, HI	j P	144d
Hawarden, IA	i K	82
Hawesville, KY	e J	68
Hawi, HI	i P	144d
Hawkins, TX	g K	84
Hawkins, WI	e E	54
Hawkinsville, GA	g C	40
Hawksbill, VA	i H	26
Hawley, MN	e K	82
Hawley, PA	f L	26
Hawthorne, FL	j D	40
Hawthorne, NV	f G	128
Haxtun, CO	k E	82
Hay, r., WI	e D	54
Hayden, AZ	k F	98
Hayden, CO	d I	98
Haydenville, OH	h D	26
Hayes, LA	l D	68
Hayes, Mount, AK	e U	142
Hayes Center, NE	k F	82
Hayesville, NC	d C	40
Hayesville, OH	g C	54
Hayfield, MN	g C	54
Hayfork, CA	d B	128
Haynes, AR	h F	68
Haynesville, LA	j C	68
Hayneville, AL	j J	68
Hays, KS	m H	82
Hays, MT	c Q	112
Hay Springs, NE	i E	82
Haystack Mountain, NV	c J	128
Haysville, KS	n J	82
Hayti, MO	f G	68
Hayti, SD	g J	82
Hayward, CA	g C	128
Hayward, WI	d D	54
Hazard, KY	b C	40
Hazel, r., VA	i I	26
Hazel Green, WI	h K	112
Hazelton, ID	h K	112
Hazelton, ND	e G	82
Hazelwood, NC	d C	40
Hazen, AR	h E	68
Hazen, ND	d F	82
Hazlehurst, GA	h D	40
Hazlehurst, MS	k F	68
Hazleton, IA	h D	54
Hazleton, PA	g K	26
Headland, AL	k K	68
Headley, Mount, MT	c J	112
Healdsburg, CA	f C	128
Healdton, OK	e I	84
Healy, AK	e T	142
Healy, KS	m G	82
Hearne, TX	i J	84
Heart, r., ND	e F	82
Heath Springs, SC	e F	40
Heathsville, VA	b J	40
Heavener, OK	h B	68
Hebbronville, TX	l F	84
Heber, AZ	j F	98
Heber, CA	l J	128
Heber City, UT	d E	98
Heber Springs, AR	g D	68
Hebron, IL	h G	54
Hebron, IN	a I	68
Hebron, MD	i K	26
Hebron, NE	k J	82
Hebron, ND	e E	82
Hecla, SD	f I	82
Hector, MN	g M	82
He Devil, ID	e I	112
Hedley, TX	e F	84
Hedrick, IA	i C	54
Heflin, AL	i K	68
Heidelberg, MS	k F	68
Helemano Stream, r., HI	e I	144c
Helena, AR	h F	68
Helena, MT	d M	112
Helena, OK	c H	84
Helenwood, TN	c B	40
Hellertown, PA	g K	26
Hells Canyon, US	e I	112
Helper, UT	e F	98
Hemet, CA	k I	128
Hemingford, NE	i D	82
Hemingway, SC	f G	40
Hemphill, TX	k C	68
Hempstead, TX	i J	84
Henderson, KY	e I	68
Henderson, MN	f B	54
Henderson, NE	k J	82
Henderson, NV	h K	128
Henderson, NC	c H	40
Henderson, TN	g H	68
Henderson, TX	j B	68
Hendersonville, NC	d D	40
Hendersonville, TN	g I	68
Hendricks, MN	g K	82
Hendricks, WV	h G	26
Henefer, UT	c E	98
Henlopen, Cape, DE	i K	26
Hennepin, IL	i F	54
Hennessey, OK	c I	84
Henniker, NH	d O	26
Henning, MN	e L	82
Henning, TN	g G	68
Henrietta, NY	d I	26
Henrietta, NC	d E	40
Henrietta, TX	f H	84
Henry, IL	i F	54
Henry, SD	g J	82
Henry, Cape, VA	c J	40
Henry, Mount, MT	b J	112
Henryetta, OK	d K	84
Henrys Fork, r., US	c F	98
Hensley, AR	h D	68
Hephzibah, GA	f D	40
Heppner, OR	e F	112
Herculaneum, MO	e E	68
Hereford, AZ	m F	98
Hereford, TX	e D	84
Herington, KS	m K	82
Herkimer, NY	d L	26
Herlong, CA	d E	128
Herman, MN	e K	82
Herman, NE	j K	82
Hermann, MO	d D	68
Hermansville, MI	e H	54
Hermanville, MS	k F	68
Hermiston, OR	e F	112
Hermitage, AR	i D	68
Hermitage, MO	e C	68
Hermleigh, TX	g F	84
Hernando, FL	k D	40
Hernando, MS	h G	68
Herndon, KS	l G	82
Herndon, PA	g J	26
Heron Lake, MN	g L	82
Herreid, SD	f G	82
Herring Cove, AK	i CC	142
Herscher, IL	i G	54
Hershey, NE	j F	82
Hershey, PA	g J	26
Hertford, NC	c J	40
Hesperia, CA	j I	128
Hesperus Mountain, CO	g H	98
Hesston, KS	m J	82
Hetch Hetchy Aqueduct, CA	g D	128
Hettinger, ND	e E	82
Heuvelton, NY	c K	26
Heyburn, ID	h L	112
Heyworth, IL	b H	68
Hialeah, FL	n F	40
Hiawassee, GA	e C	40
Hiawatha, KS	l L	82
Hiawatha, UT	e E	98
Hibbing, MN	c C	54
Hickam Air Force Base, HI	f J	144c
Hickman, KY	f G	68
Hickman, NE	k K	82
Hickory, MS	j G	68
Hickory, NC	d E	40
Hickory Flat, MS	h G	68
Hicksville, OH	f B	26
Hico, TX	h H	84
Higbee, MO	c D	68
Higgins, TX	c F	84
Higginsville, MO	c C	68
Highland, CA	j H	128
Highland, IL	d G	68
Highland, IN	a I	68
Highland, KS	l L	82
Highland Home, AL	k J	68
Highland Park, IL	h H	54
Highland Park, TX	g J	84
Highlands, NJ	g M	26
Highlands, NC	d D	40
Highlands, TX	j K	84
Highland Springs, VA	b I	40
Highmore, SD	g H	82
High Point, NC	d F	40
High Point, NJ	f L	26
High Rock Lake, NC	d F	40
High Springs, FL	j D	40
Hightstown, NJ	g L	26
Highwood, MT	c O	112
Hilbert, WI	f G	54
Hildreth, NE	k H	82
Hill City, KS	l H	82
Hill City, SD	h D	82
Hilliard, FL	i E	40
Hilliard, OH	g C	26
Hillcrest Center, CA	i G	128
Hillister, TX	l B	68
Hillman, MI	e L	54
Hills, MN	h K	82
Hillsboro, IL	c G	68
Hillsboro, KS	m J	82
Hillsboro, MO	d D	26
Hillsboro, NM	k J	98
Hillsboro, ND	d J	82
Hillsboro, OH	h C	26
Hillsboro, OR	e C	112
Hillsboro, TX	g I	84
Hillsboro, WI	g E	54
Hillsboro Canal, FL	m F	40
Hillsborough, NC	c G	40
Hillsborough, r., FL	k D	40
Hillsdale, MI	i K	54
Hillside Lake, KS	m M	82
Hillsville, VA	c F	40
Hilo, HI	j P	144d
Hilo Bay, HI	j P	144d
Hilton, NY	d I	26
Hilton Head Island, SC	g F	40
Hima, KY	b C	40
Hinchinbrook Entrance, AK	h F	60
Hinchinbrook Island, AK	f U	142
Hinckley, IL	i G	54
Hinckley, MN	d C	54
Hinckley, UT	e D	98
Hindman, KY	b D	40
Hines, OR	g F	112
Hinesville, GA	h E	40
Hingham, MA	e P	26
Hinsdale, MT	b R	112
Hinsdale, NH	e N	26
Hinton, OK	d H	84
Hinton, WV	b F	40
Hiram, ME	d P	26
Hitchcock, TX	j K	84
Hitchins, KY	i D	26
Hiwannee, MS	k H	68
Hiwassee, r., US	g K	68
Hixson, TN	g K	68
Hoback, r., WY	g O	112
Hobart, OK	d G	84
Hobbs, NM	g C	84
Hobe Sound, FL	l F	40
Hobgood, NC	c I	40
Hobson, MT	c P	112
Hocking, r., OH	h E	26
Hodge, LA	j D	68
Hodgenville, KY	e K	68
Hoehne, CO	n C	82
Hoffman, MN	f L	82
Hogansville, GA	f B	40
Hoh, r., WA	c A	112
Hohenwald, TN	g I	68
Hoisington, KS	m I	82
Hokah, MN	g C	54
Hokes Bluff, AL	i K	68
Holbrook, AZ	j F	98
Holbrook, NE	k G	82
Holden, MO	d C	68
Holden, UT	e D	98
Holden, WV	j D	26
Holdenville, OK	d J	84
Holder, FL	k D	40
Holdingford, MN	e A	54
Holdrege, NE	k H	82
Hole in the Mountain Peak, NV	d J	128
Holgate, OH	f B	26
Holladay, UT	d E	98
Holland, MI	h I	54
Holland, TX	i I	84
Hollandale, MS	i F	68
Holley, NY	d H	26
Holliday, TX	f H	84
Hollidaysburg, PA	g H	26
Hollins, VA	b G	40
Hollis, OK	e G	84
Hollister, CA	h D	128
Hollow Rock, TN	f H	68
Holly, CO	m E	82
Holly, MI	g L	54
Holly Grove, AR	h E	68
Holly Hill, FL	j E	40
Holly Hill, SC	f E	40
Holly Springs, MS	h G	68
Hollywood, FL	m F	40
Holmen, WI	f E	54
Holmes, Mount, WY	f O	112
Holstein, IA	i L	82
Holston, r., TN	c C	40
Holston High Knob, TN	i I	68
Holt, AL	i I	68
Holt, MI	h K	54
Holton, KS	l L	82
Holton, MI	g I	54
Holts Summit, MO	c D	68
Holtville, CA	l J	128
Holy Cross, AK	e O	142
Holyoke, CO	k E	82
Holyoke, MA	e N	26
Holyrood, KS	m I	82
Homedale, ID	g I	112
Homeland Park, SC	e D	40
Homer, AK	g S	142
Homer, GA	e C	40
Homer, LA	j C	68
Homer, MI	h K	54
Homer, NE	i K	82
Homer, NY	e J	26
Homer City, PA	g G	26
Homerville, GA	h D	40
Homestead, FL	n F	40
Homewood, AL	i J	68
Hominy, OK	c J	84
Homochitto, r., MS	k E	68
Homosassa, FL	k D	40
Honaker, VA	b E	40
Hondo, NM	i K	98
Hondo, TX	j G	84
Hondo, Rio, r., NM	f B	84
Honea Path, SC	e D	40
Honesdale, PA	f K	26
Honey Grove, TX	f K	84
Honey Lake, CA	d E	128
Honeyville, UT	c D	98
Honokaa, HI	a C	144a
Honokahua, HI	f J	144c
Honolulu, HI	i P	144d
Honomu, HI	j P	144d
Honouliuli, HI	f I	144c
Hood, Mount, OR	e D	112
Hood Canal, WA	c B	112
Hoodoo Peak, WA	b E	112
Hood River, OR	e D	112
Hoodsport, WA	c B	112
Hooker, OK	c E	84
Hooks, TX	i B	68
Hoolehua, HI	a B	144a
Hoonah, AK	g AA	142
Hoopa, CA	c B	128
Hooper, NE	j K	82
Hooper Bay, AK	f K	142
Hoopeston, IL	j H	54
Hoople, ND	c J	82
Hoosick Falls, NY	d M	26
Hoover Dam, US	h B	26
Hooversville, PA	g H	26
Hopatcong, NJ	g L	26
Hope, AR	i C	68
Hope, IN	c K	68
Hope, ND	d J	82
Hope, Point, AK	b K	142
Hopedale, IL	b G	68
Hopedale, LA	m G	68
Hope Mills, NC	e H	40
Hope Valley, RI	f O	26
Hopewell, VA	b I	40
Hopkins, MO	b B	68
Hopkinsville, KY	e I	68
Hopkinton, IA	h D	54
Hopland, CA	f B	128
Hoquiam, WA	d B	112
Horatio, AR	i B	68
Horicon, WI	g G	54
Hornbeak, TN	f G	68
Hornbeck, LA	k C	68
Hornbrook, CA	c C	128
Hornell, NY	e I	26
Horn Island, MS	l H	68
Horn Lake, MS	h F	68
Horse Cave, KY	e K	68
Horse Creek, WY	c K	98
Horseheads, NY	e J	26
Horseshoe Bend, AR	f E	68
Horseshoe Bend, ID	g I	112
Horton, KS	l L	82
Hortonville, WI	f G	54
Hosford, FL	i B	40
Hosmer, SD	f H	82
Hospers, IA	i L	82
Hosston, LA	j C	68
Hosta Butte, NM	f I	98
Hotchkiss, CO	f I	98
Hotevilla, AZ	i E	98
Hotham Inlet, AK	c N	142
Hot Springs, see Truth or Consequences, NM		
Hot Springs, NC	d D	40
Hot Springs, SD	h D	82
Hot Springs, VA	b G	40
Hot Springs National Park, AR	h C	68
Hot Sulphur Springs, CO	d J	98
Houghton, MI	c G	54
Houghton, NY	e H	26
Houghton Lake, MI	f K	54
Houghton Lake, MI	f K	54
Houlka, MS	h G	68
Houlton, ME	a S	26
Houma, LA	m F	68
Housatonic, MA	e M	26
House, NM	e C	84
Houston, MN	g D	54
Houston, MS	i H	68
Houston, MO	e E	68
Houston, TX	j K	84
Houston, r., LA	l C	68
Houston, Lake, TX	j K	84
Houtzdale, PA	g H	26
Hoven, SD	f H	82
Howard, KS	n K	82
Howard, PA	f I	26
Howard, SD	g J	82
Howard, WI	f G	54
Howard City, MI	g J	54
Howard Lake, MN	e A	54
Howe, IN	a K	68
Howe, TX	f J	84
Howell, MI	h L	54
Howells, NE	j J	82
Howland, ME	b R	26
Hoxie, AR	f F	68
Hoxie, KS	l G	82
Hoyleton, IL	d G	68
Hoyt Lakes, MN	c C	54
Huachuca City, AZ	m F	98
Hualalai, HI	j P	144d
Hualapai Peak, AZ	i C	98
Hubbard, IA	h B	54
Hubbard, TX	h J	84
Hubbard Creek Reservoir, TX	g G	84
Hubbard Lake, MI	f L	54
Hubbell, MI	c G	54
Hudson, IA	h C	54
Hudson, MA	e O	26
Hudson, MI	i K	54
Hudson, NH	e O	26
Hudson, NY	e M	26
Hudson, OH	f D	26
Hudson, SD	h K	82
Hudson, WI	f C	54
Hudson, WY	b H	98
Hudson, r., US	f L	26
Hudson, Lake, OK	c K	84
Hudson-Bayonet Point, FL	k D	40
Hudson Falls, NY	d M	26
Hudsonville, MI	h J	54
Huerfano, r., CO	m C	82
Huerfano Mountain, NM	h I	98
Hueytown, AL	i J	68
Hugh Butler Lake, NE	k G	82
Hughes, AK	c Q	142
Hughes, AR	h F	68
Hughes Springs, TX	i B	68
Hughesville, PA	f J	26
Hughson, CA	g E	128
Hugo, CO	l D	82
Hugo, OK	e K	84
Hugoton, KS	n F	82
Hulbert, MI	d J	54
Hulbert, OK	g A	68
Hulett, WY	g C	82
Hull, IL	h K	82
Hull, IA	h K	82
Hull, TX	i L	84
Humansville, MO	e C	68
Humbird, WI	f E	54
Humboldt, AZ	j D	98
Humboldt, IL	c H	68
Humboldt, IA	i M	82
Humboldt, KS	n L	82
Humboldt, NE	k L	82
Humboldt, SD	h J	82
Humboldt, TN	g H	68
Humboldt, r., NV	d G	128
Hume, CA	h G	128
Humeston, IA	j B	54
Humphrey, AR	h E	68
Humphrey, NE	j J	82
Humphreys, Mount, CA	j K	82
Humphreys Peak, AZ	i E	98
Humptulips, r., WA	c B	112
Hundred, WV	h F	26
Hungerford, TX	j J	84
Hungry Horse, MT	b K	112
Hungry Horse Reservoir, MT	b L	112
Hunter, ND	d J	82
Hunter, Mount, AK	e S	142
Huntersville, NC	d F	40
Huntingburg, IN	d J	68
Huntingdon, PA	g H	26
Huntingdon, TN	f H	68
Huntington, IN	b K	68
Huntington, OR	f H	112
Huntington, TX	k B	68
Huntington, UT	e F	98
Huntington, WV	i D	26
Huntington Beach, CA	k H	128
Huntland, TN	g J	68
Huntley, MT	e Q	112
Huntley, IL	h G	54
Hunt Mountain, WY	f R	112
Huntsville, AL	h J	68
Huntsville, AR	f C	68
Huntsville, MO	c D	68
Huntsville, TN	c B	40
Huntsville, TX	i K	84
Huntsville, UT	c E	98
Hurley, MS	l H	68
Hurley, NM	i H	98
Hurley, SD	h J	82
Hurley, WI	d E	54
Hurlock, MD	i K	26
Huron, CA	h E	128
Huron, OH	f D	26
Huron, SD	g I	82
Huron, r., MI	h L	54
Huron, Lake, NA	f M	54
Hurricane, UT	g C	98
Hurricane, WV	i D	26
Hurricane Cliffs, US	g C	98
Hurt, VA	b G	40
Hurtsboro, AL	j K	68
Huslia, AK	d P	142
Hustisford, WI	g G	54
Hutchinson, KS	m J	82
Hutchinson, MN	f A	54
Hutsonville, IL	c I	68
Huttig, AR	i D	68
Hutto, TX	i I	84
Huxford, AL	k I	68
Hyannis, MA	f P	26
Hyannis, NE	i F	82
Hyattville, WY	f R	112
Hyco, r., US	c H	40
Hydaburg, AK	i BB	142
Hyden, KY	b C	40
Hyde Park, NY	f M	26
Hyde Park, VT	c N	26
Hydro, OK	d H	84
Hymera, IN	c I	68
Hyndman, PA	h H	26
Hyndman Peak, ID	g K	112
Hyrum, UT	c E	98
Hysham, MT	d R	112

I

Name	Map Ref.	Page
Iaeger, WV	b E	40
Ibapah Peak, UT	e C	98
Iberia, MO	d D	68
Iceberg Pass, CO	d K	98
Icy Bay, AK	f X	142
Ida, IL	i L	54
Ida Grove, IA	i L	82
Idabel, OK	i B	68
Idaho, state, US	c D	8
Idaho City, ID	g J	112
Idaho Falls, ID	g M	112
Idaho Springs, CO	e K	98
Idalou, TX	f E	84
Idanha, OR	e C	112
Idel, MN	c C	54
Idlewild, CA	k I	128
Ignacio, CO	g I	98
Iliamna, AK	g Q	142
Iliamna Lake, AK	g Q	142
Iliff, CO	k D	82
Ilion, NY	d K	26
Ilio Point, HI	a B	144a
Illinois, r., US	f B	68
Illinois, r., IL	i F	54
Illinois, r., OR	h B	112
Illinois, r., US	c J	68
Illiopolis, IL	c G	68
Imboden, AR	f E	68
Imlay, NV	d G	128
Imlay City, MI	g L	54
Immokalee, FL	m E	40
Imperial, CA	l J	128
Imperial, NE	k F	82
Imperial, TX	h D	84
Imperial Beach, CA	l H	128
Imperial Valley, CA	l J	128

Ina, IL — d H 68
Incline Village, NV — e F 128
Independence, CA — h G 128
Independence, IA — h D 54
Independence, KS — n L 82
Independence, KY — i B 26
Independence, LA — l F 68
Independence, MO — c B 68
Independence, OR — f B 112
Independence, VA — c E 40
Independence, WI — f D 54
Independence, r., NY — d K 26
Independence Mountains, NV — c I 128
Indialantic, FL — k F 40
Indian, r., MI — d I 54
Indiana, PA — g G 26
Indiana, state, US — c I 8
Indiana Dunes National Lakeshore, IN — a I 68
Indianapolis, IN — c J 68
Indian Lake, NY — d L 26
Indianola, IA — i B 54
Indianola, MS — i F 68
Indianola, NE — k G 82
Indian Peak, UT — f C 98
Indian Peak, WY — f P 112
Indian River, MI — e K 54
Indian River, FL — k F 40
Indian Springs, NV — h J 128
Indiantown, FL — l F 40
Indio, CA — k I 128
Industry, IL — b F 68
Industry, TX — j J 84
Inez, KY — b D 40
Inez, TX — k J 84
Ingleside, TX — l I 84
Inglewood, CA — k G 128
Ingram, TX — i G 84
Inkom, ID — h M 112
Inkster, ND — c J 82
Inman, KS — m J 82
Inman, SC — d D 40
Inman Mills, SC — d D 40
Inola, OK — c K 84
Inspiration, AZ — k F 98
International Falls, MN — b B 54
Intracoastal Waterway, US — h E 40
Intracoastal Waterway, US — m B 68
Intracoastal Waterway, US — k J 84
Inverness, CA — f C 128
Inverness, FL — k D 40
Inverness, MS — i F 68
Inwood, IA — h K 82
Inyokern, CA — i H 128
Iola, KS — n L 82
Iola, WI — f F 54
Iona, ID — g N 112
Ione, CA — f E 128
Ione, OR — e F 112
Ione, WA — b H 112
Ionia, MI — h J 54
Iota, LA — l D 68
Iowa, LA — l C 68
Iowa, state, US — c H 8
Iowa, r., IA — i D 54
Iowa City, IA — i D 54
Iowa Falls, IA — h B 54
Iowa Park, TX — h H 84
Ipava, IL — b F 68
Ipswich, MA — e P 26
Ipswich, SD — f H 82
Ira, TX — g E 84
Iraan, TX — i E 84
Irene, SD — h J 82
Ireton, IA — i K 82
Irish, Mount, NV — g J 128
Iron Belt, WI — d E 54
Iron City, TN — g I 68
Irondale, AL — i J 68
Irondale, MO — e F 68
Irondequoit, NY — d I 26
Iron Mountain, MI — e G 54
Iron Mountains, US — c E 40
Iron River, MI — d G 54
Iron River, WI — d D 54
Ironton, MN — d B 54
Ironton, MO — e F 68
Ironton, OH — i D 26
Ironwood, MI — d E 54
Iroquois, SD — g J 82
Iroquois, r., US — j H 54
Irrigon, OR — e F 112
Irvine, CA — k G 128
Irvine, KY — b C 40
Irving, IL — c G 68
Irving, TX — g J 84
Irvington, KY — e J 68
Irwinton, GA — g C 40
Isabel, SD — f F 82
Isabelle, r., MN — c D 54
Isanti, MN — e B 54
Ishpeming, MI — d H 54
Island, KY — e J 68
Island Falls, ME — a R 26
Island Park, ID — f N 112
Island Park Reservoir, ID — f N 112
Island Pond, VT — c O 26
Isla Vista, CA — j F 128
Isle, MN — d B 54
Isle of Hope, GA — h E 40
Isle of Palms, SC — g G 40
Isle of Wight, VA — c J 40
Isle Royale National Park, MI — b G 54
Islesboro Island, ME — c R 26
Isleta, NM — j J 98
Isleton, CA — f E 128
Isola, MS — i F 68
Israel, r., NH — c O 26
Isto, Mount, AK — b W 142
Istokpoga, Lake, FL — l E 40
Italy, TX — g J 84
Itasca, TX — g I 84
Itasca, Lake, MN — d L 82
Ithaca, MI — g K 54
Ithaca, NY — e J 26
Itta Bena, MS — i F 68
Iuka, MS — h H 68
Iva, SC — d D 40
Ivanhoe, CA — h F 128
Ivanhoe, MN — g K 82
Ivanhoe, VA — c F 40

J
Jacinto City, TX — j K 84
Jackman, ME — b P 26
Jack Mountain, WA — b E 112
Jackpot, NV — c K 128
Jacksboro, TN — c B 40

Jacksboro, TX — f H 84
Jacks Fork, r., MO — e E 68
Jackson, AL — k l 68
Jackson, CA — f E 128
Jackson, GA — f C 40
Jackson, KY — b C 40
Jackson, LA — l E 68
Jackson, MI — h K 54
Jackson, MN — h M 82
Jackson, MS — j F 68
Jackson, MO — e G 68
Jackson, NC — c l 40
Jackson, OH — h D 26
Jackson, SC — f E 40
Jackson, TN — g H 68
Jackson, WY — a F 98
Jackson Center, OH — g B 26
Jackson Lake, WY — g O 112
Jacksonville, AL — i K 68
Jacksonville, AR — h D 68
Jacksonville, FL — i E 40
Jacksonville, IL — c F 68
Jacksonville, NC — e l 40
Jacksonville, OR — h C 112
Jacksonville, TX — h K 84
Jacksonville Beach, FL — i E 40
Jacumba, CA — l l 128
Jaffrey, NH — e N 26
Jake Creek Mountain, NV — c l 128
Jal, NM — j d 84
James, r., US — h J 82
James, r., MO — e C 68
James, r., VA — b l 40
James City, NC — d l 40
James Island, SC — g G 40
Jamesport, MO — c C 68
Jamestown, CA — g E 128
Jamestown, KS — l J 82
Jamestown, KY — f K 68
Jamestown, NY — e G 26
Jamestown, NC — d G 40
Jamestown, ND — d J 82
Jamestown, OH — h C 26
Jamestown, TN — f L 68
Jamestown Reservoir, ND — d l 82
Janesville, CA — d E 128
Janesville, MN — f B 54
Janesville, WI — h F 54
Jarales, NM — j J 98
Jarbidge, r., US — h J 112
Jarratt, VA — c l 40
Jarreau, LA — l E 68
Jarvisburg, NC — c K 40
Jasonville, IN — c l 68
Jasper, AL — i l 68
Jasper, AR — f C 68
Jasper, FL — i D 40
Jasper, GA — e B 40
Jasper, IN — d J 68
Jasper, MN — h K 82
Jasper, MO — e B 68
Jasper, TN — g K 68
Jasper, TX — l C 68
Java, SD — f H 82
Jay, FL — l l 68
Jay, OK — c L 84
Jayton, TX — f F 84
Jeanerette, LA — m E 68
Jeffers, MN — g L 82
Jefferson, GA — e C 40
Jefferson, IA — i M 82
Jefferson, NC — c E 40
Jefferson, OH — f F 26
Jefferson, OR — f B 112
Jefferson, SC — e F 40
Jefferson, SD — i K 82
Jefferson, TX — j B 68
Jefferson, WI — h G 54
Jefferson, r., MT — e M 112
Jefferson, Mount, US — f N 112
Jefferson, Mount, NV — f l 128
Jefferson, Mount, OR — f D 112
Jefferson City, MO — d D 68
Jefferson City, TN — c C 40
Jeffersonton, VA — i l 26
Jeffersontown, KY — d K 68
Jefferson Valley, GA — d C 40
Jeffersonville, IN — d H 68
Jeffersonville, OH — h C 26
Jeffrey City, WY — h E 40
Jekyll Island, GA — h E 40
Jellico, TN — f B 40
Jelm Mountain, WY — a W 142
Jemez, r., NM — i l 98
Jemez Springs, NM — i J 98
Jena, LA — k D 68
Jenkins, KY — b C 40
Jenkinsville, SC — e E 40
Jenkintown, PA — g K 26
Jenks, OK — c K 84
Jennings, FL — i C 40
Jennings, LA — l D 68
Jensen, UT — d E 98
Jensen Beach, FL — l F 40
Jerimoth Hill, RI — f O 26
Jerome, AZ — j D 98
Jerome, ID — h K 112
Jersey City, NJ — g L 26
Jersey Mountain, ID — e J 112
Jersey Shore, PA — f l 26
Jerseyville, IL — c F 68
Jessup, PA — f K 26
Jesup, GA — h E 40
Jesup, IA — h C 54
Jet, OK — c H 84
Jetmore, KS — m H 82
Jewell, IA — h B 54
Jewell, KS — l l 82
Jewell Ridge, VA — b E 40
Jewett, IL — c G 68
Jewett, TX — h J 84
Jewett City, CT — f O 26
Jim Thorpe, PA — g K 26
Joanna, SC — e D 40
Joaquin, TX — k B 68
Job Peak, NV — f E 128
Johannesburg, CA — i H 128
John Day, OR — f G 112
John Day, r., OR — e E 112
John H. Kerr Reservoir, US — c H 40
John Martin Reservoir, CO — m D 82
John Redmond Reservoir, KS — m L 82
Johnson, KS — n F 82
Johnson, NE — k L 82
Johnson, VT — c O 26
Johnsonburg, PA — f H 26
Johnson City, NY — e J 26
Johnson City, TN — c D 40
Johnson City, TX — i H 84

Johnsondale, CA — i G 128
Johnsonville, SC — f G 40
Johnston, IA — i B 54
Johnston, SC — f E 40
Johnston City, IL — e H 68
Johnstown, CO — d L 98
Johnstown, NY — d L 26
Johnstown, OH — g D 26
Johnstown, PA — g H 26
Joiner, AR — g F 68
Joliet, IL — i G 54
Joliet, MT — e Q 112
Jones, OK — d l 84
Jonesboro, AR — g F 68
Jonesboro, GA — f B 40
Jonesboro, IL — e G 68
Jonesboro, LA — j D 68
Jonesboro, TN — c D 40
Jonesburg, MO — d E 68
Jones Mill, AR — h D 68
Jonesport, ME — c S 26
Jonestown, MS — h F 68
Jonesville, LA — k E 68
Jonesville, MI — i K 54
Jonesville, NC — c F 40
Jonesville, SC — e E 40
Jonesville, VA — c C 40
Joplin, MO — e B 68
Joplin, MT — b O 112
Joppa, IL — e H 68
Jordan, MN — f B 54
Jordan, MT — c S 112
Jordan, NY — d J 26
Jordan, r., UT — d E 98
Jordan Valley, OR — h H 112
Jornado del Muerto, NM — k J 98
Joseph, OR — e H 112
Joseph City, AZ — j F 98
Joshua, TX — g l 84
Joshua Tree, CA — j l 128
Jourdanton, TX — k H 84
Joy, IL — i E 54
Joyce, LA — k D 68
J. Percy Priest Lake, TN — f J 68
Juan de Fuca, Strait of, NA — i l J 24
Judith, r., MT — c P 112
Judith Gap, MT — d P 112
Judith Mountains, MT — c P 112
Judson, SC — e D 40
Judsonia, AR — g E 68
Julesburg, CO — k E 82
Jump, r., WI — e E 54
Junction, TX — i G 84
Junction, UT — f D 98
Junction City, AR — i D 68
Junction City, KS — l K 82
Junction City, KY — e L 68
Junction City, OR — f B 112
Juneau, AK — g AA 142
Juneau, WI — g G 54
June Lake, CA — g F 128
Juniata, NE — k l 82
Juniata, r., PA — g l 26
Junior, WV — i G 26
Jupiter, FL — m F 40

K
Kaaawa, HI — e J 144c
Kaala, HI — e l 144c
Kaalaea, HI — e l 144c
Kabetogama Lake, MN — b G 54
Kachemak Bay, AK — g S 142
Kadoka, SD — h F 82
Kaena Point, HI — e l 144c
Kahaluu, HI — f J 144c
Kahana Bay, HI — e J 144c
Kahiu Point, HI — a C 144a
Kahoka, MO — b E 68
Kahoolawe, HI — b C 144a
Kahuku, HI — e J 144c
Kahuku Point, HI — e J 144c
Kahului, HI — b D 144a
Kahului Bay, HI — b D 144a
Kaibab Plateau, AZ — h D 98
Kaibito Plateau, AZ — h E 98
Kailua, HI — f J 144c
Kailua Kona, HI — j P 144d
Kaiwi Channel, HI — f J 144d
Kake, AK — h BB 142
Kaktovik, AK — a W 142
Ka Lae, HI — k P 144d
Kalaheo, HI — d G 144b
Kalama, WA — d C 112
Kalamazoo, MI — h J 54
Kalamazoo, r., MI — h l 54
Kalaupapa, HI — a C 144a
Kalaupapa National Historical Park, HI — a C 144a
Kalaupapa Peninsula, HI — a C 144a
Kalispell, MT — a K 112
Kalkaska, MI — f J 54
Kalohi Channel, HI — b C 144a
Kalona, IA — i D 54
Kalskag, AK — f N 142
Kaltag, AK — e N 142
Kamakou, HI — a C 144a
Kamas, UT — d E 98
Kamay, TX — h H 84
Kamiah, ID — d l 112
Kamishak Bay, AK — g R 142
Kampsville, IL — c F 68
Kamuela (Waimea), HI — i P 144d
Kanab, UT — g D 98
Kanab Plateau, US — g D 98
Kanaga Volcano, AK — k F 142
Kanarraville, UT — g C 98
Kanawha, IA — h B 54
Kanawha, r., WV — i D 26
Kane, IL — c F 68
Kane, PA — f H 26
Kaneohe, HI — f J 144c
Kaneohe Bay, HI — f J 144c
Kaneohe Bay Marine Corps Air Station, HI — f J 144c
Kankakee, IL — i H 54
Kankakee, r., US — a H 68
Kannapolis, NC — d F 40
Kanopolis, KS — m l 82
Kanorado, KS — l E 82
Kanosh, UT — e l 98
Kansas, IL — c l 68
Kansas, state, US — d G 8
Kansas, r., KS — l K 82
Kansas City, KS — l M 82
Kansas City, MO — c B 68
Kantishna, AK — d S 142
Kapaa, HI — c H 144b
Kaplan, LA — m D 68
Karlstad, MN — c K 82

Karnack, TX — j B 68
Karnak, IL — e H 68
Karnes City, TX — k l 84
Karthaus, PA — f H 26
Kasaan, AK — i BB 142
Kashunuk, r., AK — f L 142
Kasigluk, AK — f M 142
Kaskaskia, r., IL — d G 68
Kasota, MN — f B 54
Kasson, MN — g F 54
Katahdin, Mount, ME — b R 26
Kauai, HI — c H 144b
Kauai Channel, HI — h M 144d
Kau Desert, HI — j P 144d
Kaufman, TX — g J 84
Kauiki Head, HI — b E 144a
Kaukauna, WI — f G 54
Kaulakahi Channel, HI — c G 144b
Kaumakani, HI — d G 144b
Kaunakakai, HI — a C 144a
Kaw, OK — c J 84
Kawaihae Bay, HI — i P 144d
Kawaihoa, HI — d F 144b
Kawaikini, HI — c H 144b
Kawailoa, HI — e l 144c
Kawailoa Beach, HI — e l 144c
Kawich Peak, NV — g l 128
Kaw Lake, OK — c J 84
Kayak Island, AK — g V 142
Kaycee, WY — a J 98
Kayenta, AZ — h F 98
Kaysville, UT — c E 98
Keaau, HI — j P 144d
Keahole Point, HI — j O 144d
Kealaikahiki, Lae o, HI — b C 144a
Kealaikahiki Channel, HI — b C 144a
Kealia, HI — c H 144b
Kealakekua Bay, HI — j P 144d
Kealia, HI — c H 144b
Keams Canyon, AZ — i F 98
Keanae, HI — b D 144a
Keanapapa Point, HI — b B 144a
Kearney, MO — c B 68
Kearney, NE — k H 82
Kearns, UT — d E 98
Kearny, AZ — k F 98
Keene, KY — b B 40
Keene, NH — e N 26
Keene, TX — g l 84
Keenesburg, CO — d L 98
Keeseville, NY — c M 26
Keewatin, MN — c B 54
Keiser, AR — g F 68
Keithsburg, IL — i E 54
Keizer, OR — f B 112
Kekaha, HI — d G 144b
Kelleys Island, OH — f D 26
Kellogg, ID — c l 112
Kellogg, IA — i C 54
Kellogg, MN — f D 54
Kellyville, OK — d J 84
Kelseyville, CA — f C 128
Kelso, WA — d C 112
Kemah, TX — j K 84
Kemmerer, WY — c F 98
Kemp, TX — g J 84
Kemp, Lake, TX — f G 84
Kempner, TX — h H 84
Kenai, AK — f S 142
Kenai Peninsula, AK — g S 142
Kenansville, FL — l F 40
Kenansville, NC — e l 40
Kenbridge, VA — c H 40
Kendall, FL — n F 40
Kendall, WI — g E 54
Kendallville, IN — a K 68
Kendrick, FL — j D 40
Kendrick, ID — d l 112
Kenedy, TX — l l 84
Kenesaw, NE — k l 82
Kenilworth, UT — e F 98
Kenly, NC — d H 40
Kenmare, ND — c E 82
Kennard, TX — h K 84
Kennebec, SD — h H 82
Kennebec, r., ME — c Q 26
Kennebunk, ME — d P 26
Kennedy, AL — i l 68
Kennedy, Cape, see Canaveral, Cape, FL — k F 40
Kennedy Entrance, AK — g R 142
Kenner, LA — m F 68
Kennett, MO — f F 68
Kennett Square, PA — h K 26
Kennewick, WA — d F 112
Kenosha, WI — h H 54
Kenova, WV — i D 26
Kensal, ND — d l 82
Kensett, AR — g E 68
Kensington, KS — l H 82
Kensington Park, FL — l D 40
Kent, OH — f E 26
Kent, WA — c C 112
Kentland, IN — b l 68
Kenton, MI — d G 54
Kenton, OH — g C 26
Kenton, TN — f G 68
Kentucky, state, US — d l 8
Kentucky, r., KY — d K 68
Kentucky Lake, US — f H 68
Kentwood, LA — l F 68
Kenyon, MN — f C 54
Keokea, HI — b D 144a
Keokuk, IA — b E 68
Keokuk, r., IA — j D 54
Keosauqua, IA — j D 54
Keota, IA — i D 54
Keota, OK — d L 84
Kerby, OR — h B 112
Kerens, TX — g J 84
Kerhoven, MN — f L 82
Kerman, CA — h E 128
Kermit, TX — h C 84
Kern, r., CA — i G 128
Kernersville, NC — c F 40
Kernville, CA — i G 128
Kerrville, TX — i G 84
Kershaw, SC — e F 40
Keshena, WI — f G 54
Ketchikan, AK — i CC 142
Ketchum, ID — g K 112
Kettering, OH — h B 26
Kettle, r., NA — b P 24
Kettle, r., MN — d C 54
Kettle Falls, WA — b G 112
Keuka Lake, NY — e l 26
Kevin, MT — b N 112
Kewanee, IL — i F 54
Kewanna, IN — a J 68
Kewaskum, WI — g G 54
Kewaunee, WI — f H 54
Keweenaw Bay, MI — c G 54
Keweenaw Peninsula, MI — c G 54
Keweenaw Point, MI — c H 54
Keya Paha, r., US — i H 82
Keyes, CA — c D 84
Key Largo, FL — n F 40

Key Largo, FL — n F 40
Keyser, WV — h H 26
Keystone, IA — i C 54
Keystone, SD — h D 82
Keystone, WV — b E 40
Keystone Lake, OK — c J 84
Keysville, VA — c H 40
Keytesville, MO — c D 68
Key West, FL — o E 40
Kiamichi, r., OK — e K 84
Kiana, AK — c N 142
Kickapoo, r., WI — g E 54
Kiel, WI — g G 54
Kiester, MN — g B 54
Kihei, HI — b D 144a
Kilauea, HI — c G 144b
Kilauea Crater, HI — j P 144d
Kilauea Point, HI — c H 144b
Kilgore, TX — j B 68
Killbuck, OH — g E 26
Killdeer, ND — d E 82
Killeen, TX — h l 84
Killen, AL — h l 68
Killington Peak, VT — d N 26
Kilmarnock, VA — b J 40
Kilmichael, MS — i G 68
Kim, CO — n D 82
Kimball, MN — e A 54
Kimball, NE — j B 82
Kimball, SD — h l 82
Kimberling City, MO — f C 68
Kimberly, ID — h K 112
Kimberly, WI — f G 54
Kincaid, IL — c G 68
Kinder, LA — l D 68
Kindred, ND — e J 82
King, NC — c F 40
King and Queen Court House, VA — b J 40
King City, CA — h D 128
King City, MO — b B 68
King Cove, AK — i M 142
Kingfield, ME — c P 26
Kingfisher, OK — d l 84
King George, VA — i l 26
King Hill, ID — g J 112
King Lear Peak, NV — c G 128
Kingman, AZ — i B 98
Kingman, KS — n l 82
Kings, r., AR — f C 68
Kings, r., CA — h F 128
Kings, r., NV — c G 128
King Salmon, AK — g P 142
Kings Beach, CA — e E 128
Kings Canyon National Park, CA — h G 128
Kingsford, MI — e G 54
Kingsland, AR — i D 68
Kingsland, GA — i E 40
Kingsland, TX — i H 84
Kingsley, IA — i L 82
Kingsley, MI — f J 54
Kings Mountain, NC — d E 40
Kings Peak, UT — d F 98
Kingsport, TN — c D 40
Kingston, GA — e B 40
Kingston, MA — f P 26
Kingston, MO — c B 68
Kingston, NY — f M 26
Kingston, OH — h D 26
Kingston, OK — f J 84
Kingston, PA — f K 26
Kingston, TN — d B 40
Kingstree, SC — f G 40
Kingsville, TX — l l 84
King William, VA — b l 40
Kingwood, WV — h G 26
Kinmundy, IL — d H 68
Kinross, MI — d K 54
Kinsley, KS — n H 82
Kinsman, OH — f F 26
Kinston, AL — k J 68
Kinston, NC — d l 40
Kinzua, OR — f E 112
Kiowa, CO — l C 82
Kiowa, KS — n l 82
Kiowa, OK — e K 84
Kipnuk, AK — g L 142
Kirbyville, TX — l C 68
Kirkland, IL — h G 54
Kirkland, TX — e F 84
Kirkland, WA — c C 112
Kirklin, IN — b J 68
Kirksville, MO — b D 68
Kirkwood, IL — j E 54
Kirkwood, MO — a K 68
Kirtland, NM — h H 98
Kirwin, KS — l H 82
Kiska Island, AK — j C 143a
Kissimmee, FL — k E 40
Kissimmee, r., FL — l F 40
Kissimmee, Lake, FL — l F 40
Kit Carson, CO — m E 82
Kittanning, PA — g G 26
Kittery, ME — d P 26
Kittitas, WA — d E 112
Klamath, r., US — h C 128
Klamath, r., KY — c A 128
Klamath Falls, OR — h D 112
Klamath Mountains, US — d C 128
Klawock, AK — i BB 142
Klemme, IA — h B 54
Klickitat, WA — e D 112
Klickitat, r., WA — d D 112
Klukwan, AK — g AA 142
Knapp, WI — f G 54
Knickerbocker, TX — h F 84
Knife, r., ND — c F 82
Knights Landing, CA — f D 128
Knightstown, IN — c K 68
Knik Arm, AK — f T 142
Knippa, TX — j G 84
Knob Noster, MO — d C 68
Knox, IN — a I 68
Knox, PA — f G 26
Knoxville, GA — g C 40
Knoxville, IA — i B 54
Knoxville, IL — i E 54
Knoxville, TN — c B 40
Kobuk, AK — c P 142
Kobuk, r., AK — c N 142
Kodiak, AK — g Q 142
Kodiak Island, AK — h Q 142
Kokee State Park, HI — c G 144b
Koko Head, HI — f J 144c
Kokomo, HI — b D 144a
Kokomo, IN — b J 68
Koloa, HI — d G 144b
Kona Coast, HI — j P 144d
Konawa, OK — e J 84

Koocanusa, Lake, NA — b J 112
Koolau Range, HI — e J 144c
Koontz Lake, IN — a J 68
Koosharem, UT — f E 98
Kooskia, ID — d J 112
Kootenai (Kootenay), r., NA — i R 24
Kosciusko, MS — i G 68
Koshkonong, MO — f E 68
Kosse, TX — h J 84
Kotzebue, AK — c M 142
Kotzebue Sound, AK — c M 142
Koula, r., HI — d G 144b
Kountze, TX — l B 68
Kouts, IN — a l 68
Koyuk, AK — d N 142
Koyukuk, AK — d P 142
Koyukuk, r., AK — d Q 142
Krebs, OK — e K 84
Kremmling, CO — d J 98
Kress, TX — e E 84
Krotz Springs, LA — l E 68
Kruzof Island, AK — h AA 142
Kualapuu, HI — a B 144a
Kuee Ruins, HI — j P 144d
Kuiu Island, AK — h AA 142
Kula, HI — b C 144a
Kulm, ND — e l 82
Kumukahi, Cape, HI — j Q 144d
Kuna, ID — g l 112
Kunia, HI — f l 144c
Kupreanof Island, AK — h BB 142
Kurtistown, HI — j P 144d
Kuskokwim, r., AK — f N 142
Kuskokwim Mountains, AK — e P 142
Kutztown, PA — g K 26
Kwethluk, AK — f N 142
Kwigillingok, AK — g M 142
Kykotsmovi Village, AZ — i F 98
Kyle, SD — h E 82
Kyle, TX — j l 84

L
Laau Point, HI — a B 144a
Labadieville, LA — m F 68
La Barge, WY — b F 98
La Belle, FL — m E 40
La Belle, MO — b E 68
Lac du Flambeau, WI — d E 54
La Center, KY — e H 68
Laclede, ID — b C 112
Laclede, MO — c C 68
Lacombe, LA — l G 68
Lacon, IL — i F 54
Laconia, NH — d O 26
La Conner, WA — b C 112
Lacoochee, FL — k D 40
La Coste, TX — j G 84
Lac qui Parle, r., MN — g K 82
Lacrosse, WA — d H 112
La Crosse, IN — a J 68
La Crosse, KS — m H 82
La Crosse, VA — c H 40
Lacrosse, WA — d H 112
La Crosse, WI — g D 54
La Crosse, r., WI — g D 54
La Cygne, KS — m M 82
Ladd, IL — i F 54
Laddonia, MO — c E 68
Ladonia, TX — f K 84
Ladoga, IN — c J 68
Ladson, SC — f F 40
Ladysmith, WI — e D 54
La Farge, WI — g E 54
Lafayette, AL — j K 68
Lafayette, CA — g C 128
Lafayette, CO — l B 82
Lafayette, GA — e A 40
Lafayette, IN — b J 68
Lafayette, LA — l D 68
Lafayette, TN — f J 68
Lafourche, Bayou, r., LA — m F 68
La Grange, GA — e G 112
La Grange, KY — d K 68
La Grange, MO — b E 68
Lagrange, IN — a K 68
La Grange, NC — d l 40
La Grange, TX — j J 84
Lagrange, WY — j C 82
Laguna, NM — i l 98
Laguna Beach, CA — k H 128
Lahaina, HI — b C 144a
La Harpe, IL — j E 54
La Harpe, KS — n L 82
Lahontan Reservoir, NV — e F 128
La Huerta, NM — g B 84
Laie, HI — e J 144c
Laingsburg, MI — h K 54
Laird Hill, TX — j B 68
La Jara, CO — g K 98
La Jolla, CA — l H 128
La Junta, CO — n D 82
Lake, MS — j G 68
Lake Alfred, FL — k E 40
Lake Andes, SD — h l 82
Lake Arthur, LA — l D 68
Lake Benton, MN — g K 82
Lake Brownwood, TX — h G 84
Lake Butler, FL — i D 40
Lake Carmel, NY — f M 26
Lake Charles, LA — l C 68
Lake City, AR — g F 68
Lake City, CO — f l 98
Lake City, FL — i D 40
Lake City, IA — i M 82
Lake City, MI — f J 54
Lake City, MN — f D 54
Lake City, PA — e F 26
Lake City, SC — f G 40
Lake City, TN — c B 40
Lake Crystal, MN — g M 82
Lake Dallas, TX — f l 84
Lake Elsinore, CA — k H 128
Lakefield, MN — h L 82
Lake Forest, IL — h H 54
Lake Fork, r., UT — d F 98
Lake Geneva, WI — h G 54

Lake George, NY — d M 26
Lake Harbor, FL — m F 40
Lake Havasu City, AZ — j B 98
Lake Helen, FL — k E 40
Lakehurst, NJ — g L 26
Lake Isabella, CA — i G 128
Lake Jackson, TX — j K 84
Lakeland, FL — k E 40
Lakeland, GA — h C 40
Lake Linden, MI — c G 54
Lake Mills, IA — g B 54
Lake Mills, WI — g G 54
Lakemont, PA — g H 26
Lake Norden, SD — g J 82
Lake Odessa, MI — h J 54
Lake Oswego, OR — e C 112
Lake Ozark, MO — d D 68
Lake Park, FL — m F 40
Lake Park, MN — e K 82
Lake Placid, FL — l E 40
Lake Placid, NY — c M 26
Lake Pleasant, NY — d L 26
Lake Preston, SD — g J 82
Lake Providence, LA — j E 68
Lakes District, WA — c C 112
Lakeshore, MS — l G 68
Lakeside, AZ — j G 98
Lakeside, CA — l H 128
Lakeside, MT — b K 112
Lakeside, OR — g A 112
Lake Stevens, WA — b C 112
Laketown, UT — c E 98
Lake View, AR — h F 68
Lakeview, GA — e A 40
Lake View, IA — i L 82
Lakeview, MI — g J 54
Lake View, NY — e H 26
Lakeview, OH — g C 26
Lakeview, OR — h E 112
Lake View, SC — e G 40
Lakeview, TX — m C 68
Lakeview, TX — e F 84
Lake Village, AR — i E 68
Lakeville, MN — f B 54
Lake Wales, FL — l E 40
Lake Wilson, MN — h L 82
Lakewood, CO — e K 98
Lakewood, NJ — g L 26
Lakewood, NY — e G 26
Lakewood, OH — f E 26
Lakewood, WI — e G 54
Lakewood Park, ND — c l 82
Lakin, KS — n F 82
Lakota, IA — h M 82
Lakota, ND — c l 82
La Luz, NM — l K 98
Lamar, CO — m E 82
Lamar, MO — e B 68
Lamar, SC — e F 40
Lamar, r., WY — f P 112
La Marque, TX — j L 84
Lambert, MS — h F 68
Lambert, MT — d C 82
Lamberton, MN — g L 82
Lambertville, NJ — g L 26
Lame Deer, MT — e S 112
La Mesa, CA — l H 128
La Mesa, NM — l J 98
Lamesa, TX — g E 84
Lamine, r., MO — d D 68
La Moille, IL — i F 54
Lamoille, r., VT — c N 26
La Moine, r., IL — b F 68
Lamoni, IA — j B 54
Lamont, CA — i G 128
Lamont, IA — h C 54
Lamont, OK — c l 84
La Monte, MO — d C 68
La Moure, ND — e l 82
Lampasas, TX — h H 84
Lampasas, r., TX — h H 84
Lanai, HI — b C 144a
Lanai City, HI — b C 144a
Lanark, IL — h F 54
Lancaster, CA — j G 128
Lancaster, KY — b B 40
Lancaster, MN — b K 82
Lancaster, MO — b D 68
Lancaster, NH — c O 26
Lancaster, NY — e H 26
Lancaster, OH — h D 26
Lancaster, PA — g J 26
Lancaster, SC — e F 40
Lancaster, TX — g J 84
Lancaster, WI — h E 54
Lance Creek, WY — a L 98
Lander, WY — b H 98
Landis, NC — d F 40
Lando, SC — e F 40
Land O'Lakes, WI — d F 54
Landrum, SC — d D 40
Lanesboro, MN — g D 54
Lanett, AL — j A 40
Langdale, AL — j A 40
Langdon, ND — c l 82
Langford, SD — c l 82
Langsburg, MI — h K 54
Langston, OK — d l 84
Langley, OK — c K 84
Langley, SC — f E 40
Langlois, OR — h A 112
L'Anguille, r., AR — g F 68
L'Anse, MI — d G 54
Lansford, ND — c F 82
Lansing, IA — g D 54
Lansing, KS — l M 82
Lansing, MI — h K 54
Lantana, FL — m F 40
Laona, WI — e F 54
Lapeer, MI — g L 54
La Pine, OR — g D 112
La Plata, MD — j J 26
La Plata, MO — b D 68
La Plata Peak, CO — e H 98
Laporte, CO — d K 98
Laporte, IN — a J 68
La Porte, TX — j K 84
La Porte City, IA — h C 54
Lapwai, ID — d l 112
Laramie, WY — l B 98
Laramie, r., US — k B 98
Laramie Mountains, WY — b K 98
Larchwood, IA — h K 82
Laredo, TX — l G 84
Largo, FL — l D 40
Largo, Cañon, NM — h l 98
Larimore, ND — d J 82
Larned, KS — m H 82

Name	Map Ref.	Page
Larose, LA	m F	68
Larsen Bay, AK	h Q	142
La Rue, OH	g C	26
La Sal, UT	f G	98
La Salle, CO	d L	98
La Salle, IL	i F	54
Las Animas, CO	m D	82
Las Cruces, NM	l J	98
Lassen Peak, CA	d D	128
Lassen Volcanic National Park, CA	d D	128
Las Vegas, NV	h J	128
Las Vegas, NM	i K	98
Lathrop, MO	c B	68
Latimer, IA	h B	54
Latrobe, PA	g G	26
Latta, SC	e G	40
Lauderdale, MS	j H	68
La Union, NM	m J	98
Laurel, DE	i K	26
Laurel, FL	l D	40
Laurel, IN	c K	68
Laurel, MD	h J	26
Laurel, MS	k G	68
Laurel, MT	i J	112
Laurel, NE	i J	82
Laurel, r., KY	b B	40
Laurel Bay, SC	g F	40
Laureldale, PA	g K	26
Laurel Hill, NC	e G	40
Laurelville, OH	h D	26
Laurens, IA	i M	82
Laurens, SC	e D	40
Laurinburg, NC	e G	40
Laurium, MI	c G	54
Lavaca, r., TX	j J	84
Lava Hot Springs, ID	h M	112
La Valley, CO	g K	98
La Vergne, TN	f J	68
Laverne, OK	c G	84
La Vernia, TX	j H	84
La Veta, CO	g K	98
Lavina, MT	d Q	112
La Vista, NE	j K	82
Lavonia, GA	c E	40
Lawai, HI	d G	144b
Lawler, IA	g C	54
Lawn, TX	g G	84
Lawndale, NC	d E	40
Lawrence, IN	c J	68
Lawrence, KS	m L	82
Lawrence, MA	e O	26
Lawrence, NE	k I	82
Lawrenceburg, IN	c L	68
Lawrenceburg, KY	d L	68
Lawrenceburg, TN	g I	68
Lawrenceville, IL	d I	68
Lawrenceville, NJ	g L	26
Lawrenceville, VA	c I	40
Lawson, MO	c B	68
Lawtey, FL	i D	40
Lawton, MI	h J	54
Lawton, ND	c I	82
Lawton, OK	e H	84
Layton, UT	c E	98
Laytonville, CA	e B	128
Leachville, AR	g F	68
Lead, SD	g D	82
Leadore, ID	f L	112
Leadville, CO	e J	98
Leaf, r., MN	e L	82
Leaf, r., MS	k H	68
League City, TX	j K	84
Leakesville, MS	k H	68
Leakey, TX	j G	84
Leaksville, NC	c G	40
Lealman, FL	l D	40
Leary, GA	h B	40
Leatherman Peak, ID	f L	112
Leavenworth, KS	l M	82
Leavenworth, WA	c E	112
Leawood, MO	e B	68
Lebam, WA	d B	112
Lebanon, IN	b J	68
Lebanon, KS	l I	82
Lebanon, KY	e K	68
Lebanon, MO	e D	68
Lebanon, NH	d N	26
Lebanon, OH	h B	26
Lebanon, OR	f C	112
Lebanon, PA	g J	26
Lebanon, SD	f H	82
Lebanon, TN	f J	68
Lebanon, VA	c D	40
Lebanon Junction, KY	e K	68
Lebec, CA	j G	128
Lebo, KS	m L	82
Le Center, MN	f B	54
Le Claire, IA	i E	54
Lecompte, LA	k B	68
Lee, MA	e M	26
Leechburg, PA	g G	26
Leech Lake, MN	c A	54
Leedey, OK	d G	84
Leeds, AL	i J	68
Leeds, ND	c H	82
Leelanau Peninsula, MI	f K	54
Leesburg, FL	k E	40
Leesburg, GA	h B	40
Leesburg, VA	h I	26
Lees Summit, MO	d B	68
Leesville, LA	k C	68
Leesville, SC	f E	40
Leesville, TX	j I	84
Lee Vining, CA	g F	128
Lefors, TX	d F	84
Leggett, CA	e B	128
Le Grand, CA	g E	128
Lehi, UT	d E	98
Lehigh, IA	h A	54
Lehigh, OK	e J	84
Lehigh Acres, FL	m E	40
Leighton, PA	g H	26
Lehr, ND	f H	82
Leighton, AL	h I	68
Leipsic, OH	f C	26
Leitchfield, KY	e J	68
Leland, IL	i G	54
Leland, MI	e J	54
Leland, MS	i F	68
Leleiwi Point, HI	j P	144d
Le Mars, IA	i K	82
Lemay, MO	d F	68
Lemeta, AK	d U	142
Lemhi Pass, US	f L	112
Lemhi Range, ID	f L	112
Leming, TX	j H	84
Lemitar, NM	j J	98
Lemmon, SD	f E	82
Lemoncove, CA	h F	128
Lemon Grove, CA	l H	128
Lemont, PA	g I	26
Lemoore, CA	h F	128
Lena, IL	h F	54
Lena, WI	f G	54
Lennox, SD	h K	82
Lenoir, NC	d E	40
Lenoir City, TN	d B	40
Lenox, GA	h C	40
Lenox, IA	k M	82
Lenox, MA	e M	26
Lenox, TN	f G	68
Leola, AR	h D	68
Leola, SD	f I	82
Leon, IA	j B	54
Leon, KS	n K	82
Leon, r., TX	h I	84
Leonard, ND	e J	82
Leonard, TX	f J	84
Leonardtown, MD	i J	26
Leonville, LA	l E	68
Leoti, KS	m F	82
Lepanto, AR	g F	68
Le Roy, IL	b H	68
Le Roy, KS	m L	82
Le Roy, MN	g C	54
Le Roy, NY	e I	26
Leslie, AR	g D	68
Leslie, GA	h B	40
Leslie, MI	h K	54
Leslie, WV	i F	26
Le Sueur, MN	f B	54
Le Sueur, r., MN	f B	54
Letcher, SD	h I	82
Leucadia, CA	k H	128
Levan, UT	e E	98
Levelland, TX	f D	84
Levelock, AK	g P	142
Levering, MI	e K	54
Levisa Fork, r., US	b D	40
Levittown, NY	g M	26
Levittown, PA	g L	26
Lewes, DE	i K	26
Lewis, IA	j L	82
Lewis, KS	n H	82
Lewis, r., WA	e C	112
Lewis, Mount, NV	d I	128
Lewis and Clark Lake, US	i J	82
Lewis and Clark Range, MT	c M	112
Lewisburg, OH	h B	26
Lewisburg, PA	g J	26
Lewisburg, TN	g J	68
Lewisburg, WV	j F	26
Lewisport, KY	d J	68
Lewis Range, MT	b L	112
Lewis Run, PA	f H	26
Lewis Smith Lake, AL	h I	68
Lewiston, CA	d C	128
Lewiston, ID	d H	112
Lewiston, ME	c P	26
Lewiston, MI	f K	54
Lewiston, MN	g D	54
Lewiston, NY	d G	26
Lewiston, UT	c E	98
Lewiston Orchards, ID	d I	112
Lewistown, IL	b F	68
Lewistown, MO	b F	68
Lewistown, MT	c P	112
Lewistown, PA	g I	26
Lewisville, AR	i C	68
Lewisville, TX	f J	84
Lewisville Lake, TX	f I	84
Lexa, AR	h F	68
Lexington, GA	f C	40
Lexington, IL	j G	54
Lexington, KY	a B	40
Lexington, MA	e O	26
Lexington, MI	g M	54
Lexington, MS	i F	68
Lexington, MO	c C	68
Lexington, NE	k H	82
Lexington, NC	d F	40
Lexington, OK	d I	84
Lexington, OR	e F	112
Lexington, SC	f E	40
Lexington, TN	g H	68
Lexington, TX	i I	84
Lexington, VA	b G	40
Lexington Park, MD	i J	26
Libby, MT	b J	112
Liberal, KS	n G	82
Liberal, MO	e B	68
Liberty, IN	c L	68
Liberty, KY	e K	68
Liberty, MS	k F	68
Liberty, MO	c B	68
Liberty, NE	k K	82
Liberty, NY	f L	26
Liberty, NC	d G	40
Liberty, SC	e E	40
Liberty, TX	i L	84
Liberty Center, OH	f B	26
Liberty Hill, TX	i H	84
Libertyville, IL	h H	54
Licking, MO	e E	68
Licking, r., KY	i B	26
Lidgerwood, ND	e J	82
Lighthouse Point, FL	m F	40
Lighthouse Point, MI	e J	54
Lignite, ND	c E	82
Ligonier, IN	a K	68
Ligonier, PA	g G	26
Lihue, HI	d G	144b
Lilbourn, MO	f G	68
Lillington, NC	d G	40
Lily, KY	b B	40
Lima, MT	f M	112
Lima, NY	e I	26
Lima, OH	g B	26
Lime Springs, IA	g C	54
Limon, CO	l D	82
Linch, WY	a J	98
Lincoln, AR	g B	68
Lincoln, CA	f D	128
Lincoln, IL	b I	68
Lincoln, KS	l I	82
Lincoln, ME	b B	26
Lincoln, MI	f L	54
Lincoln, MO	d C	68
Lincoln, MT	d M	112
Lincoln, NE	k K	82
Lincoln, Mount, CO	e J	98
Lincoln City, OR	f A	112
Lincoln Park, CO	f K	98
Lincoln Park, MI	h L	54
Lincolnton, GA	f D	40
Lincolnton, NC	d E	40
Lincoln Village, CA	h J	68
Lind, WA	d G	112
Linda, CA	f D	128
Lindale, GA	e A	40
Lindale, TX	g K	84
Linden, AL	j I	68
Linden, IN	b J	68
Linden, MI	h L	54
Linden, TX	g L	84
Lindon, CO	l D	82
Lindsay, CA	h F	128
Lindsay, NE	j J	82
Lindsay, OK	e I	84
Lindsborg, KS	m J	82
Linesville, PA	f F	26
Lineville, AL	i K	68
Lineville, IA	j B	54
Lingle, WY	b L	98
Linn, KS	l J	82
Linn, MO	d E	68
Linton, IN	c I	68
Linton, ND	e G	82
Linville, NC	c E	40
Lipan, TX	g H	84
Lipscomb, TX	c F	84
Lisbon, NH	c O	26
Lisbon, ND	e J	82
Lisbon, OH	g F	26
Lisbon Falls, ME	d P	26
Lisman, AL	j H	68
Litchfield, MI	h K	54
Litchfield, MN	e A	54
Litchfield, NE	j H	82
Litchfield Park, AZ	k D	98
Litchville, ND	e I	82
Lithonia, GA	f B	40
Lititz, PA	g J	26
Little, r., US	i B	68
Little, r., AL	h K	68
Little, r., GA	f D	40
Little, r., KY	f I	68
Little, r., LA	k D	68
Little, r., OK	d J	84
Little, r., SC	e E	40
Little, r., TN	c D	40
Little Arkansas, r., KS	m I	82
Little Bear, r., UT	c E	98
Little Belt Mountains, MT	d O	112
Little Bighorn, r., US	d I	112
Little Bitterroot, r., MT	c K	112
Little Blackfoot, r., MT	d M	112
Little Blue, r., US	l K	82
Little Cedar, r., US	g C	54
Little Chute, WI	f G	54
Little Colorado, r., AZ	i E	98
Little Cottonwood, r., MN	g M	82
Little Deschutes, r., OR	g D	112
Little Diomede Island, AK	d J	142
Little Eau Pleine, r., WI	f E	54
Little Falls, MN	e A	54
Little Falls, NY	d L	26
Littlefield, TX	f D	84
Littlefork, MN	b B	54
Little Fork, r., MN	b B	54
Little Humboldt, r., NV	c H	128
Little Juniata, r., PA	g I	26
Little Kanawha, r., WV	h K	54
Little Lake, LA	m F	68
Little Mexico, WI	i D	84
Little Missouri, r., US	d D	82
Little Missouri, r., AR	i C	68
Little Muddy, r., IL	e G	68
Little Muddy, r., ND	c D	82
Little Nemaha, r., NE	k K	82
Little Osage, r., US	d B	68
Little Pee Dee, r., SC	f G	40
Little Platte, r., MO	c B	68
Little Powder, r., US	g B	98
Little Red, r., AR	g E	68
Little River, US	m I	82
Little Rock, AR	h D	68
Little Rock, IA	h L	82
Little Sable Point, MI	f E	54
Little Sac, r., MO	e C	68
Little Salkehatchie, r., SC	f F	40
Little Sandy, r., KY	i C	26
Little Sioux, r., US	i L	82
Little Snake, r., US	d H	98
Littlestown, PA	h I	26
Little Tallapoosa, r., US	f A	40
Little Tennessee, r., US	d B	40
Littleton, CO	e K	98
Littleton, NH	c O	26
Littleton, NC	c I	40
Littleton, WV	h F	26
Little Traverse Bay, MI	e J	54
Little Valley, NY	e H	26
Little Wabash, r., IL	d H	68
Little Washita, r., OK	e H	84
Little White, r., SD	h F	82
Little Wolf, r., WI	f F	54
Little Wood, r., ID	g K	112
Live Oak, CA	f D	128
Live Oak, FL	i D	40
Livermore, CA	g D	128
Livermore, IA	h A	54
Livermore, KY	e I	68
Livermore Falls, ME	c P	26
Liverpool, NY	g J	26
Livingston, AL	j H	68
Livingston, CA	g E	128
Livingston, IL	d G	68
Livingston, KY	b B	40
Livingston, LA	l F	68
Livingston, MT	e O	112
Livingston, TN	f K	68
Livingston, TX	i J	84
Livingston, WI	h E	54
Livingstone, Lake, TX	i H	84
Livingston Manor, NY	f L	26
Livonia, IN	c J	68
Livonia, MI	h L	54
Lizard Head Peak, WY	h P	112
Llano, TX	i H	84
Llano, r., TX	i H	84
Loa, UT	f E	98
Loami, IL	b I	68
Lobelville, TN	g I	68
Lockesburg, AR	h B	68
Lockhart, TX	j I	84
Lock Haven, PA	g I	26
Lockney, TX	e E	84
Lockport, IL	i H	54
Lockport, LA	m F	68
Lockport, NY	d H	26
Lockwood, MO	e C	68
Locust Fork, r., AL	h J	68
Locust Grove, OK	c K	84
Logan, OH	h D	26
Logan, UT	c E	98
Logan, WV	j E	26
Logan, r., UT	c E	98
Logandale, NV	h K	128
Logan Martin Lake, AL	i J	68
Logansport, IN	b J	68
Logansport, LA	k C	68
Loganville, GA	f C	40
Lohrville, IA	i M	82
Loleta, CA	d A	128
Lolita, TX	k J	84
Lolo, MT	d K	112
Lolo Pass, US	d K	112
Lomax, IL	j D	54
Lometa, TX	h H	84
Lomira, WI	g G	54
Lompoc, CA	j E	128
Lonaconing, MD	h H	26
London, KY	b B	40
London, OH	h C	26
London, TX	i G	84
Lone Grove, OK	e I	84
Lone Mountain, NV	f C	128
Lone Oak, KY	e H	68
Lone Oak, TX	f K	84
Lone Pine, CA	h G	128
Lone Rock, WI	g E	54
Lone Star, TX	j B	68
Lone Tree, IA	i D	54
Lone Wolf, OK	e G	84
Long Bay, US	f H	40
Long Beach, CA	k G	128
Long Beach, MS	l G	68
Long Beach, NY	g M	26
Long Beach, WA	d A	112
Longboat Key, FL	l D	40
Long Branch, r., MO	c D	68
Long Branch, NJ	h L	26
Long Creek, OR	f F	112
Long Island, NY	g N	26
Long Island Sound, US	f N	26
Long Lake, NY	d L	26
Long Lake, ND	e G	82
Longleaf, LA	k D	68
Long Leaf Park, NC	e I	40
Longmeadow, MA	e N	26
Longmont, CO	d K	98
Long Pine, NE	i H	82
Long Prairie, MN	e M	82
Long Prairie, r., MN	e M	82
Longs Peak, CO	d K	98
Long Tom, r., OR	f B	112
Longton, KS	n K	82
Longview, NC	d E	40
Longview, TX	j B	68
Longview, WA	d C	112
Longwood Park, NC	e G	40
Lonoke, AR	h E	68
Lonsdale, MN	f B	54
Loogootee, IN	d J	68
Looking Glass, r., MI	h K	54
Lookout, Cape, NC	e J	40
Lookout Mountain, US	h K	68
Lookout Mountain, OR	f E	112
Lookout Pass, US	c J	112
Lookout Ridge, AK	b O	142
Loomis, CA	k H	82
Loop, TX	g D	84
Lorain, OH	f D	26
Loraine, TX	g F	84
Lordsburg, NM	l H	98
Loreauville, LA	l E	68
Lorenzo, TX	f E	84
Loretto, KY	e K	68
Loretto, TN	g l	68
Lorimor, IA	a B	68
Loris, SC	e H	40
Lorman, MS	k E	68
Los Alamos, CA	j E	128
Los Alamos, NM	i J	98
Los Angeles, CA	j G	128
Los Angeles Aqueduct, CA	i G	128
Los Banos, CA	g E	128
Los Ebanos, TX	m H	84
Los Fresnos, TX	m I	84
Los Gatos, CA	g D	128
Los Lunas, NM	j J	98
Los Molinos, CA	d C	128
Los Padillas, NM	j J	98
Los Pinos, r., US	g I	98
Lost, r., US	h D	112
Lost, r., IN	d J	68
Lost, r., MN	d L	82
Lost, r., WV	i H	26
Lost Hills, CA	i F	128
Lostine, r., OR	e H	112
Lost Nation, IA	i E	54
Lost River Range, ID	f L	112
Lost Trail Pass, US	e L	112
Lothair, KY	b C	40
Lott, TX	h I	84
Loudon, TN	d B	40
Loudonville, OH	g D	26
Louin, MS	j G	68
Louisa, KY	a D	40
Louisa, VA	a H	40
Louisburg, KS	m M	82
Louisburg, NC	c H	40
Louise, MS	j F	68
Louise, TX	j J	84
Louise, Lake, AK	e U	142
Louisiana, MO	c E	68
Louisiana, state, US	e H	8
Louisville, AL	k K	68
Louisville, GA	f D	40
Louisville, IL	d H	68
Louisville, KY	d K	68
Louisville, MS	i G	68
Louisville, OH	k K	82
Louisville, r., NE	j J	82
Louviers, CO	e K	98
Lovelady, TX	h K	84
Lovell, WY	f Q	112
Lovelock, NV	d G	128
Lovely, KY	b D	40
Loves Park, IL	h F	54
Lovilia, IA	i C	54
Loving, NM	m M	98
Loving, TX	f H	84
Lovington, IL	c H	68
Lovington, NM	g D	84
Lowden, IA	i E	54
Lowell, AR	f B	68
Lowell, IN	a I	68
Lowell, MA	e O	26
Lowell, MI	h J	54
Lowell, OR	f C	112
Lower Kalskag, AK	f N	142
Lower Klamath Lake, CA	c D	128
Lower Paia, HI	b D	144a
Lower Red Lake, MN	d L	82
Lowmoor, VA	b G	40
Lowry City, MO	d C	68
Lowville, NY	d K	26
Loxley, AL	l l	68
Loyal, WI	f E	54
Loyalton, CA	e E	128
Lubbock, TX	f E	84
Lubec, ME	c T	26
Lucas, IA	i B	54
Lucas, KS	l I	82
Lucasville, OH	i D	26
Lucedale, MS	l H	68
Lucerne, CA	e C	128
Luck, WI	d E	54
Luckiamute, r., OR	f B	112
Ludington, MI	g l	54
Ludlow, MA	e N	26
Ludlow, VT	d N	26
Ludowic, GA	h E	40
Lueders, TX	g G	84
Lufkin, TX	k B	68
Lukeville, AZ	m D	98
Lula, MI	h F	68
Luling, TX	j l	84
Lumber, r., US	e G	40
Lumber City, GA	h D	40
Lumberport, WV	h F	26
Lumberton, MS	k G	68
Lumberton, NC	e G	40
Lumberton, TX	l B	68
Lumpkin, GA	g B	40
Luna Pier, MI	i L	54
Lund, NV	f J	128
Lundale, WV	j E	26
Lunenburg, VA	c H	40
Luray, VA	i H	26
Lusk, WY	b L	98
Lutcher, LA	l F	68
Lutesville, MO	e G	68
Luther, MI	f J	54
Luther, OK	d l	84
Luttrell, TN	c C	40
Lutz, FL	k D	40
Luverne, AL	k J	68
Lu Verne, IA	h A	54
Luverne, MN	h K	82
Luxemburg, WI	f H	54
Luxora, AR	g G	68
Lycoming Creek, r., PA	f I	26
Lydia Mills, SC	e E	40
Lyerly, GA	e A	40
Lyford, TX	m I	84
Lykens, PA	g J	26
Lyle, MN	g C	54
Lyles, TN	g I	68
Lyman, NE	j C	82
Lyman, SC	d E	40
Lyman, WY	c F	98
Lynch, KY	c D	40
Lynch, NE	i I	82
Lynchburg, OH	h C	26
Lynchburg, TN	g J	68
Lynchburg, VA	b G	40
Lynches, r., US	f G	40
Lynden, WA	b C	112
Lyndon, KS	m L	82
Lyndon, KY	d K	68
Lyndonville, VT	c N	26
Lyndora, PA	g G	26
Lynn, AL	h I	68
Lynn, IN	b L	68
Lynn, MA	e P	26
Lynn Canal, AK	g AA	142
Lynndyl, UT	e D	98
Lynn Garden, TN	c D	40
Lynn Haven, FL	l K	68
Lynnville, IA	i C	54
Lyon Mountain, NY	c M	26
Lyons, CO	d K	98
Lyons, GA	g D	40
Lyons, IN	d I	68
Lyons, KS	m I	82
Lyons, MI	h K	54
Lyons, NE	j K	82
Lyons, NY	d J	26
Lytle, TX	j H	84

M

Name	Map Ref.	Page
Maalaea Bay, HI	b D	144a
Mabank, TX	g J	84
Maben, MS	i G	68
Mableton, GA	f B	40
Mabton, WA	d F	112
MacClenny, FL	i D	40
Machias, ME	c S	26
Machias, r., ME	c S	26
Mackay, ID	g L	112
Mackinac, Straits of, MI	e K	54
Mackinac Island, MI	e K	54
Mackinac Island, MI	e K	54
Mackinaw, IL	j F	54
Mackinaw, r., IL	j F	54
Mackinaw City, MI	e K	54
Macksville, KS	m l	82
Macomb, IL	j E	54
Macon, GA	g C	40
Macon, MS	i H	68
Macon, MO	c D	68
Macon, Bayou, r., US	j E	68
Mad, r., CA	d B	128
Mad, r., OH	h B	26
Mad, r., VT	d N	26
Maddock, ND	c H	82
Madeira, MN	f A	54
Madeline Island, WI	d E	54
Madera, CA	h E	128
Madill, OK	e J	84
Madison, AL	h J	68
Madison, FL	i C	40
Madison, GA	f C	40
Madison, IN	d K	68
Madison, KS	m K	82
Madison, MN	f K	82
Madison, MO	c D	68
Madison, NE	j J	82
Madison, OH	f E	26
Madison, SD	h K	82
Madison, VA	i H	26
Madison, WV	j E	26
Madison, WI	g F	54
Madison, r., US	e N	112
Madison Heights, VA	b G	40
Madison Range, MT	e N	112
Madisonville, KY	e I	68
Madisonville, LA	l F	68
Madisonville, TN	d B	40
Madisonville, TX	i K	84
Madras, OR	f D	112
Madre, Laguna, TX	m l	84
Madrid, AL	k K	68
Madrid, IA	i B	54
Madrid, NE	k F	82
Maeser, UT	d G	98
Magazine Mountain, AR	g C	68
Magdalena, NM	j l	98
Magee, MS	k G	68
Magnolia, AR	i C	68
Magnolia, MN	h K	82
Magnolia, MS	k F	68
Mahanoy City, PA	g J	26
Mahnomen, MN	d L	82
Mahomet, IL	b H	68
Maiden, NC	d E	40
Maili, HI	f l	144c
Maine, state, US	b M	8
Maine, Gulf of, NA	c M	8
Makaha, HI	f l	144c
Makahuena Point, HI	d H	144b
Makapuu Head, HI	g E	144b
Makawao, HI	b D	144a
Makaweli, HI	d G	144b
Makika, Lua, HI	b C	144a
Malad, r., US	c D	98
Malad City, ID	h M	112
Malaga, NM	g B	84
Malakoff, TX	g J	84
Malaspina Glacier, AK	g X	142
Malcom, IA	i C	54
Malden, MO	f G	68
Malheur, r., OR	g H	112
Malheur Lake, OR	g G	112
Malin, OR	h D	112
Malmar, NM	g C	84
Malone, FL	l A	40
Malone, NY	c L	26
Malta, MT	b R	112
Malta, OH	h E	26
Malvern, AR	h D	68
Malvern, IA	j L	82
Malvern, OH	g E	26
Mamie, NC	c K	40
Mammoth, AZ	l F	98
Mammoth, WV	i E	26
Mammoth Cave National Park, KY	e J	68
Mammoth Lakes, CA	g G	128
Mammoth Spring, AR	f F	68
Mamou, LA	l D	68
Mana Point, HI	c G	144b
Manasquan, NJ	g L	26
Manassa, CO	g K	98
Manassas, VA	i l	26
Manawa, WI	f G	54
Mancelona, MI	f J	54
Manchester, CT	f N	26
Manchester, GA	g B	40
Manchester, IA	h D	54
Manchester, KY	c D	40
Manchester, MA	e P	26
Manchester, MI	h K	54
Manchester, NH	e O	26
Manchester, OH	i C	26
Manchester, TN	g J	68
Manchester, VT	d M	26
Mancos, CO	g H	98
Mancos, r., US	g H	98
Mandan, ND	e G	82
Manderson, WY	f R	112
Mandeville, LA	l F	68
Mangham, LA	j E	68
Mangum, OK	e G	84
Manhattan, KS	l K	82
Manhattan, MT	e N	112
Manila, AR	g F	68
Manila, UT	d G	98
Manistee, MI	f l	54
Manistee, r., MI	f J	54
Manistique, MI	e l	54
Manistique, r., MI	e l	54
Manito, IL	b G	68
Manitou Springs, CO	f L	98
Manitowish Waters, WI	d F	54
Manitowoc, WI	f H	54
Manitowoc, r., WI	f G	54
Mankato, KS	l l	82
Mankato, MN	f B	54
Manly, IA	g B	54
Mannford, OK	c J	84
Manning, IA	j L	82
Manning, ND	d E	82
Manning, SC	f F	40
Mannington, WV	h F	26
Manokotak, AK	g O	142
Manor, TX	i I	84
Mansfield, GA	f C	40
Mansfield, IL	b H	68
Mansfield, LA	j C	68
Mansfield, MA	e O	26
Mansfield, MO	e D	68
Mansfield, OH	g D	26
Mansfield, PA	f I	26
Mansfield, Mount, VT	c N	26
Manson, IA	i M	82
Mansura, LA	k D	68
Manteca, CA	g D	128
Manteno, IL	i H	54
Manteo, NC	d K	40
Manti, UT	e E	98
Manton, MI	f J	54
Mantorville, MN	f C	54
Mantua, OH	f E	26
Manvel, ND	c J	82
Many, LA	k C	68
Many Farms, AZ	h G	98
Maple, r., US	i l	82
Maple, r., MI	g K	54
Maple, r., MN	g B	54
Maple, r., ND	e J	82
Maple Lake, MN	e A	54
Maple Mount, KY	e l	68
Maplesville, AL	j J	68
Mapleton, IA	i L	82
Mapleton, MN	f B	54
Mapleton, ND	e J	82
Mapleton, OR	f B	112
Maquoketa, IA	h E	54
Maquoketa, r., IA	h E	54
Marais des Cygnes, r., US	d A	68
Marana, AZ	l E	98
Marathon, NY	e J	26
Marathon, TX	i C	84
Marathon, WI	f F	54
Marble, MN	c B	54
Marble, NC	d C	40
Marble Canyon, AZ	h E	98
Marble Falls, TX	i H	84
Marblehead, OH	f D	26
Marble Hill, MO	e G	68
Marble Rock, IA	h C	54
Marceline, MO	c D	68
Marcellus, MI	h J	54
Marcola, OR	f C	112
Marcus, IL	i L	82
Marcus Baker, Mount, AK	f U	142
Marcy, Mount, NY	c M	26
Marengo, IA	h G	54
Marengo, IN	d J	68
Marengo, IA	i C	54
Marenisco, MI	d F	54
Marfa, TX	i B	84
Margaretville, NY	e L	26
Margate, FL	m F	40
Margate City, NJ	h L	26
Marianna, AR	h F	68
Marianna, FL	l A	40
Maricopa, AZ	k D	98
Maricopa, CA	i F	128
Marienville, PA	f G	26
Maries, r., MO	d D	68
Marietta, GA	f B	40
Marietta, MN	f K	82
Marietta, OH	h E	26
Marietta, OK	f l	84
Marine City, MI	h M	54
Marinette, WI	e H	54
Maringouin, LA	l E	68
Marion, AL	j l	68
Marion, AR	g F	68
Marion, IL	e H	68
Marion, IN	b K	68
Marion, KY	e H	68
Marion, KS	m J	82
Marion, LA	i D	68
Marion, MI	f J	54
Marion, MS	j H	68
Marion, NC	d D	40
Marion, ND	e l	82
Marion, OH	g C	26
Marion, SC	e G	40
Marion, SD	h J	82
Marion, VA	c E	40
Marion, WI	f G	54
Marion, Lake, SC	f F	40
Marion Junction, AL	j l	68
Marion Lake, KS	m J	82
Marionville, MO	e C	68
Mariposa, CA	g F	128
Marissa, IL	d G	68
Marked Tree, AR	g F	68
Markesan, WI	g G	54
Markham, TX	k J	84
Markle, IN	b K	68
Markleeville, CA	f F	128
Marks, MS	h F	68
Marksville, LA	k D	68
Mark Twain Lake, MO	c E	68
Marlboro, NY	f M	26
Marlborough, MA	e O	26
Marlette, MI	g L	54
Marlin, TX	h J	84
Marlinton, WV	i F	26
Marlow, OK	e l	84
Marmaduke, AR	f F	68
Marmarth, ND	e D	82
Marmaton, r., US	e B	68
Marmet, WV	i E	26
Marne, MI	g J	54
Maroa, IL	b H	68
Marquand, MO	e F	68
Marquesas Keys, FL	o D	40
Marquette, KS	m J	82
Marquette, MI	d H	54
Marrero, LA	m F	68
Mars, PA	g F	26
Marseilles, IL	i G	54
Marshall, AR	g D	68
Marshall, IL	c l	68
Marshall, MI	h K	54
Marshall, MN	g L	82
Marshall, MO	c C	68
Marshall, NC	d D	40
Marshall, TX	j B	68
Marshall, r., NC	d l	40
Marshallberg, NC	e J	40
Marshalltown, IA	h C	54
Marshallville, GA	g C	40
Marshallville, OH	g E	26
Marshfield, MO	e D	68
Marshfield, WI	f E	54
Mars Hill, NC	d D	40
Marsh Island, LA	m E	68
Marsh Peak, UT	d G	98
Marshville, NC	e F	40
Marsing, ID	g l	112
Mart, TX	h J	84
Martha's Vineyard, MA	f P	26
Martin, KY	b D	40
Martin, MI	h J	54
Martin, ND	d G	82
Martin, SD	h F	82
Martin, TN	f H	68
Martindale, TX	j l	84
Martinez, CA	f C	128
Martinez, GA	f C	128
Martin Lake, AL	j K	68
Martinsburg, PA	g H	26
Martinsburg, WV	h l	26
Martins Ferry, OH	g F	26
Martinsville, IL	c l	68
Martinsville, IN	c J	68
Martinsville, VA	c G	40
Marvell, AR	h F	68
Marvine, Mount, UT	f E	98
Maryland, state, US	d K	8
Marymeal, TX	f E	84
Marys, r., NV	c J	128
Marysvale, UT	f D	98
Marysville, CA	e D	128
Marysville, KS	l K	82
Marysville, MI	h M	54
Marysville, OH	g C	26
Marysville, WA	b C	112
Maryville, MO	b B	68
Maryville, TN	d B	40
Mascot, TN	c C	40
Mascoutah, IL	d G	68
Mason, MI	h K	54
Mason, OH	h B	26
Mason, TN	g G	68
Mason, TX	i H	84
Mason City, IA	g B	54
Mason City, IL	b G	68
Mason City, NE	j H	82

Name | Map Ref. | Page

Massachusetts, state, US c L 8
Massachusetts Bay, MA e P 26
Massena, IA j M 82
Massena, NY c L 26
Massillon, OH g E 26
Massive, Mount, CO e J 98
Masterson, TX d E 84
Matador, TX e F 84
Matagorda, TX k K 84
Matagorda Bay, TX k J 84
Matagorda Island, TX k J 84
Matamoras, PA f L 26
Matanuska, r., AK f T 142
Matewan, WV b D 40
Mather, PA h F 26
Mathews, VA b J 40
Mathis, TX k I 84
Mattawa, WA d F 112
Mattawamkeag, ME b R 26
Mattawamkeag, r., ME b R 26
Matterhorn, NV c J 128
Mattoon, IL c H 68
Mattoon, WI e F 54
Mattydale, NY d J 26
Maud, OK d J 84
Maud, TX i B 68
Maui, HI b D 144a
Mauldin, SC e D 40
Maumee, OH f C 26
Maumee, r., US f B 26
Mauna Kea, HI j P 144d
Maunaloa, HI a B 144a
Mauna Loa, HI j P 144d
Maunalua Bay, HI f J 144c
Maupin, OR e D 112
Maurepas, Lake, LA i F 68
Mauston, WI g E 54
Maverick, AZ k G 98
Max, ND d F 82
Maxton, NC e G 40
Maxwell, CA e C 128
Maxwell, IA i B 54
Maxwell, NE j G 82
Maxwell, NM c B 84
May, TX h H 84
May, Cape, NJ i L 26
Maybeury, WV b E 40
Mayer, AZ j D 98
Mayersville, MS j E 68
Mayfield, KY f H 68
Mayfield, UT e E 98
Mayflower, AR h D 68
Maynard, IA h D 54
Maynardville, TN c C 40
Mayo, FL i C 40
Mayodan, NC c G 40
Mays Landing, NJ h L 26
Maysville, KY i C 26
Maysville, MO c B 68
Maysville, NC e I 40
Maysville, OK e I 84
Mayville, MI g L 54
Mayville, NY e G 26
Mayville, ND d J 82
Mayville, WI g G 54
Maywood, NE k G 82
Mazatzal Peak, AZ j E 98
Mazeppa, MN f C 54
Mazomanie, WI g F 54
Mazon, IL i G 54
McAdoo, PA g K 26
McAlester, OK e K 84
McAllen, TX m H 84
McArthur, OH h D 26
McBain, MI f J 54
McBee, SC e F 40
McCall, ID f I 112
McCall Creek, MS k F 68
McCamey, TX h D 84
McCammon, ID h M 112
McCaysville, GA e B 40
McCleary, WA c B 112
McClellanville, SC f I 40
McCloud, CA c C 128
McClure, IL e G 68
McClure, PA g I 26
McClusky, ND d G 82
McColl, SC e G 40
McComas, WV b E 40
McComb, MS k F 68
McComb, OH f C 26
McConaughy, Lake, NE j F 82
McConnellsburg, PA h I 26
McConnelsville, OH h E 26
McCook, NE k G 82
McCormick, SC f D 40
McCrory, AR g E 68
McCune, KS n L 82
McCurtain, OK d L 84
McDade, TX i I 84
McDavid, FL l I 68
McDermitt, NV c H 128
McDermott, OH i C 26
McDonald, KS l F 82
McDonough, GA f B 40
McEwen, TN f I 68
McFadden, WY c J 98
McFarland, CA i F 128
McFarland, WI g F 54
McGehee, AR i E 68
McGill, NV e K 128
McGrath, AK e Q 142
McGraw, NY e J 26
McGregor, IA g D 54
McGregor, TX h I 84
McHenry, IL h G 54
McHenry, MS l G 68
McIntosh, AL k H 68
McIntosh, MN d L 82
McIntosh, SD f F 82
McKee, KY b C 40
McKeesport, PA g G 26
McKenzie, AL k J 68
McKenzie, TN f H 68
McKenzie Bridge, OR f C 112
McKinley, Mount, AK e S 142
McKinleyville, CA d A 128
McKinney, TX f J 84
McLain, MS k H 68
McLaughlin, SD f G 82
McLaurin, MS k G 68
McLean, IL b G 68
McLean, TX d F 84
McLeansboro, IL d H 68
McLoughlin, Mount, OR h C 112
McLouth, KS l L 82
McMillan, Lake, NM g B 84
McMinnville, OR e B 112
McMinnville, TN g K 68
McNary, AZ j G 98
McNeil, AR i C 68
McNeill, MS l G 68
McPherson, KS m J 82
McQueeney, TX j H 84
McRae, AR g E 68
McRae, GA g D 40
McRoberts, KY b D 40
McVeigh, KY b D 40
McVille, ND d I 82
McWilliams, AL k I 68
Mead, NE j K 82
Mead, Lake, US h B 98
Meade, KS n G 82
Meaden Peak, CO d I 98
Meadow, TX f D 84
Meadow, UT f D 98
Meadowview, VA c E 40
Meadville, MS k F 68
Meadville, MO c C 68
Meadville, PA f F 26
Mebane, NC c G 40
Mechanic Falls, ME c P 26
Mechanicsburg, OH g C 26
Mechanicsville, IA i D 54
Mechanicsville, VA b I 40
Mechanicville, NY e M 26
Medaryville, IN a J 68
Medford, OK c I 84
Medford, OR h C 112
Medford, WI e E 54
Mediapolis, IA i D 54
Medical Lake, WA c H 112
Medicine Bow, WY c J 98
Medicine Bow, r., WY b J 98
Medicine Bow Mountains, US c J 98
Medicine Bow Peak, WY c J 98
Medicine Lake, MT c C 82
Medicine Lodge, KS n I 82
Medicine Lodge, r., US b H 84
Medina, NY d H 26
Medina, ND e H 82
Medina, OH f E 26
Medina, TX j G 84
Medina, r., TX j H 84
Medora, IN d J 68
Medora, ND e D 82
Meeker, CO d I 98
Meeks Bay, CA e E 128
Meeteetse, WY f Q 112
Megargel, TX f H 84
Meherrin, r., US c I 40
Meigs, GA h B 40
Meiners Oaks, CA j F 128
Mekoryuk, AK f K 142
Melbourne, AR f E 68
Melbourne, FL k F 40
Melbourne, IA i B 54
Melcher, IA i B 54
Mellen, WI d E 54
Mellette, SD f I 82
Melrose, MN f M 82
Melrose, NM e C 84
Melrose, WI f E 54
Melstone, MT d R 112
Melvern, KS m L 82
Melville, LA l E 68
Melvin, IL j G 54
Melvin, KY b D 40
Melvin, TX h G 84
Memphis, FL l D 40
Memphis, MI h M 54
Memphis, MO b D 68
Memphis, TN g F 68
Memphis, TX e F 84
Memphremagog, Lake, NA b N 26
Mena, AR h B 68
Menahga, MN e L 82
Menan, ID g N 112
Menard, TX i G 84
Menasha, WI f G 54
Mendenhall, MS k G 68
Mendocino, CA e B 128
Mendocino, Cape, CA d A 128
Mendon, IL b E 68
Mendon, MI h J 54
Mendota, CA h E 128
Mendota, IL i F 54
Menlo Park, CA g C 128
Menno, SD h J 82
Meno, OK c H 84
Menominee, MI e H 54
Menominee, r., US e H 54
Menomonee Falls, WI g G 54
Menomonie, WI f D 54
Mentasta Mountains, AK e W 142
Mentone, TX h C 84
Mentor, OH f E 26
Mequon, WI g H 54
Meramec, r., MO d E 68
Merced, CA g E 128
Merced, r., CA g E 128
Mercedes, TX m I 84
Mercer, MO b C 68
Mercer, PA f F 26
Mercer, WI d E 54
Mercersburg, PA h I 26
Mercury, NV h J 128
Meredith, NH d O 26
Meredith, Lake, TX d E 84
Meredosia, IL c F 68
Meriden, CT f N 26
Meridian, GA h E 40
Meridian, ID g I 112
Meridian, MS j H 68
Meridian, TX h I 84
Meridianville, AL h J 68
Merigold, MS i F 68
Merino, CO k D 82
Merkel, TX g F 84
Merlin, OR h B 112
Merna, NE j H 82
Merrill, IA i K 82
Merrill, MI g K 54
Merrill, OR h D 112
Merrill, WI e F 54
Merrillan, WI f E 54
Merrillville, IN a I 68
Merrimack, r., US d O 26
Merriman, NE i F 82
Merritt Island, FL k F 40
Mer Rouge, LA j E 68
Merryville, LA l C 68
Mertzon, TX h F 84
Mesa, AZ k E 98
Mesabi Range, MN c C 54
Mesa Mountain, CO g J 98
Mesa Verde National Park, CO g H 98
Mescalero, NM k K 98
Mesick, MI f J 54
Mesilla, NM l J 98
Mesquite, NV h K 128
Mesquite, TX g K 84
Messix Peak, UT c D 98
Metairie, LA m F 68
Metaline Falls, WA b H 112
Metamora, IL j F 54
Meteor Crater, AZ i E 98
Methow, r., WA b E 112
Metlakatla, AK i CC 142
Meto, Bayou, r., AR h E 68
Metolius, r., OR f D 112
Metropolis, IL e H 68
Metropolitan, MI d H 54
Metter, GA g D 40
Mexia, TX h J 84
Mexican Hat, UT g G 98
Mexico, ME c P 26
Mexico, MO c E 68
Mexico, NY d J 26
Mexico, Gulf of g H 8
Mexico Beach, FL j A 40
Meyers Chuck, AK i BB 142
Meyersdale, PA h G 26
Miami, AZ k F 98
Miami, FL n F 40
Miami, OK c L 84
Miami, TX d F 84
Miami Beach, FL n F 40
Miami Canal, FL m F 40
Miamisburg, OH h B 26
Miami Springs, FL n F 40
Micanopy, FL j D 40
Michigamme, r., MI d G 54
Michigan, ND c I 82
Michigan, state, US c I 8
Michigan, Lake, US f H 54
Michigan Center, MI h K 54
Michigan City, IN a J 68
Middle, r., IA a B 68
Middleboro, MA f P 26
Middlebourne, WV h F 26
Middleburg, NY e L 26
Middleburg, PA g I 26
Middlebury, VT c M 26
Middle Fabius, r., MO c D 68
Middlefield, OH f E 26
Middle Loup, r., NE j H 82
Middle Point, OH g B 26
Middleport, OH h D 26
Middlesboro, KY c C 40
Middlesex, NC d H 40
Middleton, MI g K 54
Middleton, TN g H 68
Middleton, WI g F 54
Middleton Island, AK g U 142
Middletown, CA f C 128
Middletown, CT f N 26
Middletown, DE h K 26
Middletown, IL b G 68
Middletown, IN b K 68
Middletown, KY d K 68
Middletown, MD h I 26
Middletown, NY f L 26
Middletown, OH h B 26
Middletown, PA g J 26
Middletown, RI f O 26
Middletown, VA h H 26
Middleville, MI h J 54
Midland, CA k K 128
Midland, MI g K 54
Midland, NC d F 40
Midland, SD g F 82
Midland, TX h D 84
Midlothian, TX g J 84
Midvale, ID f I 112
Midville, GA g D 40
Midway, AL j K 68
Midway, KY i B 26
Midway, TX h K 84
Midway, UT d E 98
Midway Park, NC e I 40
Midwest, WY a J 98
Midwest City, OK d I 84
Mifflinburg, PA g I 26
Milaca, MN e B 54
Milan, GA g C 40
Milan, IN c K 68
Milan, MI h L 54
Milan, MN f L 82
Milan, MO b C 68
Milan, NM i I 98
Milan, TN g H 68
Milano, TX i J 84
Milbank, SD f K 82
Milburn, OK e J 84
Mildred, PA f J 26
Miles, TX h F 84
Miles City, MT d T 112
Milford, CT f M 26
Milford, DE i K 26
Milford, IL j H 54
Milford, IN a K 68
Milford, IA h L 82
Milford, ME c R 26
Milford, MA e O 26
Milford, MI h L 54
Milford, NH e O 26
Milford, NJ g K 26
Milford, PA f L 26
Milford, UT f C 98
Milford Center, OH g C 26
Milk, r., NA b S 112
Millard, NE j K 82
Millboro, VA b G 40
Millbrook, NY f M 26
Mill City, OR f C 112
Millcreek, PA e F 26
Millcreek, UT d E 98
Mill Creek, WV i G 26
Milledgeville, GA f C 40
Milledgeville, IL i F 54
Mille Lacs Lake, MN d B 54
Millen, GA g E 40
Miller, MO e C 68
Miller, SD g I 82
Miller Mountain, NV f G 128
Miller Peak, AZ m F 98
Millersburg, KY i B 26
Millersburg, MI e K 54
Millersburg, OH g E 26
Millersburg, PA g J 26
Millers Ferry, AL j I 68
Millersport, OH h D 26
Millersville, PA h J 26
Millerton, NY f M 26
Millett, TX k G 84
Mill Hall, PA f I 26
Milligan, FL k I 68
Milligan, NE k J 82
Millington, MI g L 54
Millington, TN g G 68
Millinocket, ME b R 26
Millport, AL i H 68
Millry, AL k H 68
Mills, WY b J 98
Milltown, IN d J 68
Milltown, MT d L 112
Milltown, WI e C 54
Mill Valley, CA g C 128
Millville, NJ h K 26
Millwood, VA h H 26
Millwood Lake, AR i B 68
Milnor, ND e J 82
Milo, IA i B 54
Milo, ME b R 26
Milpitas, CA g D 128
Milroy, IN c K 68
Milroy, PA g I 26
Milton, DE i K 26
Milton, FL l I 68
Milton, IA j C 54
Milton, ND c I 82
Milton, PA f J 26
Milton, VT c M 26
Milton, WV i D 26
Milton, WI h G 54
Milton-Freewater, OR e G 112
Miltonvale, KS l J 82
Milwaukee, WI g H 54
Milwaukee, r., WI g G 54
Milwaukie, OR e C 112
Mimbres, r., NM l I 98
Mims, FL k F 40
Mina, NV f G 128
Minatare, NE j D 82
Minco, OK d I 84
Minden, LA j C 68
Minden, NE k I 82
Minden, NV f F 128
Minden, WV j E 26
Minden City, MI g M 54
Mindenmines, MO e B 68
Mineola, TX g K 84
Mineral, WA d C 112
Mineral Point, WI h E 54
Mineral Springs, AR i C 68
Mineral Wells, TX g H 84
Minersville, PA g J 26
Minersville, UT f D 98
Minerva, OH g E 26
Mineville, NY c M 26
Mingo Junction, OH g F 26
Minier, IL b G 68
Minneapolis, KS l J 82
Minneapolis, MN f B 54
Minnehaha, WA e C 112
Minneola, KS n G 82
Minneota, MN g L 82
Minnesota, state, US b H 8
Minnesota, r., MN f B 54
Minnesota Lake, MN g B 54
Minnewaukan, ND c H 82
Minocqua, WI e F 54
Minong, WI d D 54
Minonk, IL j F 54
Minot, ND c F 82
Minster, OH g B 26
Minto, AK d T 142
Minto, ND c J 82
Minturn, CO e J 98
Mio, MI f K 54
Miranda, CA d B 128
Mirando City, TX l G 84
Misenheimer, NC d E 40
Mishawaka, IN a J 68
Mishicot, WI f H 54
Mission, SD h G 82
Mission, TX m H 84
Mississinewa, r., US b K 68
Mississippi, state, US e I 8
Mississippi, r., US e H 8
Mississippi Delta, LA m G 68
Mississippi Sound, US l H 68
Mississippi State, MS i H 68
Missoula, MT d L 112
Missouri, state, US d H 8
Missouri, r., US c G 8
Missouri Valley, IA j L 82
Mitchell, IN d J 68
Mitchell, NE j D 82
Mitchell, OR f E 112
Mitchell, SD h I 82
Mitchell, Lake, AL j J 68
Mitchell, Mount, NC d D 40
Mitchellville, IA i B 54
Mize, MS k G 68
Moab, UT f G 98
Mobeetie, TX d F 84
Moberly, MO c D 68
Mobile, AL l H 68
Mobile, AZ k D 98
Mobile, r., AL l H 68
Mobile Bay, AL l H 68
Mobridge, SD f G 82
Mocksville, NC d F 40
Moclips, WA c A 112
Modesto, CA g E 128
Moenkopi, AZ h E 98
Moffit, ND e G 82
Mogollon Rim, AZ j F 98
Mohall, ND c F 82
Mohave, Lake, US k I 128
Mohawk, MI c G 54
Mohawk, r., NY e L 26
Mojave, CA i G 128
Mojave Desert, CA j H 128
Mokapu Peninsula, HI f J 144c
Mokelumne, r., CA f D 128
Molalla, OR e C 112
Moline, IL i E 54
Moline, KS n K 82
Molino, FL l I 68
Molokai, HI a C 144a
Momence, IL i H 54
Mona, UT e E 98
Monaca, PA g F 26
Monadnock Mountain, NH e N 26
Monahans, TX h D 84
Monango, ND e I 82
Monarch, SC e E 40
Monarch Pass, CO f J 98
Moncks Corner, SC g F 40
Mondovi, WI f D 54
Monero, NM h J 98
Monessen, PA g G 26
Monett, MO f C 68
Monette, AR g F 68
Monico, WI e F 54
Monida Pass, US f M 112
Monitor Range, NV f I 128
Monitor Valley, NV f I 128
Monmouth, IL j E 54
Monmouth, OR f B 112
Mono Lake, CA f G 128
Monon, IN b J 68
Monona, IA g D 54
Monona, WI g F 54
Monongahela, r., US h G 26
Monroe, GA f C 40
Monroe, IA i B 54
Monroe, LA j D 68
Monroe, MI i L 54
Monroe, NE j J 82
Monroe, NY f L 26
Monroe, NC e E 40
Monroe, OR f B 112
Monroe, UT f D 98
Monroe, VA b G 40
Monroe, WA c D 112
Monroe, WI h F 54
Monroe City, IN d I 68
Monroe City, MO c E 68
Monroe Lake, IN c J 68
Monroeville, AL k I 68
Monroeville, IN b L 68
Monroeville, OH f D 26
Monroeville, PA g G 26
Monson, ME b Q 26
Montague, CA c C 128
Montague, MI g I 54
Montague, TX f I 84
Montague Island, AK f U 142
Montana, state, US b D 8
Montauk, NY f O 26
Montauk Point, NY f O 26
Mont Belvieu, TX j L 84
Montclair, CA j H 128
Montclair, NJ g L 26
Monteagle, TN g K 68
Montecito, CA j F 128
Montegut, LA m F 68
Montello, NV c K 128
Montello, WI g F 54
Monterey, CA h D 128
Monterey, TN f K 68
Monterey, VA i G 26
Monterey Bay, CA h D 128
Montesano, WA d B 112
Montevallo, AL i J 68
Montevideo, MN g L 82
Monte Vista, CO g J 98
Montezuma, GA h B 40
Montezuma, IN c I 68
Montezuma, IA i C 54
Montezuma, KS n G 82
Montfort, WI h E 54
Montgomery, AL j J 68
Montgomery, LA k D 68
Montgomery, MN f B 54
Montgomery, PA f J 26
Montgomery, TX i K 84
Montgomery, WV i E 26
Montgomery City, MO d E 68
Monticello, AR i E 68
Monticello, FL i C 40
Monticello, GA f C 40
Monticello, IL b H 68
Monticello, IN b J 68
Monticello, IA h D 54
Monticello, KY f L 68
Monticello, MN e B 54
Monticello, MS k F 68
Monticello, MO b E 68
Monticello, NY f L 26
Monticello, UT g G 98
Monticello, WI h F 54
Montour Falls, NY e J 26
Montoursville, PA f J 26
Montpelier, ID h N 112
Montpelier, IN g A 26
Montpelier, MS i H 68
Montpelier, OH f B 26
Montpelier, VT c N 26
Montreal, WI d E 54
Montrose, CO f I 98
Montrose, IA j D 54
Montrose, MI g L 54
Montrose, PA f K 26
Montrose, SD h J 82
Montross, VA i J 26
Montvale, VA b G 40
Monument, OR f F 112
Monument Peak, ID h K 112
Monument Valley, US g F 98
Moody, TX h I 84
Moorcroft, WY g C 82
Moore, ID g L 112
Moore, MT d P 112
Moore, OK d I 84
Moore, TX j G 84
Moorefield, WV h H 26
Moore Haven, FL m E 40
Mooreland, OK c G 84
Mooresville, IN c J 68
Mooresville, NC d F 40
Moorhead, MN e K 82
Moorhead, MS i F 68
Mooringsport, LA j C 68
Moosehead Lake, ME b Q 26
Moose Lake, MN d C 54
Mooselookmeguntic Lake, ME c P 26
Moose Pass, AK f T 142
Mora, MN e B 54
Mora, NM i K 98
Mora, r., NM h K 98
Moran, KS n L 82
Moran, MI e K 54
Moran, TX g G 84
Moravia, IA j C 54
Moravia, NY e J 26
Moreau, r., SD f F 82
Moreauville, LA k E 68
Morehead, KY i C 26
Morehead City, NC e J 40
Morehouse, MO f G 68
Moreland, GA f B 40
Moreland, KY e L 68
Morenci, AZ k G 98
Morenci, MI i K 54
Morgan, GA h B 40
Morgan, MN g M 82
Morgan, TX g I 84
Morgan, UT c E 98
Morgan City, AL h J 68
Morgan City, LA m E 68
Morganfield, KY e I 68
Morgan Hill, CA g D 128
Morganton, NC d E 40
Morgantown, IN c J 68
Morgantown, KY e J 68
Morgantown, MS k E 68
Morgantown, WV h G 26
Morganza, LA l E 68
Moriah, Mount, NV e K 128
Moriarty, NM j J 98
Morley, MI g J 54
Morning Sun, IA i D 54
Moro, OR e E 112
Morocco, IN b I 68
Moroni, UT e E 98
Morrill, NE j D 82
Morrilton, AR g D 68
Morris, IL i G 54
Morris, MN f L 82
Morris, OK d K 84
Morrison, IL i F 54
Morrisonville, IL c G 68
Morristown, AZ k D 98
Morristown, IN c K 68
Morristown, MN f B 54
Morristown, SD f F 82
Morristown, TN c C 40
Morrisville, NY e K 26
Morrisville, PA g L 26
Morrisville, VT c N 26
Morro Bay, CA i E 128
Morrow, LA l D 68
Morse, LA l D 68
Morse, TX c E 84
Morton, IL j F 54
Morton, MN g M 82
Morton, MS j G 68
Morton, TX f D 84
Morton, WA d C 112
Mortons Gap, KY e I 68
Morven, GA i C 40
Morven, NC e F 40
Moscow, ID d I 112
Moselle, MS k G 68
Moses Lake, WA c F 112
Moses Point, AK d M 142
Mosheim, TN c D 40
Mosinee, WI f F 54
Mosquero, NM d C 84
Mosquito Creek Lake, OH f F 26
Moss Point, MS l H 68
Mott, ND e E 82
Moulton, AL h I 68
Moulton, IA j C 54
Moulton, TX j I 84
Moultrie, GA h C 40
Moultrie, Lake, SC f F 40
Mound Bayou, MS i F 68
Mound City, IL e G 68
Mound City, KS m M 82
Mound City, MO b A 68
Mound City, SD f G 82
Moundridge, KS m J 82
Mounds, IL e G 68
Mounds, OK d J 84
Moundsville, WV h F 26
Moundville, AL j I 68
Mountain, WI e G 54
Mountainair, NM j J 98
Mountainaire, AZ i E 98
Mountain Brook, AL i J 68
Mountain City, GA e C 40
Mountain City, NV c J 128
Mountain City, TN c E 40
Mountain Creek, AL j J 68
Mountain Grove, MO e D 68
Mountain Home, AR f D 68
Mountain Home, ID g J 112
Mountain Iron, MN c C 54
Mountain Lake, MN h M 82
Mountain Pine, AR h C 68
Mountain Point, AK i CC 142
Mountain View, AR g D 68
Mountain View, CA g C 128
Mountain View, MO f E 68
Mountain View, OK d H 84
Mountain View, WY c F 98
Mountain View, WY b J 98
Mountain Village, AK e M 142
Mount Airy, MD h I 26
Mount Airy, NC c F 40
Mount Angel, OR e C 112
Mount Ayr, IA k M 82
Mount Calm, TX h J 84
Mount Carmel, IL d I 68
Mount Carmel, PA g J 26
Mount Carroll, IL h F 54
Mount Clare, WV h F 26
Mount Clemens, MI h M 54
Mount Desert Island, ME c R 26
Mount Dora, FL k E 40
Mount Edgecumbe, AK h AA 142
Mount Enterprise, TX k B 68
Mount Gay, WV j D 26
Mount Gilead, NC d F 40
Mount Gilead, OH g D 26
Mount Holly, NC d E 40
Mount Holly Springs, PA g I 26
Mount Hope, KS n J 82
Mount Hope, WV j E 26
Mount Horeb, WI g F 54
Mount Ida, AR h C 68
Mount Jackson, VA i H 26
Mount Jewett, PA f H 26
Mount Juliet, TN f J 68
Mount Kisco, NY f M 26
Mount Lebanon, PA g F 26
Mount Morris, IL h F 54
Mount Morris, MI g L 54
Mount Morris, NY e I 26
Mount Olive, IL c G 68
Mount Olive, MS k G 68
Mount Olive, NC d H 40
Mount Olivet, KY i B 26
Mount Orab, OH h C 26
Mount Pleasant, IA j D 54
Mount Pleasant, MI g K 54
Mount Pleasant, NC d F 40
Mount Pleasant, PA g G 26
Mount Pleasant, SC g G 40
Mount Pleasant, TN g I 68
Mount Pleasant, TX f L 84
Mount Pleasant, UT e E 98
Mount Pulaski, IL b G 68
Mount Rainier National Park, WA d D 112
Mount Savage, MD h H 26
Mount Shasta, CA c C 128
Mount Sterling, IL c F 68
Mount Sterling, KY a C 40
Mount Sterling, OH h C 26
Mount Union, PA g I 26
Mount Vernon, AL k H 68
Mount Vernon, GA g D 40
Mount Vernon, IL d H 68
Mount Vernon, IN e I 68
Mount Vernon, IA i D 54
Mount Vernon, KY b B 40
Mount Vernon, MO e C 68
Mount Vernon, OH g D 26
Mount Vernon, OR f F 112
Mount Vernon, SD h I 82
Mount Vernon, TX f K 84
Mount Vernon, WA b C 112
Mount Victory, OH g C 26
Mount Wolf, PA g J 26
Moville, IA i K 82
Moweaqua, IL c G 68
Moyie Springs, ID b I 112
Mud, r., KY e J 68
Mud, r., WV i D 26
Muddy, r., NV h K 128
Muenster, TX f I 84
Mukilteo, WA c C 112
Mukwonago, WI h G 54
Mulberry, AR g B 68
Mulberry, FL l E 40
Mulberry, IN b J 68
Mulberry, r., AR g C 68
Mulberry Fork, r., AL i I 68
Mulchatna, r., AK f Q 142
Muldoon, TX j I 84
Muldraugh, KY e K 68
Muldrow, OK g B 68
Muleshoe, TX e D 84
Mulhall, OK c I 84
Mullan, ID c J 112
Mullen, NE i F 82
Mullens, WV b E 40
Mullett Lake, MI e K 54
Mullica, r., NJ h L 26
Mullin, TX h H 84
Mullins, SC e G 40
Mullinville, KS n H 82
Mulvane, KS n J 82
Mumford, TX i J 84
Muncie, IN b K 68
Muncy, PA f J 26
Munday, TX f G 84
Mundelein, IL h G 54
Munford, TN g G 68
Munfordville, KY e K 68
Munising, MI d I 54
Munsons Corners, NY e J 26
Munuscong Lake, NA d K 54
Murchison, TX g K 84
Murdo, SD h G 82
Murfreesboro, AR h C 68
Murfreesboro, NC c I 40
Murfreesboro, TN g J 68
Murphy, ID g I 112
Murphy, NC d B 40
Murphys, CA f E 128
Murphysboro, IL e G 68
Murray, IA i B 54
Murray, KY f H 68
Murray, UT d E 98
Murray, Lake, SC e E 40
Murray City, OH h D 26
Murrayville, IL c F 68
Muscatatuck, r., IN d J 68
Muscatine, IA i D 54
Muscle Shoals, AL h I 68
Muscoda, WI g E 54
Muskegon, MI g I 54
Muskegon, r., MI d A 26
Muskegon Heights, MI g I 54
Muskingum, r., OH h E 26
Muskogee, OK d K 84
Musselshell, r., MT c R 112
Mustang Island, TX l J 84
Mustinka, r., MN f K 82
Myerstown, PA g J 26
Myrtle Beach, SC f H 40
Myrtle Creek, OR g B 112
Myrtle Grove, FL l I 68
Myrtle Point, OR g A 112
Myrtletowne, CA d A 128
Mystic, CT f O 26
Mystic, IA j C 54
Myton, UT d F 98

N

Naalehu, HI j P 144d
Nabesna, AK e W 142
Naches, r., WA d D 112
Naco, AZ m G 98
Nacogdoches, TX k B 68
Nahma, MI e I 54
Nahunta, GA h E 40
Nairn, LA m G 68
Nakalele Point, HI a C 144a
Naknek, AK g P 142
Namakan Lake, NA b C 54
Namekagon, r., WI d C 54
Nampa, ID g I 112
Nanakuli, HI f I 144c
Nanticoke, PA f J 26
Nanticoke, r., US i K 26
Nantucket, MA f P 26
Nantucket Island, MA f P 26
Nantucket Sound, MA f P 26
Nanty Glo, PA g H 26
Napa, CA f C 128
Napakiak, AK f N 142
Na Pali Coast State Park, HI c G 144b
Napaskiak, AK f N 142
Naperville, IL i G 54
Naples, FL m E 40
Naples, ID b I 112
Naples, NY e I 26
Naples, TX f L 84
Napoleon, ND e H 82
Napoleon, OH f B 26
Napoleonville, LA m E 68
Nappanee, IN a J 68
Nara Visa, NM d C 84
Narrows, VA b F 40
Nash, TX i B 68
Nashua, IA h C 54
Nashua, MT b S 112
Nashua, NH e O 26
Nashville, AR i C 68
Nashville, GA h C 40
Nashville, IL d G 68
Nashville, IN c J 68
Nashville, MI h J 54
Nashville, NC d I 40
Nashville, TN f J 68
Nashwauk, MN c B 54
Nassau, NY e M 26
Nassawadox, VA b K 40
Natalia, TX j H 84
Natchez, MS k E 68
Natchitoches, LA k C 68
National City, CA l H 128
Natoma, KS l H 82
Naturita, CO f H 98
Naugatuck, CT f M 26
Nauvoo, IL j D 54
Navajo, NM i G 98
Navajo, r., US g J 98
Navajo Mountain, UT g F 98
Navajo Reservoir, US h I 98
Navarre, OH g E 26
Navasota, TX i J 84
Navasota, r., TX h J 84
Navassa, NC e H 40
Navidad, r., TX j J 84
Naylor, MO f F 68
Nazareth, PA g K 26
Neah Bay, WA b A 112
Near Islands, AK j A 143a
Nebo, IL c F 68
Nebo, Mount, UT e E 98
Nebraska, state, US c F 8
Nebraska City, NE k L 82
Necedah, WI f E 54
Neche, ND c J 82
Neches, TX h K 84
Neches, r., TX l B 68
Nederland, TX m C 68
Neebish Island, MI d K 54

Name	Map Ref.	Page
Needle Mountain, WY	f P	112
Needles, CA	j K	128
Needville, TX	j K	84
Neenah, WI	f G	54
Negaunee, MI	d H	54
Nehalem, r., OR	e B	112
Nehawka, NE	k L	82
Neihart, MT	d O	112
Neillsville, WI	f E	54
Nekoosa, WI	f F	54
Neligh, NE	i I	82
Nelson, NE	k I	82
Nelsonville, OH	h D	26
Nemadji, r., US	d C	54
Nemaha, NE	k L	82
Nenana, AK	d T	142
Nenana, r., AK	d T	142
Neodesha, KS	n L	82
Neoga, IL	c H	68
Neola, IA	j L	82
Neola, UT	d F	98
Neopit, WI	f G	54
Neosho, MO	f B	68
Neosho, r., US	f B	68
Nephi, UT	e E	98
Neptune, NJ	g L	26
Neptune Beach, FL	i E	40
Ness City, KS	m H	82
Nettleton, MS	h H	68
Neuse, r., NC	e J	40
Nevada, IA	h B	54
Nevada, MO	e B	68
Nevada, OH	g C	26
Nevada, state, US	d C	8
Nevada, Sierra, CA	f F	128
Nevada City, CA	e D	128
New, r., NA	i J	128
New, r., US	b F	40
New, r., SC	g F	40
New, r., TN	c B	40
New Albany, IN	d K	68
New Albany, MS	h G	68
New Albin, IA	g D	54
Newark, AR	g E	68
Newark, DE	h K	26
Newark, NJ	d I	26
Newark, NY	d I	26
Newark, OH	g D	26
Newark Valley, NY	e J	26
New Athens, IL	d G	68
New Augusta, MS	k G	68
Newaygo, MI	g J	54
New Baden, IL	d G	68
New Baltimore, MI	h M	54
New Bedford, MA	f P	26
Newberg, OR	e C	112
New Berlin, IL	c G	68
New Berlin, NY	e K	26
New Berlin, WI	h G	54
Newbern, AL	j I	68
New Bern, NC	d I	40
Newbern, TN	f G	68
Newberry, FL	j D	40
Newberry, MI	d J	54
Newberry, SC	e E	40
New Bethlehem, PA	f G	26
New Bloomfield, PA	g I	26
New Boston, IL	i E	54
New Boston, OH	i D	26
New Boston, TX	i B	68
New Braunfels, TX	j H	84
New Bremen, OH	g B	26
New Britain, CT	f N	26
New Brockton, AL	k K	68
New Brunswick, NJ	g L	26
New Buffalo, MI	i I	54
Newburg, MO	e E	68
Newburgh, IN	e I	68
Newburgh, NY	f L	26
Newburyport, MA	e P	26
New Carlisle, IN	b K	68
Newcastle, CA	f D	128
New Castle, CO	e I	98
New Castle, DE	h K	26
New Castle, IN	c K	68
New Castle, KY	d K	68
Newcastle, NE	i K	82
Newcastle, OK	d I	84
New Castle, PA	f F	26
Newcastle, TX	f H	84
New Castle, VA	b F	40
Newcastle, WY	h C	82
New City, NY	f M	26
Newcomerstown, OH	g E	26
New Concord, OH	h E	26
New Cumberland, WV	f G	26
New Edinburg, AR	i D	68
New Effington, SD	f K	82
New Egypt, NJ	g L	26
Newell, IA	i L	82
Newell, SD	g D	82
Newell, WV	f G	26
New Ellenton, SC	f E	40
Newellton, LA	j E	68
New England, ND	e E	82
Newfane, NY	d H	26
Newfane, VT	e N	26
New Florence, MO	d E	68
New Florence, PA	g G	26
Newfound Gap, US	d C	40
New Franklin, MO	c D	68
New Freedom, PA	h J	26
New Giarus, WI	h F	54
Newgulf, TX	j K	84
Newhalem, WA	b D	112
Newhalen, AK	g Q	142
Newhall, CA	j I	128
New Hampshire, state, US	c L	8
New Hampton, IA	g C	54
New Harmony, IN	d I	68
New Hartford, CT	f N	26
New Hartford, IA	h C	54
New Haven, CT	f N	26
New Haven, IL	e H	68
New Haven, IN	a K	68
New Haven, KY	e K	68
New Haven, MO	d E	68
New Haven, WV	i E	26
Newhebron, MS	k G	68
New Holland, OH	h C	26
New Holland, PA	h J	26
New Holstein, WI	g G	54
New Hope, AL	h H	68
New Iberia, LA	l E	68
New Jersey, state, US	c L	8
New Johnsonville, TN	f I	68
New Kensington, PA	g G	26
New Kent, VA	b J	40
Newkirk, OK	c I	84
Newland, NC	c E	40
New Leipzig, ND	e F	82
New Lexington, OH	h D	26
New Lisbon, WI	g E	54
Newllano, LA	k C	68
New London, CT	f N	26
New London, IA	j D	54
New London, MN	f M	82
New London, MO	c E	68
New London, NH	e N	26
New London, OH	f D	26
New London, TX	j B	68
New London, WI	f G	54
New Madrid, MO	f G	68
Newman, CA	g D	128
Newman, IL	c I	68
Newman Grove, NE	j J	82
New Market, AL	h J	68
New Market, IA	k M	82
New Market, VA	i H	26
Newmarket, NH	d P	26
New Martinsville, WV	h F	26
New Meadows, ID	f I	112
New Mexico, state, US	e E	8
New Milford, CT	f M	26
New Milford, PA	f K	26
Newnan, GA	f B	40
New Orleans, LA	m F	68
New Oxford, PA	h J	26
New Paltz, NY	f L	26
New Paris, OH	h B	26
New Philadelphia, OH	g E	26
New Pine Creek, OR	i E	112
New Plymouth, ID	g I	112
Newport, AR	g E	68
Newport, IN	c I	68
Newport, KY	h B	26
Newport, ME	c Q	26
Newport, NH	d N	26
Newport, NC	e J	40
Newport, OR	f A	112
Newport, PA	g I	26
Newport, RI	f O	26
Newport, TN	d C	40
Newport, VT	c N	26
Newport, WA	b H	112
Newport Beach, CA	k H	128
Newport News, VA	c J	40
New Port Richey, FL	k D	40
New Prague, MN	f E	54
New Providence, TN	f I	68
New Richland, MN	g B	54
New Richmond, OH	i E	26
New Richmond, WI	e C	54
New Roads, LA	l E	68
New Rochelle, NY	g M	26
New Rockford, ND	d H	82
Newry, SC	e D	40
New Salem, ND	f F	82
New Sharon, IA	i C	54
New Smyrna Beach, FL	j F	40
New Stuyahok, AK	g P	142
North Fork, CA	g F	128
New Tazewell, TN	c C	40
Newtok, AK	f L	142
Newton, GA	h B	40
Newton, IL	d H	68
Newton, IA	i B	54
Newton, KS	m J	82
Newton, MA	e O	26
Newton, MS	j G	68
Newton, NJ	f L	26
Newton, NC	d E	40
Newton, TX	l C	68
Newton Falls, NY	c L	26
New Town, ND	d E	82
New Ulm, MN	g M	82
New Ulm, TX	j J	84
New Vienna, OH	h C	26
Newville, PA	g I	26
New Vineyard, ME	c P	26
New Washington, OH	g D	26
New Waverly, TX	i K	84
New Whiteland, IN	c J	68
New Wilmington, PA	f F	26
New York, NY	g L	26
New York, state, US	c K	8
New York Mills, MN	e L	82
New York State Barge Canal, NY	d H	26
Nezperce, ID	d I	112
Niagara, WI	f H	54
Niagara Falls, NY	d G	26
Niangua, r., MO	e D	68
Niantic, IL	c G	68
Niceville, FL	l J	68
Nicholasville, KY	b B	40
Nicholls, GA	h D	40
Nicholson, MS	k F	68
Nicholson, PA	f K	26
Nickerson, KS	m I	82
Nicolet, Lake, MI	d K	54
Nicollet, MN	f A	54
Niihau, HI	d F	144b
Nikolski, AK	j I	142
Niland, CA	k J	128
Niles, IL	h H	54
Niles, MI	i I	54
Niles, OH	f F	26
Ninety Six, SC	e D	40
Ninilchik, AK	f S	142
Ninnescah, r., KS	n J	82
Niobrara, NE	i I	82
Niobrara, r., US	i I	82
Niota, TN	d B	40
Nipomo, CA	i E	128
Nisqually, r., WA	d C	112
Nisswa, MN	e E	82
Nitro, WV	i E	26
Nixa, MO	f B	68
Nixon, NV	e F	128
Nixon, TX	j I	84
Noatak, AK	c M	142
Noble, IL	d H	68
Noble, OK	d I	84
Noblesville, IN	c J	68
Nocatee, FL	l E	40
Nocona, TX	i I	84
Nodaway, r., US	b A	68
Noel, MO	f B	68
Nogales, AZ	m F	98
Nokomis, FL	l D	40
Nokomis, IL	c G	68
Nolichucky, r., US	c C	40
Nolin, r., KY	e J	68
Nolin Lake, KY	e J	68
Nome, AK	d L	142
Nondalton, AK	f Q	142
Nooksack, r., WA	b C	112
Noonan, ND	c D	82
Noorvik, AK	c N	142
Nora Springs, IA	g B	54
Norborne, MO	c C	68
Norcatur, KS	l G	82
Norcross, GA	f A	40
Nordheim, TX	k I	84
Norfolk, NE	i H	82
Norfolk, VA	c J	40
Norfork Lake, US	f D	68
Norlina, NC	c H	40
Normal, AL	h J	68
Normal, IL	c H	68
Norman, AR	h C	68
Norman, OK	d I	84
Norman, Lake, NC	d F	40
Normangee, TX	h J	84
Norman Park, GA	h C	40
Norphlet, AR	i C	68
Norridgewock, ME	c Q	26
Norris, TN	c B	40
Norris City, IL	e H	68
Norris Lake, TN	c C	40
Norristown, PA	g K	26
North, SC	f E	40
North, r., AL	i I	68
North, r., VA	i B	54
North Adams, MA	e M	26
North Albany, OR	f B	112
Northampton, MA	e N	26
Northampton, PA	g K	26
North Anna, r., VA	b I	40
North Anson, ME	c Q	26
North Asheboro, NC	d G	40
North Atlanta, GA	f B	40
North Augusta, SC	f E	40
North Baltimore, OH	f C	26
North Bend, NE	j K	82
North Bend, OR	f A	112
North Bennington, VT	e M	26
North Berwick, ME	d P	26
North Branch, MI	g L	54
North Branch, MN	e C	54
North Canadian, r., OK	d J	84
North Canton, GA	e B	40
North Canton, OH	g E	26
North Carolina, state, US	d K	8
North Cascades National Park, WA	b D	112
North Charleston, SC	g G	40
North Chicago, IL	h H	54
North College Hill, OH	h B	26
North Collins, NY	e H	26
North Conway, NH	c O	26
North Creek, NY	d M	26
North Crossett, AR	i E	68
North Dakota, state, US	b F	8
North East, MD	h K	26
North East, PA	e G	26
North English, IA	i C	54
North Fabius, r., MO	b D	68
Northfield, MN	f B	54
Northfield, NH	d N	26
Northfield, VT	c N	26
North Fond du Lac, WI	g G	54
North Fork, CA	g F	128
North Fork, r., US	f D	68
North Fort Myers, FL	m E	40
North Freedom, WI	g F	54
North Glenn, CO	e L	98
North Gulfport, MS	l G	68
North Henderson, NC	c H	40
North Hero, VT	c M	26
North Highlands, CA	f D	128
North Judson, IN	a J	68
North Kenai, AK	f S	142
North Kingsville, OH	e H	26
North La Junta, CO	n D	82
North Las Vegas, NV	h J	128
North La Veta Pass, CO	g K	98
North Liberty, IA	h C	54
North Little Rock, AR	h D	68
North Logan, UT	c E	98
North Loon Mountain, ID	e J	112
North Loup, NE	j I	82
North Loup, r., NE	j I	82
North Mamm Peak, CO	e I	98
North Manchester, IN	a K	68
North Manitou Island, MI	e I	54
North Mankato, MN	f A	54
North Miami, FL	n F	40
North Miami Beach, FL	n F	40
North Muskegon, MI	g J	54
North Myrtle Beach, SC	f H	40
North New River Canal, FL	m F	40
North Newton, KS	m J	82
North Ogden, UT	c E	98
North Palisade, CA	g G	128
North Palm Beach, FL	m F	40
North Park, IL	h F	54
North Platte, NE	j G	82
North Platte, r., US	c F	8
North Pole, AK	d U	142
Northport, AL	i I	68
Northport, MI	e J	54
Northport, WA	b H	112
North Powder, OR	e H	112
North Richland Hills, TX	g I	84
North Rim, AZ	h D	98
North Salt Lake, UT	d E	98
North Santiam, r., OR	f B	112
North Terre Haute, IN	c I	68
North Troy, VT	c N	26
North Tunica, MS	h F	68
North Vernon, IN	d K	68
Northville, NY	d L	26
North Wilkesboro, NC	c E	40
North Windham, ME	d P	26
Northwood, IA	g B	54
Northwood, ND	d J	82
North Yamhill, r., OR	e B	112
North Zulch, TX	i J	84
Norton, KS	l H	82
Norton, VA	c D	40
Norton Shores, MI	g J	54
Norton Sound, AK	e L	142
Nortonville, KS	l L	82
Norwalk, CT	g M	26
Norwalk, IA	i B	54
Norwalk, OH	f D	26
Norway, IA	i D	54
Norway, MI	e H	54
Norway, ME	c P	26
Norwich, CT	f N	26
Norwich, KS	n J	82
Norwich, NY	e K	26
Norwood, CO	f H	98
Norwood, MA	e O	26
Norwood, MN	f B	54
Norwood, NC	d F	40
Norwood, OH	h B	26
Norwoodville, IA	i B	54
Notasulga, AL	j K	68
Notch Peak, UT	e C	98
Notrees, TX	h D	84
Nottawa, MI	h J	54
Nottoway, VA	b H	40
Nottoway, r., VA	c I	40
Novato, CA	f C	128
Novice, TX	h G	84
Novinger, MO	b D	68
Nowata, OK	c K	84
Nowitna, r., AK	d Q	142
Nowood, r., WY	f R	112
Noxapater, MS	j G	68
Noxen, PA	f J	26
Noxon, MT	b E	112
Noxubee, r., US	i H	68
Nucla, CO	f H	98
Nueces, r., TX	l I	84
Nulato, AK	d G	142
Numila, HI	d G	144b
Nunapitchuk, AK	f M	142
Nunda, NY	e I	26
Nunivak Island, AK	f K	142
Nunnelly, TN	g I	68
Nursery, TX	k I	84
Nutrioso, AZ	k G	98
Nutter Fort, WV	h F	26
Nyack, NY	f M	26
Nyssa, OR	g I	112

O

Name	Map Ref.	Page
Oacoma, SD	h H	82
Oahe, Lake, US	f G	82
Oahu, HI	e J	144c
Oak Bluffs, MA	f P	26
Oakboro, NC	d F	40
Oak City, NC	d I	40
Oak City, UT	e D	98
Oak Creek, CO	d J	98
Oak Creek, r., AZ	j E	98
Oakdale, CA	g E	128
Oakdale, LA	l D	68
Oakdale, NE	i J	82
Oakdale, TN	d B	40
Oakes, ND	e I	82
Oakesdale, WA	c H	112
Oakfield, ME	a R	26
Oakfield, NY	d H	26
Oakfield, WI	g G	54
Oak Grove, LA	k E	68
Oak Harbor, WA	b C	112
Oak Hill, FL	k F	40
Oak Hill, MI	f I	54
Oak Hill, OH	i D	26
Oak Hill, WV	i E	26
Oakhurst, CA	g F	128
Oakhurst, TX	i K	84
Oak Knolls, CA	j E	128
Oakland, CA	g C	128
Oakland, IL	c H	68
Oakland, IA	j L	82
Oakland, ME	c Q	26
Oakland, MD	h G	26
Oakland, MS	h G	68
Oakland, NE	j K	82
Oakland, OR	g B	112
Oakland City, IN	d I	68
Oakland Park, FL	m F	40
Oak Lawn, IL	i H	54
Oaklawn, KS	n J	82
Oakley, ID	h L	112
Oakley, KS	l G	82
Oakman, AL	i I	68
Oak Park, IL	i H	54
Oakridge, OR	g C	112
Oak Ridge, TN	c B	40
Oaktown, IN	d I	68
Oak View, CA	j F	128
Oakwood, OH	f B	26
Oakwood, TX	h K	84
Oatman, AZ	i B	98
Obed, r., TN	c B	40
Oberlin, IL	l G	82
Oberlin, LA	l D	68
Oberlin, OH	f E	26
Obion, TN	f G	68
Obion, r., TN	f G	68
Oblong, IL	c I	68
O'Brien, OR	h B	112
Ocala, FL	j D	40
Oceana, WV	b E	40
Ocean Cape, AK	g Y	142
Ocean City, MD	i K	26
Ocean City, NJ	h L	26
Oceano, CA	i E	128
Ocean Park, WA	d A	112
Oceanside, CA	k H	128
Ocean Springs, MS	l H	68
Ocheyedan, IA	h L	82
Ochlockonee, GA	h B	40
Ochlockonee, r., US	i B	40
Ocilla, GA	h C	40
Ocmulgee, r., GA	h C	40
Ocoee, FL	k E	40
Ocoee (Toccoa), r., US	d B	40
Oconee, r., GA	g D	40
Oconomowoc, WI	g G	54
Oconto, WI	f H	54
Oconto, r., WI	f G	54
Oconto Falls, WI	f G	54
Ocracoke, NC	d K	40
Ocracoke Island, NC	d K	40
Odebolt, IA	i L	82
Odell, IL	i G	54
Odell, NE	k K	82
Odell, TX	e G	84
Odem, TX	l I	84
Odessa, MO	d C	68
Odessa, TX	h D	84
Odessa, WA	c G	112
Odon, IN	d J	68
O'Donnell, TX	g E	84
Odum, GA	h D	40
Oelwein, IA	h D	54
O'Fallon, MO	d F	68
Ogallala, NE	j F	82
Ogden, IA	h A	54
Ogden, KS	l K	82
Ogden, UT	c E	98
Ogdensburg, NY	c K	26
Ogeechee, r., GA	g D	40
Ogilvie, MN	e B	54
Oglesby, IL	i F	54
Oglesby, TX	h I	84
Oglethorpe, GA	g B	40
Ogunquit, ME	d P	26
Ohio, IL	i F	54
Ohio, state, US	c J	8
Ohio, r., US	d I	8
Ohio City, OH	g B	26
Oil City, LA	j C	68
Oil City, PA	f G	26
Oil Creek, r., PA	f G	26
Oildale, CA	i F	128
Oilton, OK	c J	84
Oilton, TX	l H	84
Oil Trough, AR	g E	68
Ojai, CA	j F	128
Okanogan, WA	b F	112
Okanogan, r., NA	b F	112
Okarche, OK	d I	84
Okawville, IL	d G	68
Okeechobee, FL	l F	40
Okeechobee, Lake, FL	m F	40
Okeene, OK	c H	84
Okefenokee Swamp, US	i D	40
Okemah, OK	d J	84
Okemos, MI	h K	54
Oklahoma, state, US	d G	8
Oklahoma City, OK	d I	84
Oklawaha, FL	j E	40
Oklee, MN	d L	82
Okmulgee, OK	d K	84
Okolona, AR	i C	68
Okolona, KY	d K	68
Okolona, MS	h H	68
Ola, AR	g C	68
Olancha, CA	h G	128
Olancha Peak, CA	h G	128
Olanta, SC	f E	40
Olar, SC	f E	40
Olathe, CO	f I	98
Olathe, KS	m M	82
Olcott, NY	d H	26
Olden, TX	g H	84
Old Faithful Geyser, WY	f O	112
Old Forge, NY	d L	26
Old Forge, PA	f K	26
Oldham, SD	g J	82
Old Harbor, AK	h R	142
Old Hickory Lake, TN	f J	68
Old Orchard Beach, ME	d P	26
Old Saybrook, CT	f N	26
Old Town, ME	c R	26
Old Trap, NC	c J	40
Olean, NY	e H	26
Olin, IA	h D	54
Olive Branch, MS	h G	68
Olive Hill, KY	i C	26
Olivehurst, CA	f D	128
Oliver Springs, TN	c B	40
Olivet, MI	h J	54
Olivet, SD	h J	82
Olivia, MN	g M	82
Olla, LA	k D	68
Olney, IL	d H	68
Olney, TX	f H	84
Olpe, KS	m K	82
Olton, TX	e D	84
Olustee, FL	i D	40
Olustee, OK	e G	84
Olympia, WA	c C	112
Olympic Mountains, WA	c B	112
Olympic National Park, WA	c B	112
Olympus, Mount, WA	c B	112
Omaha, NE	j L	82
Omaha, TX	i B	68
Omak, WA	b F	112
Omar, WV	b E	40
Omega, GA	h C	40
Omro, WI	f G	54
Onaga, KS	l K	82
Onamia, MN	e B	54
Onancock, VA	b K	40
Onarga, IL	i G	54
Onawa, IA	i K	82
Onaway, MI	e K	54
Oneco, FL	l D	40
One Hundred and Two, r., MO	c B	68
Oneida, IL	i E	54
Oneida, KY	b C	40
Oneida, NY	d K	26
Oneida, TN	c B	40
Oneida Lake, NY	d K	26
O'Neill, NE	i I	82
Onekama, MI	f I	54
Oneonta, AL	i J	68
Oneonta, NY	e K	26
Onida, SD	g G	82
Onset, MA	f P	26
Onslow Bay, NC	e I	40
Ontario, CA	j H	128
Ontario, OH	g D	26
Ontario, OR	f I	112
Ontario, Lake, NA	b I	8
Ontonagon, MI	d F	54
Ontonagon, r., MI	d F	54
Oolitic, IN	d J	68
Oologah, OK	c K	84
Oologah Lake, OK	c K	84
Oostburg, WI	g H	54
Opelika, AL	j K	68
Opelousas, LA	l D	68
Opheim, MT	b S	112
Ophir, UT	d D	98
Opp, AL	k J	68
Opportunity, MT	d E	112
Opportunity, WA	c H	112
Oquawka, IL	j E	54
Oracle, AZ	l F	98
Oran, MO	f G	68
Orange, MA	e N	26
Orange, TX	l C	68
Orange, VA	a H	40
Orangeburg, SC	f E	40
Orange City, FL	k E	40
Orange City, IA	h K	82
Orange Cove, CA	h F	128
Orange Grove, TX	l I	84
Orange Lake, FL	j D	40
Orange Park, FL	i E	40
Orangeville, UT	e E	98
Orbisonia, PA	g H	26
Orchard, NE	i I	82
Orchard City, CO	f I	98
Orchard Homes, MT	d K	112
Orchard Mesa, CO	e H	98
Orchard Park, NY	e H	26
Orchard Valley, WY	e L	98
Ord, NE	j I	82
Orderville, UT	g D	98
Ordway, CO	n C	82
Ore City, TX	j B	68
Oregon, IL	h F	54
Oregon, MO	c B	68
Oregon, OH	e C	26
Oregon, state, US	b B	8
Oregon City, OR	e B	112
Orem, UT	d E	98
Orfordville, WI	h F	54
Organ Needle, NM	l J	98
Orick, CA	c A	128
Orient, IA	j A	54
Oriental, NC	d J	40
Orion, IL	i E	54
Oriskany, NY	d K	26
Orland, CA	e C	128
Orlando, FL	k E	40
Orleans, CA	c B	128
Orleans, IN	d J	68
Orleans, MA	f Q	26
Orleans, NE	k H	82
Orleans, VT	c N	26
Ormond Beach, FL	j E	40
Orofino, ID	d I	112
Oro Grande, CA	j H	128
Orono, ME	c R	26
Oroville, CA	e D	128
Oroville, WA	b F	112
Oroville, Lake, CA	e D	128
Orrick, MO	c B	68
Orrin, ND	c G	82
Orrs Island, ME	d Q	26
Orrville, AL	j I	68
Orrville, OH	g E	26
Orting, WA	c C	112
Ortonville, MN	f K	82
Orwell, OH	f F	26
Osage, IA	g C	54
Osage, WY	h C	82
Osage, r., MO	d D	68
Osage Beach, MO	d D	68
Osage City, KS	m L	82
Osakis, MN	f L	82
Osawatomie, KS	m M	82
Osborne, KS	l I	82
Osburn, ID	c J	112
Osceola, AR	g G	68
Osceola, IA	i B	54
Osceola, MO	d C	68
Osceola, NE	j J	82
Osceola Mills, PA	g H	26
Oscoda, MI	f L	54
Osgood, IN	c K	68
Oshkosh, NE	j E	82
Oshkosh, WI	f G	54
Oskaloosa, IA	i C	54
Oskaloosa, KS	l L	82
Osseo, MN	i I	82
Ossabaw Island, GA	g E	40
Osseo, WI	f D	54
Ossian, IN	b K	68
Ossian, IA	g D	54
Ossining, NY	f M	26
Ossipee, NH	d O	26
Oswego, IL	i G	54
Oswego, KS	n L	82
Oswego, NY	d J	26
Oswego, r., NY	d J	26
Osyka, MS	k F	68
Othello, WA	d F	112
Otis, CO	k E	82
Otis, KS	m H	82
Otsego, MI	h J	54
Otselic, r., NY	e K	26
Ottawa, IL	i G	54
Ottawa, KS	m L	82
Ottawa, OH	f B	26
Otter Creek, FL	j D	40
Otter Lake, MI	g L	54
Otter Tail, r., MN	e K	82
Otterville, MO	d C	68
Ottumwa, IA	i C	54
Ouachita, r., US	b C	68
Ouachita, Lake, AR	h C	68
Ouachita Mountains, US	h B	68
Ouray, CO	f I	98
Ouray, Mount, CO	f J	98
Outer Island, WI	c E	54
Outlook, MT	c C	82
Overbrook, KS	m L	82
Overland Park, KS	m M	82
Overton, NE	k H	82
Overton, NV	h K	128
Overton, TX	j B	68
Ovett, MS	k G	68
Ovid, MI	g K	54
Ovid, NY	e J	26
Owasso, OK	c K	84
Owatonna, MN	f B	54
Owego, NY	e J	26
Owen, WI	f E	54
Owens, r., CA	h F	128
Owensboro, KY	e I	68
Owens Creek, MI	h H	128
Owensville, IN	d I	68
Owensville, MO	d E	68
Owenton, KY	d L	68
Owingsville, KY	i C	26
Owl Creek Mountains, WY	g Q	112
Owosso, MI	h K	54
Owyhee, NV	c I	112
Owyhee, r., US	g H	112
Owyhee, Lake, OR	g I	112
Oxford, AL	i K	68
Oxford, IN	b I	68
Oxford, IA	i D	54
Oxford, KS	n J	82
Oxford, ME	c P	26
Oxford, MD	i J	26
Oxford, MS	h G	68
Oxford, NY	e K	26
Oxford, NC	c H	40
Oxford, OH	h B	26
Oxford, PA	h K	26
Oxford, WI	g F	54
Oxford Junction, IA	i E	54
Oxnard, CA	j F	128
Ozark, AL	k K	68
Ozark, AR	g C	68
Ozark, MO	f C	68
Ozark Plateau, US	f C	68
Ozark Reservoir, AR	g B	68
Ozarks, Lake of the, MO	d D	68
Ozona, TX	i E	84

P

Name	Map Ref.	Page
Paauilo, HI	i P	144d
Pablo, MT	c K	112
Pace, FL	l I	68
Pace, MS	i F	68
Pacific, MO	d F	68
Pacifica, CA	g C	128
Pacific Grove, CA	h D	128
Pacific Ocean	f B	8
Pacolet, r., SC	e E	40
Pacolet Mills, SC	e E	40
Paden City, WV	h F	26
Padre Island, TX	l I	84
Paducah, KY	f H	68
Paducah, TX	f F	84
Page, AZ	h E	98
Page, ND	d J	82
Pageland, SC	e F	40
Pagoda Peak, CO	d I	98
Pagosa Springs, CO	g J	98
Paguate, NM	i I	98
Pahala, HI	j P	144d
Pahoa, HI	j Q	144d
Pahokee, FL	m F	40
Pahrump, NV	h J	128
Pahvant Range, UT	f D	98
Paia, HI	b D	144a
Paige, TX	i I	84
Pailolo Channel, HI	a C	144a
Painesdale, MI	c G	54
Painesville, OH	f E	26
Paint, r., MI	d G	54
Painted Desert, AZ	i E	98
Painted Rock Reservoir, AZ	k D	98
Paint Rock, TX	h G	84
Paint Rock, r., AL	h J	68
Paintsville, KY	b D	40
Paisley, OR	h E	112
Palaau State Park, HI	a B	144a
Palacios, TX	k J	84
Palaoa Point, HI	b C	144a
Palatka, FL	j E	40
Palestine, AR	h F	68
Palestine, IL	c I	68
Palestine, TX	h K	84
Palestine, Lake, TX	g K	84
Palikea, HI	f I	144c
Palisade, CO	e H	98
Palisade, NE	k F	82
Palisades, ID	g N	112
Palisades Reservoir, US	g N	112
Palm Bay, FL	k F	40
Palm Beach, FL	m F	40
Palmdale, CA	j G	128
Palm Desert, CA	k I	128
Palmer, AK	f T	142
Palmer, MA	e N	26
Palmer, MS	k G	68
Palmer, NE	j I	82
Palmer, TN	g K	68
Palmer, TX	g J	84
Palmer Lake, CO	f L	98
Palmerton, PA	g K	26
Palmetto, FL	l D	40
Palmetto, GA	f B	40
Palmetto, LA	l E	68
Palm Springs, CA	k I	128
Palmyra, IL	c G	68
Palmyra, MO	c E	68
Palmyra, NY	d I	26
Palmyra, PA	g J	26
Palmyra, VA	b H	40
Palo Alto, CA	h C	128
Palo Flechado Pass, NM	h K	98
Palomar Mountain, CA	k I	128
Palo Pinto, TX	g H	84
Palouse, WA	d H	112
Palouse, r., US	d G	112
Palo Verde, CA	k K	128
Pamlico, r., NC	d J	40
Pamlico Sound, NC	d K	40
Pampa, TX	f E	84
Pamplico, SC	f G	40
Pamunkey, r., VA	b I	40
Pana, IL	c G	68
Panaca, NV	g K	128
Panacea, FL	i B	40
Panama, IL	c G	68
Panama, OK	g B	68
Panama City, FL	l K	68
Panamint Range, CA	h H	128
Pangburn, AR	g E	68
Panguitch, UT	g D	98
Panhandle, TX	d E	84
Paniau, HI	d F	144b
Panola, AL	k J	68
Panora, IA	i A	54
Paola, KS	m M	82
Paoli, IN	d J	68
Paoli, OK	e I	84
Paonia, CO	f I	98
Papaikou, HI	j P	144d
Papawai Point, HI	b C	144a
Papillion, NE	j K	82
Parachute, CO	e H	98
Paradise, CA	e D	128
Paradise, MT	c K	112
Paradise, NV	h J	128
Paradise Valley, AZ	k E	98
Paradise Valley, NV	c H	128
Paragonah, UT	g D	98
Paragould, AR	f F	68
Parchment, MI	h J	54
Pardeeville, WI	g F	54
Paria, r., US	h E	98
Paris, AR	g C	68
Paris, ID	h N	112
Paris, IL	c I	68
Paris, KY	i B	40
Paris, ME	c P	26
Paris, MO	c D	68
Paris, TN	f H	68
Paris, TX	f K	84
Park, r., ND	c J	82
Park City, KS	n J	82
Park City, MT	e Q	112
Park City, UT	d E	98
Parkdale, OR	e D	112
Parker, AZ	j B	98
Parker, CO	f L	98
Parker, ID	f K	68
Parker, SD	h J	82
Parker Dam, CA	k K	128
Parkersburg, IL	d H	68
Parkersburg, IA	h C	54
Parkersburg, WV	h E	26
Parkers Prairie, MN	e L	82
Park Falls, WI	e E	54
Park Forest, IL	i H	54
Parkland, WA	c C	112
Parkland, IN	a C	112
Park Range, CO	d I	98
Park Rapids, MN	e L	82
Park River, ND	c J	82
Parkrose, OR	e C	112
Parksley, VA	b K	40
Parkston, SD	h J	82
Parkville, MD	h J	26
Parkville, MO	c B	68
Parkwater, WA	c H	112
Parle, Lac qui, MN	f K	82
Parma, ID	g I	112
Parma, MO	f G	68
Parma, OH	f E	26
Parowan, UT	g D	98
Parrish, AL	i I	68
Parrish, FL	l D	40
Parshall, ND	d F	82
Parsons, KS	n L	82
Parsons, TN	g I	68
Parsons, WV	h G	26
Pasadena, CA	j G	128
Pasadena, TX	j L	84
Pascagoula, MS	l H	68

Name — Map Ref. Page

Pascagoula, r., MS I H 68
Pasco, WA d F 112
Pascoag, RI f O 26
Paso Robles, CA i E 128
Pasquotank, r., NC c J 40
Passadumkeag, ME b R 26
Passaic, NJ g L 26
Pastora Peak, AZ h G 98
Patagonia, AZ m F 98
Patchogue, NY g M 26
Pateros, WA b F 112
Paterson, NJ g L 26
Pathfinder Reservoir, WY b J 98
Patoka, IL d G 68
Patoka, r., IN d I 68
Patten, ME b R 26
Patterson, CA g D 128
Patterson, GA h O 40
Patterson, LA m E 68
Patterson, NC d F 40
Pattison, MS k F 68
Patton, PA g H 26
Pattonsburg, MO b B 68
Patuxent, r., MD i J 26
Paul, ID h L 112
Paulding, MS j G 68
Paulding, OH f B 26
Paulina Peak, OR g D 112
Paullina, IA i L 82
Pauloff Harbor (Pavlof Harbor), AK i M 142
Pauls Valley, OK e I 84
Pauwela, HI b D 144a
Pavillion, WY a H 98
Pavo, GA h B 40
Paw Creek, NC d F 40
Pawhuska, OK c J 84
Pawnee, OK c G 68
Pawnee, OK c J 84
Pawnee, r., KS m H 82
Pawnee City, NE k K 82
Pawnee Rock, KS m I 82
Paw Paw, IL i G 54
Paw Paw, MI h J 54
Paw Paw, WV h H 26
Paw Paw Lake, MI h I 54
Pawtucket, RI f O 26
Paxton, IL j G 54
Paxton, NE j F 82
Payette, ID f I 112
Payette, r., ID g I 112
Payne, OH f B 26
Paynesville, MN f M 82
Payson, AZ j E 98
Payson, IL c E 68
Payson, UT d E 98
Pea, r., US k J 68
Peabody, KS m J 82
Peabody, MA e P 26
Peace, r., FL I E 40
Peach Creek, WV j E 26
Peach Orchard, AR f D 40
Peach Springs, AZ i C 98
Peale, Mount, UT f G 98
Pearce, AZ m G 98
Pearisburg, VA b F 40
Pearl, IL c F 68
Pearl, MS j F 68
Pearl, r., US l G 68
Pearland, TX j K 84
Pearl City, HI f J 144c
Pearl Harbor, HI f J 144c
Pearl Harbor Naval Station, HI f J 144c
Pearl Peak, NV d J 128
Pearl River, LA l G 68
Pearl River, NY f L 26
Pearsall, TX k G 84
Pearsoll Peak, OR h B 112
Pearson, GA h D 40
Pecan Bayou, r., TX h G 84
Pecan Gap, TX f K 84
Pecatonica, IL h F 54
Pecatonica, r., US h F 54
Peck, MI g M 54
Pecos, NM i K 98
Pecos, TX h C 84
Pecos, r., US j E 84
Pedernales, r., TX i G 84
Peebles, OH i C 26
Pee Dee, r., US d F 40
Peekskill, NY f M 26
Pe Ell, WA d B 112
Peerless, MT b T 112
Peetz, CO k D 82
Pekin, IL j F 54
Pekin, IN d J 68
Pelahatchie, MS j G 68
Pelham, AL i J 68
Pelham, GA h B 40
Pelican, r., MN e K 82
Pelican Lake, WI e F 54
Pelican Rapids, MN e K 82
Pella, IA i C 54
Pell City, AL i J 68
Pellston, MI e K 54
Peloncillo Mountains, US l G 98
Pemadumcook Lake, ME b R 26
Pembina, ND c J 82
Pembine, WI e H 54
Pembroke, GA g E 40
Pembroke, KY f I 68
Pembroke, ME c S 26
Pembroke, NC e D 40
Pembroke, VA b F 40
Pembroke Pines, FL m F 40
Pemigewasset, r., NH d O 26
Pen Argyl, PA g K 26
Penasco, NM h K 98
Peñasco, Rio, r., NM l K 98
Pence, WI d E 54
Pender, NE i K 82
Pendleton, IN c K 68
Pendleton, OR e G 112
Pendleton, SC e D 40
Pend Oreille, r., NA f O 113
Pend Oreille, Lake, ID b I 112
Penfield, PA f H 26
Penitas, TX m H 84
Penn Hills, PA g G 26
Pennington Gap, VA c C 40
Pennsboro, WV h F 26
Penns Grove, NJ h K 26
Pennsylvania, state, US c K 8
Penn Yan, NY e I 26
Penobscot, r., ME b R 26
Penobscot Bay, ME c R 26
Pensacola, FL l I 68
Pensacola Bay, FL l I 68
Pensaukee, WI f G 54
Pentagon Mountain, MT c L 112
Pentwater, MI g I 54
Penwell, TX h D 84

Peoria, AZ k D 98
Peoria, IL j F 54
Peoria Heights, IL j F 54
Peotone, IL i H 54
Pepin, WI f C 54
Pepin, Lake, US f C 54
Pequot Lakes, MN d A 54
Peralta, NM j J 98
Perdido, AL k I 68
Perdido, r., US l I 68
Perdido Bay, US l I 68
Pere Marquette, r., MI g J 54
Perham, MN e L 82
Peridot, AZ k F 98
Perkasie, PA g K 26
Perkins, OK d I 84
Perkinston, MS l G 68
Perrin, TX f H 84
Perris, CA k H 128
Perry, FL l C 40
Perry, GA g C 40
Perry, IA i A 54
Perry, KS l L 82
Perry, MI h K 54
Perry, MO c E 68
Perry, NY e H 26
Perry, OK c I 84
Perry, UT c D 98
Perry Lake, KS l L 82
Perrysburg, OH f C 26
Perrysville, OH g D 26
Perryton, TX c F 84
Perryville, AK i O 142
Perryville, AR g D 68
Perryville, KY b B 40
Perryville, MO e G 68
Persia, IA i A 54
Perth Amboy, NJ g L 26
Peru, IL i F 54
Peru, IN b J 68
Peru, NE k L 82
Peru, NY c M 26
Peshtigo, WI e H 54
Peshtigo, r., WI e G 54
Petal, MS k G 68
Petaluma, CA f C 128
Petenwell Lake, WI f F 54
Peterborough, NH e O 26
Peterman, AL k I 68
Petersburg, AK h BB 142
Petersburg, IL b G 68
Petersburg, IN d I 68
Petersburg, MI i L 54
Petersburg, NE j I 82
Petersburg, TN g J 68
Petersburg, TX f E 84
Petersburg, VA b I 40
Petersburg, WV h I 26
Peterson, IA i L 82
Petit Bois Island, US l H 68
Petit Jean, r., AR g C 68
Petoskey, MI e K 54
Petrified Forest National Park, AZ j G 98
Petrolia, TX e H 84
Petros, TN c B 40
Pettus, TX k I 84
Pheba, MS i H 68
Phelps, NY e I 26
Phelps, WI d F 54
Phenix City, AL g A 40
Philadelphia, MS j G 68
Philadelphia, NY c K 26
Philadelphia, PA h K 26
Philadelphia, TN d B 40
Phil Campbell, AL h I 68
Philip, SD g F 82
Philipp, MS i F 68
Philippi, WV h F 26
Philipsburg, MT d L 112
Philipsburg, PA g H 26
Phillips, ME c P 26
Phillips, TX d E 84
Phillips, WI e E 54
Phillipsburg, KS l H 82
Phillipsburg, NJ g K 26
Philmont, NY e M 26
Philo, IL b H 68
Philo, OH h E 26
Philomath, OR f B 112
Phoenix, AZ k D 98
Phoenix, NY d J 26
Phoenixville, PA g K 26
Picacho, AZ l E 98
Picayune, MS l G 68
Picher, OK c L 84
Pickens, MS j G 68
Pickens, SC e D 40
Pickens, WV i F 26
Pickensville, AL i H 68
Pickford, MI d K 54
Pickstown, SD h I 82
Pickwick Lake, US h H 68
Piedmont, AL i K 68
Piedmont, MO e F 68
Piedmont, SC e D 40
Pierce, CO d L 98
Pierce, ID d J 112
Pierce, NE i J 82
Pierce City, MO f B 68
Pierceton, IN a K 68
Pierpont, SD g G 82
Pierre, SD g G 82
Pierre, Bayou, r., LA k C 68
Pierre Part, LA m E 68
Pierson, FL j E 40
Pierz, MN e A 54
Pigeon, MI g L 54
Pigeon, r., US d C 40
Pigeon, r., US i J 54
Pigeon, r., MI e K 54
Pigeon Forge, TN d C 40
Pigg, r., VA c F 40
Piggott, AR f F 68
Pike, r., WI e K 54
Pikes Peak, CO f K 98
Pikesville, MD h J 26
Piketon, OH h C 26
Pikeville, KY b D 40
Pikeville, TN g K 68
Pilger, NE i J 82
Pilot Grove, MO d D 68
Pilot Knob, MO e F 68
Pilot Mountain, NC c F 40
Pilot Peak, NV f H 128
Pilot Point, TX f J 84
Pilot Rock, OR e G 112
Pilot Station, AK f M 142
Pima, AZ l F 98
Pinardville, NH e O 26
Pinckney, MI h L 54

Pinckneyville, IL d G 68
Pinconning, MI g L 54
Pine, r., MI f L 54
Pine, r., WI e G 54
Pine Apple, AL k J 68
Pine Barrens, NJ h L 26
Pine Bluff, AR h D 68
Pine Bluffs, WY j C 82
Pine Bush, NY f L 26
Pine Castle, FL k E 40
Pine City, MN e C 54
Pine Creek Lake, OK e K 84
Pinedale, CA h F 128
Pinedale, WY b G 98
Pine Grove, PA g J 26
Pine Grove, WV h F 26
Pine Hill, AL k I 68
Pine Hills, FL k E 40
Pinehurst, GA g C 40
Pinehurst, ID e I 112
Pinehurst, NC d G 40
Pine Island, MN f C 54
Pine Island, FL m D 40
Pineland, TX i B 68
Pinellas Park, FL l D 40
Pine Mountain, WY i P 112
Pine Prairie, LA l D 68
Pine Ridge, SD h E 82
Pinetop, AZ j G 98
Pinetops, NC d I 40
Pine Valley, UT f C 98
Pineville, KY c C 40
Pineville, LA k D 68
Pineville, MO f B 68
Pineville, NC d F 40
Pineville, WV b E 40
Pinewood, SC f F 40
Piney, r., TN g I 68
Piney Woods, MS j G 68
Pinnacle Buttes, WY a I 98
Pinson, AL i J 68
Pioche, NV g K 128
Pioneer, OH f B 26
Pipestone, MN g K 82
Piqua, OH g B 26
Pirtleville, AZ m G 98
Pisgah Forest, NC d D 40
Pisinemo, AZ l D 98
Pismo Beach, CA i E 128
Pit, r., CA d C 128
Pittsboro, MS i G 68
Pittsboro, NC d G 40
Pittsburg, KS n M 82
Pittsburg, TX g L 84
Pittsburgh, PA g G 26
Pittsfield, IL c F 68
Pittsfield, ME c Q 26
Pittsfield, MA e M 26
Pittsfield, NH d O 26
Pittsford, MI i K 54
Pittston, PA f K 26
Pittsview, AL g A 40
Pixley, CA i F 128
Placerville, CA f E 128
Plain City, OH g C 26
Plain City, UT c D 98
Plain Dealing, LA j C 68
Plainfield, CT f O 26
Plainfield, IN c J 68
Plainfield, NJ g L 26
Plainfield, WI f F 54
Plains, GA g B 40
Plains, KS n G 82
Plains, MT c K 112
Plains, TX f D 84
Plainview, MN f C 54
Plainview, NE i J 82
Plainview, TX e E 84
Plainville, IN d I 68
Plainville, KS l H 82
Plainwell, MI h J 54
Plaistow, NH e O 26
Planada, CA g E 128
Plankinton, SD h I 82
Plano, IL i G 54
Plano, TX f J 84
Plantation, FL m F 40
Plant City, FL k D 40
Plantersville, AL j J 68
Plantersville, MS h H 68
Plantsite, AZ k G 98
Plaquemine, LA l E 68
Platte, SD h I 82
Platte, r., MN d A 54
Platte, r., NE j E 82
Platte, r., WI h E 54
Platte Center, NE j J 82
Platte City, MO c B 68
Platteville, CO d L 98
Platteville, WI h E 54
Plattsburg, MO c B 68
Plattsburgh, NY c M 26
Plattsmouth, NE j L 82
Playas Lake, NM m H 98
Plaza, ND c F 82
Pleasant, Lake, AZ k D 98
Pleasant Gap, PA g I 26
Pleasant Garden, NC d G 40
Pleasant Grove, UT d E 98
Pleasant Hill, IL c F 68
Pleasant Hill, LA k C 68
Pleasant Hill, MO d B 68
Pleasanton, KS m M 82
Pleasanton, TX k H 84
Pleasant Plains, IL b G 68
Pleasantville, IA i B 54
Pleasantville, NJ h L 26
Pleasantville, PA f G 26
Plentywood, MT c C 82
Plevna, MT e C 82
Plover, r., WI f F 54
Plumerville, AR g D 68
Plummer, ID c I 112
Plymouth, CA f E 128
Plymouth, IL b F 68
Plymouth, IN a J 68
Plymouth, MA f P 26
Plymouth, MI h K 54
Plymouth, NH d O 26
Plymouth, NC d I 40
Plymouth, PA f K 26
Plymouth, WI g H 54
Pocahontas, AR f E 68
Pocahontas, IL d G 68
Pocahontas, IA i M 82
Pocatalico, r., WV i E 26
Pocatello, ID h M 112
Pocola, OK g B 68
Pocomoke, r., US j K 26
Pocomoke City, MD i L 26
Pocono Mountains, PA f K 26
Pocono Summit, PA f K 26
Point, TX g K 84
Point Arena, CA f B 128

Point Au Fer Island, LA m E 68
Point Comfort, TX k J 84
Pointe a la Hache, LA m H 68
Point Hope, AK b K 142
Point Imperial, AZ h E 98
Point Marion, PA h G 26
Point Pleasant, NJ g L 26
Point Pleasant, WV i D 26
Pojoaque Valley, NM i J 98
Polacca, AZ i F 98
Polihale State Park, HI c G 144b
Polk, NE j J 82
Polk, PA f G 26
Polkton, NC d F 40
Pollock, LA k D 68
Pollock, SD f G 82
Polo, IL i F 54
Polo, MO c B 68
Polson, MT c K 112
Pomerene, AZ m F 98
Pomeroy, IA i M 82
Pomeroy, OH h D 26
Pomeroy, WA d H 112
Pomme de Terre, r., MN f K 82
Pomme de Terre, r., MO e C 68
Pomona, CA j H 128
Pomona, KS m L 82
Pomona Park, FL j E 40
Pompano Beach, FL m F 40
Pompton Lakes, NJ f L 26
Ponca, NE i K 82
Ponca City, OK c I 84
Ponce de Leon, FL l K 68
Ponchatoula, LA l F 68
Pond, r., KY e l 68
Pondcreek, OK c l 84
Pondosa, CA c D 128
Pontchartrain, Lake, LA l F 68
Pontiac, IL j G 54
Pontiac, MI h L 54
Pontotoc, MS h H 68
Pontotoc, TX i H 84
Pony, MT e N 112
Pooler, GA g E 40
Poolville, TX g I 84
Pope, MS h G 68
Poplar, MT c B 82
Poplar, WI d D 54
Poplar, r., MN d K 82
Poplar Bluff, MO f F 68
Poplarville, MS l G 68
Popple, r., WI e G 54
Poquoson, VA b J 40
Porcupine, r., NA c W 142
Portage, UT c D 98
Portage, WI g F 54
Portage, r., OH f C 26
Portageville, MO f G 68
Portal, GA g E 40
Portal, ND c E 82
Portales, NM e C 84
Port Allegany, PA f H 26
Port Allen, LA l E 68
Port Angeles, WA b B 112
Port Aransas, TX l I 84
Port Arthur, TX m C 68
Port Austin, MI f M 54
Port Barre, LA l E 68
Port Byron, IL i E 54
Port Charlotte, FL m D 40
Port Chester, NY f M 26
Port Clinton, OH f D 26
Port Clyde, ME d Q 26
Porte Crayon, Mount, WV i G 26
Port Edwards, WI f F 54
Porter, OK d K 84
Porter, TX i K 84
Porterville, CA h F 128
Porterville, MS j H 68
Port Gamble, WA c C 112
Port Gibson, MS k F 68
Port Graham, AK g S 142
Port Henry, NY c M 26
Port Hope, MI g M 54
Port Huron, MI h M 54
Port Isabel, TX m I 84
Port Jervis, NY f L 26
Portland, AR i E 68
Portland, IN b L 68
Portland, ME d P 26
Portland, MI h K 54
Portland, ND d J 82
Portland, OR e C 112
Portland, TN f J 68
Portland, TX l I 84
Portland Canal, NA b D 24
Port Lavaca, TX k J 84
Port Leyden, NY d K 26
Port Lions, AK h R 142
Port Neches, TX m C 68
Portneuf, r., ID h M 112
Port Norris, NJ h K 26
Port O'Connor, TX k J 84
Portola, CA e E 128
Port Orange, FL j F 40
Port Orchard, WA c C 112
Port Orford, OR h A 112
Port Richey, FL k D 40
Port Royal, PA g I 26
Port Royal, SC g F 40
Port Saint Joe, FL l A 40
Port Saint Lucie, FL l F 40
Port Sanilac, MI g M 54
Portsmouth, NH d P 26
Portsmouth, OH i C 26
Portsmouth, VA c J 40
Port Sulphur, LA m G 68
Port Townsend, WA b C 112
Portville, NY f H 26
Port Wakefield, AK g R 142
Port Washington, WI g H 54
Port Wentworth, GA g E 40
Port Wing, WI d D 54
Porum, OK d K 84
Posen, MI e L 54
Possum Kingdom Lake, TX g H 84
Post, TX f E 84
Postelle, TN d B 40
Post Falls, ID c I 112
Postville, IA g D 54
Poteau, OK g B 68
Poteau, r., US g B 68
Poteet, TX k H 84
Poth, TX k H 84
Potholes Reservoir, WA c F 112
Potlatch, ID d I 112
Potomac, IL b l 68

Potomac, r., US i J 26
Potomac Heights, MD i l 26
Potosi, MO e F 68
Potsdam, NY c L 26
Potter, NE j D 82
Potterville, MI h K 54
Potts Camp, MS h G 68
Pottstown, PA g J 26
Pottsville, PA g J 26
Potwin, KS n J 82
Poughkeepsie, NY f M 26
Poulan, GA h C 40
Poulsbo, WA c C 112
Poultney, VT d M 26
Pound, VA b D 40
Poway, CA l H 128
Powder, r., US b E 8
Powder, r., OR f H 112
Powderly, KY e l 68
Powderly, TX f K 84
Powell, WY f Q 112
Powell, r., US c C 40
Powell, Lake, US g F 98
Powell, Mount, CO e J 98
Powellhurst, OR e C 112
Powellton, WV i E 26
Powers, MI e H 54
Powers, OR h A 112
Powers Lake, ND c E 82
Powhatan, LA k C 68
Powhatan, VA b l 40
Powhatan Point, OH h F 26
Poyen, AR h D 68
Poygan, Lake, WI f G 54
Poynette, WI g F 54
Prague, NE j K 82
Prague, OK d J 84
Prairie, r., MN c B 54
Prairie, r., WI e F 54
Prairie City, IL j E 54
Prairie City, IA i B 54
Prairie City, OR f G 112
Prairie du Chien, WI g D 54
Prairie du Sac, WI g F 54
Prairie Grove, AR g B 68
Prairie View, TX i K 84
Prairie Village, KS m M 82
Pratt, KS n l 82
Prattsburg, NY e l 26
Prattville, AL j J 68
Premont, TX l H 84
Prentice, WI e E 54
Prentiss, MS k G 68
Prescott, AZ j D 98
Prescott, AR i C 68
Prescott, WI f C 54
Presho, SD h G 82
Presidio, TX j B 84
Presque Isle, ME f E 26
Presque Isle, PA e F 26
Preston, GA g B 40
Preston, ID h N 112
Preston, IA h E 54
Preston, KS n l 82
Preston, MN g C 54
Prestonsburg, KY b D 40
Pretty Prairie, KS n l 82
Price, TX j B 84
Price, UT e F 98
Price, r., UT e F 98
Prichard, AL l H 68
Priddy, TX h H 84
Pribilof Islands, AK h l 142
Priest, r., ID b l 112
Priest Lake, ID b l 112
Priest River, ID b l 112
Primera, TX m l 84
Primghar, IA h L 82
Prince Frederick, MD i J 26
Prince George, VA b l 40
Prince of Wales, Cape, AK d J 142
Prince of Wales Island, AK i BB 142
Princess Anne, MD i L 26
Princeton, CA e C 128
Princeton, IL i F 54
Princeton, IN d l 68
Princeton, KY e l 68
Princeton, ME b S 26
Princeton, MN e B 54
Princeton, MO b C 68
Princeton, NJ g L 26
Princeton, NC d H 40
Princeton, WV b E 40
Princeton, WI f F 54
Princeville, IL j F 54
Princeville, NC d l 40
Prince William Sound, AK f U 142
Prineville, OR f E 112
Pritchett, CO n E 82
Proctor, MN d C 54
Proctor, VT d M 26
Project City, CA d C 128
Prophetstown, IL i F 54
Prospect, OH g C 26
Prosser, WA d F 112
Protection, KS n H 82
Provencal, LA k C 68
Providence, KY e l 68
Providence, RI f O 26
Providence, UT c E 98
Provincetown, MA e P 26
Provo, UT d E 98
Provo, r., UT d E 98
Pryor, OK c K 84
Prudhoe Bay, AK a T 142
Pueblo, CO f L 98
Pueblo of Acoma, NM i l 98
Pueo Point, HI b F 144b
Puerco, r., US i G 98
Puerco, Rio, r., NM i l 98
Puget Sound, WA c C 112
Puhi, HI d H 144b
Pukalani, HI b D 144a
Pulaski, NY d J 26
Pulaski, TN g l 68
Pulaski, VA b F 40
Pulaski, WI f G 54
Pullman, WA d H 112
Punaluu, HI e J 144c
Punta Gorda, FL m D 40
Punxsutawney, PA g H 26
Purcell, OK d l 84
Purcell Mountains, NA g R 24
Purcellville, VA h l 26
Purdy, MO f C 68
Purvis, MS k G 68
Putnam, CT f O 26
Putnam, TX g G 84
Putney, GA h B 40
Putney, VT e N 26

Pu'uhonua o Honaunau National Historical Park, HI j P 144d
Puukohola National Historic Site, HI i P 144d
Puukolii, HI b C 144a
Puunene, HI b D 144a
Puxico, MO f F 68
Puyallup, WA c C 112
Puyallup, r., WA d C 112
Pye Islands, AK g S 142
Pymatuning Reservoir, US f F 26
Pyote, TX h C 84
Pyramid Lake, NV d F 128

Q

Quabbin Reservoir, MA e N 26
Quakertown, PA g K 26
Quanah, TX e G 84
Quantico, VA i l 26
Quarryville, PA h J 26
Quartz Hill, CA j G 128
Quartz Mountain, OR g C 112
Quartzsite, AZ k B 98
Quebeck, TN g K 68
Queen City, MO b D 68
Queen City, TX i B 68
Quemado, NM j H 98
Quemado, TX k F 84
Questa, NM h K 98
Quilcene, WA c C 112
Quimby, IA i L 82
Quinault, r., WA c B 112
Quincy, CA e E 128
Quincy, FL i B 40
Quincy, IL c E 68
Quincy, MA e O 26
Quincy, MI i K 54
Quincy, WA c F 112
Quinhagak, AK g N 142
Quinlan, TX g J 84
Quinn, r., NV c G 128
Quinter, KS l G 82
Quinton, OK d K 84
Quitaque, TX e E 84
Quitman, GA i C 40
Quitman, MS j H 68
Quitman, TX g K 84
Qulin, MO f F 68

R

Rabbit Ears Pass, CO d J 98
Raccoon, r., IA a C 68
Race Point, MA e P 26
Racine, WI h H 54
Radcliff, KY e K 68
Radford, VA b F 40
Raeford, NC e G 40
Raft, r., US h L 112
Raft River Mountains, UT c C 98
Ragland, AL i J 68
Rahway, NJ g L 26
Raiford, FL i D 40
Rainelle, WV j F 26
Rainier, Mount, WA d D 112
Rainy, r., NA c N 82
Rainy Lake, NA b B 54
Raisin, r., MI i K 54
Raleigh, MS j G 68
Raleigh, NC d H 40
Ralls, TX f E 84
Ralston, NE j K 82
Ralston, PA f J 26
Ramah, NM i H 98
Ramer, AL j J 68
Ramona, CA l l 128
Ramona, OK c K 84
Ramona, SD g J 82
Rampart, AK d S 142
Ramseur, NC d G 40
Ramsey, IL c G 68
Ranburne, AL i K 68
Ranches of Taos, NM h K 98
Ranchester, WY f R 112
Rancho Cordova, CA f D 128
Randleman, NC d G 40
Randlett, OK e H 84
Randolph, AZ l E 98
Randolph, ME d P 26
Randolph, NE i J 82
Randolph, NY e H 26
Randolph, UT c E 98
Randolph, VT d N 26
Random Lake, WI g H 54
Rangely, CO d H 98
Ranger, TX g H 84
Rankin, IL b l 68
Rankin, TX h E 84
Ranlo, NC d E 40
Ransom, KS m H 82
Ranson, WV h l 26
Rantoul, IL b H 68
Raoul, GA e C 40
Rapid, r., MN c B 54
Rapid, r., MI b A 54
Rapidan, r., VA i l 26
Rapid City, MI f J 54
Rapid City, SD g E 82
Rapid River, MI e l 54
Rappahannock, r., VA b J 40
Rathbun Lake, IA j B 54
Rathdrum, ID c l 112
Rat Islands, AK k D 143a
Raton, NM g K 84
Raton Pass, NM o C 82
Rattlesnake, MT d L 112
Raven, VA b E 40
Ravena, NY e M 26
Ravenden, AR f E 68
Ravenna, KY g l 68
Ravenna, MI g J 54
Ravenna, NE j l 82
Ravenna, OH f E 26
Ravenswood, WV i E 26
Ravenwood, MO c B 68
Rawlins, WY c l 98
Ray, ND c E 82
Raymond, IL c G 68
Raymond, MN f L 82
Raymond, MS j F 68
Raymond, WA d B 112
Raymondville, TX m l 84
Rayne, LA l D 68
Rayville, LA j E 68

Reading, MI i K 54
Reading, OH h B 26
Reading, PA g J 26
Readlyn, IA h C 54
Readstown, WI g E 54
Realitos, TX l H 84
Reardan, WA c H 112
Rector, AR f F 68
Red, r., US e H 8
Red, r., KY b C 40
Red, r., NM h K 98
Red, r., US e G 54
Red Bank, NJ g L 26
Red Bank, TN g K 68
Red Banks, MS h G 68
Red Bay, AL h H 68
Redbay, FL l K 68
Red Bluff, CA d C 128
Red Boiling Springs, TN f K 68
Red Bud, IL d G 68
Red Cedar, r., MI h K 54
Red Cedar, r., WI e D 54
Red Cliff, CO e J 98
Red Cloud, NE k l 82
Red Devil, AK f P 142
Redding, CA d C 128
Redeye, r., MN e L 82
Redfield, IA j M 82
Redfield, SD g l 82
Red Hook, NY f M 26
Redkey, IN b K 68
Redlake, MN d L 82
Red Lake, r., MN d K 82
Red Lake Falls, MN d K 82
Redlands, CA j H 128
Redlands, CO e H 98
Red Level, AL k J 68
Red Lick, MS k F 68
Red Lion, PA h J 26
Red Lodge, MT e P 112
Redmond, OR f D 112
Redmond, UT e E 98
Redmond, WA c C 112
Red Mountain, CA c B 128
Red Mountain Pass, CO g l 98
Red Oak, IA j L 82
Red Oak, OK e K 84
Redondo Beach, CA k G 128
Red Rock, r., MT f M 112
Red Rock, Lake, IA i B 54
Red Springs, NC e G 40
Redwater, r., MT d B 82
Red Wing, MN f C 54
Redwood, r., MN g L 82
Redwood City, CA g C 128
Redwood Falls, MN g L 82
Redwood National Park, CA c A 128
Redwood Valley, CA e B 128
Reed City, MI g J 54
Reeder, ND e E 82
Reedley, CA h F 128
Reedsburg, WI g E 54
Reeds Peak, NM k l 98
Reedsport, OR g A 112
Reedsville, WI f H 54
Reese, MI g L 54
Reese, r., NV d H 128
Reeseville, WI g G 54
Reform, AL i H 68
Refugio, TX k l 84
Regent, ND e E 82
Rehoboth Beach, DE i K 26
Reidsville, GA g D 40
Reidsville, NC c G 40
Reinbeck, IA h C 54
Reisterstown, MD h J 26
Reliance, WY c G 98
Remer, MN c B 54
Remington, IN a l 68
Remington, VA i l 26
Remsen, IA i L 82
Remus, MI g K 54
Rend Lake, IL d H 68
Renick, WV j F 26
Reno, NV e F 128
Renovo, PA f l 26
Rensselaer, IN b l 68
Rensselaer, NY e M 26
Renton, WA c C 112
Renville, MN g L 82
Renwick, IA h B 54
Repton, AL k l 68
Republic, KS l J 82
Republic, MI d H 54
Republic, MO f C 68
Republic, WA b G 112
Republican, r., US l J 82
Reserve, LA l F 68
Reserve, NM k H 98
Revillagigedo Island, AK i CC 142
Revillo, SD f K 82
Rexburg, ID g N 112
Rexford, KS l G 82
Rexford, MT b J 112
Reyes, Point, CA f B 128
Reyno, AR f E 68
Reynolds, GA g B 40
Reynolds, ND d J 82
Reynoldsville, PA f H 26
Rhame, ND e D 82
Rhine, GA h C 40
Rhinebeck, NY f M 26
Rhinelander, WI e F 54
Rhode Island, state, US c L 8
Rhode Island Sound, US f O 26
Rib Lake, WI e E 54
Rice, TX g J 84
Rice Lake, WI e D 54
Riceville, IA g C 54
Richards, TX i K 84
Richardson, TX f J 84
Richardton, ND e E 82
Richey, MT d B 82
Richfield, ID g K 112
Richfield, MN f B 54
Richfield, PA g l 26
Richfield, UT e E 98
Richfield Springs, NY e L 26
Richford, VT c N 26
Rich Hill, MO e B 68
Richland, GA g B 40
Richland, MI h J 54
Richland, MO e D 68
Richland, TX h J 84
Richland Center, WI g E 54
Richlands, NC e l 40
Richlands, VA b E 40

Name	Map Ref.	Page
Richland Springs, TX	h H	84
Richmond, CA	g C	128
Richmond, IN	c L	68
Richmond, KS	m L	82
Richmond, KY	b B	40
Richmond, ME	c Q	26
Richmond, MI	h M	54
Richmond, MN	f M	82
Richmond, MO	c C	68
Richmond, TX	j K	84
Richmond, UT	c E	98
Richmond, VT	c N	26
Richmond, VA	b I	40
Richmond Heights, FL	n F	40
Richmond Highlands, WA	c C	112
Richmondville, NY	e L	26
Rich Square, NC	c I	40
Richton, MS	k H	68
Richwood, OH	g C	26
Richwood, WV	i F	26
Rico, CO	g H	98
Riddle, OR	h B	112
Riddle Mountain, OR	g G	112
Ridgecrest, CA	i H	128
Ridge Farm, IL	c I	68
Ridgefield, CT	f M	26
Ridgeland, MS	j F	68
Ridgeland, SC	g F	40
Ridgely, TN	f G	68
Ridgeville, SC	f F	40
Ridgeway, MO	b C	68
Ridgeway, WI	g F	54
Ridgway, CO	e H	98
Ridgway, IL	e H	68
Ridgway, PA	f H	26
Riegelwood, NC	e H	40
Rienzi, MS	h H	68
Riffe Lake, WA	d C	112
Rifle, CO	e I	98
Rifle, r., MI	f K	54
Rigby, ID	g N	112
Riggins, ID	e I	112
Riley, KS	i K	82
Rillito, AZ	l E	98
Rimersburg, PA	f G	26
Rincon, GA	g E	40
Rincon, NM	l I	98
Ringgold, GA	e A	40
Ringgold, LA	j C	68
Ringling, OK	e I	84
Ringsted, IA	h M	82
Rio, WI	g F	54
Rio Dell, CA	d A	128
Rio Grande City, TX	m H	84
Rio Grande, see Grande, Rio, r., NA		
Rio Grande, r., NA	f G	8
Rio Hondo, TX	m I	84
Rio Rancho, NM	i J	98
Rio Vista, CA	f D	128
Ripley, MS	h H	68
Ripley, NY	e G	26
Ripley, OH	i C	26
Ripley, TN	g G	68
Ripley, WV	i E	26
Ripon, CA	g D	128
Ripon, WI	f E	54
Ririe, ID	g N	112
Rising Star, TX	g H	84
Rising Sun, IN	d L	68
Rising Sun, MD	h J	26
Risingsun, OH	f C	26
Rison, AR	i D	68
Ritter, Mount, CA	g F	128
Rittman, OH	g E	26
Ritzville, WA	c G	112
Rivanna, r., VA	b H	40
Riverbank, CA	g E	128
Riverdale, CA	h F	128
Riverdale, ND	d F	82
River Falls, AL	k J	68
River Falls, WI	f C	54
Riverhead, NY	g N	26
Rivermont, NC	d I	40
River Road, OR	h B	112
Riverside, CA	k H	128
Riverside, IA	i D	54
Riverside, TX	i K	84
Riverton, IL	c G	68
Riverton, NE	k I	82
Riverton, UT	d E	98
Riverton, VA	i H	26
Riverton, WY	a H	98
Riverton Heights, WA	c C	112
River View, AL	j K	68
Riverview, FL	l D	40
Riverview, KS	n J	82
Rives, TN	f G	68
Rivesville, WV	h F	26
Riviera, AZ	l B	98
Riviera, TX	l I	84
Riviera Beach, FL	m F	40
Roachdale, IN	c J	68
Roan Cliffs, US	e G	98
Roan Mountain, TN	c D	40
Roanoke, AL	i K	68
Roanoke, IN	j F	54
Roanoke, IN	b K	68
Roanoke, VA	b G	40
Roanoke (Staunton), r., US	d K	40
Roanoke Island, NC	d K	40
Roanoke Rapids, NC	c I	40
Roan Plateau, US	e F	98
Roaring Springs, PA	g H	26
Roaring Springs, TX	f F	84
Robbins, NC	d G	40
Robbins, TN	c B	40
Robbinsville, NC	d C	40
Robeline, LA	k C	68
Robersonville, NC	d I	40
Roberta, GA	g B	40
Roberta Mills, NC	d F	40
Robert Lee, TX	h F	84
Roberts, ID	g M	112
Roberts, MT	e P	112
Roberts Creek Mountain, NV	e I	128
Robertsdale, AL	l I	68
Robertsdale, PA	g H	26
Robert S. Kerr Lake, OK	d K	84
Robinson, IL	c I	68
Robinson, TX	h I	84
Robstown, TX	l I	84
Roby, TX	g F	84
Rochelle, GA	h C	40
Rochelle, IL	i F	54
Rochelle, TX	h G	84
Rochester, IN	a J	68
Rochester, MI	h L	54
Rochester, MN	f C	54
Rochester, NH	d P	26
Rochester, NY	d I	26
Rochester, TX	f G	84
Rock, MI	d H	54
Rock, r., US	i F	54
Rock, r., US	h K	82
Rockcastle, r., KY	b B	40
Rock Creek Butte, OR	f G	112
Rockdale, IL	i I	54
Rockdale, TX	i I	84
Rock Falls, IL	i F	54
Rockford, AL	j J	68
Rockford, IL	h F	54
Rockford, IA	g C	54
Rockford, MI	g J	54
Rockford, OH	g B	26
Rockford, TN	d C	40
Rock Hall, MD	h J	26
Rock Hill, SC	e E	40
Rockingham, NC	e G	40
Rock Island, IL	i E	54
Rockland, ND	c H	82
Rockland, ID	h M	112
Rockland, ME	c Q	26
Rockland, MA	e P	26
Rockland, MI	d F	54
Rockledge, FL	k F	40
Rocklin, CA	f D	128
Rockmart, GA	e A	40
Rockport, KY	e J	68
Rockport, ME	c Q	26
Rockport, MA	e P	26
Rock Port, MO	b A	68
Rockport, TX	k I	84
Rock Rapids, IA	h K	82
Rock River, WY	c K	98
Rocksprings, TX	i F	84
Rock Springs, WY	c G	98
Rockton, IL	h F	54
Rock Valley, IA	h K	82
Rockville, IN	c I	68
Rockville, MD	h I	26
Rockwall, TX	g J	84
Rockwell, IA	h B	54
Rockwell, NC	d F	40
Rockwell City, IA	i M	82
Rockwood, ME	b Q	26
Rockwood, PA	h G	26
Rockwood, TN	d B	40
Rocky, OK	d G	84
Rocky, r., NC	d G	40
Rocky Ford, CO	m D	82
Rocky Mount, NC	d I	40
Rocky Mount, VA	c G	40
Rocky Mountain, MT	c M	112
Rocky Mountain National Park, CO	k B	82
Rocky Mountains, NA	b D	8
Roda, UT	c D	40
Rodeo, NM	m G	98
Rodney, MS	k E	68
Roeland Park, KS	l M	82
Roff, OK	e J	84
Rogers, AR	f B	68
Rogers, TX	i I	84
Rogers, Mount, VA	c E	40
Rogers City, MI	e L	54
Rogers Lake, CA	j H	128
Rogersville, AL	h I	68
Rogersville, TN	c C	40
Rogue, r., MI	g J	54
Rogue, r., OR	h A	112
Rogue River, OR	h B	112
Roland, AR	h D	68
Roland, IA	h B	54
Rolette, ND	c H	82
Rolfe, IA	i M	82
Roll, AZ	l C	98
Rolla, KS	n F	82
Rolla, MO	e E	68
Rolla, ND	c H	82
Rolling Fork, MS	j F	68
Rolling Fork, r., KY	e K	68
Roma, TX	m G	84
Rome, GA	e A	40
Rome, IL	j F	54
Rome, MS	i F	68
Rome, NY	d K	26
Romeo, MI	h L	54
Romney, WV	h H	26
Ronan, MT	c K	112
Ronceverte, WV	b F	40
Roodhouse, IL	c F	68
Roosevelt, AZ	k E	98
Roosevelt, MN	c L	82
Roosevelt, OK	e G	84
Roosevelt, UT	d G	98
Root, r., MN	g D	54
Root, r., WI	h E	54
Roper, NC	d J	40
Ropesville, TX	f D	84
Rosalia, WA	c H	112
Rosamond, CA	j G	128
Roscoe, SD	f H	82
Roscoe, TX	g F	84
Roscommon, MI	f K	54
Rose, Mount, NV	e F	128
Roseau, MN	c L	82
Roseau, r., NA	b K	82
Roseboro, NC	e H	40
Rosebud, MT	d S	112
Rosebud, SD	h G	82
Rosebud, TX	h J	84
Roseburg, OR	g B	112
Rosebush, MI	g K	54
Rose City, MI	f K	54
Rosedale, IN	c I	68
Rosedale, LA	l E	68
Rosedale, MS	i E	68
Rose Hill, NC	e H	40
Rose Hill, VA	c C	40
Roseland, LA	l F	68
Rosenberg, TX	j K	84
Rosepine, LA	l C	68
Roseville, CA	f D	128
Roseville, IL	i E	54
Roseville, MI	h M	54
Roseville, MN	e B	54
Roseville, OH	h D	26
Rosholt, SD	f K	82
Rosholt, WI	f E	54
Rosiclare, IL	e H	68
Roslyn, WA	c E	112
Rosman, NC	d D	40
Rossford, OH	f C	26
Rossiter, PA	g H	26
Ross Lake, NA	b D	112
Ross R. Barnett Reservoir, MS	j F	68
Rossville, GA	e A	40
Rossville, IL	b I	68
Rossville, IN	b J	68
Rossville, KS	l L	82
Roswell, GA	e B	40
Roswell, NM	f B	84
Rotan, TX	g F	84
Rothsay, MN	e K	82
Rothschild, WI	f F	54
Rotterdam, NY	e M	26
Rough, r., KY	e J	68
Rough River Lake, KY	e J	68
Roulette, PA	f H	26
Round Lake, MN	h L	82
Round Mountain, NV	f H	128
Round Rock, TX	i I	84
Roundup, MT	d Q	112
Rouses Point, NY	b M	26
Rowena, TX	h F	84
Rowland, NC	e G	40
Rowlesburg, WV	h G	26
Roxboro, NC	c H	40
Roxie, MS	k E	68
Roxton, TX	f K	84
Roy, NM	d B	84
Roy, UT	c D	98
Roy, WA	c C	112
Royal, IA	h L	82
Royal Center, IN	b J	68
Royal City, WA	d F	112
Royale, Isle, MI	b G	54
Royal Gorge, CO	f K	98
Royal Oak, MI	h L	54
Royalton, MN	e A	54
Royse City, TX	g J	84
Royston, GA	e C	40
Ruby, AK	d Q	142
Ruby, r., MT	e M	112
Ruby Dome, NV	d J	128
Ruby Mountains, NV	d J	128
Ruby Valley, NV	d J	128
Rudyard, MI	d K	54
Rudyard, MT	b O	112
Rufus, OR	e E	112
Ruidoso, NM	k K	98
Ruidoso, Rio, r., NM	k K	98
Ruidoso Downs, NM	k K	98
Rule, TX	f G	84
Ruleville, MS	i F	68
Rulo, NE	k L	82
Rum, r., MN	e B	54
Rumford, ME	c P	26
Runge, TX	k I	84
Rupert, ID	h L	112
Rupert, WV	j F	26
Rural Hall, NC	c F	40
Rural Retreat, VA	c E	40
Rush, r., ND	d J	82
Rush, r., WI	f C	54
Rush Center, KS	m H	82
Rush City, MN	e C	54
Rushford, MN	g D	54
Rushmore, MN	h L	82
Rush Springs, OK	e I	84
Rushville, IL	b F	68
Rushville, IN	c K	68
Rushville, NE	i E	82
Rusk, TX	h K	84
Ruskin, FL	l D	40
Russell, IA	j B	54
Russell, KS	m I	82
Russell, KY	i D	26
Russell, MN	g L	82
Russell, PA	f G	26
Russells Point, OH	g C	26
Russell Springs, KY	e K	68
Russellville, AL	h I	68
Russellville, AR	g C	68
Russellville, KY	f J	68
Russellville, MO	d D	68
Russian, r., CA	f B	128
Russiaville, IN	b J	68
Rustburg, VA	b G	40
Ruston, LA	j D	68
Ruth, MS	k F	68
Ruth, NV	e K	128
Rutherford, TN	f H	68
Rutherfordton, NC	d E	40
Ruthton, MN	g L	82
Ruthven, IA	h M	82
Rutland, IL	e J	82
Rutland, ND	d N	26
Rutland, VT	d N	26
Rutledge, GA	f C	40
Rutledge, TN	c C	40
Ryan, OK	e I	84
Ryder, ND	d F	82
Ryderwood, WA	d B	112
Ryegate, MT	d P	112
Rye Patch Reservoir, NV	d G	128
S		
Sabetha, KS	l L	82
Sabina, OH	h C	26
Sabinal, TX	j G	84
Sabine, r., US	e H	8
Sabine Lake, US	m C	68
Sabine Pass, US	m C	68
Sable, Cape, FL	n E	40
Sabula, IA	h E	54
Sac, r., MO	c C	68
Sacajawea Peak, OR	e H	112
Sacaton, AZ	k E	98
Sac City, IA	i M	82
Sackets Harbor, NY	c J	26
Saco, ME	d P	26
Saco, MT	b R	112
Saco, r., US	d P	26
Sacramento, CA	f D	128
Sacramento, r., CA	f D	128
Sacramento, r., NM	k H	98
Sacramento Mountains, NM	k K	98
Sacramento Valley, CA	d C	128
Sacred Heart, MN	g L	82
Saddle Mountain, CO	f K	98
Saegertown, PA	f F	26
Safford, AZ	l G	98
Sagamore, PA	g H	26
Sagavanirktok, r., AK	b T	142
Sagerton, TX	f G	84
Saginaw, MI	g L	54
Saginaw, r., MI	g L	54
Saginaw Bay, MI	g L	54
Saguache, CO	f J	98
Sahuarita, AZ	m F	98
Saint Albans, VT	c N	26
Saint Albans, WV	i E	26
Saint Andrews, SC	f F	40
Saint Anne, IL	i H	54
Saint Ansgar, IA	g B	54
Saint Anthony, ID	g N	112
Saint Augustine, FL	j E	40
Saint Catherines Island, GA	h E	40
Saint Charles, AR	h E	68
Saint Charles, ID	h N	112
Saint Charles, IL	i G	54
Saint Charles, MN	g C	54
Saint Charles, MO	d F	68
Saint Charles Mesa, CO	m C	82
Saint Clair, MI	h M	54
Saint Clair, MO	d F	68
Saint Clair, r., NA	h M	54
Saint Clair, Lake, NA	h M	54
Saint Clair Shores, MI	h M	54
Saint Clairsville, OH	g F	26
Saint Cloud, FL	k E	40
Saint Cloud, MN	e A	54
Saint Croix, r., US	e C	54
Saint Croix Falls, WI	e C	54
Saint David, AZ	m F	98
Saint David, IL	j E	54
Saint Edward, NE	j J	82
Saint Elias, Cape, AK	g V	142
Saint Elias, Mount, NA	f X	142
Saint Elias Mountains, NA	f X	142
Saint Elmo, IL	c H	68
Saint Francis, KS	l F	82
Saint Francis, SD	h G	82
Saint Francis, WI	h H	54
Saint Francis, r., US	h F	68
Saint Francisville, LA	l E	68
Sainte Genevieve, MO	e F	68
Saint George, SC	f F	40
Saint George, UT	g C	98
Saint George Island, AK	h J	142
Saint George Island, FL	j B	40
Saint Helena, CA	f C	128
Saint Helena Sound, SC	g F	40
Saint Helens, OR	e C	112
Saint Helens, Mount, WA	d C	112
Saint Ignace, MI	e K	54
Saint Ignatius, MT	c K	112
Saint James, MI	e J	54
Saint James, MN	h M	82
Saint James, MO	e E	68
Saint James, NY	g M	26
Saint Jo, TX	f I	84
Saint John, KS	m I	82
Saint John, ND	c H	82
Saint John, WA	c H	112
Saint Johns, AZ	j G	98
Saint Johns, MI	g K	54
Saint Johns, r., FL	i E	40
Saint Johnsbury, VT	c N	26
Saint Joseph, IL	b H	68
Saint Joseph, LA	k E	68
Saint Joseph, MI	h I	54
Saint Joseph, MN	e A	54
Saint Joseph, MO	c B	68
Saint Joseph, TN	g I	68
Saint Joseph, r., US	i K	54
Saint Joseph, r., US	i I	54
Saint Lawrence, r., NA	b M	8
Saint Lawrence Island, AK	e I	142
Saint Louis, MI	g K	54
Saint Louis, MO	d F	68
Saint Louis, r., US	d C	54
Saint Louis Park, MN	f B	54
Saint Lucie Canal, FL	l F	40
Saint Maries, ID	c I	112
Saint Marks, FL	i B	40
Saint Martinville, LA	l E	68
Saint Mary, MO	e G	68
Saint Marys, AK	e M	142
Saint Marys, GA	i E	40
Saint Marys, KS	l K	82
Saint Marys, OH	g B	26
Saint Marys, PA	f H	26
Saint Marys, WV	h E	26
Saint Marys, r., NA	d K	54
Saint Marys, r., US	g B	26
Saint Marys, r., US	i E	40
Saint Matthew Island, AK	f H	142
Saint Matthews, KY	d K	68
Saint Matthews, SC	f F	40
Saint Meinrad, IN	d J	68
Saint Michael, AK	e M	142
Saint Michaels, MD	i J	26
Saint Nazianz, WI	f H	54
Saint Paris, OH	g C	26
Saint Paul, IN	c K	68
Saint Paul, KS	n L	82
Saint Paul, MN	f B	54
Saint Paul, NE	j I	82
Saint Paul, VA	c D	40
Saint Paul Island, AK	h I	142
Saint Pauls, NC	e H	40
Saint Peter, MN	f B	54
Saint Petersburg, FL	l D	40
Saint Regis, MT	c J	112
Saint Regis Falls, NY	c L	26
Saint Robert, MO	e D	68
Saint Simons Island, GA	h E	40
Saint Simons Island, Cape, GA	h E	40
Saint Stephen, SC	f G	40
Saint Thomas, ND	c J	82
Saint Vincent, ND	c J	82
Sakakawea, Lake, ND	d E	82
Saks, AL	i K	68
Salado, Rio, r., NM	j I	98
Salamanca, NY	e H	26
Salamonie, r., IN	b K	68
Sale Creek, TN	g K	68
Salem, AR	f E	68
Salem, IL	d H	68
Salem, IN	d J	68
Salem, IA	j D	54
Salem, KY	d I	68
Salem, MA	e P	26
Salem, MO	e D	68
Salem, NH	d P	26
Salem, NJ	h K	26
Salem, NY	d M	26
Salem, OH	g F	26
Salem, OR	f B	112
Salem, SD	g J	82
Salem, UT	d E	98
Salem, VA	b F	40
Salem, WV	h F	26
Salida, CO	f K	98
Salina, KS	m J	82
Salina, UT	f E	98
Salinas, CA	h D	128
Salinas, r., CA	h D	128
Saline, MI	h L	54
Saline, r., AR	i D	68
Saline, r., IL	e H	68
Saline, r., KS	m I	82
Saline Bayou, r., LA	j C	68
Salisbury, MD	i J	26
Salisbury, MO	c D	68
Salisbury, NC	d F	40
Salisbury, PA	h G	26
Salish Mountains, MT	b K	112
Salitpa, AL	k H	68
Salkehatchie, r., SC	f E	40
Sallisaw, OK	d L	84
Salmon, ID	e L	112
Salmon, r., ID	e I	112
Salmon, r., NY	d K	26
Salmon, r., OR	e D	112
Salmon Mountains, CA	c B	128
Salmon River Mountains, ID	e J	112
Salome, AZ	k C	98
Salt, r., US	g N	112
Salt, r., AZ	k E	98
Salt, r., KY	d K	68
Salt, r., MO	c E	68
Saltillo, MS	h H	68
Salt Lake City, UT	d E	98
Salton City, CA	k J	128
Salton Sea, CA	k J	128
Saltville, VA	c E	40
Saluda, SC	e E	40
Saluda, VA	b J	40
Saluda, r., SC	e E	40
Salvador, Lake, LA	m F	68
Salyer, CA	d B	128
Salyersville, KY	b C	40
Samaria, ID	h M	112
Samoset, FL	l D	40
Sam Rayburn Reservoir, TX	k B	68
Samson, AL	k J	68
Samtown, LA	k D	68
San Andreas, CA	f E	128
San Andres Mountains, NM	l J	98
San Angelo, TX	h F	84
San Anselmo, CA	g C	128
San Antonio, NM	i J	98
San Antonio, r., TX	k I	84
San Antonio, Mount, CA	j H	128
San Antonio Bay, TX	k I	84
San Antonio Mountain, NM	h J	98
San Antonio, Rio, r., US	h J	98
San Augustine, TX	k B	68
San Augustin Pass, NM	l J	98
San Benito, TX	m I	84
San Benito, r., CA	h D	128
San Bernardino, CA	j H	128
San Bernardino Mountains, CA	j I	128
San Blas, Cape, FL	j A	40
Sanborn, IA	h L	82
Sanborn, MN	g L	82
San Bruno, CA	g C	128
San Carlos, AZ	k F	98
San Carlos, CA	g C	128
San Clemente, CA	k H	128
San Clemente Island, CA	l G	128
Sand Coulee, MT	c N	112
Sanders, AZ	j G	98
Sanderson, TX	i D	84
Sandersville, GA	g D	40
Sandersville, MS	k G	68
Sand Fork, WV	i F	26
Sand Hill, r., MN	d K	82
Sand Hills, NE	j F	82
Sandia Crest, NM	i J	98
San Diego, CA	l H	128
San Diego, r., CA	l I	128
San Diego Aqueduct, CA	k H	128
Sand Island, HI	f J	144c
Sandoval, IL	d G	68
Sandpoint, ID	b I	112
Sand Springs, OK	c J	84
Sand Springs, TX	g E	84
Sandston, VA	b I	40
Sandstone, MN	d C	54
Sandusky, MI	g M	54
Sandusky, OH	f D	26
Sandusky, r., OH	f C	26
Sandwich, IL	i G	54
Sandwich, MA	f P	26
Sandy, OR	e C	112
Sandy, UT	d E	98
Sandy, r., ME	c Q	26
Sandy Hook, KY	b C	40
Sandy Hook, MS	k G	68
Sandy Hook, NJ	h L	26
Sandy Springs, GA	f B	40
San Elizario, TX	m J	98
San Felipe Pueblo, NM	i J	98
San Fernando, CA	j G	128
Sanford, CO	g K	98
Sanford, FL	k E	40
Sanford, ME	d P	26
Sanford, MI	g K	54
Sanford, NC	d G	40
Sanford, TX	d E	84
Sanford, Mount, AK	e V	142
San Francisco, CA	g C	128
San Francisco, r., US	k H	98
San Francisco Bay, CA	g C	128
San Gabriel, r., TX	i I	84
San Gabriel Mountains, CA	j G	128
Sangamon, r., IL	b F	68
Sanger, CA	h F	128
Sanger, TX	f I	84
Sangerville, ME	b Q	26
San Gorgonio Mountain, CA	j I	128
Sangre de Cristo Mountains, US	g K	98
Sanibel Island, FL	m D	40
San Isidro, TX	m H	84
San Jacinto, CA	k I	128
San Jacinto, West Fork, r., TX	i K	84
San Joaquin, r., CA	g D	128
San Joaquin Valley, CA	h E	128
San Jon, NM	e C	84
San Jose, CA	g D	128
San Jose, IL	b F	68
San Jose, NM	i K	98
Saline, r., NM	i D	98
San Jose Island, TX	k J	84
San Juan Bautista, CA	h D	128
San Juan Islands, WA	b C	112
San Juan Mountains, CO	g I	98
San Leandro, CA	g C	128
San Luis, AZ	l B	98
San Luis, CO	g K	98
San Luis Obispo, CA	i E	128
San Luis Peak, CO	g J	98
San Luis Reservoir, CA	g D	128
San Luis Valley, CO	g J	98
San Manuel, AZ	l F	98
San Marcos, TX	j I	84
San Marcos, r., TX	j I	84
San Mateo, CA	g C	128
San Mateo, FL	j E	40
San Mateo, NM	i I	98
San Miguel, CA	i E	128
San Miguel, r., CO	f H	98
San Nicolas Island, CA	k F	128
San Pablo Bay, CA	f C	128
San Pedro, TX	l I	84
San Pedro, r., NA	l F	98
San Pedro Channel, CA	k G	128
San Pedro Peaks, NM	h J	98
San Pitch, r., UT	e E	98
Sanpoil, r., WA	b G	112
San Rafael, CA	g C	128
San Rafael, NM	i I	98
San Rafael, r., UT	f F	98
San Rafael Desert, UT	f F	98
San Rafael Swell, UT	f F	98
San Saba, TX	h H	84
San Saba, r., TX	i G	84
San Simon, AZ	l G	98
San Simon, r., AZ	l G	98
Santa Ana, CA	k H	128
Santa Anna, TX	h G	84
Santa Barbara, CA	j F	128
Santa Barbara Channel, CA	j E	128
Santa Catalina, Gulf of, CA	l G	128
Santa Catalina Island, CA	k G	128
Santa Clara, CA	g D	128
Santa Clara, UT	g C	98
Santa Cruz, CA	h C	128
Santa Cruz, r., NA	l E	98
Santa Cruz Island, CA	j F	128
Santa Fe, NM	i K	98
Santa Fe, r., NM	i J	98
Santa Fe Baldy, NM	i K	98
Santa Lucia Range, CA	h D	128
Santa Margarita, CA	i E	128
Santa Maria, CA	j E	128
Santa Monica, CA	j G	128
Santa Monica Bay, CA	k G	128
Santaquin, UT	d E	98
Santa Rosa, CA	f C	128
Santa Rosa, NM	e B	84
Santa Rosa, TX	m I	84
Santa Rosa Beach, FL	l J	68
Santa Rosa Island, CA	k E	128
Santa Rosa Island, FL	l J	68
Santa Rosa Range, NV	c H	128
Santa Ynez, r., CA	j E	128
Santee, CA	l I	128
Santee, r., SC	f G	40
Santiam Pass, OR	f D	112
Santo, TX	g H	84
Santo Domingo Pueblo, NM	i J	98
San Ygnacio, TX	l G	84
Sapello, r., NM	i K	98
Sapelo Island, GA	h E	40
Sapulpa, OK	d J	84
Saragosa, TX	h C	84
Saraland, AL	l H	68
Saranac, MI	h J	54
Saranac, r., NY	c M	26
Saranac Lake, NY	c L	26
Sarasota, FL	l D	40
Saratoga, CA	g C	128
Saratoga, TX	i L	84
Saratoga, WY	c J	98
Saratoga Springs, NY	d M	26
Sarcoxie, MO	e B	68
Sardis, AL	j J	68
Sardis, GA	g E	40
Sardis, MS	h G	68
Sardis, TN	g H	68
Sardis Lake, MS	h G	68
Sarepta, LA	j C	68
Sargent, GA	f B	40
Sargent, NE	j H	82
Sarita, TX	l I	84
Sarles, ND	c I	82
Sartell, MN	e A	54
Sasakwa, OK	e J	84
Saspamco, TX	j H	84
Sassafras, KY	b C	40
Sassafras Mountain, US	d D	40
Satanta, KS	n G	82
Satellite Beach, FL	k F	40
Satsuma, AL	l H	68
Saucier, MS	l G	68
Saugatuck, MI	h I	54
Saugerties, NY	e M	26
Sauk, r., MN	e A	54
Sauk Centre, MN	f M	82
Sauk City, WI	g F	54
Sauk Rapids, MN	e A	54
Saukville, WI	g G	54
Sault Sainte Marie, MI	d K	54
Sauquoit, NY	d K	26
Sausalito, CA	g C	128
Savage, MD	i J	26
Savage, MT	d T	112
Savanna, IL	h E	54
Savanna, OK	e K	84
Savannah, GA	g E	40
Savannah, MO	c B	68
Savannah, TN	g H	68
Savannah, r., US	g E	40
Savonga, AK	e I	142
Savoy, TX	f J	84
Sawatch Range, CO	e J	98
Sawyer, ND	c F	82
Saxis, VA	b K	40
Saxon, WI	d E	54
Saxton, PA	h I	26
Saybrook, IA	b H	68
Saylorville Lake, IA	i B	54
Sayre, OK	d G	84
Sayre, PA	e J	26
Sayreville, NJ	g L	26
Scammon, KS	n L	82
Scandia, KS	l J	82
Scanlon, LA	m J	68
Scapegoat Mountain, MT	c M	112
Scappoose, OR	e C	112
Schaller, IA	i L	82
Schenectady, NY	e M	26
Schertz, TX	j H	84
Schlater, MS	i F	68
Schleswig, IA	i L	82
Schofield, WI	f F	54
Schofield Barracks, HI	e I	144c
Schoharie, NY	e L	26
Schoolcraft, MI	h J	54
Schriever, LA	m F	68
Schulenburg, TX	j J	84
Schuyler, NE	j J	82
Schuyler, VA	b H	40
Schuylkill, r., PA	g K	26
Schuylkill Haven, PA	g J	26
Scio, OH	g E	26
Scio, OR	f C	112
Scipio, UT	e D	98
Scobey, MT	b T	112
Scooba, MS	j H	68
Scotia, NE	i I	82
Scotia, NY	e M	26
Scotland, SD	h J	82
Scotland, TX	f H	84
Scotland Neck, NC	c I	40
Scotlandville, LA	l E	68
Scott, MS	i E	68
Scott, r., CA	c C	128
Scott, Mount, OR	h C	112
Scott City, KS	m G	82
Scott City, MO	e G	68
Scottdale, PA	g G	26
Scott Mountain, ID	f J	112
Scottsbluff, NE	j D	82
Scottsboro, AL	h J	68
Scottsburg, IN	d K	68
Scottsdale, AZ	k E	98
Scotts Hill, TN	g H	68
Scottsville, KY	f J	68
Scottville, MI	g I	54
Scranton, IA	h M	82
Scranton, ND	e D	82
Scranton, PA	f K	26
Screven, GA	h D	40
Scribner, NE	j K	82
Scurry, TX	g J	84
Seaboard, NC	c I	40
Seadrift, TX	k J	84
Seaford, DE	i K	26
Seaforth, MN	d D	82
Seagraves, TX	g D	84
Sea Islands, US	i E	40
Sea Isle City, NJ	h L	26
Seale, AL	j K	68
Sealevel, NC	e J	40
Sealy, TX	j J	84
Searchlight, NV	i K	128
Searcy, AR	g E	68
Searsport, ME	c R	26
Seaside, CA	h D	128
Seaside, OR	e B	112
Seaside Park, NJ	h L	26
Seattle, WA	c C	112
Sebago Lake, ME	d P	26
Sebastian, TX	m I	84
Sebastopol, CA	f C	128
Sebastopol, MS	j G	68
Sebeka, MN	e L	82
Sebewaing, MI	g L	54
Sebree, KY	e I	68
Sebring, FL	l E	40
Section, AL	h K	68
Security, CO	m C	82
Sedalia, MO	d C	68
Sedan, KS	n K	82
Sedgefield, NC	d F	40
Sedgwick, CO	k E	82
Sedgwick, KS	n J	82
Sedona, AZ	j E	98
Sedro Woolley, WA	b C	112
Seeley Lake, MT	c L	112
Seelyville, IN	c I	68
Seguin, TX	j I	84
Segundo, CO	n C	82
Seibert, CO	l E	82
Seiling, OK	c H	84
Selah, WA	d E	112
Selawik, AK	c N	142
Selby, SD	f G	82
Selbyville, DE	i K	26
Selden, KS	l G	82
Seldovia, AK	g S	142
Selfridge, ND	e G	82
Seligman, AZ	i D	98
Seligman, MO	f B	68
Selinsgrove, PA	g J	26
Selkirk Mountains, NA	f P	24
Sellers, SC	e G	40
Sellersburg, IN	d K	68
Sells, AZ	m E	98
Selma, AL	j I	68
Selma, CA	h F	128
Selma, NC	d H	40
Selmer, TN	g H	68
Selmont, AL	j I	68
Seminary, MS	k G	68
Seminoe Reservoir, WY	b J	98
Seminole, OK	d J	84
Seminole, TX	g D	84
Seminole, Lake, US	i B	40
Senath, MO	f F	68
Senatobia, MS	h G	68
Seneca, IL	i G	54
Seneca, KS	l K	82
Seneca, MO	e B	68
Seneca, OR	f G	112
Seneca, SC	e D	40
Seneca Falls, NY	e J	26
Seneca Lake, NY	e J	26
Senoia, GA	f B	40
Sentinel, OK	d G	84
Sepulga, r., AL	k J	68
Sequatchie, r., TN	d A	40
Sequim, WA	b B	112
Sequoia National Park, CA	h G	128
Sergeant Bluff, IA	i K	82
Seth Ward, TN	e E	84
Severn Park, MD	i J	26
Severy, KS	n K	82
Sevier, r., UT	e D	98
Sevier Desert, UT	e D	98
Sevier Lake, UT	f C	98
Sevierville, TN	d C	40
Seville, FL	j E	40
Seville, OH	g E	26
Sewanee, TN	g K	68
Seward, AK	f T	142
Seward, NE	k J	82
Seward Peninsula, AK	d M	142
Seymour, CT	f M	26
Seymour, IN	d J	68
Seymour, IA	j B	54
Seymour, MO	e D	68
Seymour, TX	f G	84
Seymour, WI	f G	54
Seymourville, LA	l E	68
Shady Cove, OR	h C	112

Name	Map Ref.	Page

Shady Grove, FL i C 40
Shadyside, OH h F 26
Shafer Butte, ID g I 112
Shafter, CA i F 128
Shageluk, AK e O 142
Shaker Heights, OH f E 26
Shakopee, MN f B 54
Shaktoolik, AK d N 142
Shallotte, NC f H 40
Shallowater, TX f E 84
Shamokin, PA g J 26
Shamrock, FL j C 40
Shamrock, TX d F 84
Shannon, GA e A 40
Shannon, IL h F 54
Shannon, MS h H 68
Shannontown, SC f F 40
Sharon, ND d J 82
Sharon, PA f F 26
Sharon, TN f H 68
Sharon, WI h G 54
Sharon Springs, KS m F 82
Sharpe, Lake, SD g H 82
Shasta, CA d C 128
Shasta, r., CA c C 128
Shasta, Mount, CA c C 128
Shasta Lake, CA d C 128
Shattuck, OK c G 84
Shaw, MS i F 68
Shawano, WI f G 54
Shawnee, KS l M 82
Shawnee, OH h D 26
Shawnee, OK d J 84
Shawneetown, IL e H 68
Sheboygan, WI g H 54
Sheboygan, r., WI g H 54
Sheboygan Falls, WI g H 54
Sheenjek, r., AK c W 142
Sheep Mountain, WY g O 112
Sheffield, AL h I 68
Sheffield, IA i F 54
Sheffield, IA h B 54
Sheffield, PA f G 26
Sheffield, TX i E 84
Shelbina, MO c D 68
Shelburn, IN c I 68
Shelburne Falls, MA e N 26
Shelby, IA j L 82
Shelby, MI g I 54
Shelby, MS i F 68
Shelby, MT b N 112
Shelby, NE j J 82
Shelby, NC d E 40
Shelby, OH g G 26
Shelbyville, IL c H 68
Shelbyville, IN c K 68
Shelbyville, KY d K 68
Shelbyville, MO c D 68
Shelbyville, TN g J 68
Shelbyville, Lake, IL c H 68
Sheldon, IA h L 82
Sheldon, MO e B 68
Shelikof Strait, AK h Q 142
Shelley, ID g M 112
Shell Lake, WI e D 54
Shellman, GA h B 40
Shell Rock, IA h C 54
Shell Rock, r., US g B 54
Shellsburg, IA h D 54
Shelton, CT f M 26
Shelton, NE k I 82
Shelton, WA c B 112
Shemya Station, AK j B 143a
Shenandoah, IA k L 82
Shenandoah, PA g J 26
Shenandoah, VA h I 26
Shenandoah, r., US h I 26
Shenandoah National Park, VA i H 26
Shepherd, MI g K 54
Shepherd, TX l A 68
Shepherdstown, WV h I 26
Shepherdsville, KY e K 68
Sherburn, MN h M 82
Sherburne, NY e K 26
Sheridan, AR h D 68
Sheridan, IN b J 68
Sheridan, MT e M 112
Sheridan, OR e B 112
Sheridan, TX j J 84
Sheridan, WY f S 112
Sherman, NY e G 26
Sherman, TX f J 84
Sherman Mills, ME b R 26
Sherman Station, ME b R 26
Sherrard, IL i E 54
Sherrill, NY d K 26
Sherwood, AR h D 68
Sherwood, ND c F 82
Sherwood, OH f B 26
Sherwood, TN g K 68
Sherwood Shores, TX i H 84
Sheyenne, ND d H 82
Sheyenne, r., ND e J 82
Shickley, NE k J 82
Shickshinny, PA f J 26
Shidler, OK c J 84
Shields, r., MT e O 112
Shillington, PA g K 26
Shiloh, OH f E 26
Shiner, TX j I 84
Shinglehouse, PA f H 26
Shinnston, WV h F 26
Shiocton, WI f G 54
Shipman, VA b H 40
Shippensburg, PA g I 26
Shiprock, NM h H 98
Ship Rock, NM h H 98
Shirley, IN c K 68
Shishmaref, AK c K 142
Shively, KY d K 68
Shivwits Plateau, AZ h C 98
Shoals, IN d J 68
Shorewood, WI g H 54
Shortsville, NY e I 26
Shoshone, ID h K 112
Shoshone, r., WY h Q 112
Shoshone Basin, WY h Q 112
Shoshone Mountains, NV f H 128
Shoshoni, WY a H 98
Show Low, AZ j F 98
Shreve, OH g D 26
Shreveport, LA i C 68
Shrewsbury, MA e O 26
Shubuta, MS k H 68
Shuksan, Mount, WA b D 112
Shullsburg, WI h E 54
Shungnak, AK c P 142
Shuqualak, MS j H 68
Siasconset, MA f Q 26
Sibley, IA h L 82
Sibley, LA i C 68
Sibley, MS k E 68
Sicily Island, LA k E 68
Sidnaw, MI d G 54

Sidney, IL b H 68
Sidney, IA k L 82
Sidney, MT d C 82
Sidney, NE j E 82
Sidney, NY d J 26
Sidney, OH g B 26
Sidney Lanier, Lake, GA e C 40
Sidon, MS i F 68
Sierra Blanca, TX m K 98
Sierra Blanca Peak, NM k K 98
Sierra Vista, AZ m F 98
Siesta Key, FL l D 40
Signal Mountain, TN g K 68
Signal Peak, UT g C 98
Sigourney, IA i C 54
Sigurd, UT f E 98
Sikeston, MO f G 68
Silas, AL k H 68
Siler City, NC d G 40
Siletz, OR f B 112
Siletz, r., OR f B 112
Siloam Springs, AR f B 68
Silsbee, TX l B 68
Silver, TX g F 84
Silver Bay, MN c D 54
Silver Bell, AZ l E 98
Silver City, NM i H 98
Silver City, NV d G 40
Silver Creek, MS k G 68
Silver Creek, NE j J 82
Silver Creek, NY e G 26
Silverdale, WA c C 112
Silver Lake, KS l L 82
Silver Lake, MN f A 54
Silver Lake, OR g D 112
Silver Lake, WI h G 54
Silver Spring, MD i I 26
Silver Star Mountain, WA b E 112
Silvertip Mountain, MT c L 112
Silverton, CO g I 98
Silverton, OR e C 112
Silverton, TX e E 84
Simi Valley, CA j G 128
Simla, CO l C 82
Simmesport, LA l E 68
Simms, MT c N 112
Simpson, LA k C 68
Simpsonville, SC e D 40
Simsbury, CT f N 26
Sinclair, WY c I 98
Sinclair, Lake, GA f C 40
Singer, LA l C 68
Sinnamahoning, PA f H 26
Sinton, TX k I 84
Sioux Center, IA h K 82
Sioux City, IA i K 82
Sioux Falls, SD h J 82
Sioux Rapids, IA i L 82
Sipsey, r., AL i I 68
Siskiyou Mountains, US c B 128
Siskiyou Pass, OR h C 112
Sisquoc, r., CA j F 128
Sisseton, SD f J 82
Sissonville, WV i E 26
Sister Bay, WI e H 54
Sisters, OR f D 112
Sistersville, WV h F 26
Sitka, AK h AA 142
Skagit, r., WA b D 112
Skagway, AK g AA 142
Skellytown, TX d E 84
Skiatook, OK c J 84
Skidmore, TX k I 84
Skilak Lake, AK f S 142
Skillet Fork, r., IL d H 68
Skokie, IL h H 54
Skowhegan, ME c Q 26
Skull Valley, AZ j D 98
Skuna, r., MS i G 68
Skunk, r., IA j D 54
Skykomish, r., WA c D 112
Skyland, NC d D 40
Slater, IA c C 54
Slater, MO c C 68
Slaton, TX f E 84
Slaughter, LA l E 68
Slayton, MN h L 82
Sledge, MS h F 68
Sleepy Eye, MN g M 82
Slidell, LA l G 68
Sligo, PA f G 26
Slinger, WI g G 54
Slippery Rock, PA f F 26
Sloan, IA i K 82
Sloan, NV i J 128
Slocomb, AL k K 68
Smackover, AR i D 68
Smethport, PA f H 26
Smiley, TX j I 84
Smith, r., US c F 40
Smith, r., CA c A 128
Smith, r., MT c N 112
Smith, r., OR g B 112
Smith Center, KS l I 82
Smithers, WV i E 26
Smithfield, NC d H 40
Smithfield, UT c E 98
Smithfield, VA c J 40
Smithland, KY e H 68
Smith Mountain Lake, VA b G 40
Smith River, CA c A 128
Smiths, AL j K 68
Smiths Grove, KY e J 68
Smithton, MO d C 68
Smithville, GA h B 40
Smithville, MS h H 68
Smithville, MO c B 68
Smithville, TN g J 68
Smithville, TX i I 84
Smoky Dome, ID h J 112
Smoky Hill, r., US m J 82
Smoot, WY b F 98
Smyrna, DE h K 26
Smyrna, GA f B 40
Smyrna, TN g J 68
Snake, r., US d G 112
Snake, r., MN e B 54
Snake, r., NE i E 82
Snake River Plain, ID g L 112
Snake Valley, US e L 128
Sneads, FL i B 40
Sneedville, TN b C 40
Snelling, CA g C 128
Snohomish, WA c C 112
Snoqualmie Pass, WA c D 112
Snover, MI g M 54
Snow Hill, MD i K 26
Snow Hill, NC d I 40
Snowmass Mountain, CO e I 98

Snow Peak, WA b G 112
Snowyside Peak, ID g K 112
Snyder, OK e H 84
Snyder, TX g F 84
Soap Lake, WA c F 112
Social Circle, GA f C 40
Society Hill, SC e G 40
Socorro, NM j J 98
Socorro, TX m J 98
Soda Lake, CA i I 128
Soda Springs, ID h N 112
Soddy-Daisy, TN g K 68
Sodus, NY d I 26
Solana, FL m E 40
Soldiers Grove, WI g E 54
Soldotna, AK f S 142
Soledad, CA h D 128
Solen, ND e G 82
Solomon, AZ l G 98
Solomon, KS m J 82
Solomon, r., KS l J 82
Solon, IA i D 54
Solon, ME c Q 26
Solon Springs, WI d D 54
Solvang, CA j E 128
Solvay, NY d J 26
Somers, MT b K 112
Somerset, CO f I 98
Somerset, KY b B 40
Somerset, MA f O 26
Somerset, OH h D 26
Somerset, PA g G 26
Somerset, TX j H 84
Somerset, WI e C 54
Somers Point, NJ h L 26
Somersworth, NH e P 26
Somerton, AZ l B 98
Somerville, NJ g L 26
Somerville, TN g G 68
Somerville, TX i J 84
Somerville Lake, TX i J 84
Somo, r., WI e F 54
Sonoma, CA f C 128
Sonora, CA g E 128
Sonora, TX i F 84
Sontag, MS k F 68
Soo, see Sault Sainte Marie, MI d K 54
Sopchoppy, FL i B 40
Soperton, GA g D 40
Sophia, WV b B 40
Sorrento, LA l F 68
Soso, MS k G 68
Souderton, PA g K 26
Soughegan, r., NH g G 26
Souris, r., NA b G 82
Sourlake, TX l B 68
South, r., IA a C 68
Southampton, NY g L 26
South Anna, r., VA b I 40
Southaven, MS h F 68
South Bald Mountain, CO d K 98
South Baldy, NM k I 98
South Bay, FL m F 40
South Beloit, IL h F 54
South Bend, IN a J 68
South Bend, WA d B 112
South Boston, VA b H 40
Southbridge, MA e N 26
South Burlington, VT e M 26
South Carolina, state, US e J 8
South Channel, MI e K 54
South Charleston, WV i E 26
South Coffeyville, OK c K 84
South Dakota, state, US c F 8
Southern Pines, NC c G 40
South Fabius, r., MO a E 68
South Fallsburg, NY f L 26
Southfield, MI h L 54
South Fork, CO g J 98
South Fulton, TN f H 68
Southgate, MI h L 54
South Hadley, MA e N 26
South Haven, KS n J 82
South Haven, MI h J 54
South Henderson, NC c H 40
South Hero, VT c M 26
South Hill, VA c H 40
South Holston Lake, US c D 40
South Houston, TX j K 84
Southington, CT f N 26
South International Falls, MN b H 82
South Kenosha, WI h H 54
South Lake Tahoe, CA f F 128
Southland, TX f E 84
Southlawn, IL c G 68
South Lyon, MI h L 54
South Medford, OR h C 112
South Miami, FL n F 40
South Mills, NC c J 40
South Milwaukee, WI h H 54
South Mountain, ID h I 112
South Naknek, AK g P 142
South Ogden, UT c E 98
South Paris, ME c P 26
South Pass, WY h Q 112
South Pekin, IL b F 68
South Pittsburg, TN g K 68
South Platte, r., US c F 8
Southport, FL i K 40
Southport, IN c J 68
Southport, NY e J 26
Southport, NC d I 40
South Portland, ME d P 26
South Range, MI d G 54
South Rockwood, MI h L 54
South San Francisco, CA g C 128
South Sioux City, NE i K 82
South Superior, WY c H 98
South Torrington, WY c N 98
South Tucson, AZ l F 98
South West City, MO f B 68
Southwest Harbor, ME c R 26
South Whitley, IN a K 68
South Williamson, KY b D 40
South Windham, ME d P 26
South Yamhill, r., OR e B 112
Spalding, NE j I 82
Spanish Fork, UT d E 98
Spanish Peak, OR f E 112
Sparkman, AR i D 68
Sparks, GA h C 40
Sparks, NV e F 128
Sparland, IL i F 54
Sparlingville, MI h M 54
Sparrows Point, MD h J 26
Sparta, GA f D 40

Sparta, IL d G 68
Sparta, KY d L 68
Sparta, MI g J 54
Sparta, NJ f L 26
Sparta, NC c E 40
Sparta, TN g K 68
Sparta, WI g E 54
Spartanburg, SC e E 40
Spearfish, SD g D 82
Spearman, TX c E 84
Spearville, KS n H 82
Speedway, IN c J 68
Spencer, AK e M 142
Spencer, IA h L 82
Spencer, IN d I 68
Spencer, NE i I 82
Spencer, NC d F 40
Spencer, SD h J 82
Spencer, TN g K 68
Spencer, WV i E 26
Spencerville, OH g B 26
Sperryville, VA i H 26
Spicer, MN f M 82
Spickard, MO b C 68
Spillville, IA g D 54
Spindale, NC d E 40
Spirit Lake, ID c I 112
Spirit Lake, IA h L 82
Spiro, OK g B 68
Spofford, TX j F 84
Spokane, WA c H 112
Spokane, r., US c G 112
Spoon, r., IL b F 68
Spooner, WI e D 54
Spotsylvania, VA i I 26
Sprague, WA c H 112
Sprague, r., OR h D 112
Spray, OR f F 112
Spreckelsville, HI b D 144a
Spring, r., US c G 68
Spring, r., AR f E 68
Spring City, TN d B 40
Spring City, UT e E 98
Springdale, AR f B 68
Springdale, SC f E 40
Springdale, UT g D 98
Springdale, WA b H 112
Spring Dale, WV b F 40
Springer, NM c B 84
Springerville, AZ j G 98
Springfield, CO f E 82
Springfield, FL i K 40
Springfield, GA g E 40
Springfield, IL c G 68
Springfield, KY e K 68
Springfield, MA e N 26
Springfield, MN g M 82
Springfield, MO e C 68
Springfield, OH h C 26
Springfield, SC f E 40
Springfield, SD i J 82
Springfield, TN f J 68
Springfield, VT d N 26
Spring Glen, UT e F 98
Spring Green, WI g E 54
Spring Grove, MN g D 54
Spring Grove, PA h J 26
Springhill, LA i C 68
Spring Hill, TN g I 68
Spring Hope, NC d H 40
Spring Lake, NC d H 40
Spring Mountains, NV h J 128
Springtown, TX g I 84
Springvale, ME d P 26
Spring Valley, CA l I 128
Spring Valley, IL i F 54
Spring Valley, MN g C 54
Spring Valley, NY f L 26
Spring Valley, WI f C 54
Springview, NE i H 82
Springville, AL i J 68
Springville, CA h G 128
Springville, IA h D 54
Springville, NY e H 26
Springville, UT d E 98
Spruce Knob, WV i G 26
Spruce Mountain, AZ j D 98
Spruce Mountain, NV d K 128
Spruce Pine, AL h I 68
Spruce Pine, NC d D 40
Spur, TX f F 84
Spurger, TX l B 68
Squaw Peak, MT c K 112
Squire, WV b E 40
Stacyville, IA g C 54
Stafford, KS n I 82
Stafford, VA i I 26
Stafford Springs, CT f N 26
Stambaugh, MI d G 54
Stamford, CT f M 26
Stamford, NY e L 26
Stamford, TX g G 84
Stamford, Lake, TX f G 84
Stamps, AR i C 68
Standard, WV i H 26
Standardsville, VA i H 26
Stanberry, MO b B 68
Standard, AK d T 142
Standish, MI g L 54
Stanfield, AZ k E 98
Stanfield, OR e F 112
Stanford, KY b B 40
Stanford, MT c O 112
Stanhope, IA h B 54
Stanislaus, r., CA g E 128
Stanley, NC d E 40
Stanley, ND c E 82
Stanley, VA i H 26
Stanley, WI f E 54
Stanton, IA j L 82
Stanton, KY b C 40
Stanton, MI g J 54
Stanton, NE j J 82
Stanton, ND f G 82
Stanton, TN g G 68
Stanton, TX h E 84
Stantonsburg, NC d H 40
Stanwood, WA b C 112
Staples, MN e M 82
Stapleton, AL l I 68
Stapleton, NE j G 82
Star, MS j F 68
Star, NC d F 40
Starbuck, MN f L 82
Starbuck, WA d G 112
Star City, AR h E 68
Star City, IN b J 68
Stargo, AZ k G 98
Starke, FL j D 40
Starkville, MS i H 68
State Center, IA h B 54
State College, PA g I 26
State Line, MS j I 68
Stateline, NV f F 128

Statenville, GA i C 40
State Road, NC c F 40
Statesboro, GA g E 40
Statesville, NC d F 40
Staunton, IL c G 68
Staunton, VA i G 26
Stayton, OR f C 112
Steamboat Mountain, WY c H 98
Steamboat Springs, CO d J 98
Stearns, KY c B 40
Stebbins, AK e M 142
Steele, MO f G 68
Steele, ND e H 82
Steeleville, IL d G 68
Steelville, MO e E 68
Stella, NE k L 82
Stephen, MN c K 82
Stephens, AR i C 68
Stephens City, VA h H 26
Stephenson, MI e H 54
Stephenville, TX g H 84
Sterling, AK f S 142
Sterling, CO k D 82
Sterling, IL i F 54
Sterling, KS m I 82
Sterling, NE k K 82
Sterling, ND f K 82
Sterling City, TX h F 84
Sterlington, LA i D 68
Steubenville, OH h F 26
Stevenson, AL h K 68
Stevenson, WA e D 112
Stevens Pass, WA c D 112
Stevens Point, WI f F 54
Stevens Village, AK c T 142
Stevensville, MI h I 54
Stevensville, MT d K 112
Stewardson, IL c H 68
Stewart, MN f A 54
Stewartstown, PA h J 26
Stewartsville, MO c B 68
Stewartville, MN g C 54
Stickney, SD h I 82
Stigler, OK d K 84
Stillmore, GA g D 40
Stillwater, MN e C 54
Stillwater, OK c I 84
Stillwater, r., MT e P 112
Stillwell, OK g B 68
Stimson, Mount, MT b L 112
Stinking Water Creek, r., NE k F 82
Stinnett, TX d E 84
Stirling City, CA e D 128
Stirrat, WV b D 40
Stockbridge, GA f B 40
Stockbridge, MI h K 54
Stockdale, TX j I 84
Stockett, MT c N 112
Stockton, AL l I 68
Stockton, CA g D 128
Stockton, IL h E 54
Stockton, KS l H 82
Stockton, MO e C 68
Stockton, UT d D 98
Stockton Plateau, TX i D 84
Stockton Reservoir, MO e C 68
Stockton Springs, ME c R 26
Stockville, NE k G 82
Stoneboro, PA f F 26
Stonefort, IL e H 68
Stone Harbor, NJ h L 26
Stone Mountain, GA f B 40
Stoneville, NC c G 40
Stonewall, LA j C 68
Stonewall, MS j H 68
Stonewall, OK e J 84
Stonington, IL c G 68
Stonington, ME c R 26
Stony, r., MN c D 54
Stony Point, NC d E 40
Stony Point, NY f L 26
Storm Lake, IA i L 82
Storrs, CT f N 26
Story, WY f S 112
Story City, IA h B 54
Stoughton, MA e O 26
Stoughton, WI h F 54
Stover, MO d D 68
Stow, OH f E 26
Stowe, VT c N 26
Stowell, TX m B 68
Strasburg, CO d D 82
Strasburg, ND g G 82
Strasburg, OH g E 26
Strasburg, PA h J 26
Strasburg, VA i H 26
Stratford, CA h F 128
Stratford, CT f M 26
Stratford, IA h B 54
Stratford, OK d J 84
Stratford, TX c D 84
Stratford, WI f E 54
Strathmore, CA h F 128
Stratton, CO l E 82
Stratton, ME b P 26
Stratton, NE k F 82
Strawberry, r., AR f E 68
Strawberry, r., UT d F 98
Strawberry Mountain, OR f G 112
Strawberry Point, IA h D 54
Strawn, TX g H 84
Streator, IL i G 54
Streeter, ND e H 82
Streetman, TX h J 84
Streetsboro, OH f E 26
Strong, AR i D 68
Strong, r., MS j G 68
Strong City, KS m K 82
Stronghurst, IL c E 68
Stroud, OK d I 84
Stroudsburg, PA g K 26
Strum, WI f D 54
Struthers, OH f F 26
Stryker, OH f B 26
Stuart, FL m F 40
Stuart, IA j M 82
Stuart, NE i H 82
Stuart, VA c F 40
Stuarts Draft, VA i G 26
Sturgeon, MO c D 68
Sturgeon, r., MI e K 54
Sturgeon Bay, WI e H 54
Sturgis, KY e I 68
Sturgis, MI i J 54
Sturgis, MS i G 68
Sturgis, SD g D 82

Sturtevant, WI h H 54
Stuttgart, AR h E 68
Styx, r., AL l I 68
Sublette, KS n G 82
Sucarnoochee, r., US i H 68
Sudan, TX e D 84
Suffolk, VA c J 40
Sugar, r., US h F 54
Sugar, r., NH d N 26
Sugar City, ID g N 112
Sugarcreek, PA f G 26
Sugar Grove, VA b E 40
Sugar Hill, GA e B 40
Sugar Island, MI d K 54
Sugar Land, TX j K 84
Sugarloaf Mountain, ME b P 26
Sulligent, AL i H 68
Sullivan, IL c H 68
Sullivan, IN c I 68
Sullivan, MO d E 68
Sulphur, LA l C 68
Sulphur, OK e J 84
Sulphur, r., US i B 68
Sulphur Springs, TX f K 84
Sulphur Springs Valley, AZ m G 98
Sultan, WA c D 112
Sumas, WA a C 112
Summerfield, FL j D 40
Summerfield, NC c G 40
Summersville, WV i F 26
Summerton, SC f F 40
Summertown, TN g I 68
Summerville, GA e A 40
Summerville, SC f F 40
Summit, MS k F 68
Summit, SD f J 82
Summit Mountain, NV e I 128
Summit Peak, CO g J 98
Sumner, IA h C 54
Sumner, MS i F 68
Sumner, WA c C 112
Sumrall, MS k G 68
Sumter, SC f F 40
Sun, r., MT c M 112
Sunbright, TN c B 40
Sunburst, MT b N 112
Sunbury, NC c J 40
Sunbury, OH g D 26
Sunbury, PA g J 26
Suncook, NH d O 26
Suncook, r., NH d O 26
Sundance, WY f V 112
Sundown, TX f D 84
Sunflower, MS i F 68
Sunflower, Mount, KS l E 82
Sunland Park, NM l J 98
Sunnyside, UT e F 98
Sunnyvale, CA g C 128
Sun Prairie, WI g F 54
Sunray, TX c E 84
Sunrise, WY b L 98
Sunrise Manor, NV h J 128
Sunset, LA l D 68
Sunset, TX f I 84
Sunset Beach, HI e I 144c
Sunset Heights, TX h D 84
Suntrana, AK e T 142
Sun Valley, ID g K 112
Superior, AZ k E 98
Superior, MT c K 112
Superior, NE k I 82
Superior, WI d C 54
Superior, Lake, NA c H 54
Surf City, NJ h L 26
Surgoinsville, TN c D 40
Suring, WI f G 54
Surprise, AZ k D 98
Surprise Valley, US c E 128
Surrency, GA h D 40
Surrey, ND c F 82
Surry, VA b J 40
Susanville, CA d E 128
Susitna, AK e S 142
Susitna, r., AK e S 142
Susquehanna, PA f K 26
Susquehanna, r., US h J 26
Sussex, NJ f L 26
Sussex, VA c I 40
Sutherland, IA i L 82
Sutherland, NE j F 82
Sutherlin, OR g B 112
Sutter, CA e D 128
Sutter Creek, CA f E 128
Sutton, AK f T 142
Sutton, NE k J 82
Sutton, WV i F 26
Suttons Bay, MI f J 54
Suwannee, r., US j C 40
Swainsboro, GA g D 40
Swan, r., MN c B 54
Swanee, see Suwannee, r., US
Swan Lake, MT c L 112
Swannanoa, NC d D 40
Swanquarter, NC d J 40
Swan Range, MT c L 112
Swansboro, NC e I 40
Swansea, SC f E 40
Swanton, OH f C 26
Swanton, VT c M 26
Swanville, MN e A 54
Swartz Creek, MI h L 54
Swasey Peak, UT d C 98
Swea City, IA h M 82
Swedish Knoll, UT e E 98
Sweeny, TX k K 84
Sweet Briar, VA b G 40
Sweet Home, OR f C 112
Sweet Home, TX j I 84
Sweet Springs, MO d C 68
Sweetwater, TN d B 40
Sweetwater, TX g F 84
Sweetwater, r., WY h R 112
Swepsonville, NC c G 40
Swifton, AR g F 68
Sycamore, GA h C 40
Sycamore, IL i G 54
Sycamore, OH g C 26
Sycan, r., OR h D 112
Sykesville, MD h J 26
Sykeston, ND d H 82
Sylacauga, AL i J 68
Sylva, NC d D 40
Sylvan Grove, KS l I 82
Sylvania, GA g E 40
Sylvania, OH f C 26
Sylvester, GA h C 40
Sylvester, TX g F 84
Sylvia, KS n I 82

Syracuse, IN a K 68
Syracuse, KS n F 82
Syracuse, NE k K 82
Syracuse, NY d J 26

T

Table Rock, NE k K 82
Table Rock Lake, US f C 68
Tabor, IA k L 82
Tabor, SD i J 82
Tabor City, NC e H 40
Tacna, AZ l C 98
Tacoma, WA c C 112
Taconic Range, US e M 26
Taft, CA i F 128
Taft, OK d K 84
Taft, TX l I 84
Tahlequah, OK d L 84
Tahoe, Lake, US e E 128
Tahoe City, CA e E 128
Tahoe Valley, CA f E 128
Tahoka, TX f E 84
Tahquamenon, r., MI d J 54
Tajique, NM j J 98
Taku Glacier, AK g AA 142
Talbotton, GA g B 40
Talco, TX f K 84
Talent, OR h C 112
Talihina, OK e K 84
Talkeetna, AK e S 142
Talladega, AL i J 68
Tallahassee, FL i B 40
Tallahatchie, r., MS i F 68
Tallapoosa, GA f A 40
Tallapoosa, r., US j J 68
Tallassee, AL j K 68
Tallmadge, OH f E 26
Tallula, IL c G 68
Tallulah, LA i E 68
Talmage, CA e B 128
Talmage, NE k K 82
Taloga, OK c H 84
Talpa, TX h G 84
Tama, IA i C 54
Tamaqua, PA g K 26
Tamarac, r., MN c J 82
Tamaroa, IL d G 68
Tamiami Canal, FL n E 40
Tamms, IL e G 68
Tampa, FL l D 40
Tampa Bay, FL l D 40
Tampico, IL i F 54
Tanacross, AK e W 142
Tanana, AK d R 142
Tanana, r., AK d S 142
Taneytown, MD h I 26
Tangier, VA b K 40
Tangipahoa, r., US k F 68
Tanner, AL h J 68
Taos, MO d D 68
Taos, NM h K 98
Taos Pueblo, NM h K 98
Tappahannock, VA b J 40
Tappen, ND e H 82
Tar, r., NC d I 40
Tarboro, NC d I 40
Tarentum, PA g G 26
Targhee Pass, US f N 112
Tarkio, MO b A 68
Tarkio, r., US k L 82
Tarpon Springs, FL k D 40
Tarrant City, AL i J 68
Tarzan, TX g E 84
Tate, GA e B 40
Tatitlek, AK f U 142
Tatum, NM j C 84
Tatum, TX j B 68
Taum Sauk Mountain, MO e F 68
Taunton, MA f O 26
Tavares, FL k E 40
Tavernier, FL n F 40
Tawakoni, Lake, TX g J 84
Tawas City, MI f L 54
Taylor, AZ j F 98
Taylor, NE j H 82
Taylor, PA f K 26
Taylor, TX i I 84
Taylor, Mount, NM i I 98
Taylors, SC e D 40
Taylorsville, IN c K 68
Taylorsville, KY d K 68
Taylorsville, MS k G 68
Taylorsville, NC d E 40
Taylorville, IL c G 68
Tazewell, TN c C 40
Tazewell, VA b E 40
Tchefuncta, r., LA l F 68
Tchula, MS i F 68
Teague, TX h J 84
Teche, Bayou, r., LA l E 68
Tecopa, CA i I 128
Tecumseh, MI h L 54
Tecumseh, NE k K 82
Tecumseh, OK d J 84
Teec Nos Pos, AZ h G 98
Tehachapi, CA i G 128
Tehachapi Pass, CA i G 128
Tekamah, NE j K 82
Tekoa, WA c H 112
Tekonsha, MI h K 54
Telescope Peak, CA h H 128
Tell City, IN e I 68
Teller, AK d K 142
Tellico, r., US d B 40
Tellico Plains, TN d B 40
Telluride, CO g I 98
Temecula, CA k H 128
Tempe, AZ k E 98
Temperance, MI i L 54
Temple, OK e H 84
Temple, TX h I 84
Tenaha, TX k B 68
Tenakee Springs, AK h AA 142
Tenino, WA d C 112
Tenkiller Ferry Lake, OK d K 84
Tennessee, state, US d I 8
Tennessee, r., US d I 8
Tennille, GA g D 40
Tensas, r., LA k E 68
Tensed, ID c I 112
Ten Sleep, WY f R 112
Ten Thousand Islands, FL n E 40
Terlingua, TX j C 84
Terra Alta, WV h G 26
Terra Bella, CA h F 128
Terral, OK f I 84
Terrebonne Bay, LA m F 68
Terre Haute, IN c I 68
Terrell, TX g J 84
Terrell Hills, TX j H 84
Terry, MS j F 68

Name	Map Ref.	Page
Terry, MT	e B	82
Terry Peak, SD	g D	82
Tescott, KS	l J	82
Tesuque, NM	i K	98
Tetlin, AK	e W	142
Tetlin Lake, AK	e W	142
Teton, ID	g N	112
Teton, r., MT	c N	112
Tetonia, ID	g N	112
Teton Range, WY	g O	112
Teutopolis, IL	c H	68
Texarkana, AR	i B	68
Texarkana, TX	i B	68
Texas, state, US	e G	8
Texas City, TX	j L	84
Texhoma, OK	c E	84
Texico, NM	e C	84
Texline, TX	c C	84
Texoma, Lake, US	f J	84
Thalia, TX	f G	84
Thatcher, AZ	l G	98
Thayer, KS	n L	82
Thayer, MO	f E	68
Thealka, KY	b D	40
Thebes, IL	e G	68
The Dalles, OR	e D	112
Thedford, NE	j G	82
The Everglades, FL	m F	40
The Flat Tops, CO	d I	98
Theodore, AL	l H	68
Theodore Roosevelt Lake, AZ	k E	98
Theresa, NY	c K	26
Thermopolis, WY	a H	98
Thibodaux, LA	m F	68
Thief, r., MN	c K	82
Thief River Falls, MN	c K	82
Thielsen, Mount, OR	g C	112
Thomas, OK	d H	84
Thomas, WV	h G	26
Thomasboro, IL	b H	68
Thomaston, AL	j I	68
Thomaston, CT	f M	26
Thomaston, GA	g B	40
Thomaston, ME	c Q	26
Thomasville, AL	k I	68
Thomasville, GA	i C	40
Thomasville, NC	d F	40
Thompson, IA	g B	54
Thompson, r., US	c C	68
Thompson Falls, MT	c J	112
Thompson Pass, AK	f V	142
Thompsonville, MI	f J	54
Thomson, GA	f D	40
Thomson, IL	i E	54
Thonotosassa, FL	k D	40
Thoreau, NM	i H	98
Thornapple, r., WI	e D	54
Thorndale, TX	i I	84
Thornton, AR	i D	68
Thornton, CO	e L	98
Thornton, TX	h J	84
Thorntonville, TX	h D	84
Thorp, WI	f E	54
Thorsby, AL	j J	68
Thousand Lake Mountain, UT	f E	98
Thousand Oaks, CA	j G	128
Three Fingered Jack, OR	f D	112
Three Forks, MT	e N	112
Three Lakes, WI	e F	54
Three Oaks, MI	i I	54
Three Rivers, MI	i J	54
Three Rivers, TX	k H	84
Three Sisters, OR	f D	112
Throckmorton, TX	f G	84
Thunder Bay, MI	e L	54
Thunder Bay, r., MI	e L	54
Thunderbolt, GA	g E	40
Thurmont, MD	h I	26
Tibbie, AL	k H	68
Tice, FL	m E	40
Tickfaw, LA	l F	68
Tickfaw, r., US	l F	68
Ticonderoga, NY	d M	26
Tidioute, PA	f G	26
Tie Plant, MS	i G	68
Tierra Amarilla, NM	h J	98
Tiffany Mountain, WA	b F	112
Tiffin, OH	f C	26
Tifton, GA	h C	40
Tiftona, TN	d A	40
Tignall, GA	f D	40
Tilden, IL	d G	68
Tilden, NE	i J	82
Tilden, TX	k H	84
Tillamook, OR	e B	112
Tillmans Corner, AL	l H	68
Tillson, NY	f L	26
Tilton, IL	b I	68
Tilton, NH	d O	26
Tiltonsville, OH	g F	26
Timber Lake, SD	f F	82
Timmonsville, SC	e G	40
Tims Hill, WI	d E	54
Timpson, TX	k B	68
Tims Ford Lake, TN	g J	68
Tinsley, MS	j F	68
Tioga, ND	c E	82
Tioga, PA	f I	26
Tioga, r., US	f I	26
Tionesta, PA	f G	26
Tionesta Creek, r., PA	f G	26
Tioughnioga, r., NY	e J	26
Tippecanoe, r., IN	a J	68
Tipton, CA	h F	128
Tipton, IN	b J	68
Tipton, IA	i D	54
Tipton, MO	d D	68
Tipton, OK	e G	84
Tiptonville, TN	f G	68
Tishomingo, MS	h H	68
Tishomingo, OK	e J	84
Tiskilwa, IL	i F	54
Titonka, IA	g A	54
Tittabawassee, r., MI	g K	54
Titusville, FL	k F	40
Titusville, PA	f G	26
Tivoli, TX	k J	84
Toano, VA	b J	40
Toast, NC	c F	40
Tobacco, r., MI	c J	54
Tobias, NE	k J	82
Tobyhanna, PA	f K	26
Toccoa, GA	e C	40
Toccoa (Ocoee), r., US	e B	40
Togiak, AK	g N	142
Togwotee Pass, WY	g O	112
Toiyabe Range, NV	e H	128
Toksook Bay, AK	f L	142
Toledo, IL	c H	68
Toledo, IA	i C	54
Toledo, OH	f C	26
Toledo, OR	e B	112
Toledo Bend Reservoir, US	k C	68
Tolleson, AZ	k D	98
Tolono, IL	c H	68
Toluca, IL	i F	54
Tomah, WI	g E	54
Tomahawk, WI	e E	54
Tomball, TX	i K	84
Tombigbee, r., US	k H	68
Tombstone, AZ	m F	98
Tompkinsville, KY	f K	68
Toms, r., NJ	g L	26
Toms River, NJ	h L	26
Tonasket, WA	b F	112
Tonawanda, NY	d H	26
Tonganoxie, KS	l L	82
Tongue, r., US	e S	112
Tongue, r., ND	e J	82
Tongue, r., TX	f F	84
Tonica, IL	i F	54
Tonkawa, OK	c I	84
Tonopah, NV	f H	128
Tooele, UT	d D	98
Toomsboro, GA	g C	40
Topawa, AZ	m E	98
Topeka, KS	l L	82
Toppenish, WA	d E	112
Topsham, ME	d Q	26
Torch Lake, MI	e J	54
Tornillo, TX	m J	98
Toronto, KS	n L	82
Toronto, OH	g F	26
Toronto, SD	g K	82
Torrance, CA	k G	128
Torrington, CT	f M	26
Torrington, WY	i C	82
Totagatic, r., WI	d D	54
Toulon, IL	i F	54
Toutle, r., WA	d C	112
Tow, TX	i H	84
Towanda, KS	n K	82
Towanda, PA	f J	26
Tower, MN	c C	54
Tower City, ND	e J	82
Tower City, PA	g J	26
Tower Hill, IL	c H	68
Town and Country, WA	c H	112
Towner, ND	c G	82
Townsend, MT	d N	112
Towson, MD	h J	26
Toyah, TX	h C	84
Tracy, CA	g D	128
Tracy, MN	g L	82
Tracy City, TN	g K	68
Tradewater, r., KY	e I	68
Traer, IA	h C	54
Trammel, VA	b D	40
Traverse, Lake, US	f K	82
Traverse City, MI	f J	54
Travis, Lake, TX	i H	84
Tremont, IL	j F	54
Tremont, PA	g J	26
Tremonton, UT	c D	98
Trempealeau, WI	f D	54
Trempealeau, r., WI	f D	54
Trenton, FL	j D	40
Trenton, GA	e A	40
Trenton, KY	f I	68
Trenton, MO	b C	68
Trenton, NE	k F	82
Trenton, NJ	g L	26
Trenton, NC	d I	40
Trenton, TN	g H	68
Trenton, TX	f J	84
Trentwood, WA	c H	112
Tres Montosas, NM	j I	98
Trevorton, PA	g J	26
Trezevant, TN	f H	68
Triangle, VA	i I	26
Tribune, KS	m F	82
Trilby, FL	k D	40
Trimont, MN	h M	82
Trinidad, CO	n C	82
Trinidad, TX	g J	84
Trinity, TX	i K	84
Trinity, r., CA	d B	128
Trinity, r., TX	i L	84
Trinity Bay, TX	j L	84
Trion, GA	e A	40
Tripoli, IA	h C	54
Tripp, SD	h J	82
Triumph, LA	m G	68
Trona, CA	i H	128
Tropic, UT	g D	98
Trotwood, OH	h B	26
Troup, TX	g K	84
Trout, LA	k D	68
Trout Creek, MI	d F	54
Trout Creek Pass, CO	f I	98
Troutville, VA	b G	40
Troy, AL	k K	68
Troy, ID	d I	112
Troy, IN	e J	68
Troy, KS	l L	82
Troy, MO	d F	68
Troy, MT	b J	112
Troy, NH	e N	26
Troy, NY	e M	26
Troy, NC	d G	40
Troy, OH	g B	26
Troy, PA	f J	26
Troy, TN	f H	68
Troy, TX	h I	84
Troy Peak, NV	f K	128
Truchas, NM	h K	98
Truchas Peak, NM	h K	98
Truckee, CA	e E	128
Truckee, r., US	e E	128
Truman, MN	h M	82
Trumann, AR	g F	68
Trumansburg, NY	e J	26
Trumbull, CT	f M	26
Truscott, TX	f G	84
Truth or Consequences (Hot Springs), NM	k I	98
Tryon, NE	j G	82
Tryon, NC	d D	40
Tubac, AZ	m E	98
Tuba City, AZ	h E	98
Tuckerman, AR	g E	68
Tuckerton, NJ	h L	26
Tucson, AZ	l F	98
Tucumcari, NM	d C	84
Tug Fork, r., US	a D	40
Tugidak Island, AK	h Q	142
Tulare, CA	h F	128
Tulare, SD	g I	82
Tularosa, NM	k H	98
Tularosa, r., NM	k H	98
Tularosa Valley, NM	l J	98
Tule, r., CA	h F	128
Tulelake, CA	c E	128
Tule Valley, UT	e C	98
Tulia, TX	e F	84
Tullahoma, TN	g J	68
Tullos, LA	k D	68
Tulsa, OK	c K	84
Tuluksak, AK	f M	142
Tumble Mountain, MT	e O	112
Tumwater, WA	c C	112
Tunica, MS	h F	68
Tunkhannock, PA	f K	26
Tunnel Hill, GA	e A	40
Tunnelton, WV	h G	26
Tuntutuliak, AK	f M	142
Tununak, AK	f L	142
Tupelo, MS	h H	68
Tupelo, OK	e J	84
Tupper Lake, NY	c L	26
Turkey, TX	e F	84
Turkey, r., IA	h D	54
Turkey Creek, r., NE	k J	82
Turlock, CA	g E	128
Turon, KS	n I	82
Turrell, AR	g F	68
Turtle-Flambeau Flowage, WI	d E	54
Turtle Lake, ND	d G	82
Turtle Lake, WI	d C	54
Tusas, Rio, r., NM	h J	98
Tuscaloosa, AL	i I	68
Tuscarora Mountain, PA	g I	26
Tuscarora Mountains, NV	d I	128
Tuscola, IL	c H	68
Tuscola, TX	g G	84
Tuscumbia, AL	h I	68
Tuscumbia, MO	d D	68
Tuskegee, AL	j K	68
Tustumena Lake, AK	f S	142
Tuttle, ND	d H	82
Tuttle, OK	d H	84
Tuttle Creek Lake, KS	l K	82
Tutwiler, MS	h F	68
Twentynine Palms, CA	j I	128
Twin Bridges, MT	e M	112
Twin Falls, ID	h K	112
Twin Lakes, GA	i C	40
Twin Lakes, WI	h G	54
Twinsburg, OH	f E	26
Twin Valley, MN	d K	82
Twisp, WA	b E	112
Two Harbors, MN	c D	54
Two Medicine, r., MT	f N	112
Two Rivers, WI	f H	54
Tybee Island, GA	g F	40
Tye, TX	g G	84
Tygh Valley, OR	e D	112
Tyler, MN	g K	82
Tyler, TX	g K	84
Tylertown, MS	k F	68
Tyndall, SD	h J	82
Tyonek, AK	f S	142
Tyrone, OK	c E	84
Tyrone, PA	g H	26
Ty Ty, GA	h C	40

U

Name	Map Ref.	Page
Ubly, MI	g M	54
Ucon, ID	g N	112
Udall, KS	n J	82
Uhrichsville, OH	g E	26
Uinta, r., UT	d F	98
Uinta Mountains, UT	d F	98
Ukiah, CA	e B	128
Ukiah, OR	e G	112
Ulen, MN	d K	82
Ullin, IL	e G	68
Ulm, MT	c N	112
Ulysses, KS	n F	82
Ulysses, NE	j J	82
Umatilla, FL	k E	40
Umatilla, OR	e F	112
Umatilla, r., OR	e F	112
Umpqua, r., OR	g B	112
Unadilla, GA	g C	40
Unadilla, NY	e K	26
Unadilla, r., NY	e K	26
Unalakleet, AK	e N	142
Unalaska, AK	j K	142
Uncompahgre, r., CO	f I	98
Uncompahgre Peak, CO	f I	98
Uncompahgre Plateau, CO	f H	98
Underwood, ND	d F	82
Unicoi, TN	c D	40
Unimak Island, AK	i L	142
Unimak Pass, AK	i L	142
Union, IL	h B	54
Union, LA	l F	68
Union, MS	j G	68
Union, MO	d E	68
Union, NJ	g L	26
Union, OR	e H	112
Union, SC	e E	40
Union, WA	c B	112
Union, WV	b F	40
Union City, IN	b K	68
Union City, MI	h J	54
Union City, OH	g B	26
Union City, PA	f G	26
Union City, TN	f G	68
Union Gap, WA	d E	112
Union Grove, WI	h G	54
Union Park, FL	k E	40
Union Point, GA	f C	40
Union Springs, AL	j K	68
Union Springs, NY	e J	26
Uniontown, AL	j I	68
Uniontown, KY	e I	68
Uniontown, PA	h G	26
Unionville, MI	g L	54
Unionville, MO	b C	68
United, PA	g G	26
United States, NA	d	8
Universal City, TX	j H	84
University, MS	h G	68
University City, MO	d F	68
University Heights, OH	f E	26
University Park, NM	l J	98
University Park, TX	g J	84
Upham, ND	c G	82
Upland, NE	k I	82
Upolu Point, HI	i P	144d
Upper Arlington, OH	g C	26
Upper Darby, PA	h K	26
Upper Iowa, r., US	g D	54
Upper Klamath Lake, OR	h D	112
Upper Lake, CA	e C	128
Upper Red Lake, MN	c M	82
Upper Sandusky, OH	g C	26
Upton, KY	e K	68
Upton, WY	g C	82
Urania, LA	k D	68
Uravan, CO	f H	98
Urbana, AR	i D	68
Urbana, IL	b H	68
Urbana, MO	e C	68
Urbana, OH	g C	26
Urbandale, IA	a C	68
Uriah, AL	k I	68
Urich, MO	d B	68
Ursa, IL	b E	68
Usk, WA	b H	112
Utah, state, US	d D	8
Utah Lake, UT	d E	98
Ute, IA	i L	82
Utica, KS	m G	82
Utica, MI	h L	54
Utica, MS	j F	68
Utica, NE	k J	82
Utica, NY	d K	26
Utica, OH	g D	26
Utopia, TX	j G	84
Uvalda, GA	f C	40
Uvalde, TX	j G	84

V

Name	Map Ref.	Page
Vacaville, CA	f D	128
Vaiden, MS	i G	68
Vail, CO	e J	98
Vail, IA	i L	82
Valatie, NY	e M	26
Valders, WI	f H	54
Valdese, NC	d E	40
Valdez, AK	f U	142
Valdosta, GA	i C	40
Vale, OR	g H	112
Valentine, NE	i G	82
Valentine, TX	i B	84
Valier, IL	d G	68
Valier, MT	b M	112
Vallecitos, NM	h J	98
Vallejo, CA	f C	128
Valles Caldera, NM	i H	98
Valley, AL	i K	68
Valley, NE	j K	82
Valley Bend, WV	i G	26
Valley Center, KS	n J	82
Valley City, ND	e J	82
Valley Falls, KS	l L	82
Valley Farms, AZ	l E	98
Valley Head, AL	h K	68
Valley Head, WV	i F	26
Valley Mills, TX	h I	84
Valley Springs, SD	h K	82
Valley Station, KY	d K	68
Valley View, TX	f I	84
Valliant, OK	e K	84
Valmeyer, IL	d F	68
Valparaiso, FL	l J	68
Valparaiso, IN	a I	68
Valparaiso, NE	j K	82
Valsetz, OR	f B	112
Van, TX	g K	84
Van Alstyne, TX	f I	84
Van Buren, AR	g B	68
Van Buren, ME	e F	24
Van Buren, MO	f E	68
Vanceboro, ME	b S	26
Vanceburg, KY	i C	26
Vancleave, MS	l H	68
Vancouver, WA	e C	112
Vancouver, Cape, AK	f L	142
Vancouver, Mount, NA	f Y	142
Vandalia, IL	d G	68
Vandalia, MO	c E	68
Vandalia, OH	h B	26
Vanderbilt, MI	e K	54
Vanderbilt, TX	k J	84
Vandergrift, PA	g G	26
Vandervoort, AR	h B	68
Van Horn, TX	h C	84
Van Horne, IA	h C	54
Van Lear, KY	b D	40
Vandale, AR	g F	68
Vansant, VA	b D	40
Van Vleck, TX	j K	84
Van Wert, OH	g B	26
Vardaman, MS	i G	68
Varnville, SC	g E	40
Vass, NC	d G	40
Vassar, MI	g L	54
Vaughn, NM	j K	98
Veazie, ME	c R	26
Veblen, SD	f J	82
Veedersburg, IN	b I	68
Vega, TX	d D	84
Veguita, NM	j J	98
Velma, OK	d H	84
Velva, ND	c G	82
Veniaminof, Mount, AK	h O	142
Venice, FL	l D	40
Venice, LA	m G	68
Ventura, CA	j F	128
Venus, TX	g I	84
Verde, r., AZ	k E	98
Verden, OK	d H	84
Verdi, NV	e F	128
Verdigre, NE	i I	82
Verdigris, r., US	c K	84
Verdon, NE	k L	82
Vergennes, VT	c M	26
Vermejo, r., NM	h L	98
Vermilion, OH	f C	26
Vermilion, r., IL	i G	54
Vermilion, r., LA	m D	68
Vermilion, r., MN	b C	54
Vermilion Bay, LA	m D	68
Vermilion Lake, MN	c C	54
Vermillion, SD	i K	82
Vermillion, r., SD	h K	82
Vermont, IL	j E	54
Vermont, state, US	c L	8
Vernal, UT	d G	98
Verndale, MN	e L	82
Verona, MS	h H	68
Verona, WI	g F	54
Vernon, AL	h H	68
Vernon, CT	f N	26
Vernon, FL	l I	68
Vernon, IN	d K	68
Vernon, TX	e G	84
Vernon, UT	d D	98
Vernonia, OR	e B	112
Vero Beach, FL	l F	40
Versailles, IN	c K	68
Versailles, KY	d L	68
Versailles, MO	d D	68
Versailles, OH	g B	26
Vesta, MN	g L	82
Vestaburg, MI	f K	54
Vestavia Hills, AL	i J	68

W

Name	Map Ref.	Page
Vevay, IN	d K	68
Vian, OK	d L	84
Viborg, SD	h J	82
Viburnum, MO	e E	68
Vicco, KY	c B	40
Vici, OK	c G	84
Vicksburg, MI	h J	54
Vicksburg, MS	j F	68
Victor, ID	g N	112
Victor, IA	i C	54
Victor, MT	d K	112
Victoria, KS	m H	82
Victoria, TX	k I	84
Victoria, VA	b H	40
Victorville, CA	j H	128
Vidalia, GA	g D	40
Vidalia, LA	k E	68
Vidor, TX	l B	68
Vienna, GA	g C	40
Vienna, IL	e H	68
Vienna, MD	i K	26
Vienna, MO	d E	68
Vienna, SD	g J	82
Vienna, VA	h E	26
Village, OK	d I	84
Villa Grove, IL	c H	68
Villanueva, NM	i K	98
Villa Rica, GA	f B	40
Villas, NJ	h L	26
Ville Platte, LA	l D	68
Villisca, IA	k M	82
Vina, CA	e C	128
Vinalhaven, ME	c R	26
Vincennes, IN	d I	68
Vincent, AL	i J	68
Vinegar Hill, OR	f G	112
Vine Grove, KY	e K	68
Vineland, NJ	h K	26
Vinemont, AL	h J	68
Vineyard Haven, MA	f P	26
Vinita, OK	c K	84
Vinton, IA	h C	54
Vinton, LA	l C	68
Vinton, VA	b G	40
Viola, IL	i E	54
Viola, WI	g E	54
Virden, IL	c G	68
Virden, NM	l G	98
Virgil, KS	n K	82
Virgilina, VA	c H	40
Virgin, r., US	h B	98
Virginia, IL	c F	68
Virginia, MN	c C	54
Virginia, state, US	d K	8
Virginia Beach, VA	c K	40
Virginia City, MT	e N	112
Virginia City, NV	f F	128
Viroqua, WI	g E	54
Visalia, CA	h F	128
Vista, CA	k H	128
Vivian, LA	j C	68
Voca, TX	h G	84
Volcano, HI	j P	144d
Volga, IA	h D	54
Volga, SD	g K	82
Voyageurs National Park, MN	b C	54
Vredenburgh, AL	k I	68
Vsevidof, Mount, AK	j J	142
Vulcan, MI	e H	54
Wabash, IN	b K	68
Wabash, r., US	e I	68
Wabasha, MN	f C	54
Wabasso, FL	l F	40
Wabasso, MN	g L	82
Wabeno, WI	e G	54
Waccamaw, r., US	f H	40
Wachapreague, VA	b K	40
Wacissa, FL	i C	40
Waco, TX	h I	84
Waconda Lake, KS	l I	82
Waconia, MN	f B	54
Waddington, NY	c K	26
Wadena, MN	e L	82
Wadesboro, NC	e F	40
Wadley, AL	i K	68
Wadley, GA	g D	40
Wadsworth, NV	e F	128
Wadsworth, OH	f E	26
Waelder, TX	j I	84
Wagner, SD	h I	82
Wagoner, OK	c K	84
Wagon Mound, NM	i L	98
Wahiawa, HI	e l	144c
Wahoo, NE	j K	82
Wahpeton, ND	e K	82
Waialeale, HI	e l	144b
Waialua, HI	e l	144b
Waialua Bay, HI	e l	144c
Waianae, HI	f l	144c
Waianae Range, HI	f l	144c
Waianapanapa State Park, HI	b D	144d
Waihee, HI	b C	144d
Waikapu, HI	b C	144d
Waikiki Beach, HI	f J	144c
Wailua, HI	b C	144d
Wailua River State Park, HI	c H	144a
Wailuku, HI	b C	144d
Waimanalo, HI	f J	144c
Waimea, HI	b C	144d
Waimea Canyon, HI	c G	144a
Waimea Canyon State Park, HI	c G	144a
Wainwright, AK	a N	142
Waipahu, HI	f l	144c
Waipio Acres, HI	f l	144c
Waite Park, MN	e A	54
Waitsburg, WA	d G	112
Waka, TX	c J	84
Wakarusa, IN	a J	68
Wakarusa, r., KS	m L	82
WaKeeney, KS	l H	82
Wakefield, KS	l J	82
Wakefield, NE	i J	82
Wakefield, VA	b J	40
Wake Forest, NC	c H	40
Wake Village, TX	i B	68
Wakita, OK	c H	84
Wakonda, SD	h I	82
Walcott, IA	i E	54
Walcott, ND	d F	82
Walden, CO	d J	98
Walden, NY	f L	26
Walden Ridge, TN	f K	68
Waldo, AR	i C	68
Waldoboro, ME	c Q	26
Waldorf, MD	i I	26
Waldport, OR	f A	112
Waldron, AR	h B	68
Waldron, IN	c K	68
Waldron, MI	i K	54
Wales, AK	d J	142
Walhalla, ND	c J	82
Walhalla, SC	e C	40
Walker, IA	h D	54
Walker, MN	c A	54
Walker, r., NV	e G	128
Walker Lake, NV	f G	128
Walkersville, MD	h I	26
Walkerton, IN	a J	68
Walkertown, NC	c F	40
Walkerville, MT	d M	112
Wall, SD	h E	82
Wallace, ID	c J	112
Wallace, NE	k F	82
Wallace, NC	e I	40
Walla Walla, WA	d G	112
Waller, TX	i K	84
Wallingford, CT	f N	26
Wallingford, VT	d N	26
Wallis, TX	j J	84
Wallowa, OR	e H	112
Wallowa, r., OR	e H	112
Wallowa Mountains, OR	e H	112
Walls, MS	h F	68
Wallula, Lake, US	d G	112
Walnut, IA	a A	68
Walnut, IL	i F	54
Walnut, KS	n L	82
Walnut, MS	h H	68
Walnut, NC	d D	40
Walnut, r., KS	n J	82
Walnut Cove, NC	c F	40
Walnut Grove, MN	g L	82
Walnut Grove, MS	j G	68
Walnut Ridge, AR	f F	68
Walnut Springs, TX	g I	84
Walpole, NH	d N	26
Walsenburg, CO	g L	98
Walsh, CO	n E	82
Walterboro, SC	g F	40
Walter F. George Lake, US	h A	40
Walters, OK	e H	84
Waltersville, MS	j F	68
Walthall, MS	i G	68
Waltham, MA	e O	26
Walthill, NE	i K	82
Walton, IN	b J	68
Walton, KY	i B	68
Walton, NY	e K	26
Walworth, WI	h G	54
Wamego, KS	l K	82
Wampsville, NY	d K	26
Wampum, PA	g F	26
Wamsutter, WY	i R	112
Wanamingo, MN	f C	54
Wanblee, SD	h F	82
Wanchese, NC	d K	40
Wanette, OK	e I	84
Wapakoneta, OH	g B	26
Wapanucka, OK	e J	84
Wapato, WA	d E	112
Wapello, IA	i D	54
Wappingers Falls, NY	f M	26
Wapsipinicon, r., US	i C	54
War, WV	b E	40
Ward Cove, AK	b C	24
Warden, WA	d F	112
Ware, MA	e N	26
Ware, r., MA	e N	26
Wareham, MA	f P	26
Ware Shoals, SC	e D	40
Warminster, PA	g K	26
Warm Springs, GA	g B	40
Warm Springs, MT	d M	112
Warm Springs, OR	f D	112
Warm Springs, r., OR	a G	40
Warner, NH	d O	26
Warner Lakes, OR	h F	112
Warner Mountains, US	c E	128
Warner Peak, OR	h F	112
Warner Robins, GA	g C	40
Warr Acres, OK	d I	84
Warren, AR	i D	68
Warren, IL	h F	54
Warren, IN	b K	68
Warren, MI	h L	54
Warren, OH	f F	26
Warren, PA	f G	26
Warrens, WI	f E	54
Warrensburg, MO	d C	68
Warrensburg, NY	d M	26
Warrenton, GA	f D	40
Warrenton, MO	d E	68
Warrenton, NC	c H	40
Warrenton, OR	d B	112
Warrenton, VA	i I	26
Warrington, FL	l I	68
Warrior, AL	i J	68
Warroad, MN	b L	82
Warsaw, IL	j D	54
Warsaw, IN	a K	68
Warsaw, KY	i A	68
Warsaw, MO	d C	68
Warsaw, NY	e H	26
Warsaw, NC	d H	40
Warsaw, OH	g D	26
Warsaw, VA	b J	40
Wartburg, TN	c B	40
Wartrace, TN	g J	68
Warwick, RI	f O	26
Wasatch Plateau, UT	f E	98
Wasatch Range, UT	d E	98
Wasco, CA	i F	128
Wasco, OR	e E	112
Waseca, MN	f B	54
Washburn, IL	j F	54
Washburn, ND	d F	82
Washburn, WI	d E	54
Washington, DC	i I	26
Washington, GA	f D	40
Washington, IL	j F	54
Washington, IN	d I	68
Washington, IA	i D	54
Washington, KS	l J	82
Washington, LA	l D	68
Washington, MO	d E	68
Washington, NJ	g K	26
Washington, NC	d I	40
Washington, PA	g F	26
Washington, UT	g C	98
Washington, VA	b I	40
Washington, state, US	b B	8
Washington, Mount, NH	c O	26
Washington Court House, OH	h C	26
Washington Island, WI	e I	54
Washington Terrace, UT	c E	98
Washita, r., US	e J	84
Washtucna, WA	d G	112
Wasilla, AK	f T	142
Waskom, TX	j B	68
Waterbury, CT	f M	26
Waterbury, VT	c N	26
Wateree, r., SC	f F	40
Wateree Lake, SC	e F	40
Waterford, CA	g E	128
Waterford, PA	f G	26
Waterloo, AL	h I	68
Waterloo, IL	d F	68
Waterloo, IA	h C	54
Waterloo, NY	e J	26
Waterloo, WI	g G	54
Waterman, IL	i G	54
Waterproof, LA	k E	68
Watersmeet, MI	d F	54
Waterton-Glacier International Peace Park, NA	b L	112
Watertown, NY	d K	26
Watertown, SD	g J	82
Watertown, WI	g G	54
Water Valley, MS	h G	68
Waterville, KS	l K	82
Waterville, ME	c Q	26
Waterville, MN	f B	54
Waterville, OH	f C	26
Waterville, WA	c E	112
Watervliet, NY	e M	26
Watford City, ND	d D	82
Wathena, KS	l M	82
Watkins Glen, NY	e J	26
Watkinsville, GA	f C	40
Watonga, OK	d H	84
Watonwan, r., MN	g M	82
Watrous, NM	i L	98
Watseka, IL	i H	54
Watson, town, PA	f J	26
Watsonville, CA	h D	128
Watts Bar Lake, TN	d B	40
Watts Mills, SC	e D	40
Waubay, SD	f J	82
Wauchula, FL	l E	40
Wauconda, WA	b F	112
Waugh Mountain, ID	e K	112
Waukegan, IL	h H	54
Waukesha, WI	h G	54
Waukomis, OK	c I	84
Waukon, IA	g D	54
Waunakee, WI	g F	54
Wauneta, NE	k F	82
Waupaca, WI	f F	54
Waupun, WI	g G	54
Waurika, OK	e I	84
Wausa, NE	i J	82
Wausau, WI	e F	54
Wausaukee, WI	e H	54
Wauseon, OH	f B	26
Wautoma, WI	f F	54
Wauwatosa, WI	g G	54
Wauzeka, WI	g E	54
Waveland, MS	l G	68
Waverly, AL	j K	68
Waverly, IL	c G	68
Waverly, IA	h C	54
Waverly, MN	f A	54
Waverly, MO	c C	68
Waverly, NE	k K	82
Waverly, NY	e J	26
Waverly, OH	h D	26
Waverly, TN	f I	68
Waverly, VA	b I	40
Waverly Hall, GA	g B	40
Waxahachie, TX	g J	84
Waxhaw, NC	e F	40
Waycross, GA	h D	40
Wayland, IA	j D	54
Wayland, KY	b D	40
Wayland, MI	h J	54
Wayland, NY	e I	26
Waylyn, SC	g G	40
Wayne, MI	h L	54
Wayne, NE	i J	82
Wayne, OK	d I	84
Wayne, WV	i D	26
Wayne City, IL	d H	68
Waynesboro, GA	f D	40
Waynesboro, MS	k H	68
Waynesboro, PA	h I	26
Waynesboro, TN	g I	68
Waynesboro, VA	a H	40
Waynesburg, PA	h F	26
Waynesville, IL	j G	54
Waynesville, MO	e C	68
Waynesville, NC	d D	40
Waynoka, OK	c H	84
Weatherford, OK	d H	84
Weatherford, TX	g I	84
Weatherly, PA	g K	26
Weaubleau, MO	e C	68
Weaver, AL	i K	68
Weaverville, CA	d C	128
Weaverville, NC	d D	40
Webb, MS	i F	68
Webb City, MO	e B	68
Weber, r., UT	d E	98
Webster, FL	k D	40
Webster, MA	f O	26
Webster, SD	f I	82
Webster, WI	d C	54
Webster City, IA	h B	54
Webster Springs, WV	i F	26
Wedowee, AL	i K	68
Weed, CA	c C	128
Weedsport, NY	d J	26
Weedville, PA	f H	26
Weems, VA	b J	40
Weeping Water, NE	k K	82
Weimar, TX	j I	84
Weiner, AR	g F	68
Weippe, ID	d J	112
Weir, KS	n M	82
Weir, MS	i G	68
Weirsdale, FL	k E	40
Weirton, WV	e F	26
Weiser, ID	f I	112
Weiser, r., ID	f I	112
Weisner Mountain, AL	h K	68
Weiss Lake, US	h K	68
Welaka, FL	j E	40
Welch, OK	c K	84
Welch, WV	i E	26
Welcome, MN	h M	82
Welcome, SC	e D	40
Weldon, IL	j G	54
Weldon, NC	c I	40
Weldon, r., US	b C	68
Weleetka, OK	d J	84

Name	Map Ref.	Page
Wellborn, FL	i D	40
Wellborn, TX	i J	84
Wellfleet, MA	f P	26
Wellington, CO	d K	98
Wellington, KS	n J	82
Wellington, MO	c C	68
Wellington, OH	f D	26
Wellington, TX	e F	84
Wellington, UT	e F	98
Wellman, IA	i D	54
Wellman, TX	f D	84
Wells, MI	e H	54
Wells, MN	g B	54
Wells, NV	c K	128
Wells, NY	d L	26
Wells, TX	k B	84
Wellsboro, PA	f I	26
Wellsburg, IA	h C	54
Wellsburg, WV	g F	26
Wellston, OH	h D	26
Wellston, OK	d I	84
Wellsville, KS	m L	82
Wellsville, MO	c E	68
Wellsville, NY	e I	26
Wellsville, OH	g F	26
Wellsville, UT	c E	98
Wellton, AZ	I B	98
Welsh, LA	I D	68
Wenatchee, WA	c E	112
Wenatchee, r., WA	c E	112
Wenatchee Mountains, WA	c E	112
Wendell, ID	h K	112
Wendell, NC	d H	40
Wenden, AZ	k C	98
Wendover, UT	d B	98
Wenona, IL	i F	54
Wentworth, NC	c G	40
Wentworth, SD	h K	82
Weskan, KS	m F	82
Weslaco, TX	m I	84
Wesley, IA	g B	54
Wesleyville, PA	e F	26
Wessington, SD	g I	82
Wessington Springs, SD	g I	82
Wesson, MS	k F	68
West, MS	i G	68
West, TX	h I	84
West, r., VT		
West Alexandria, OH	h B	26
West Allis, WI	g G	54
Westbay, FL	I K	68
West Bay, TX	j L	84
West Bend, IA	i M	82
West Bend, WI	g G	54
West Blocton, AL	i I	68
West Branch, IA	i D	54
West Branch, MI	f K	54
Westbrook, ME	d P	26
Westbrook, MN	g L	82
Westbrook, TX	g E	84
West Burlington, IA	j D	54
West Butte, MT	b N	112
Westby, MT	c C	82
Westby, WI	g E	54
West Carlisle, PA	f E	84
West Chester, PA	h K	26
Westcliffe, CO	f K	98
West Columbia, SC	f E	40
West Columbia, TX	j K	84
West Concord, MN	f C	54
West Des Moines, IA	i B	54
West Elk Mountains, CO		
West Elk Peak, CO	f I	98
West End, AR	h D	68
West End, NC	d G	40
Westerly, RI	f O	26
Western, NE	k J	82
Westernport, MD	h G	26
Westerville, OH	g D	26
West Fargo, ND	e K	82
Westfield, IL	c H	68
Westfield, IN	b J	68
Westfield, MA	e N	26
Westfield, NJ	g L	26
Westfield, NY	e G	26
Westfield, PA	f I	26
Westfield, WI	g F	54
West Fork, AR	g B	68
West Frankfort, IL	e H	68
West Glacier, MT	b L	112
West Hamlin, WV	i D	26
West Hartford, CT	f N	26
Westhaven, CA	c A	128
West Haven, CT	f N	26
West Helena, AR	h F	68
Westhoff, TX	j I	84
Westhope, ND	g L	82
West Jefferson, NC	c E	40
West Jefferson, OH	h C	26
West Jordan, UT	d E	98
West Kingston, RI	f O	26
West Lafayette, IN	b J	68
West Lafayette, OH	g E	26
Westlake, LA	I C	68
West Laramie, WY	c K	98
West Lebanon, IN	b I	68
West Liberty, IA	i D	54
West Liberty, KY	b C	40
West Liberty, OH	g C	26
West Melbourne, FL	k F	40
West Memphis, AR	g F	68
West Mifflin, PA	g G	26
Westminster, CO	e K	98
Westminster, MD	h J	26
Westminster, SC	e C	40
West Monroe, LA	j D	68
Westmont, PA	g H	26
Westmoreland, KS	I K	82
Westmoreland, TN	f J	68
Westmorland, CA	k J	128
West Nishnabotna, r., IA	k L	82
Weston, CO	g L	98
Weston, ID	h N	112
Weston, MO	c B	68
Weston, NE	j K	82
Weston, OH	f C	26
Weston, OR	e G	112
Weston, WV	h F	26
West Orange, TX	I C	68
West Paris, ME	c P	26
West Pensacola, FL	I I	68
Westphalia, KS	m L	82
West Plains, MO	f E	68
West Point, CA	f E	128
West Point, GA	g A	68
West Point, IA	j D	54
West Point, KY	e K	68
West Point, MS	i H	68
West Point, NE	j K	82
West Point, NY	f M	26
West Point, VA	b J	40
West Point Lake, US	f A	68
Westport, CT	f M	26
Westport, IN	c K	68
Westport, OR	d B	112
Westport, WA	d A	112
West Portsmouth, OH	i C	26
West Richland, WA	d F	112
West Rutland, VT	d M	26
West Sacramento, CA	f D	128
West Salem, IL	d H	68
West Salem, OH	g D	26
West Salem, WI	g D	54
West Slope, OR	e C	112
West Spanish Peak, CO	g L	98
West Terre Haute, IN	c I	68
West Union, IA	h D	54
West Union, OH	i C	26
West Union, WV	h F	26
West Unity, OH	f B	26
West Valley, MT	d L	112
West Valley City, UT	d E	98
Westville, IN	a J	68
Westville, OK	d J	84
Wetmore, KS	I L	82
Wet Mountains, CO	f K	98
Wetumka, OK	d J	84
Wetumpka, AL	j J	68
Wewahitchka, FL	i A	40
Wewoka, OK	d J	84
Weyauwega, WI	f G	54
Weymouth, MA	e P	26
Wharton, TX	j J	84
Wharton, WV	j E	26
What Cheer, IA	i C	54
Whatley, AL	k I	68
Wheatland, CA	e D	128
Wheatland, IA	i E	54
Wheatland, WY	b L	98
Wheatley, AR	h E	68
Wheaton, IL	a H	68
Wheaton, MD	h I	26
Wheaton, MN	f K	82
Wheat Ridge, CO	e K	98
Wheeler, MS	h H	68
Wheeler, TX	d F	84
Wheeler Air Force Base, HI	f I	144c
Wheeler Lake, AL	h I	68
Wheeler Peak, CA	f F	128
Wheeler Peak, NV	f E	128
Wheeler Peak, NM	h K	98
Wheeling, WV	g F	26
Wheelwright, KY	b D	40
Whidbey Island, WA	c E	112
Whigham, GA	i B	40
Whitakers, NC	c I	40
White, GA	e B	40
White, SD	g K	82
White, r., NA	e X	142
White, r., US	h E	68
White, r., US	h G	82
White, r., US	d G	98
White, r., AZ	k F	98
White, r., IN	d I	68
White, r., NV	g K	128
White, r., VT	d N	26
White, r., WI	e C	54
White Bear Lake, MN	e B	54
White Bluff, TN	f I	68
White Butte, ND	e D	82
White Castle, LA	I E	68
White City, KS	m K	82
White Cloud, MI	g J	54
White Deer, TX	d E	84
White Earth, r., ND	c E	82
Whiteface, TX	f D	84
Whiteface, r., MN	c C	54
Whiteface Mountain, NY	c M	26
Whitefield, NH	n O	26
Whitefish, MT	b K	112
Whitefish, r., MI	g H	54
Whitefish Bay, WI	g H	54
Whitefish Point, MI	d K	54
Whitefish Point, MI	d J	54
White Hall, AR	h D	68
White Hall, IL	c F	68
Whitehall, MI	g I	54
Whitehall, MT	e M	112
Whitehall, NY	d M	26
Whitehall, WI	f D	54
White Haven, PA	f K	26
White House, TN	f J	68
Whitehouse, TX	g K	84
White Lake, SD	h I	82
White Lake, WI	e E	54
White Lake, LA	m D	68
White Mountain, AK	d M	142
White Mountain Peak, CA	g G	128
White Mountains, US	g G	128
White Mountains, NH	n N	26
White Oak, TX	j B	68
White Pass, NC	g AA	142
White Pigeon, MI	i J	54
White Pine, MI	d F	54
White Pine, TN	c C	40
White Plains, NY	f M	26
White Plains, NC	c F	40
Whiteriver, AZ	k G	98
White River, SD	h G	82
White River Junction, VT	d N	26
Whiterocks, r., UT	d G	98
White Salmon, WA	d E	112
White Salmon, r., WA	d E	112
Whitesboro, TX	f J	84
Whitesburg, KY	b D	40
White Settlement, TX	g I	84
White Springs, FL	i D	40
White Sulphur Springs, MT	d O	112
White Sulphur Springs, WV	b F	40
Whitesville, KY	e J	68
Whitesville, WV	j E	26
Whiteville, NC	e H	40
Whiteville, TN	g G	68
Whitewater, KS	n J	82
Whitewater, MT	b R	112
Whitewater, WI	g H	54
Whitewater, r., US	c K	68
Whitewater, r., MO	c D	68
Whitewater Baldy, NM	k H	98
Whitewood, SD	g D	82
Whitewright, TX	f J	84
Whiting, IA	i K	82
Whiting, KS	I L	82
Whiting, WI	f F	54
Whitley City, KY	c B	40
Whitman, MA	e P	26
Whitmire, SC	e E	40
Whitmore Village, HI	e I	144c
Whitney, TX	h I	84
Whitney, Lake, TX	h I	84
Whitney, Mount, CA	h G	128
Whitney Point, NY	e K	26
Whittemore, IA	h M	82
Whittemore, MI	f L	54
Whittier, AK	f T	142
Whittier, NC	d C	40
Whitwell, TN	g K	68
Wibaux, MT	e C	82
Wichita, KS	n J	82
Wichita, r., TX	e H	84
Wichita Falls, TX	f H	84
Wichita Mountains, OK	e H	84
Wickenburg, AZ	k D	98
Wickliffe, KY	f G	68
Widen, WV	i F	26
Wiergate, TX	k C	68
Wiggins, CO	b K	98
Wiggins, MS	I G	68
Wilber, NE	k K	82
Wilbur, WA	c G	112
Wilburton, OK	e K	84
Wilcox, NE	k H	82
Wilcox, PA	f H	26
Wilder, ID	g I	112
Wildersville, TN	g H	68
Wild Rice, r., MN	e B	82
Wild Rice, r., ND	e J	82
Wildrose, ND	c D	82
Wild Rose, WI	f F	54
Wildwood, NJ	i L	26
Wilkerson Pass, CO	e K	98
Wilkes-Barre, PA	f K	26
Wilkesboro, NC	c E	40
Willacoochee, GA	h C	40
Willamette, r., OR	e C	112
Willamina, OR	e B	112
Willapa, r., WA	d B	112
Willapa Bay, WA	d A	112
Willard, MO	e C	68
Willard, NM	j J	98
Willard, OH	f D	26
Willard, UT	c D	98
Willcox, AZ	I G	98
Willcox Playa, AZ	I G	98
William Bill Dannelly Reservoir, AL	j I	68
Williams, AZ	i D	98
Williams, CA	e C	128
Williams, IA	h B	54
Williams, MN	c M	82
Williams Bay, WI	h G	54
Williamsburg, IA	i C	54
Williamsburg, KY	c B	40
Williamsburg, PA	g H	26
Williamsburg, VA	b J	40
Williamson, NY	d I	26
Williamson, WV	b D	40
Williamsport, IN	b I	68
Williamsport, PA	f I	26
Williamston, MI	h K	54
Williamston, NC	d I	40
Williamston, SC	e D	40
Williamstown, KY	i B	26
Williamstown, MA	e M	26
Williamstown, NJ	h L	26
Williamstown, VT	c N	26
Williamstown, WV	h E	26
Williamsville, IL	c G	68
Willimantic, CT	f N	26
Willingboro, NJ	g L	26
Willis, TX	i K	84
Williston, FL	j D	40
Williston, ND	c D	82
Williston, SC	f E	40
Willisville, IL	e G	68
Willits, CA	e B	128
Willmar, MN	f L	82
Willoughby, OH	f E	26
Willow, AK	f S	142
Willow, r., MN	d B	54
Willow, r., WI	e C	54
Willow City, ND	c G	82
Willow Creek, CA	d B	128
Willow Creek, MT	e N	112
Willowick, OH	f E	26
Willow Lake, SD	g J	82
Willows, CA	e C	128
Willow Springs, MO	f E	68
Willshire, OH	g B	26
Wills Point, TX	g J	84
Wilmar, AR	i E	68
Wilmer, AL	I H	68
Wilmer, TX	g J	84
Wilmette, IL	h H	54
Wilmington, DE	h K	26
Wilmington, IL	i G	54
Wilmington, NC	e I	40
Wilmington, OH	h C	26
Wilmington, VT	e N	26
Wilmore, KY	b B	40
Wilmot, AR	i E	68
Wilmot, SD	f K	82
Wilsall, MT	e N	112
Wilson, AR	g F	68
Wilson, KS	m I	82
Wilson, LA	I E	68
Wilson, NC	d H	40
Wilson, OK	e I	84
Wilson, TX	f E	84
Wilson, r., OR	e B	112
Wilson, Mount, CA	j G	128
Wilson, Mount, CO	g I	98
Wilson, Mount, NV	f K	128
Wilson Lake, AL	h I	68
Wilson Lake, KS	m I	82
Wilsonville, NE	k G	82
Wilton, ME	c P	26
Wilton, NH	e O	26
Wilton, ND	e H	82
Wilton, WI	g E	54
Wimauma, FL	j D	40
Wimberley, TX	i H	84
Wimbledon, ND	d I	82
Winamac, IN	a J	68
Winchendon, MA	e N	26
Winchester, ID	d I	112
Winchester, IL	c F	68
Winchester, IN	b L	68
Winchester, KY	b B	40
Winchester, TN	g J	68
Winchester, VA	h H	26
Wind, r., WY	g Q	112
Windber, PA	g H	26
Wind Cave National Park, SD	h D	82
Winder, GA	f C	40
Wind Lake, WI	h G	54
Windom, MN	h L	82
Windom Peak, CO	g I	98
Window Rock, AZ	i G	98
Wind River Peak, WY	h P	112
Wind River Range, WY	g P	112
Windsor, CA	f C	128
Windsor, CO	d L	98
Windsor, CT	f N	26
Windsor, IL	c H	68
Windsor, MO	d C	68
Windsor, NC	d J	40
Windsor, VT	d N	26
Windsor, VA	c J	40
Windsor Forest, GA	h E	40
Windsor Locks, CT	f N	26
Windthorst, TX	f H	84
Windy Peak, CO	f J	98
Windy Peak, WA	b F	112
Winfield, AL	h I	68
Winfield, IA	i D	54
Winfield, KS	n K	82
Winfield, MO	d F	68
Winfield, WV	i E	26
Wing, ND	d G	82
Wingate, NC	e F	40
Wingo, KY	f H	68
Winifred, MT	c P	112
Wink, TX	h C	84
Winkelman, AZ	I F	98
Winlock, WA	d C	112
Winnebago, IL	h F	54
Winnebago, MN	g A	54
Winnebago, NE	i K	82
Winnebago, r., IA	g A	54
Winnebago, Lake, WI	f G	54
Winneconne, WI	f G	54
Winnemucca, NV	d H	128
Winnetka, IL	h H	54
Winnett, MT	c Q	112
Winnfield, LA	k D	68
Winnibigoshish, Lake, MN	c A	54
Winnie, TX	m B	68
Winnipesaukee, Lake, NH	d O	26
Winnsboro, LA	j E	68
Winnsboro, SC	e E	40
Winnsboro, TX	g K	84
Winnsboro Mills, SC	e E	40
Winona, KS	I F	82
Winona, MI	d G	54
Winona, MN	f D	54
Winona, MS	i G	68
Winona, MO	e E	68
Winona Lake, IN	a K	68
Winooski, VT	c M	26
Winooski, r., VT	c N	26
Winside, NE	i J	82
Winslow, AZ	i F	98
Winslow, ME	c Q	26
Winsted, CT	f M	26
Winsted, MN	f A	54
Winston, FL	k D	40
Winston, OR	g B	112
Winston-Salem, NC	c F	40
Winter, WI	e D	54
Winter Garden, FL	k E	40
Winter Harbor, ME	c R	26
Winterhaven, CA	I K	128
Winter Haven, FL	k E	40
Wintering, r., ND	e G	82
Winter Park, FL	k E	40
Winter Park, NC	e I	40
Winterport, ME	c R	26
Winters, CA	f D	128
Winters, TX	h G	84
Winterset, IA	i A	54
Winterville, GA	e E	40
Winterville, MS	i E	68
Winterville, NC	d I	40
Winthrop, IA	h D	54
Winthrop, ME	c Q	26
Winthrop, MN	f A	54
Winthrop, WA	b F	112
Winthrop Harbor, IL	h H	54
Winton, NC	c J	40
Wiscasset, ME	c Q	26
Wisconsin, state, US	c I	8
Wisconsin, r., WI	g E	54
Wisconsin, Lake, WI	f E	54
Wisconsin Dells, WI	g F	54
Wisconsin Rapids, WI	f F	54
Wisdom, MT	e L	112
Wise, VA	c D	40
Wishek, ND	e H	82
Wishram, WA	e E	112
Wisner, LA	k E	68
Wisner, NE	j K	82
Wister, OK	h B	68
Withlacoochee, r., US	i C	40
Witt, IL	c G	68
Wittenberg, WI	f F	54
Woburn, MA	e O	26
Wolbach, NE	j I	82
Wolcott, IN	b I	68
Wolcott, NY	d J	26
Wolcottville, IN	a K	68
Wolf, r., MN	c B	54
Wolf, r., KS	I L	82
Wolf, r., MS	i G	68
Wolf, r., WI	f G	54
Wolf Creek, MT	c M	112
Wolf Creek, OR	h B	112
Wolf Creek Lake, KS	m L	82
Wolf Creek Pass, CO	g J	98
Wolfeboro, NH	d O	26
Wolfe City, TX	f J	84
Wolfforth, TX	f D	84
Wolf Lake, MI	g I	54
Wolf Point, MT	b T	112
Wolsey, SD	g I	82
Wolverine, MI	e K	54
Wonderland, CA	d D	128
Wonewoc, WI	g E	54
Wood, SD	h G	82
Wood, r., NE	k H	82
Wood, r., WY	g P	112
Woodall Mountain, MS	h H	68
Woodbine, GA	i E	40
Woodbine, IA	i L	82
Woodbine, NJ	h L	26
Woodbridge, VA	i I	26
Woodburn, OR	e C	112
Woodbury, CT	f M	26
Woodbury, GA	g B	40
Woodbury, NJ	h K	26
Woodbury, TN	g J	68
Woodhull, IL	i E	54
Woodlake, CA	h F	128
Woodland, CA	f D	128
Woodland, ME	b S	26
Woodland, WA	d C	112
Woodland Park, CO	f K	98
Woodlawn, IL	e H	68
Woodrow, NC	d I	40
Woodruff, AZ	j F	98
Woodruff, SC	e D	40
Woodruff, WI	e F	54
Woods, Lake of the, NA	b M	82
Woodsboro, TX	k I	84
Woodsfield, OH	h E	26
Woods Hole, MA	f P	26
Woodson, TX	f G	84
Woodstock, GA	e B	40
Woodstock, IL	h G	54
Woodstock, NY	e L	26
Woodstock, VT	d N	26
Woodstock, VA	i H	26
Woodsville, NH	c N	26
Woodville, AL	h J	68
Woodville, FL	i B	40
Woodville, GA	f C	40
Woodville, MS	k E	68
Woodville, OH	f C	26
Woodville, TX	I B	84
Woodward, IA	h B	54
Woodward, OK	c G	84
Woodworth, LA	k D	68
Woolmarket, MS	I H	68
Woonsocket, RI	e O	26
Woonsocket, SD	g I	82
Wooster, OH	g E	26
Worcester, MA	e O	26
Worden, MT	e Q	112
Worland, WY	f R	112
Wortham, TX	h J	84
Worthington, IN	c J	68
Worthington, MN	h L	82
Worthington, OH	g C	26
Worthington Peak, NV	g I	128
Wounded Knee, SD	h E	82
Wrangell, AK	h BB	142
Wrangell, Cape, AK	j A	143a
Wrangell Island, AK	h BB	142
Wrangell Mountains, AK	f W	142
Wray, CO	k E	82
Wrens, GA	f D	40
Wright, Mount, MT	c M	112
Wright City, MO	d E	68
Wright City, OK	e K	84
Wright Patman Lake, TX	i B	68
Wrightson, Mount, AZ	m F	98
Wrightstown, WI	f G	54
Wrightsville, GA	g D	40
Wrightsville Beach, NC	e I	40
Wrightwood, CA	j H	128
Wrigley, TN	g I	68
Wyaconda, MO	b E	68
Wyaconda, r., MO	b E	68
Wyalusing, PA	f J	26
Wyandotte, MI	h L	54
Wyatt, MO	f G	68
Wyeville, WI	f E	54
Wykoff, MN	g C	54
Wylie, TX	f J	84
Wylie, Lake, US	c D	40
Wymore, NE	k K	82
Wyndmere, ND	e J	82
Wynne, AR	g F	68
Wynnewood, OK	e I	84
Wynona, OK	c J	84
Wynot, NE	i J	82
Wyocena, WI	g F	54
Wyodak, WY	g B	82
Wyoming, IL	i F	54
Wyoming, MN	h D	54
Wyoming, MI	h J	54
Wyoming, state, US	c E	8
Wytheville, VA	c E	40

X

| Xenia, IL | d H | 68 |
| Xenia, OH | h C | 26 |

Y

Yadkin, r., NC	d F	40
Yadkinville, NC	c F	40
Yahara, r., WI	h F	54
Yainax Butte, OR	h D	112
Yakima, WA	d E	112
Yakima, r., WA	d F	112
Yakobi Island, AK	g Y	142
Yakutat, AK	g Y	142
Yakutat Bay, AK	g X	142
Yale, MI	g M	54
Yale, OK	d I	84
Yale, Mount, CO	f J	98
Yalobusha, r., MS	i G	68
Yampa, CO	d J	98
Yampa, r., CO	d J	98
Yamsay Mountain, OR	h D	112
Yanceyville, NC	c G	40
Yankeetown, FL	j D	40
Yankton, SD	i J	82
Yarmouth, ME	d P	26
Yatesboro, PA	g G	26
Yates Center, KS	n L	82
Yates City, IL	j E	54
Yazoo, r., MS	j F	68
Yazoo City, MS	i F	68
Yellow, r., US	i J	68
Yellow, r., IN	a J	68
Yellow, r., IA	g D	54
Yellow, r., WI	e C	54
Yellow Medicine, r., MN	g L	82
Yellowstone, r., US	b E	8
Yellowstone Falls, WY	f O	112
Yellowstone Lake, WY	f O	112
Yellowstone National Park, WY	f O	112
Yellowstone National Park, US	f O	112
Yellville, AR	f D	68
Yemassee, SC	g F	40
Yerington, NV	f F	128
Yermo, CA	j I	128
Yeso, NM	e B	84
Yoakum, TX	j I	84
Yockanookany, r., MS	j G	68
Yocona, r., MS	h G	68
Yoncalla, OR	g B	112
Yonkers, NY	g M	26
York, AL	j H	68
York, NE	k J	82
York, ND	c H	82
York, PA	h J	26
York, SC	e E	40
York, r., VA	b J	40
Yorktown, IN	b L	68
Yorktown, TX	k I	84
Yorktown, VA	b J	40
Yorkville, IL	i G	54
Yorkville, NY	d K	26
Yosemite National Park, CA	g F	128
Yosemite National Park, CA	g F	128
Young, AZ	j F	98
Youngstown, FL	i A	40
Youngstown, NY	d G	26
Youngstown, OH	f F	26
Youngsville, LA	I E	68
Youngsville, NC	c H	40
Youngsville, PA	f G	26
Yountville, CA	f C	128
Ypsilanti, MI	h L	54
Yreka, CA	c C	128
Yuba, r., CA	e D	128
Yuba City, CA	e D	128
Yucaipa, CA	j H	128
Yucca, AZ	j B	98
Yucca Valley, CA	j I	128
Yukon, OK	d I	84
Yukon, r., NA	e N	142
Yukon Flats, AK	c U	142
Yuma, AZ	I B	98
Yuma, CO	k E	82

Z

Zachary, LA	I E	68
Zama, MS	j G	68
Zanesville, OH	h D	26
Zap, ND	d F	82
Zapata, TX	m G	84
Zarembo Island, AK	h BB	142
Zavalla, TX	k B	68
Zearing, IA	h B	54
Zebulon, GA	f B	40
Zebulon, NC	d H	40
Zeeland, MI	h I	54
Zeeland, ND	f H	82
Zeigler, IL	e G	68
Zelienople, PA	f F	26
Zephyr, TX	h H	84
Zephyrhills, FL	k D	40
Zillah, WA	d E	112
Zilwaukee, MI	g L	54
Zion, IL	h H	54
Zion National Park, UT	g C	98
Zionsville, IN	c J	68
Zolfo Springs, FL	I E	40
Zumbro, r., MN	f C	54
Zumbrota, MN	f C	54
Zuni, NM	i H	98
Zuni, r., US	j G	98
Zwolle, LA	k C	68